By the same author

SIX HUNDRED MILLION CHINESE, 1957
WHEN CHINA WAKES, 1966

THE
JAPANESE
CHALLENGE

ROBERT GUILLAIN

translated from the French by
PATRICK O'BRIAN

J. B. Lippincott Company
Philadelphia and New York

CONTENTS

CONTENTS

1.

The Race to the Year 2000

It was two and a half years since I had been in Japan, and as usual I found Tokyo almost unrecognizable. It is the city I know best in the world; I have lived there for years and years, and every district, every street corner, has a particular meaning for me. Yet my knowledge of it is by no means complete, for the town is in a continual state of evolution, and from one stay to the next I find greater and even more rapid changes. Once again, this time I had everything to learn afresh.

I had already been astonished when I came at the time of the Olympic Games in 1964. Tokyo literally rebuilt itself for this great international gathering, and the transformations that had been carried out in two or three years positively amazed an old Tokyo hand like me. Everybody expected that after the Games the Japanese capital would take a breathing spell. Not at all. The boom in building and modernization went on and grew stronger—an even more surprising spectacle at the present moment when one remembers that from the economic point of view the two very important years after the Games were periods of stagnation and even of recession. The news that reached foreign countries from Japan was either gloomy or anxious: the dispatches spoke of crisis, great difficulties, an economic slump.

What a staggering surprise for the returning visitor! So this was what their crisis amounted to! In the depths of their depression these astonishing Japanese had gone on building as hard as they could. I lost my way in the ever-increasing network of high-speed expressways that ran in every direction across the enormous city; I could no longer tell where I was among the new, continually spreading lines of the underground railway. Whole districts had suddenly vanished before the attack of the bulldozers; others had come into being during the last year or two. Streets where I had once fought my way through appalling traffic jams were no longer recognizable; they were five times wider, and the cars raced along in an even flow. Many old landmarks in this enormous city were no longer any use as points of reference, for they were entirely swamped by huge new buildings that changed the appearance of everything. I was quite bewildered by the proliferation of new places which are the new "musts"—new hotels, shops, museums, clubs, restaurants and so on. And I had never seen a Tokyo so vividly alive, with such tight-packed and obviously prosperous crowds, with such a dense flow of traffic and such a striking appearance of being a very great capital.

This is the aspect of Tokyo—its noise, its crowds, its turmoil—that will form the newcomer's first impression of the city. But it is a deceptive appearance, only half the picture; apart from the Western-style districts and the modern avenues there is still a vast, almost villagelike Tokyo consisting of wooden houses in a labyrinth of little, very narrow, very Japanese streets. Everything is to be found in this city: Chicago and old Japan, tall buildings and bamboo houses, modern complexity and the poetry and grace of the Orient, astonishing alternations between the mechanized West and the unmoving East, instant changes of scene. There is that daily miracle which abruptly wipes out the city's saddening daylight ugliness and turns it into the wonderful, blazing, nighttime Tokyo. And above all, there is the perpetual cycle of transformation as year after year the city grows and changes.

Shinjuku provides a striking example of Tokyo's mutation. It was a well-known working-class district, a haunt of the "with it" young and penniless intellectuals. Until 1963 its western side was nothing but an unwholesome maze of Japanese hovels, enlivened here and there by a row of cafés that provided indifferent sake and skewers of grilled chicken. Just before the Olympic Games bulldozers appeared and turned the whole place into a building site, though what was to be built was not exactly known. On my visit in 1967 I was astonished to find that it had turned into an ultramodern district—one that will be able to compete with Marunouchi, the famous business center in the heart of the capital.

The new Shinjuku is built around a huge square, and the façades of the immense buildings that line its four sides are made of glass and stainless steel. There is an enormous railway station; there are two very large department stores, some banks, various insurance companies, and huge office buildings. The square, with its whirling streams of traffic, has some curious features of its own. From its asphalt there arise prodigious sloping funnels, like those of a modern liner but made of concrete. Farther on there is an immense depression, and into this, running down spiral ramps, the cars either disappear beneath the surface or rise up, coming into the air from the lower depths. For in fact beneath the square there is another square—an enormous underground space, all of which, apart from a central court, is kept solely for pedestrians. A third level, below this, provides parking for a very large number of cars.

Here, beneath the ground and under a concrete sky held up by hundreds of pillars and lit by neon, the pedestrians keep up a continual flow of movement, day and night, like a human anthill. Shinjuku is an exchange point where two and a quarter million people a day move between the capital and the suburbs. During the rush hour—nine in the morning—two hundred thousand people cross the underground square. A positive network of underground streets branches from it, and until eleven in the evening they are full of life, with hundreds of brightly lit shops, stalls, cafés and restaurants all thronged with customers.

What is more, the buildings around the square, including the station, thrust great numbers of galleries and passages down into its depths, and in order to draw off the crowds they provide all the most recent kinds of elevators and escalators, both up and down.

The Shinjuku terminal actually includes four or five stations, since a whole system of public and private railroads and subways comes together here in one enormous junction. The terminal building itself contains an important store, whole stories of offices, theaters, movie houses, restaurants and countless little shops of every kind. The foreign visitor is astonished when he sees how life has been made easier for the housewife and the customer—travelers can get out of their train literally inside the store. Shinjuku is by no means an isolated example; this linking of a station and a department store is rather the rule than otherwise, and it is so in all the important cases, such as Tokyo Central Station. In fact, the Ikebukuro station, a little beyond Shinjuku, is surrounded by four big department stores, each one of them almost the size of Macy's.

I could describe a whole series of these impressive changes affecting entire districts—changes that have even transformed the business center of the capital itself, where the Marunouchi quarter, which is to Tokyo what the City is to London, has undergone a total metamorphosis. Marunouchi was built at the beginning of the century, and its architects, imitating London, put up old-fashioned red-brick buildings not without a certain odd charm in that Japanese city. Today the whole district consists of metal, glass and concrete giants, their outsides as luxurious as their interiors, and this powerful, American-looking architectural complex rears its splendidly modern mass right next to the ancient moats of the neighboring Imperial Palace.

Shinjuku, Marunouchi and the rest are but a few among the countless examples of change in Tokyo—a change that is growing faster and faster every day. The face of the Japanese capital has been deeply altered by the astonishing and very sudden revolution of the high-speed expressways. There are freeways in the very heart of the city; and as there was no room for them at ground level they have been built in the air, high above the ordinary traffic. They first appeared in 1962. Until then Tokyo had been bogging down in the chaos of its own traffic; and the problem seemed to be growing more and more hopeless. The flow consisted of an enormous and particular mixture of trucks, private cars, trolleys, three-wheeled delivery vans, light trucks, tricycles, buses and sightseeing vehicles, and it caused both enormous traffic jams and countless accidents—in brief, it was the noisiest and the most dangerous traffic in the world. To its alarm and distress, the huge town realized that for a brief moment in 1945 it had had a perfect opportunity for carrying out its revolution, and that it had thrown this chance away. For in fact by the end of the war American planes had flattened Tokyo almost as thoroughly as the atomic bomb had flattened Hiroshima, and it would have been easy to rebuild the city on entirely new lines. Unintelligently it rose again upon its former plan, part of which went back to the Japan of feudal days; and the mistake was all the more heartbreaking since this was the second time it had been made (the first was after the 1923 earthquake). From that point onward it seemed impossible that things could ever be put right, and the position was made all the worse by the government's sluggishness and by the fact that the municipality, up to its neck in red tape, was incapable of movement. The people of Tokyo watched the approach of the 1964 Olympic Games with alarm. They could already see the enormous bottlenecks that would prevent anyone from reaching the stadiums, jams that would be all the worse because it seemed the authorities had made the additional error of holding the Games in the very middle of the city.

At this juncture the long red serpents began to make their appearance: metal beams poised high above the little one-storied Japanese houses on enormous columns. Their function was to carry new elevated expressways, and they took shape very quickly, covering great distances and following the most daring lines. The most surprising thing about them, something that could never have happened except in Japan, was that no one could tell who had decided to have them built, or when. There had been no public discussion either in the municipal council or in parliament. However, in the end it was learned that the man responsible for the expressways was none other than the minister in charge of the Olympic Games, Ichiro Kono, a man who was full of drive and who at that time hoped he might soon be premier. (He died before getting there.) And the world in general praised both his energetic action and his secret preparation for it—any publicity would probably have brought the plan to nothing, and it would quite certainly have caused frightful land speculation.

There was another surprise, too: for years and years the authorities had excused their do-nothing policy by saying that expropriation was impossibly complex; but now the builders of the expressways were given powers that enabled them to demolish whole blocks at the merest stroke of a pen, to disembowel entire districts, to make inroads upon the parks, to leap over historical monuments, to make various streets and avenues five times broader, removing the inhabitants on either side for the whole length, with the promise of rehousing them in taller buildings on the widened boulevards. The opening of the Games was at hand; just before D-day itself the expressways were ready. The problem had been solved and the revolution accomplished. Once again Japan had shown that it was the home of sudden decision after long-enduring patience.

Once the Olympic Games were over and the brilliant Kono was dead, the general opinion was that the building of the famous elevated ex-

pressways would stop. But not at all. Today the network is still growing fast, tracing out a well-conceived system of circling-roads and great
radial lines. It is possible to travel on them for miles and miles, high
above roof level, no longer seeing anything of the ordinary Japanese
districts, whose lightly built wooden houses only rise a single story; in
the modern central districts of taller buildings the driver runs along
at the height of the fourth or fifth floor. And not a traffic light anywhere! In the very heart of the city these expressways sometimes
provide astonishing perspectives, with their ramps, their overpasses
and the involutions of their traffic interchanges. In other places, and
still for miles on end, the expressways plunge beneath the ordinary
level of the traffic, either in the cuts that have replaced the former
canals (Tokyo used to have great numbers of them) or in endless
tunnels. At present the world's biggest underground traffic interchange
is to be found in the middle of Tokyo.

The revolution of the expressways is paralleled by that of the underground railway. For the Olympic Games, Tokyo provided itself with
more than thirty miles of new lines in two years, and the network is
still growing. At the beginning of 1968 there were nearly fifty-four
miles in service and nearly forty-four under construction. What other
country can say as much? Here again the Japanese builders set about
their task with impressive dash and enterprise. They simplified the
problem; and generally speaking they made their subway not by
driving a tunnel but by opening a trench along the great avenues. The
street was ripped up, the subway was installed in a kind of strip mine,
and then a lid of concrete was put back on top of it all.

The most surprising aspect was that over very considerable lengths
of street the digging of the subway did not stop the traffic, at least
not during the daytime. The trench was covered over with a wooden
flooring made of countless massive beams side by side, and the traffic
went on running in the usual way, from morning to night, apart from
the tremendous echoing din. At about nine in the evening hundreds
of workmen removed the beams, and climbed down into the trench,
and went on working there under floodlights. At five in the morning
the beams were put back and the traffic began running once more.

According to the plans, Tokyo will have about 125 miles of subway
before 1975, and the system will be able to carry five to six million
passengers a day. Osaka also has its underground railway, which spread

very fast in order to deal with Expo '70, which opened in March of 1970. Nagoya, between Osaka and Tokyo, is the fastest-growing town in the whole country, and Nagoya too is beginning to develop its subway.

In addition to the huge underground square at Shinjuku, there are subterranean complexes being hollowed out under nearly all the more enterprising parts of the capital; as soon as a horizontal shaft has been driven, it at once becomes an underground stream of pedestrians and a hive of stores and little shops. The Ginza district, which is the most fashionable in Tokyo and the liveliest, took advantage of the building of the subway to treat itself to a series of long subterranean galleries; they form a delightful labyrinth that is bewildering to newcomers but wonderfully amusing with its innumerable shops, its color, the gaiety of the young who fill its streets, and the unexpected way the system branches off in every direction. The price of a square foot of land in Tokyo is the highest in the world; to make the most of it, new buildings not only rise ten or twelve floors above the surface but also go down three, four or even more beneath it, so as to find room for parking lots and maintenance staff. In addition to that they also have underground offices, restaurants, meeting rooms and so on, and of course those omnipresent little shops. A thoroughly Japanese detail: in order to recruit their staff—almost 100 percent of them are girls—some of these buried shops offer free vitamin pills, vitaminized face cream and artificial sunbathing every week.

If you go to Japan, just for the fun of it hail a taxi and ask the driver to take you to the French restaurant called Maxim's. You don't have to tell him the address; he knows it. The cab will go to the middle of Ginza and there it will suddenly plunge underground. It will follow a spiral ramp down to the fourth level below the surface and then it will stop. You get out, and there you are at Maxim's of 3, rue Royale; but a subterranean rue Royale, made in Japan, with the name of the street up on the wall, the lamp post, the corner of the pavement and the façade—an exact, slightly reduced copy of the famous Paris restaurant. And the inside is all of a piece with the outside: a faithful replica of the Parisian original.

But let us go back to the surface and speak of another revolution, the construction of enormous buildings. "When are they going to stop throwing up these huge modern blocks? Or when are they at least going to slow down?" That question arose again and again during the first Japanese boom of 1955 to 1960, when these buildings began to go up in considerable numbers. Today it is clear that in fact there is no foreseeable end and that the question was meaningless. The truth of the matter is that what is going on at present is part of a process with a great extension in time; it is the change-over from a former epoch in which Japanese houses consisted of a single wooden story, as they had from the earliest days, to a modern age in which they are built of lasting materials—stone, metal, concrete—as they are in the other great cities in the world, and built high. The continual increase in the population of the capital, the rising price of building sites, the growth of the economy, the Olympic Games—all these are other factors that have given a steadily increasing impulse to construction. Neither the end of the Games nor the slump that followed stopped the building boom, and when the economy recovered it went on at an even greater pace. The enormous city provided a great many facilities for the Games, among them several architectural masterpieces, such as Kenzo Tange's famous swimming pool, as well as half a dozen big ultra-modern hotels; not content with that, Tokyo is adding new buildings at a great speed, buildings that change its whole appearance more and more radically every day.

Offhand I could name several important new hotels, three magnificent theaters whose size and equipment equal or surpass their most up-to-date European rivals, some enormous buildings such as the offices of the great *Mainichi* newspaper or those of the Japanese employers' federation (Keidanren), whose wealth and modernity bring America to mind, an ambitious Catholic cathedral (another of Tange's creations), several big swimming pools, and great apartment houses, not to mention the flood of medium-sized buildings that are everywhere thrusting back the little wooden houses of a former age.

Two other achievements belong to quite a different order of things. The first is the quietly magnificent new Imperial Palace, rebuilt in that great wooded, landscaped area which is still a kind of forbidden city in the very heart of the capital. Here modern architects have employed modern materials, using them in a traditional architecture that nevertheless reflects the attitudes of today. The decoration makes great use of the time-honored Japanese materials, especially wood, but it does so on a very much larger scale than is the case with ordinary buildings of the traditional style; and it is said that the interior of the palace is strikingly splendid. Its green roofs seem to float among the pines, and all around it wonderful Japanese gardens have been laid out; as a welcome sign of "democratization," part of the wooded park has been opened to the public.

The second of these spectacular achievements and the most revolutionary of all is the construction of Tokyo's first skyscrapers. A huge thirty-five-story building was put up by the powerful Mitsui industrial group in the middle of the administrative district. Another, more recently completed, is five hundred feet high, with about forty stories above ground. The Japanese boast that they have taken up the special challenge of the earthquake and that their architects have now solved all the relevant problems. Special building techniques and materials unite the solidity of monolithic construction with elasticity, and this allows the raising of very tall buildings that will stand the strain of the strongest known or foreseeable quakes. The Japanese architects say that the decisive advances in this field have been made by bringing computers to bear on the movements that take place during earthquakes, on the reactions of the materials used in building, and on the shifting and vibration of the whole mass.

I know from experience what a fairly strong earthquake is like on the seventh floor of an ordinary modern building in Ginza, since my office was there for a long while. All at once I felt as though I were on the deck of a ship, or rather on the top of a windblown tree; through the windows I saw the urban landscape sliding from right to left and then back again, while at the same time the earthquake rattled the metal window frames, making a tremendous din. When I call this incident to mind I do not feel at all inclined to be caught by a *jishin* (the Japanese for an earthquake) when I am visiting the fortunate tenant of some apartment on a thirty-fifth floor.

One must not judge a country by its capital, and this applies as much to Japan as anywhere else. Tokyo is not Japan, or at least it is only a very special Japan. Still, the provinces are also modernizing themselves at a great pace, and the transformation of Tokyo is part and parcel of a system of material change that is turning the whole archipelago upside down. For example, as one travels along the Tokyo–Osaka axis, which might be called the backbone of Japan, one sees the prodigious amount of work that has either been finished in the last four or five years or is still under way—work that is moving even faster since the economic revival. Driving out of Tokyo is no longer a risky or even very dangerous adventure; one is no longer in a chaotic, murderous turmoil of traffic, surrounded by "kamikaze of the wheel," always providing one chooses the new roads; the Yokohama expressway, for instance, has three lanes, or rather six—three in one direction and three in the other.

One of the first surprises for an observer like me, used to these suburbs and to the thickly populated countryside, is to see how the houses and even whole villages have recently changed color. Everywhere there are blue tiles, green tiles, light brown, pink or yellow walls, bright patches of color, whereas formerly Japanese suburbs and villages were always dim and dark, gray or black. This is the outward sign of a threefold phenomenon of modernization. To begin with, a great number of the houses are new, and they bear witness to the rapid spread of dwellings over areas that were until recently open hills or rice fields. Secondly—and this particularly interesting transformation becomes apparent only when one looks closely—many of the new-looking houses are in fact old ones that have been completely done over, refurbished and often enlarged. A Japanese house has a life of twenty years or less; after that it has to be restored or even rebuilt. After the war the ruined Japanese held out for about twenty years in their old gray houses—houses that grew more and more dilapidated. But then came the economic boom and the general rise in the standard of living. For thousands and thousands of Japanese the decisive moment of the rise was when their worn-out dwellings could at last be renewed, rebuilt on the old foundations as quickly as possible. And thirdly, it was at this particular juncture that the factories began the mass production and marketing of modern building materials for the Japanese house—tiles with colored glazes, plastic-covered plywood, outside walls made of a synthetic product resembling wood, hollow bricks, concrete blocks, corrugated metal of various patterns and so forth.

To all this must be added the great number of dwellings that consist of rapidly assembled prefabricated parts. Building the little Japanese house is no longer a complex, highly skilled fitting together of wooden sections, straw mats, and heavy lead-colored tiles. Without losing many of its particularly Japanese and particularly charming characteristics, the private house has become something not unlike a European summer villa; it is in appearance more fragile than ever, but it is perhaps more lasting than its predecessors. And, too—often a disagreeable sight—there is the rapid spread of apartment buildings constructed of permanent or semipermanent materials: mere rabbit hutches, put up without the least care for aesthetic considerations, with the one idea of crowding as many tenants as possible into a small space.

Everything in the way of factories, workshops and warehouses is being modernized, too. In earlier days it was usual to see industrial buildings or godowns (all over the Far East a warehouse is called a godown) made of unpainted boards, blackened by the weather. These have almost entirely disappeared, and nowadays steel frameworks, concrete, and sheet metal are the rule. Many of the big factories are brand new and very good looking, and in addition to these there are great numbers of small industrial concerns that have obviously renewed and modernized their buildings and equipment.

And everywhere, all along the main lines of communication, the expanding cities are eating into the surrounding countryside: houses, workshops, telegraph poles and huge cable-bearing towers invade the rice fields; hills are disemboweled or bulldozed into terraces for housing sites; factories spring up everywhere; and everywhere the builders are at work.

Road improvement, of course, is an inseparable part of this development. For many years I knew a Japan with appalling roads, among the worst in the world. Today, good modern roads stretch in every direction—partly owing to the long-delayed coming of age of the private automobile, but more importantly as a result of the slump of 1964–1965, which induced the government at long last to take over from private finance, which was then slackening. For close to twenty years the Japanese government had done much less than private industry in the way of investment, and its indifference to the road system was only one instance of its lack of care for the country's whole infrastructure. Now, in addition to the splendid Yokohama expressway, there is the completely remade Tokyo–Osaka highway, the Tokaido. It is no longer an outstanding feat to drive from Tokyo to Kyoto, the center of Japan of former days; and the great main road has been provided with two alternatives—one an expressway along the Pacific coast by way of Atami, a seaside resort, and Shizuoka, a town well known for its green tea, and the other running inland through the mountain valleys to Nagoya, thence to the mercantile city of Osaka, and so to Kobe, the great port of central Japan. Toll roads are increasing, and they now cover about 550 miles. The road system as a whole is being recast; between 1963 and 1967 more than 25,000 miles of road were reconditioned, and there are to be 2,200 miles of new superhighways by 1975. Though road construction cannot keep up with traffic growth, it is being undertaken with impressive speed.

The Olympic Games seemed to mark the highest point that the Japanese building industry (public works and construction) would reach during the years after the war. But in fact its activity has not diminished, and according to statistics its annual rate of growth is still 20 percent. The Kajima Construction Company, whose base is in Tokyo, stands third among the world's building contractors.

The national development plan includes a whole program of bridges and submarine tunnels for linking Honshu, the main island, with its three great neighbors, and this program is already being carried out. Japanese engineers say that the country will no longer be an archipelago. Travelers will move from one island to another without having to get out of the train. In the north the poverty-stricken, storm-lashed coast of the Strait of Tsugaru, dotted with ancient fishing villages, has already been turned upside down by an undertaking that may well be one of the century's finest accomplishments in civil engineering. This is what the London *Times* called "Japan's channel tunnel." The idea is to drive a tunnel under the sea, joining the main island with its great northern neighbor, Hokkaido; it will be three times as deep as the proposed tunnel between England and France, and it will be the longest in the world—twenty-two and a half miles. This "channel tunnel" is coming into being far quicker than the English one. Work began in 1963, and a pilot shaft was finished in 1969. The whole tunnel will be built by 1975, and trains running under the sea will take the place of the ferryboat, only too well known for its many shipwrecks in winter and during the typhoon season.

At the other end of Japan there is already an underwater tunnel; it was made several years ago and runs from the main island to the sunlit shores of Kyushu, the great southern island less than two miles away. The tunnel carries the railway, and recently a parallel shaft was driven for an expressway. The system will be completed by a suspension bridge. This is already begun; eventually it will cross the strait two hundred feet above sea level. And, finally, another suspension bridge is planned for the middle of the archipelago, running across to the great island of Shikoku; it is now being prepared, and they say that it will be built before 1971. There are many other outstanding achievements that could be mentioned, such as a mammoth bridge which now serves the Yawata steel mills in Kyushu, or that series of five great bridges, still in this same southern island, which knits together the individual islets of an enchanting archipelago as well as the charming coast that surrounds it; these are the Amakusa islands, a new region for tourists and one they find delightful.

Many daring hydroelectric dams have been built all over the mountains. A striking example is the recent and already very well-known Kurobe dam, right in the middle of the Japanese Alps. Its builders succeeded (unfortunately this is not always the case) in carrying out their enormous works without badly spoiling the wonderful landscape of deep gorges. This is a place of great natural beauty, far from the beaten track, and it is well worth a visit, particularly when autumn lights up the red maples on the mountains all around.

Throughout the country, from north to south, the engineers aim at discovering or even creating new building sites. In order to do this they win land from the only direction that is still open to them—the sea itself. Huge areas have been reclaimed by damming and draining techniques that are even more efficient than those used by the Dutch in the Zuider Zee. This is particularly the case in Tokyo Bay. The beaches dear to the people of Tokyo for their Sunday outings, and those where the fishermen used to have their strange edible-seaweed plantations, have now been pushed far out into the bay; and on the new shores builders have taken the place of the fishermen.

The great port of Kobe, near Osaka, always suffered from being hemmed in on a narrow corridor between the mountains and the sea; now it is providing itself with more space by the simple method of destroying the mountain behind the town and flinging it into the sea in front. It is an astonishing undertaking that will go on for several years. A tremendous battery of ultramodern machines—drills, huge bulldozers, rock crushers, grinders and so on—attack the mountain and literally pulverize it. The next thing to do is throw the huge mass of sand and stone thus produced into the water. But between the shattered mountain and the sea there lies the town. So engineers drilled a kind of subway under Kobe and installed a huge conveyor belt that moves the material in a fast, uninterrupted flow. At the other end waits a regiment of enormous trucks; each in turn takes its load of pulverized mountain, tips it into the water, a little farther off each time, and slowly the sea withdraws. This operation is being carried out at the end of the town, where the industrial suburbs lie. Fortunately the rest of Kobe does not see the huge white gash in the background but retains a beautiful screen of wooded mountains on its landward side.

Great numbers of factories are being built on these new industrial polders, and it is for the sake of the factories that they have been created all along the Pacific and on the shores of the Inland Sea, especially in the bays of Nagoya and Osaka, which are most favorably situated for industry. More and more often, the great industrial complexes, particularly in steel, are building their works "with their feet in the water," right on the edge of the sea. The artificial shores are good, but Japan has natural shores that are even better—shores that allow the construction of deepwater piers very close to the works, where ships can come in and load or discharge their cargoes directly. The archipelago's coastline is so indented that it has a total length of nearly seventeen thousand miles; the Japanese calculate that there are 202 yards of shore for every square mile of territory. This is twice as much as the figure for England and twelve times that for the United States; it is of course a very considerable advantage for a country that lives on its external trade. So what is going on at present is a twofold development: on the one hand that of the great traditional ports and on the other that of what might be called private harbors—ports belonging to industrial firms installed along the winding coastline, close to sheltered deepwater anchorages.

To some degree the whole of Japan is becoming a port over great lengths of its coast, thanks to the development of harbor installations. In several regions the great ports themselves are moving toward one another. This is the case with Yokohama, Tokyo and Kawasaki, which serve the most important industrial district in the country and are tending to merge into one enormous harbor. The ports of Nagoya and Yokkaichi are almost joined by a scattering of smaller harbors; and so are those of Kobe, Amagasaki and Osaka, which serve the second great industrial region. In the same way the southern ports of Dokai, Kokura, Moji and Shimonoseki tend to unite in one huge complex whose activity keeps pace with the astonishing rhythm of Japanese economic growth. At present there are plans for the building of a single enormous breakwater that will be common to the ports in the Bay of Tokyo that I have mentioned; and another in Osaka Bay. But the Japanese government, anxious to diminish congestion in these regions, encourages the dispersion of industry and of the harbor facilities that go with it.

This galloping industrialization is the most important phenomenon in modern Japan, and it is changing the whole physical appearance of the country. Until recently it was reckoned that there were four great industrial regions: the region of Tokyo–Yokohama (30 percent of the working population and 35 percent of the country's industrial production); of Nagoya; then, somewhat farther south, of Osaka–Kobe; and lastly the southern region of north Kyushu, built around the new city of Kitakyushu, the product of the fusion of four towns that contained the most important steel mills in the archipelago. For some years now there have been two new developments. The first is the rise of heavy industry in the two central regions—Nagoya and Osaka—which had formerly concentrated on light manufactures and which are now turning more and more toward metallurgy, chemical industries and the like. The second is the emigration of industry from these four main centers and the rapid crystallization of new industrial regions in the intermediate areas. Thus a fifth region has come into existence on the shores of the Inland Sea, between Kobe and Hiroshima; this is the Mizushima–Okayama region, and it is said that the ironworks being built there will be the most important in the world.

The sixth and seventh regions are taking shape on the eastern side of Kyushu, and an eighth is being formed on Shikoku, the least developed of the big Japanese islands, in the neighborhood of Tokushima, which commands one of the two passages from the Inland Sea to the Pacific. In 1963 the national development plan called for thirteen "new industrial towns," most of them in the new regions I have just mentioned. There are special advantages for investors in these developing centers, particularly where the investment is concerned with ironworks, oil and its derivatives, synthetic fibers and paper.

Industrialization goes hand in hand with fast-moving urbanization—with the rapid growth of existing towns and the building of new ones. The population of Japan has passed the 100 million mark, and by an odd coincidence it did so just as modern Japan reached its hundredth anniversary, in 1967. The last detailed census showed 98,281,955 inhabitants on October 1, 1965. As opposed to the militaristic Japan of earlier days, modern industrial Japan no longer has a very rapidly increasing birthrate. At present the increase is only a little over a million a year, and in this respect the country is no longer growing any faster than the advanced Western countries. On the other hand there is a most remarkable internal movement of the population. More and more rapidly the people are leaving the country for the cities, while at the same time the villages are growing until they too become towns. Japan's problem is no longer that of a population explosion but that of a population shift, a large-scale movement toward the towns.

The extent of this urban concentration is shown by the fact that half the inhabitants of Japan, or roughly 50 million of them, live in an area that amounts to no more than 1.25 percent of the country's total surface. About 60 million of them live in the three great industrial regions whose centers are Tokyo, Nagoya and Osaka. (This does not mean that they are all employed in industry; there are some who still work the land. In 1967 the town dwellers numbered 53 million and the country dwellers 47 million.) The regions where the density of population exceeds ten thousand to the square mile and which Japanese statistics call "concentrated population areas" have a rate of growth three times higher than the national average. The urbanized belts surrounding Tokyo, Nagoya and Osaka increased in area by 20 to 25 percent in the five years from 1961 to 1965. The fastest growth is found in the towns of more than half a million inhabitants. Tokyo has more than 15 million people, and every year 300,000 more move in.

Another way of realizing the fast-growing preponderance of the towns is to look at the employment figures. Immediately after World War II the workers in the primary sector (agriculture, forestry, fishing) amounted to nearly 50 percent of the total. Japan's first wave of postwar modernization brought this figure down to 30 percent by 1961. It had dropped to under 20 percent by 1967.

Another aspect of the movement toward towns and industry is the continually increasing concentration of the population on the "outward" side of the country, the Pacific side, at the expense of the "inner" side, which looks toward the Sea of Japan. The 1965 census showed an increase of population in twenty-one prefectures out of forty-eight; twenty of these were prefectures on the outward side. All the prefectures on the Sea of Japan except for one were in decline. In ten, the diminution over five years exceeded 4 percent, and in the worst case it reached 8 percent. Thus we have a strongly marked geographical division between a modern, industrialized, urbanized, overpopulated Japan and a "backwoods" Japan which is also a backward Japan or at least an underdeveloped one, not unlike the "old Japan" of former days, a rural country of village dwellers, much more sparsely inhabited; and this is a division that is growing more and more distinct.

Of the plan for thirteen new industrial towns I have mentioned, only two are on the Sea of Japan side. This unequal sharing of the country's economic activity gives rise to serious problems and shows that still further radical improvements are needed in the development of the archipelago. Among the drawbacks of the present situation is the tendency of management and head offices in business, government administration, universities, public transport and so on, to concentrate in the three urban centers of Nagoya, Osaka and above all Tokyo. The capital is becoming the overgrown head of an ill-balanced body.

At all events, urbanization is inevitable in Japan. And the same applies to the accompanying phenomenon which results from the invasion of the countryside and the swelling of the towns so that they push out, meet one another, and form a single urban mass—the phenomenon that has been called conurbation. Take a car and start off from, let us say, Omiya, a place fifteen miles north of Tokyo. Drive due south. Omiya; the enormous suburbs of Tokyo; the capital itself; then Kawasaki, a town of half a million inhabitants; then Yokohama, with nearly two million; and then a whole string of other places beyond until you reach Yokosuka, a naval base now used by the United States. All this will have been one single endless built-up area, and after some hours you will reach the last town without ever having caught so much as a glimpse of the countryside. In the same way one of Tokyo's many tentacles stretches far out toward the southwest, following the Tokaido, the great highway that runs along the Pacific.

The urbanization of the countryside can be felt very distinctly as far as Shizuoka, well over a hundred miles from the capital.

In central Japan the great cities of Osaka, Sakai, Amagasaki and Kobe are almost entirely joined in one vast urban sprawl. Invaded by ever-increasing numbers of houses belonging to people from these overpopulated cities, the countryside between Osaka and Kyoto or Osaka and Nara is beginning to vanish altogether. And it is much the same, as I have already said, around the steel mills in the north of Kyushu, the southern island.

Another factor may have a bearing on the invasion of the Japanese countryside: the earthquakes. It seems to me that it is an important factor for the worse, but I have not heard it mentioned in Japanese discussions of the problem. The overpopulated country of Japan is also a country shaken by seismic tremors. These two factors, overpopulation and earthquakes, combine to cause the houses to be spread out over a greater area than in an ordinary country and to require a greater number of individual houses, small and lightly built. Many-storied houses and of course very tall buildings are quite out of the average man's reach, and it will be a great while before they are seen anywhere outside certain special districts in the main cities. It is likely that all this makes for faster conurbation.

As for the future, the Japanese futurologists look upon vast conurbation on a national scale as something quite unavoidable. All along the coastal strip that runs from Tokyo to beyond Osaka, the present urban clusters will merge to form one gigantic ribbon city stretching over more than three hundred miles.

They calculate that in one generation—that is to say, before the year 2000—80 million Japanese will be gathered together in this endless town, which they call the Tokaido region. It will group 70 percent of the prospective population. The ends and the middle of the strip will be marked by three enormous bulges, the three metropolises of Tokyo, Osaka and Nagoya.

According to an official statement, Tokyo numbered 11,200,717 inhabitants on January 1, 1968. The forecasters reckon that by 1985, well before the end of the century, it will have 33 million. Osaka, with 18 million, will have grown bigger than the present Tokyo. Nagoya will have about 10 million. The Japanese already have a name for the supercity that will absorb all these huge cities into its prodigious urban nebula, a word they have adopted for the occasion: Megalopolis, or the Tokaido Megalopolis. Even now it is taking shape under our very eyes, for about 60 million people are already living in this Tokaido region—that is to say, more than half the present population of the archipelago. The specialists give advance warning of the huge difficulties that will soon arise from this staggering rate of growth and that are indeed arising already. To plan and guide this coming development, they call for the setting up of a megalopolitan authority.

What do the Japanese themselves think about this Japan of tomorrow? Is the coming Megalopolis planned and foreseen only by a handful of megalomaniacs? Is the average Japanese still unaware of the current that is carrying him along and the direction in which he is going? Nothing of the sort; indeed, rather the opposite is true. In Japan it is a whole nation that knows it is heading for the future, a whole society that is turned toward the coming years. The only way of fully understanding the nature of this country's transformation— its force and energy—is to go there and see the drive and zeal of the men who are carrying it through. In the West we are still too apt to look upon the Japanese as people who are coming along behind us on the road of progress, people who are still held back and handicapped by the remoteness and the strangeness of their islands. In short, we think of them as people who are doing their best to catch up with us, but who find it rather hard. But this is no longer true at all. They have overtaken us and gone on ahead.

What is more, in an evolving Japan, the Japanese themselves are changing fast. Fresh attitudes are appearing in both their private and their collective behavior. Youth, weight of numbers, and eagerness to be doing—these are three characteristics that have always struck the visiting foreigner as soon as he mingles with Tokyo's remarkable crowds. These characteristics are more marked than ever, but in a way their tone, their color, has undergone a fundamental change. Formerly it was that of pessimism. Now it is that of optimism. On these countless faces, all of which seem to be twenty years old (oh, the human rivers of the streets, stations, public places, bearing along that myriad of pebble-round faces, and the incessant flow of black heads, wave after wave of them!), the tension and bitterness of earlier days have given way to a serene confidence and often indeed to a visible delight in life. Of course there are also some that show confusion, distress, anger against the present times and the world in general. But this has become the exception. In the military period, I knew a Japanese nation systematically drilled by its leaders into a pessimistic view, both of its present and its future. Our islands are too poor and too small, they said, and there are too many of us; so let us prepare ourselves for crises, unavoidable conflicts and necessary wars. For a short while after the defeat Japan wondered whether the sky were not going to cloud over again, but then quite soon the wind changed. Indeed, it is possible to date the moment of this change exactly.

I was in Japan in 1960 when Hayato Ikeda, the prime minister (he is now dead), told the country that the national income was going to double in ten years and that it would do so in a period of unexampled growth and prosperity. It was said that his forecast was unwise; and maybe there was some truth in that, for it had an inflationary effect on the economy. But one thing is certain: the speech galvanized the Japanese and showed them a sudden new vision of their future. For the first time a prime minister had told them not to prepare for fresh sacrifices but to get ready for a better life. For the first time he had showed them not a Japan stifled by overpopulation and persecuted by an unsympathetic outer world but a Japan in which a hundred million Japanese would manage to live very well on their four islands—a hundred million Japanese on friendly terms with the rest of the world and trading peacefully with it. Soon afterward there was no longer any doubt that by 1970 Japan's national income would in fact have more than doubled. And although individual incomes have not increased as fast as that, they are growing all the time. The great majority of the people have never fared so well; their standard of living has never been so high.

Their pleasure in this is accompanied by a certain pride. To be sure, there are still a good many dark places in the general picture, but it is clear to everybody that Japan has advanced over a broad front and has advanced rapidly, often outstripping Western countries long admired for their superiority. Not so very long ago a Japanese visiting Europe for the first time would be bowled over by the discovery of a bigger, stronger, happier world than his own; and when he went home, his own country would seem to him backward, narrow, cramped and wanting in power. Today there can be no doubt that for the Japanese traveler New York, Paris, London and Rome have lost something of their former standing. Of course the traveler does appreciate their beauty and their culture, but when he compares them with Japan he finds to his surprise that Western countries are not advancing so fast, that Western capital cities leave him with a feeling of old-fashionedness and lack of progress, and that only when he gets home does he come into contact with modernity, life and activity once more. In short, for someone looking at the world from Tokyo, it is the Westerners who seem to be dragging the slow weight of the past and the Asians who are hurrying wholeheartedly and rapidly along the road to the year 2000.

It is a fact that in twenty or thirty years we shall be obliged to live in a world that has been radically changed by the scientific and technical revolutions of our time; and it is therefore urgently necessary for us to set about transforming our institutions, to do so fast, and to do so right away. This is something that the Japanese have understood better than we. The American alliance has played a decisive part in their attitude, but not, I think, the part that is often attributed to it. There is a great deal of talk about the Americanization of Japan, of the degree of mimicry and mutation that will eventually turn the country into a copy of the United States. For my part I do not believe in this; indeed, I will go so far as to say that I do not see this Americanized Japan coming into existence at all. Although the country has certainly been deeply marked by its contact with the United States, Japan remains very much itself; it "nipponizes" what it takes from America much more than it is itself Americanized.

But it is truer to say that above and beyond the image of America and the West (both of them in a state of change), Japan is irresistibly attracted by the image of the year 2000, by the wonderful dawn of that third millennium toward which it is traveling on a road parallel to that taken by the United States and the Western powers. The true part played by the American alliance in this adventure is rather that of a powerful stimulus, a most efficient spur. The Japanese discovered the postwar economic transformations of the United States earlier and more thoroughly than the Americans' European allies; and this they did partly because their defeat brought them closer to America, partly because their wretched condition urged them to learn from America and to adopt American solutions, and partly because they were certainly cleverer than Europeans in making use of American aid without being overwhelmed or turned into a satellite. In short, the Japanese managed to turn the American challenge to their own advantage.

Unceasing change, speed of change, modernity always carried to the highest possible degree, personal mobility: these are a few of the characteristics of the new age that the Japanese have taken to their hearts with such staggering ease.

Change: the modern Japanese is a being for whom everything is in a constant state of flux—the landscape he sees, the street he lives in, his house, his place of work, his job, his pattern of life. His district is turned upside down, his house is given a new story or perhaps it is pulled down and rebuilt, his garden vanishes and a garage takes its place, his office is no longer in a wooden hut but in a huge ultramodern building, his factory is continually modified; but none of this seems to worry him—he just takes it in his stride.

Speed of change: it looks as though the now-vanishing ancient Japan bequeathed the new country a legacy—the strongly held idea of what it used to call "this fleeting world" or "the impermanence of things." But whereas the old world derived a sad, resigned submissiveness from this notion, the new appears to look upon it as a cause for rejoicing and for hastening the change with an insatiable appetite for even greater speed. As an example of this altered attitude: There used to be a little piece of very old Tokyo still in existence on an island in the mouth of the Sumida River; it was a genuine fishing village right in the middle of the city. You had to take a ferry to get there, just as people had always done, and the passage was free. Suddenly the island was an island no more. In a few months an "Olympic" expressway had leaped the stream, linking the two banks, sweeping away the old houses and filling the tranquillity with the roar of trucks and automobiles. I am only a citizen of Tokyo by adoption, but who else felt a pang in his heart? *Shikata-ga-nai*, say the Japanese, meaning that there is nothing to be done about it. But this Japanese *nichevo* that one hears so often no longer expresses resignation. It is full of active approval for everything that is new; it is the young people's retort of "Too bad" when softhearted old dodderers lament the disappearance of the past.

Modernity: that is the passion of this ancient country which is in the act of growing young again. The grandsons of the samurai outdo most of the West in the use of all gadgets; they are thoroughly at home with automation and with all the mechanical, electrical, synthetic wonders of this mechanized world. Take television, for example. They got their teeth into it early and in short order developed seven channels, color television on four of them, all the news in color, and, by 1967, seven hours of color a day. In that year there were over 1.2 million color sets in Japan; three years later, an estimated 5.5 million offering ten hours of color. A black-and-white set costs the equivalent of about $93; color, about $300. Many homes have several television sets, including portable and miniature versions. Many hotels have one in every room. And there are twenty hours of programs a day, from six in the morning on.

A fraction over 94 percent of Japanese homes have television, and other household machines of every kind are widely used too; there are washing machines in 75 percent of the houses, sewing machines in 76.6 percent, refrigerators in 61.6 percent, vacuum cleaners in 41.2 percent. In the country television is even more general than it is in the towns, since it is the perfect amusement for peasants, even the poorest among them. The figures prove it: 99.1 percent of peasant families have television! In the towns there is another domestic appliance which, in view of Japan's oppressively damp summer heat, is understandably widely used—the air conditioner. It is not only theaters, movie houses, big stores, hotels and offices that are air-conditioned, but countless public and private places, including great numbers of boutiques, little restaurants, and cafés, as well as thousands and thousands of homes.

There is an extraordinarily widespread ownership of cameras, both for still and moving pictures. The cameras are infinitely varied, usually good, and cheaper than they are in the West; and the Japanese are exceedingly keen and, what is more, skillful photographers. Then again, Japan has a far bigger public for transistor radios, tape recorders, walkie-talkies and so on. As for "community gadgets "such as escalators and electronically controlled doors, they are much more usual than in the West, particularly the escalators. And lastly there is the telephone, to which the Japanese are passionately attached.

Another field in which Japanese progress in modernity is evident is that of synthetic substances and materials of all kinds—the man-made fibers, which will soon allow them to be dressed almost entirely in artificial textiles, and plastics of every sort, which are gradually re-placing wood, metal, paper, leather and so forth. The everyday world is being positively invaded by plastics; they have even made their way into the traditional equipment of the Japanese house, and already it is possible to see *tatami* (mats) made of synthetic materials. (Whether this is a change for the better or not is quite a different question.)

There is still another field in which they are moving faster than Westerners are: this is the modernization and the mechanization of mass tourism. In twenty years' time there will scarcely be a Japanese lake without its tourist-laden hydroplanes, its high-speed catamarans, its jet- or aerial-propeller-driven boats; no accessible peak without its cable car; no well-known mountain without its funicular. The first hovercraft were in service in Japan at a time when they were still in the developmental stage in all other countries. As early as the begin-ning of 1968 a kind of little wheelless car that traveled on a cushion of air was on the market, and its price was no more than 370,000 yen (under $900).

As a journalist I was also quite astonished at the modern facilities that great newspapers, radio and television put at my Japanese col-leagues' disposition. In 1962, which was by no means yesterday, I went to have a look at Nagoya, a great, rapidly expanding city, and I was met at the station by fellow journalists from the *Chubu Nippon Shimbun* (the Central Japan Newspaper), which is the main pro-vincial daily of those parts. They said, "Instead of taking the car, what do you say to getting into the paper's helicopter and going for a flight over the town right away?" Of course I agreed enthusiastically, and my visit to Nagoya began by a view of the city from the sky. I learned in passing that this same newspaper also owned three planes that were used both for news reporting and for distribution. And journalists out on a story in the remoter parts of the province used little radios to dictate their copy straight to the paper's central desk. In Tokyo, the *Asahi*, the biggest paper in the country (its circulation is an almost unbelievable nine million a day, the world's highest), owns a dozen planes, run by a staff of over forty. The *Asahi* also prints one of its many regional editions by radioing a photographic reproduction of the Tokyo edition. The Hokkaido edition is produced in this way, and the technique means that in twenty minutes an exact copy of a page of the Tokyo paper comes off the presses in Sapporo, the capital of the

great northern island, where incidentally, the Winter Olympics of 1972 are to be held.

It is likely that before long Japan will be ahead of all other countries as far as daring journalistic innovations are concerned. For example, the Japanese are doing research upon the television set of tomorrow: this will not only supply the viewer with a colored picture but also with a printed newspaper that the set itself will produce right there in the house by telephotography. Clearly this overwhelming eagerness for modernity will very soon do away with the archipelago's last strongholds of backwardness and stagnation.

Another thing that makes the course of change and progress even faster is the extraordinary mobility of the people themselves. The Japanese are perpetually traveling about their own country, and they do so from the earliest age. The primary schools' program includes taking the children to see the country's great cities and its most famous sights. Every year the pupils, even those from the villages, can form part of a group that tours one of the regions of Japan for several days, led by their teachers; and all at moderate cost. By the time they have finished school they have a personal, firsthand experience of their country's geography and of its main artistic treasures. The grown-ups in their turn are most enthusiastic travelers, and for vacations or business missions they usually travel in groups. This same intense eagerness to see things, this same restlessness, also sends them out on voyages of discovery all over the world. Anyone who uses the great airlines knows that next to the Americans the Japanese are their most usual customers.

A most striking picture of this personal mobility is provided by the New Tokaido electrified railroad, which runs from Tokyo to Osaka, the capital of central Japan. The ordinary railroad, the Old Tokaido, was slow and overcrowded, so alongside it they built a new line for ultramodern "superexpresses." This new line is built high over the ordinary road and rail traffic, and there is not a single grade crossing or point switch anywhere along its whole length. It carries passenger trains only; no freight. Technically it is a masterpiece: it has nine bridges, each over five hundred yards long, in addition to twelve tunnels of well over a mile; all traffic is electronically controlled; and automation is carried to the highest degree. The one thing that everybody remembered when it was opened in 1963 was that Japan now had the fastest trains in the world. And in fact the superexpress runs the 345 miles between Tokyo and Osaka in a record time of three hours and ten minutes, with two stops. At times its speed is greater than 125 miles an hour, and it may reach peaks of 150 to 160 miles an hour. The cost for a one-way first-class ticket is the equivalent of about $16, and there is no need to book seats ahead of time because of the remarkable frequency of trains. In 1968, there were seventy-six trips on weekdays and eighty-five on Sundays. They carried an average daily number of 180,000 travelers. (On August 15, an important holiday, there were as many as 300,000.)

The passengers on the 345-mile superexpress trip look like people who are merely going to their offices. They carry very little baggage, usually no more than a plain leather—or plastic—briefcase. Many of them make the return journey the same day. Most are thoroughly used to the trip and go back and forth twice or three times a week.

This personal mobility, this easy, rapid traveling, is doing away with the former rigid barriers between the world of Tokyo and that of the provinces. It favors decentralization, and it is a potent factor in the country's new development. The New Tokaido is already being lengthened, for the Japanese never rest on their laurels; the extension to Okayama, farther south, is well along, and early in the 1970's the superexpress will run as far as Hiroshima. Later it will reach Kyushu, the southern island. Plans are being made to carry it on in the other direction, northward; and when within ten years' time this line is working, it will stimulate the development of the still backward northern parts of Japan.

To crown all this, the Japanese engineers envisage the building of a network of superexpress lines radiating in all directions from Tokyo. The inhabitants of the satellite towns around the capital will no longer have to spend an hour and a half or two hours getting to their jobs as they do at present, but half or one third of that time.

The New Tokaido superexpress is no longer really a train; it is already a subway. A subway on a national scale—the supersubway of the Megalopolis of the year 2000 that is now coming into existence on the shores of the Pacific.

Yet even when this forward-looking Japan and its headlong career toward the future have been thoroughly described, the picture is neither true nor complete without a view of the firmly present "old Japan," solidly rooted in its traditional immobility and weighed down by the burden of the past. For Japan is a whole tissue of contradictions. As soon as some statement, firmly based upon observed evidence, is put forward, a conflicting and equally well-based statement can be advanced either to nullify or refute it. This is because the nation is perpetually torn between opposites, between extreme positions. In any other country these oppositions would seem both irreconcilable and intolerable, but the Japanese adjust to them. What is more, they even derive part of their energy from this perpetual division, part of their drive from the fact of always being between two contrary poles. It is as though they were electrified by it.

In Japanese life there are the most surprising contrasts to be seen at every turn. Fifty miles from the enormous ribbon city where the superexpresses hurtle through a steel and concrete landscape, the backward rural world of Japan displays its whitewood and its straw from one end of the archipelago to the other.

In the life of a Japanese citizen, the behavior of a Westernized twentieth-century man can give way in a few moments to the Oriental way of life and to premodern attitudes. A new folklore has sprung up around the gadgets and automation of mechanized Japan, but it has in no way destroyed the old folklore of the Japan of the rice fields. A full-blown ultramodern industry competes with America or Europe, but beneath or behind it there can be seen another industrial structure at a lower or different level—that of the still traditional and Asian crafts and of the countless little firms that are scarcely affected by modern organization. On the Pacific side of the country a new world turned toward the future and toward international horizons is developing at breakneck speed; on the opposite side, facing the Sea of Japan, is the stagnation of the Japanese backwoods, as they are called in Tokyo, the Japan "in the shadow of the mountains," which remains an ancient underdeveloped world, closed in upon itself.

To be sure, the Japanese often complain of this lack of balance and of these inequalities, but it is a state of affairs that frightens and irritates them less than it would us. And what is much more to the point, the existence of these striking differences of level between the various sectors in the economic and social life is an integral part of the country's system of development. It is one of the requirements for its economic makeup, a basic factor in its drive for modernization.

The Japanese leaders' first rule of progress is to thrust forward to the utmost extent on the widest possible front, and to occupy the advanced positions as fast as they can; if a whole section of the economy finds it hard to follow or even falls behind, that is just too bad. Like generals sending the vanguard deep into enemy territory without waiting for the bulk of the army, the leaders believe that what really matters is the spearhead, the thrust that will eventually carry all the rest along behind it. In international competition Japan has to keep abreast of the most advanced countries, without waiting for its more backward sectors to catch up. The country has to make sure of acquiring the most up-to-date techniques, even if they are very expensive, and it is willing to accept the continued existence of a poor, needy section of the community. It feels that although the members of that section may not be enriched personally, they will nevertheless profit by the greater wealth and the progress of society as a whole.

Most Japanese share this outlook, and there are many instances of it in daily life. Who are the people in the futuristic surroundings of the underground Shinjuku square that I described earlier? Who are the countless pedestrians in that busy hive? For the most part they are people who have obviously just come from some modest or even penurious home, people who live in the traditional way—straw mats and paper windows—in their suburbs or their villages, and who for that very reason are all the more pleased because as part of the general community they have access to the comfort, the mechanical wonders, the facilities and the beauties of modern life in their extraordinary city of Tokyo.

Besides, this uneven development and these discrepancies in the country's progress are by no means a modern phenomenon. Japan has been carrying on in this way for a hundred years. Indeed, it was one of the most striking features of the country's approach to the modern world when the Emperor Meiji came to the throne and Japan determined to catch up with the countries of the West.

2.

Japan's Hundredth Birthday

In Tokyo, on September 12, 1872, the authorities of the new regime set up by the young Emperor Meiji were all present in the Shimbashi station, its pink brick and gleaming cement all brand new. The new Japan was four years old, and already it was opening its first railroad. The assembly was made up solely of men, but most of them still had on kimonos with long brown or black silk skirts, and some were wearing the two terrible swords of the samurai. When the train with its short many-doored carriages drew into the platform, all these important people took off their shoes before getting in, just as one is required to do on the first step of a Japanese house. The engine gave a cheerful hoot, the train began to move along the narrow-gauge line, and in no more than fifty-seven minutes it ran the eighteen or nineteen miles through the rice fields between Tokyo and the port of Yoko-hama. At the far end the court and the government were greeted with great pomp; they stepped out of the train delighted but embarrassed—all these elegant people were in their socks, because the shoes had stayed, carefully and correctly lined up, on the platform in Tokyo!

There are many other stories about these heroic beginnings. For example, there were the court ladies who sent to Paris (Paris even then!) for evening dresses and who appeared at some grand dinner wearing corsets for the first time, put on with the utmost difficulty over the dresses. These touching awkwardnesses and mistakes were thoroughly understandable; the new Japan was only just getting under way, trying with unbelievable eagerness to modernize itself as quickly as it possibly could.

Now that they had emerged from two centuries of seclusion, during which all contact with the "Southern Barbarians" (the Western nations) had been forbidden and any voyage abroad had been a crime that carried the death penalty, these warriors with their two swords were obsessed with the idea of westernizing themselves through and through.

Although they were suddenly taking to Western ways and Western machinery, it was not out of love for the West, as some might have supposed, but rather as a means of learning how to withstand its assault. Like the Emperor Meiji himself, these new leaders were nationalists, and the reason they were opening the doors so wide was that they did not want the West to break them down. By opening the doors themselves they would be able to learn from the white men and to imitate their weapons.

For the "white peril" was at its height. The carving up of China had begun: the Western powers had taken Peking and sacked the Summer Palace. The English, French, Germans and Russians were continually increasing their pressure on Asia, sending expeditions all over the great continent, from Cochin-China to Siberia. The smoke-belching "black ships" had been prowling along the Japanese coasts since 1846. In 1854 Commodore Perry, representing the United States, had broken down Japanese isolation and had forced the country to sign a treaty. In 1863 an Anglo-French fleet had shelled the town of Kagoshima in retaliation for the murder of an English businessman. In 1866 the English had assembled a powerful fleet before Hyogo (now Kobe) to oblige the Japanese to sign a commercial treaty and to grant a favorable tariff. Japan, with no ships, no army, no industry and no money, could not risk a war that would lead to the same disaster that China had experienced. So the first of the Emperor Meiji's acts was to summon the foreign ambassadors and to declare that they were "his welcome guests," at the same time promising that the Westerners should be protected from all violence.

It was a drastic change; and this Japan now opening itself to foreign influence was a Japan that in fact hated foreigners. This was but one of the many paradoxes of the Meiji restoration. The feudal nobles had carried it out, but in order to unite the country and give it a strong government they had done away with their whole feudal system. They were the upholders of an aristocratic and authoritarian regime, but to make the nation into a single entity and to create the Japanese state they were now wiping out all social barriers that would prevent the rise of deserving citizens, even the humblest of them. In short, Japan was making use of the technique of total reversal the better to defend itself. This was not the first time in its history that it had done so; nor, as we now know, was it to be the last.

And this decision brought about the first "Japanese miracle" of our period—the "noncolonization" of the Land of the Rising Sun. At a time when colonial conquest was overwhelming Africa, invading Asia, and reducing China to slavery, Japan managed to avert the danger. Japan managed to treat with the West as an independent country and to agree to invasion by Western methods and techniques alone—an invasion that was under Japanese supervision and that was calculated to strengthen Japanese independence.

A little while ago the Japanese celebrated the hundredth anniversary of their entry upon the world stage, and they did so with a justifiable pride. Modern Japan was a hundred years old in 1968. For it was on January 3, 1868, that the Emperor Mutsuhito, who had succeeded his father on the throne one year before, proclaimed that the power of the Tokugawa shogun was at an end and announced the restoration of the imperial authority. In the customary way his reign was at once given a splendid name: it was termed that of Meiji—that is to say, the reign of enlightened government—and later, at the time of his death in 1912, the name was applied to the emperor himself. Until the "Meiji restoration," as the Japanese call it, the imperial power had been in eclipse for centuries. The country was in fact ruled by a second monarch, a kind of military dictator; this was the shogun, and he stood at the apex of the pyramid of feudal clans (the literal meaning of *shogun* is "general"). What amounted to a positive dynasty—the Tokugawa family—had wielded this parallel authority since the beginning of the seventeenth century. The shogun, its head, lived at Edo (now Tokyo) in a heavily fortified palace, while the emperor, himself the descendant of a dynasty whose beginnings were lost in the mist of legend, was no more than a powerless ruler, almost forgotten in his palace at Kyoto, the ancient capital.

The erosion of the shogun's authority, the ferment brought about by the pressure of the Western nations, the decay of the social and economic system in a country that had been shut away too long, the revolt of a number of the feudal vassals—these were some of the reasons why the old order fell to pieces, after disturbances lasting some fifteen years. On the whole it was not at all a bloodstained revolution. The shogun himself was not put to death; he and his family stepped into the background. Few Japanese know it, but his great-grandson, Tsunetaka Tokugawa, who is now around thirty, works in a shipping firm whose head office is in Tokyo. The Emperor Meiji (or Mutsuhito at that time) was only sixteen in 1868, but he brought to the throne a strong mind, matured by recent events and open to new and daring ideas. He had an outstanding talent for surrounding himself with very capable advisers; they were also young men, though not as young as the emperor, and they too were filled with a passionate desire to bring the new Japan into existence.

It would be possible to draw fascinating comparisons between the Japanese experience and that which China went through during the same period. The mandarins who governed China were scholars, refined and conservative, who had nothing but contempt and dislike for the Western barbarians. They scornfully rejected all contact and declined to receive foreign embassies in Peking. The very most they would do was to allow the foreigners to open a few factories, as long as they were kept apart and at a distance. In Japan the ruling class had military origins, for it was recruited from the families of the samurai. It was very much aware of the military power of the West, and at the same time it was eager for Japan to be so strong that the country's sovereignty would be assured.

The Japan of the samurai therefore felt a mixture of admiration and dread for the "Southern Barbarians." Confronted with the West, the country decided to open its gates and let the foreigners in, so as to learn their methods and discover their secrets. In Peking the old Dowager Empress Tz'u-hsi stubbornly went on refusing to have anything to do with the modern world until the Middle Kingdom fell to pieces; she held out against "the powers" until the sack of Peking in 1902. In Kyoto, as early as 1868, the young Emperor Meiji had stepped resolutely into the present age. On April 6, 1868, he took his coronation oath, and in it he proclaimed, "We shall summon assemblies, and in ruling the nation We shall have regard to public opinion. . . . Knowledge will be sought out among the nations of the world, and thus the well-being of the empire will be ensured."

Old China, that centralized state governed by the most ancient and long-lasting administration the world had ever known, fell wholly apart under the blows of the foreigner. But under this same impact of the West, Japan, which had until that time been a patchwork of many clans, became a united nation by the working of what might be called fusion or crystallization; here the Western graft took at once upon the old Japanese stock—ideas, methods, and military, economic and governmental systems. In China, on the contrary, everything Western in origin died away or went bad, and this state of affairs continued for half a century and more, right up to the China of Mao Tse-tung. A first cause for this decay was the fact that the Chinese brought foreigners into their finance and their economy, something that the Japanese took great care never to do.

There is also a valid comparison to be made between Mao's China of today and Meiji's Japan of yesterday. In either case we have a rising generation of revolutionaries flinging themselves into action at a very early age. But in Japan these were revolutionaries who at once started constructive work. They did not blow up the old world with all its traditions, its outlook, and its way of life. Far from it: they protected the old world by locking it away, sheltering it behind walls erected for the purpose. At the same time they were determined to build up a new world beside it, a world on the Western model. They plunged into the unparalleled, unprecedented experiment of a country with a twofold civilization, one in which every Japanese lives half his time as an Occidental and half as an Oriental, moving from the one world to the other with a nimble ease that we find astonishing.

In China the attitude of the Communist revolution toward the culture of the ancient world is altogether different. To be sure, it does restore and protect the monuments of the past, and it does open splendid museums to preserve its archaeological treasures and to show them to the people. But in fact the legacy of the past is itself rejected, relegated to the past; it is no longer alive—it no longer has any place in the life of today. This rejection reached its height with the launching of the cultural revolution in 1966: "the old ways"—that is to say, the old way of life, the old ways of thinking and the old beliefs—were to be swept away, and all that remains of them is systematically attacked. The new Chinese will not be twofold men like the Japanese; it is essential that everything in their makeup should be fresh and that it should belong solely to the new era opened by Maoism. Then again, in China (another contrast with the Japanese revolution), Mao Tse-tung and his companions had spent the greatest part of their lives fighting to destroy the old world and to sweep the huge amount of rubbish away; they were already old when they came to power and began building. Their strength was failing at a time when almost everything was still to be accomplished.

It is striking to see the China of today struggling with certain problems that the Japan of one hundred years ago had already begun to solve. It is true that the Chinese could retort that the Japanese answer was in its essence an over-easy solution—just the imitation of the West. China has a far more revolutionary ambition, which is no less than the discovery of a new formula for an ideal society. Why should there be only one model on earth, the Western model? We have always done things in a different way from the West, the Chinese might say, and we have always done them better. So they will have nothing to do with any of the formulas that have already been tried out, nothing to do with those of China's past or with those of the West, ancient or modern; for what they mean to do is build up a model world that has been reinvented by China itself.

However this may be, at present the Japanese are studying the history of their beginnings with passionate interest, looking for the answers to all manner of questions. What were the secret reasons for their success at first? Why did disaster come upon them little more than thirty years after the reign of Meiji? The Emperor Meiji and the men who worked with him—were they to some degree responsible? Can the Japanese experiment serve as an example for other nations? Can it, for instance, provide answers to the problems of those countries that are now trying to emerge from a state of underdevelopment?

The Japanese are by no means all in agreement about how these questions should be answered, but there seems to be at least one undeniable conclusion that emerges very clearly from this inspection of the past: From the very beginning Japan displayed exceptional talents for living in the modern epoch. In particular, it has been discovered that feudal Japan was much more "modern" than was generally supposed. Although it was subdivided in a patchwork of clans, even before the Meiji era the country displayed a high degree of cohesion, with an outstanding racial and linguistic unity. As early as Tokugawa times, communications in Japan were busy and highly developed; there were many roads and an efficient, sophisticated postal service. The economy was at the stage that comes just before the modern system: it already had nationwide markets for a number of products such as rice, sake, and shoyu (a sauce that is much used in Japanese cookery), and it had firmly based and highly developed monetary and banking institutions.

A point of fundamental importance is that public education had reached a remarkable stage of development under the old regime. It has recently been found that by the end of the Tokugawa period, in 1867, more than 40 percent of the population could read and write. Education had even reached the working classes, and in a great many of the villages there was a "temple school" kept by a monk, where the peasant children, even girls, were taught reading, writing and the use of the abacus (*soroban*) from the age of six. At a higher level, the samurai, who for the most part were no longer fighting men (it was a time of profound peace) but clan civil servants, were educated in the Confucian doctrines; they were encouraged to develop their gifts and to specialize—in contrast to the China of the mandarins, where general literary culture was very highly esteemed, but not specialization or technical ability. The clans competed among themselves for the services of the ablest and most highly educated samurai, for with the fear of a foreign invasion the need for capable men was even greater. The watchwords that became so well known as national slogans in the Meiji era in fact originated among the clans before the restoration. "Enrich the nation and strengthen the army" (*fukoku kyohei*), for example; or this, which has such a modern ring, "Encourage industry and increase production" (*shokusan kogyo*).

Each clan was already a kind of little state with a high degree of administrative centralization, and in each the samurai, who were not landowners and who now had no military power, made up an organized body of officials, their salary being paid in rice. The clans as a whole were under the firm authority of the ruling clan, that of the Tokugawas, and of its chief, the shogun. Japan was still feudal, but this was a strongly centralized feudalism—a state of affairs that was of great help in the setting up of the new order under the Emperor Meiji, for allegiance was easily and effectively transferred from the clan to the nation. When all is said and done, Emperor Meiji did not bring Japan out of feudalism; all he did was to lead the country along the second half of a road that was to some degree already open.

To modern eyes another feature is very striking: from the beginning Japan managed to "take off" economically while relying on itself alone, not allowing itself to be tempted or overwhelmed by foreign aid. It is a most remarkable fact that Japan never turned to foreign capital. Between the restoration and the end of the century there was only one solitary Japanese industrial loan raised in the West, and that was a loan of something under a million pounds sterling to help in the building of the Yokohama railroad. The basic reason for this attitude was dread of a foreign penetration that might endanger the nation's independence. Emperor Meiji's ministers, cautious and well-informed statesmen, knew what had happened in Egypt and Turkey, countries that had run into debt and had then squandered the money they borrowed in Europe, thus giving a handle to foreign intervention.

On the other hand Japan never hesitated to make use of Western experts and technicians; there were a great many of them, they were well chosen, they were very well paid, and they played an exceedingly important part in the development of the country.

The Japanese, too, were clever enough to import the best foreign machines. They were often accused of copying them and of being nothing but imitators, but this accusation takes no account of the fact that imitation and the acquisition of imported techniques is an unavoidable first stage in the development of any backward country. The Japanese were remarkably gifted in the rapid taking over of new skills (few underdeveloped countries can say as much) and even in the systematic improvement of them—a particularly Japanese talent. This had been so even in the Japan of feudal times; the Portuguese taught the Japanese to make weapons, and it was not long before the pupils outdid their masters. There was a battle at Shimabara in 1637, at which the Japanese produced artillery that was better than anything existing in Europe at the time—that is to say, immediately before the reign of Louis XIV. (Japan soon lost the art of gunmaking, however, for during the time the country was closed to foreigners arms were laid aside.)

Industry in Japan has moved by successive stages: first, the importation of machinery made abroad; second, the manufacture of foreign-designed machinery in Japan, the Japanese having acquired the patents; and last, the manufacture of Japanese-designed machinery in Japan itself. In some sectors, particularly that of machine tools, the importing stage went on until 1945.

Remarkable speed of economic growth is not a purely modern phenomenon in Japan. It made its appearance at the end of the nineteenth century, and it grew more marked from the beginning of the twentieth. During the thirty years between 1870 and 1900 the Japanese laid the foundations of their industry, thanks to the rapid setting up of a strong government, of universal education, of a full range of financial institutions, and of a well-developed transportation network. The traditional industries expanded fast, and then the last fifteen years of the nineteenth century witnessed the rise of modern industry. From the time of the victory over China in 1895 the country was in full economic revolution. The monetary system was strengthened, Tokyo adopted the gold standard, and Japanese capitalism became part of the worldwide system. A little after 1900 Japan reached the stage of being self-sufficient in textiles. After the victory over Czarist Russia in the war of 1904–1905 there came the real "take off."

Japan's backwardness in relation to the West was to be done away with in little over a quarter of a century. If, in calculating the expansion rate for this period, we adopt the coefficient of 100 for the year 1900, the figure for 1937 is nearly 2,000. Between 1900 and 1940 the output of manufactures increased by twelve times, which is four times greater than the growth observed in the rest of the world. Investment was very heavy indeed and the formation rate of capital exceedingly high. It is evident that Japan, a country of small personal incomes, was making a prodigious effort. Should it also be said that Japan was profiting by its "colonial robberies" in Korea or Taiwan to a certain extent? According to the specialists, Japan poured more wealth into the economy of these countries than it took out.

Both in the economic and the political fields, the beginning of the twentieth century stands out as a golden age in Japanese history. During the years 1905 to 1913 there was a boom; after a short depression the boom began again in 1915, thanks to World War I, and went on until 1920. There was still progress from 1920 to 1929, though it was not without setbacks (the earthquake of 1923, agricultural difficulties); 1929, the beginning of the great American depression, was the first of three bad years for the Japanese. But the 1931 devaluation encouraged exports, and although politically the years 1931 to 1937 were disastrous (they were marked by the rise of militarism and by movement in the direction of war), economically they were good. Exports doubled, thus provoking European protectionism. By this time Japan had reached the height of its expansion. The *zaibatsu* (literally, the "money powers"), a ruling group of great families that shared large-scale industry and commerce between them, strengthened their hold, a hold that was still as powerful as that of the army. From the very beginning of the war in the Pacific, the Americans discovered that Japanese technology was much more advanced than they had thought, striking examples being the effectiveness of the Japanese fleet and the high quality of its air force, which, among others, included the Zero fighter.

At this period the outside world underestimated Japan because the Japanese goods sold abroad were of the shoddiest quality whereas the finer products of Japanese industry never left the country, for the very good reason that they were the secret manufactures of the state-controlled armament factories, meant for the army and the navy, the most demanding of customers. In 1905 Admiral Togo won Japan's first naval victory, defeating the Russian fleet at Tsushima with ships that were made in England, but immediately afterwards Japan provided itself with an excellent fleet made in Japan; and in 1906 the battleship *Satsuma* was rated the biggest in the world. The descendants of the samurai were already making a dangerous combination of their talent for technology and their talent for war. More than one instance of this could be mentioned: there were the torpedoes, which made their way into world history at Port Arthur; or, that first of all military telegrams, the one which brought about the victory of Tsushima. And we need scarcely speak of the first mobile field kitchens or the first trench warfare, both of which were to be seen on the Korean front in the Russo-Japanese War.

But let us go back to the beginning of the Meiji era, when this twist, this bias toward militarism, was absent. It was the time of initial successes, a time when there were shadows in the picture, to be sure, but when the brighter aspects completely outweighed them; and this general advance may be attributed essentially to one first cause—the high quality of leadership. The Meiji generation was outstanding in all fields; government, industry, national defense, arts and letters. The leaders were great men because they had been shaped by the new Japan's revolution—thirty years of fundamental change from the middle of the century—and because they were acted upon by powerful historic forces. They in turn truly shaped their own period. These men who left a lasting mark on the country formed a brilliant group, from Iwakura, the first of the Meiji era statesmen, and his successor, Prince Ito, the father of the constitution, to Itagaki and Okuma, the first upholders of civil rights. And there were many others—Saigo, the reactionary soldier; Matsukata, the financier; General Yamagata, the founder of the imperial army; Sanjo, Okubo, Kido and other great figures of the restoration; or, leaving politics aside, men like Iwasaki, the founder of the Mitsubishi trust, or the writers Tsubouchi and Mori, or that most influential philosopher Fukuzawa, and so on. The Japanese of today are not always uncritically admiring of them, but they do admit that these men had the great merit of seeing what needed to be done and of doing it.

They were far more given to empirical realism than to idealism, and they were tough characters on the whole; but they were strong-minded men and they were united by one passionate desire, that of creating the Japanese nation. For this they wanted above all a strong state. When they endowed the country with a constitution (having got along very well without one during the first twenty years of their government), it was to set up a markedly conservative and oligarchic state. The constitution provided the emperor with considerable power, but this power returned through him to the little ruling group that governed in his name. The parliament was elected not by the people but by the restricted vote of a favored section; and in any case the people, strongly attached as they were to the family system and to their rural traditions, were in a way even more conservative than their leaders.

On the other hand, at the beginning of the Meiji era the leaders displayed unusually progressive ideas in an area of essential importance for the country's development—that of education. They at once insisted upon compulsory primary education and the system of grouped, state-controlled schools. Rich and poor, even peasants' children, went to school upon an entirely equal footing—a liberalism that had no equivalent in the Europe of that time. The new leaders themselves came for the most part from the lower reaches of the samurai class,

and even before the restoration they had begun to oust the aristocrats
of the clans. Social barriers fell, and every man had the possibility of
rising fast; in this way the community made sure of recruiting the
finest talents. Very soon higher education was open to them—Tokyo
University, for example, and the military and naval colleges, where
there was not the least social discrimination.

Meanwhile it often happened that the new men entrusted with the
building up of the economy had, in addition to their zeal, only the
most elementary knowledge of their subject. This was the case with
Matsukata, for example: he had studied in France under Léon Say,
Jean-Baptiste Say's grandson, and he based himself upon this somewhat indifferent model. Still, he did manage to stabilize the currency,
bring in the gold standard, and found the Bank of Japan. With many
of these men, wealth of ideas counterbalanced lack of experience;
though indeed the experience soon came, for they plunged very early
into action. A striking instance is that remarkable man Shibusawa, one
of the leading figures in the development of industry. He set up the
First National Bank of Japan in Tokyo, basing it upon American
models, and he became its president at the age of twenty-three or
twenty-four. He replaced water power by steam, imported English
weaving machinery, founded the first great spinning mills in Osaka and
introduced imported cotton to take the place of that grown in Japan.
Until about 1920 he remained one of the leaders in the building up
of the economy, a man overflowing with new ideas, interested in every
branch of industry, organizing and advising without growing rich himself, and, into the bargain, begetting countless children—"All by the
same wife," say his admirers, laughing, and among his descendants
they point to innumerable highly talented university professors and
technologists.

In the lower levels of this new industry there was a comparable zeal
and drive. One illustration is to be found in a recently discovered diary
of a girl who worked in the first modern silk-spinning mill, which was
set up at Tomioka, on one of the poor southern islands, by some
French engineers from Lyons. In her diary, Hideko Wada recorded
the mill's history. An old and poor samurai was the factory's makeshift
manager; he tried to engage peasant girls as mill hands, but their parents would not have it because the factory had a steam engine and a
tall, smoking chimney. "They mean to suck our daughters' blood,"

said the peasants. Next the manager turned to the daughters of the samurai—the same refusal. In the end one did accept, and she was his own daughter. Upon this some others, including Hideko, followed her example. They were all about sixteen or seventeen, and it was they who ran the mill, with heroic feats of energy, ingenuity and economy. An aged craftsman tried to make them follow his three-hundred-year-old technique. Hideko refused. She took a skein of silk, worked it up in her own way, and sent it to the inspectors in Yokohama; it was she who won—her product was better than any of the others' and her methods were adopted. By the time she had been working for a year she managed to put aside five yen, a trifling sum. She asked her father to buy her a kimono. "No," said her father; instead, he spent the five yen on dried beans as a present for the mill girls' dormitory. "Papa was right!" wrote Hideko in her diary. The Africans, Indians and others of today might follow this example of employer–employee relations.

But in general, the fate of the workers at the beginning of the Meiji period was hardly enviable, and the way they were treated cannot possibly be held up for imitation. Industrialization was carried out by means of an intensive exploitation of the peasants and the countryside, where the poorer tenants handed over half their harvest to the landowner. It is true that there was great progress in agriculture, and the yield per acre reached striking figures. But the new fiscal legislation imposed a land tax, and while the state reinvested its produce in industry, the drain of money cruelly diminished the resources of the countryside. Another form of exploitation occurred in the employment of women. In many of the factories, and above all in the textile mills— the center of the infant Japanese capitalism—the workers were women, most of them daughters of poor peasants earning themselves a dowry before they married. Until 1930 half the labor force in the factories was female. And for all the workers, men and women too, the wages were terribly low, the working conditions often unbelievably harsh, and the workers completely without protection. This was the result of the overpopulated countryside spilling into the towns, giving the employers an inexhaustible pool of cheap labor that could be tapped at will for industry (as later it was tapped for war). There was not yet anything that could rightly be called a working class; only a mass of wandering workers whom the factories did not even attempt to retain, since at any moment they could engage others in their place.

Life, even up to the level of the middle class, was hard and quite remarkably frugal. Individual incomes were very low, whereas the nation's economy was growing very fast—this is a particularly Japanese sort of contrast, and one that went on well beyond the Meiji period. It is a contrast that says much about the cost of progress—an advance that was paid for very heavily indeed in intense effort and in every kind of sacrifice.

But in any case success did not long outlast the Emperor Meiji, who died in 1912 at the age of sixty. In 1909 the wind had already begun to change, for in that year Prince Ito was assassinated at Harbin by a Korean patriot who was determined to revenge the recent subjugation of his country. Other evil omens were General Nogi's suicide and his will, which cried out against the moral confusion of the times. After World War I, the Japanese success was to change to disaster within the space of five and twenty years. How can this astonishing decline be explained?

The Japanese Marxists say that the praise traditionally accorded to the first emperor of modern times is quite misplaced; they damn the Meiji era in all respects, for, say they, it already contained within it the seeds of the militaristic fascist period. Those former feudal nobles could not possibly be genuine revolutionaries, they say. They tried to carry through an industrial revolution without a social revolution. They set up a so-called democracy which in fact preserved antidemocratic institutions and states of mind: the privilege of birth and wealth, a hierarchy based upon the lord-vassal relationship, the anachronistic monarchy, a clan system in which the military clique was already thrusting forward for domination. Japan's staggering success was therefore undermined by the contradictions of an era that was still in the stage before true capitalism and which remained essentially feudal.

But together with some other observers, including Japanese historians and critics, I am inclined to think that this is an oversimplified explanation, one that does no more than denounce a kind of original sin by the name of feudalism. In fact, both the men and the problems seem more complex and worthy of a more detailed analysis. Turning first to the men, we notice that as the first Meiji generation gave way to the second there was a decline in quality—a decline that continued with the third generation in the next reign, which was that of the

Emperor Taisho (1912 to 1926). A brilliant cluster of statesmen created Meiji's Japan; but that Japan, in its turn, produced few statesmen of the first ability. Apart from a few exceptions such as Saionji and Katsura, the newcomers were usually bureaucrats who had been formed by a political life that had grown ordinary and commonplace, particularly after the Russo-Japanese War. The parliamentary system as it then existed produced little more than indifferent run-of-the-mill policies. Under the influence of the constitution and of the well-known imperial rescript on education that shaped the younger generations, public life had become hidebound, rigid. The system produced admirable executives but not many men who were capable of hitting upon well-chosen long-term policies and aims. There was bankruptcy at the top level.

The state was dividing itself into rival groups; there was no one above these parties strong enough to decide between them and to impose his decision, nor was there any constitutional machinery that could resolve their differences. The new generation was not united by the adventure of revolution as the first had been; it was split apart by the imperfectly understood rise of conflicting ideologies. With the appearance of fresh categories, such as the intelligentsia composed of university teachers and writers, the members of the learned professions, businessmen and so on, society became increasingly diversified.

The military clan made the most of this muddle. For a long while the army had been of great importance to the state, since the infant nation had to have a defender; but the army had moved on from that position to become an aggressive power, one that took the offensive both at home and abroad. Political parties had made their appearance, and during the twenties democracy did make a certain amount of progress, but now the army and the drive for militarism was competing with it. The army arrogated to itself the right of direct access to the emperor, passing over the heads of the civilian ministers. When the "Manchuria incident" occurred in 1931, all was over for democracy; from that moment on the "clan of the morning coats" was inferior to the "clan of the uniforms." From then on the soldiers and the militarists were to impose their brutal domination upon the Japanese people—an admirable people, to be sure, but one entirely devoid of political maturity.

Now it so happened that the post-Meiji period was also one in which new problems arose on every hand, and to an ever-increasing extent it was the unintelligent military leaders who insisted upon supplying the answers. To begin with there were the exceedingly acute social difficulties arising from over-hasty industrialization, from the sudden cancerlike growth of the towns, from the birth and rise of an industrial proletariat, from the stripping of the countryside and from underemployment and lack of work. The sudden powerful rise of the new Japan had been accompanied by a greatly increased birthrate: in round figures, the population grew from about 30 million at the beginning of the Meiji era to 44 million in 1900; between 1900 and 1940 it rose to 73 million. The growth of the economy was almost entirely nullified by this human inflation. At the same time modernization made Japan increasingly dependent on the outer world, and the country was obliged to import and export ever greater quantities of goods. But Japan's exports came up against the tariff walls of the great powers, which were worried by the advent of this new competitor; and there was no certainty about Japan's access to raw materials, since this access depended largely on the attitude of Japan's rivals. Thanks to their colonial empires, it was the Western powers that had a virtual monopoly of raw materials.

As the military leaders saw it, these social, demographic and political questions could have only military solutions: conscription to absorb the unemployed, armaments to give work to industry, and colonial conquest to ensure supplies and markets. Japan gradually accustomed itself to looking upon the use of force as a solution to difficulties both at home and abroad. Once Manchuria had been conquered in 1931, Japan's advance was firmly linked to aggression upon the continent of Asia. Still worse, judging by events in Europe, it was supposed that the current of world history was flowing in the direction of the various kinds of fascism. Japan backed Hitler, convinced that this would secure the country a lion's share in the coming partition of the world. Choked by economic sanctions and entangled in its alliance with the Axis powers, Japan ended up by plunging into the insane adventure of Pearl Harbor.

August, 1945. Not only had Hiroshima been wiped out by the atomic holocaust but Tokyo, Yokohama, Osaka, Nagoya, Kobe and all the other great cities, as well as a hundred towns or more, had been razed by the terrible incendiary raids of the American air force. Japan surrendered. The country was dying of hunger. Its factories were dead. Its vanquished, humbled fighting men were no more than ragged crowds of unemployed. The victorious enemy landed, and for the first time in its history the soil of Japan was trodden by a foreign army. Defeat, wretchedness and the occupation might have impelled the country toward fresh forms of violence—resistance to the Americans, secret preparations for revenge, a rapid slide toward communism. For it would be an easy step to pass from military to Muscovite totalitarianism. But to the conquerors' astonishment nothing of the kind occurred; instead, the country flung itself with open arms upon everything it had just been fighting against—friendship with America, democracy, collaboration with the West, total disarmament.

Was it mere outward show, a superficial conversion that would not last? Not in the least. There was a complete and fundamental change, for this is a country that deals with the great turning points in its history not by evolving but rather by making a total transformation. It was a profoundly altered Japan that emerged into view, one that had been deeply and lastingly marked by the lessons of its errors and its misfortunes. In this postwar Japan, as compared with the Japan of the military era, there were three outstanding new features. The first was a genuine, deeply felt pacifism, arising from the terrible ordeal the country had been through. The second was a newly discovered freedom, one that the Japanese were to love more and more as they grew increasingly aware of its advantages during their recovery in the years after the war. And the last was the brand-new optimism that I have already spoken about, an optimism that assures them that their cramped archipelago can provide a living for all its inhabitants, whatever they may have supposed before.

Yet, as has always been the case throughout Japanese history, this country, so given to abrupt transformation, is also conscious of an abiding continuity, an invisible thread that runs through its successive stages. The reversal of 1945 should not surprise us; it was only another version of the reversal of 1867 when the country was brought face to face with the irresistible West. Here, in 1945, was a "new Japan," but in more than one respect it was a second, revised and corrected edition of Meiji's. Furthermore, at its helm there was a statesman, Yoshida, whose dynamic personality was reminiscent of the ministers and the genro—the elder statesmen—of the Emperor Meiji. Japan returned to the right road just at the point where it had left it. Because of the willpower and diligence of a whole nation intensely eager to do what is right, the country was once more becoming the "model pupil."

Japan learned in the school of misfortune, and the country became passionately against any involvement whatsoever with adventure. Postwar Japan wanted no powerful army any more. It refused to consider being concerned in the military enterprises of other countries, especially the United States. It did its utmost to diminish the growth of its population. But after all, if Japan exploded over Asia when it had 70 million inhabitants, was it not necessarily fated to do so again when it reached the 100-million mark and went beyond it? The answer to that urgent question began to appear about 1960. It can be summed up in a few words: The Japanese explosion is still in fact going on, but it has changed its direction. It has turned inward. A new adventure has begun, but this time it is a peaceful one.

The first result is that the detonating mixture of lack of room and an overflowing population now makes the energy of the Japanese act upon a rigidly confined space. The country that is undergoing the explosion is Japan itself.

The second is that in order to make a success of it the Japanese are obliged to use the dynamite method—that is to say, they have to fling themselves into a very fast-moving and violent effort. This, again, is perfectly in accordance with their traditions. Their insatiable appetite for action has come to the surface again, but with this difference: the actors who occupy the front of the stage are no longer the vanished soldiers but the engineers; the men who count are no longer the generals with their samurai swords but the new technocrats in their fine wool suits and silk ties. The dash and spirit that are so characteristic of this country and that give it its style are not extinguished but now find their expression in countless different ways—above all in the breakneck pace of industrialization and modernization.

Does this new impetuosity expose the Land of the Rising Sun to fresh dangers? It would be a pity if that were so, but it would also be yet another example of Japan's consistency throughout its transformations. Will the technocrats and managers of today do better than the post-Meiji generals? Will they do well not only in the carrying out of orders and in action but also in the conception of a philosophy and the choice of long-term policies? Will an over-hasty expansion tend to burn out the country's economic machinery and bring about grave misfortunes? Will Japanese competition abroad revive the frightened protectionist reactions of former times? The coming twenty years or so will probably bring answers to these questions.

3.

The Government
of the Managers

The average Japanese is better informed on economic
affairs than we Westerners are, and he takes more interest in them.
He is prepared for this by an education that lays more stress upon
action and technology. Furthermore, the newspapers are more help
to him than ours are to us—all observers are struck by the high quality
of Japanese economic journalism and by its wide circulation. Even
the changing landscape of his daily life that I spoke about at the beginning of this book is "economic"—that is to say, made of images
of a powerful material activity, from the continual gigantic soaring of
steel frameworks into the urban sky to the tireless multiplication of
shops and the overflowing plenty of consumer goods.

All this means that Japan has almost entirely forgotten its former
outlook, the former attitude of mind of a poor and Spartan nation in
which the good citizen had no right to think of his own well-being;
and this is a very deep change indeed. At present the average Japanese
citizen is intensely concerned with raising his own standard of living,
and he is now discovering that it is possible to reach a goal that would
once have seemed illusory: an opulent society, based upon consumption, comfort and leisure. This does not diminish his drive, his zeal for
work. Far from it. He knows that it is a plan that calls for long-con-
tinued, unslackening effort. Manufacture, build, produce—you would
say that was his entire life, his one great interest, almost his obsession.
The whole Japanese community is ruled—governed—by a single task,
that of making the economic machinery run, and it is this factor that

determines the character of the government—that decides who shall be chosen to rule.

Who does rule Japan? The question was often asked in the past, and even now one hears it from time to time, for it is not the clearest of subjects. In Japan it is almost the tradition to have the central power divided among several ruling groups, or to have what might be called a false-bottomed government, "a government behind the curtain," as the Japanese put it—that is to say, a government behind the government. The shogun used to rule behind the emperor, and often enough there was someone behind the shogun who wielded the real power. In the Japan of the restoration and then again at the beginning of the twentieth century there was some degree of division of the power between the various cliques, and this lasted up until the time when it became the sole property of the militarists, the real rulers of the country.

Since 1967 Japan's government has been headed by Premier Eisaku Sato, the leader of the conservative Liberal-Democratic Party. But to what degree does this government in fact govern Japan? The answer is far from simple. Obviously the premier with his cabinet form only one of the prime movers, and not the most important one, either. There are others—parliament, the civil service, the great employers, the trade unions. The ministers are the people who are most in view, but these other influences play an important part in the running of the country. This is particularly true of the civil service, or the "bureaucracy," as it is often called. Even before the war its role was considerable indeed, and since that time it has become even more important, for it was relatively untouched by the fighting and by the postwar purges, and now it no longer has to withstand the competition of the military party. But naturally, in this country where the economy is paramount, the greatest share of power goes to those who run it—that is to say, to the great employers, the top executives, the managers of this industrial Japan that is in full expansion. It is they who decide upon the main lines of approach, and it is they who can move the most important control levers, since their hand is already upon the one that governs the motor that drives all the rest—industry itself.

These, the managers of the economy, are the top men of what the Japanese call the *zaikai*—literally, "financial circles," or the world of big business. (The Americans still call them the *zaibatsu*—"money powers"—a term they discovered at the time of the occupation but which is both out of date and derogatory; it belonged to the period when a few great families owned the huge trusts.) The *zaikai*, or their leaders, are the government behind the government. It is of very little importance that the constitution does not acknowledge their existence and that they do not constitute a neatly organized body. This is Japan, a country in which the outlines of the institutions, like those of the landscape, are often vague and ill defined.

It would scarcely be possible to make an exact list of the men who constitute the high economic command, and perhaps they themselves would not agree on its composition if they were asked. It is not always the same men who meet and make their decisions. Nor is there any precise definition of their role, any more than there is of their relations with the government in power. They do not form a kind of supercabinet, with regular meetings and an agenda, nor do they interfere directly in the process of government—still less in that of day-to-day affairs. They direct, they manage, from a distance and a height. They are a corporate power behind or above the government, a body whose advice and influence in fact tells the cabinet what it ought to do; the cabinet cannot go against its wishes. In the last analysis it will sometimes be found that decisions and directives more important than anything that could be decided by the cabinet will emerge from a luncheon at the Industry Club or from the ultramodern building of the Federation of Economic Organizations.

Some members of the top economic command are well known to the public in general. There is Taizo Ishizaka, for example, who was president of the Federation of Economic Organizations until 1968, and Kogoro Uemura, his successor, or men such as Shigeo Nagano, the steel tycoon, and Makoto Usami, the governor of the Bank of Japan. There are others who rarely come into the limelight, and often enough their names are completely unknown in the country; the Japanese are perfectly well aware of the power wielded by such groups as Mitsui or Mitsubishi, but they certainly could not give the names of their leading men. The most important of these men, known and unknown, make up the high command of the Keidanren (short for Keizai Dantai Rengokai), the Federation of Economic Organizations, the most powerful of the employers' associations in Japan. Its members include about a hundred of the very biggest companies in metalworking, electrical equipment, textiles, oil, banking and so forth, and more than seven hundred and fifty other important firms. It is the meeting place for the rulers of the economy, and this has earned it the privilege of being allowed to submit to the government a summary of the opinions of the economic world upon subjects of common interest. A clause in its charter significantly states that, where economic policy is concerned, "the organization will not only submit motions and resolutions to the Diet and the government, but will also cooperate in the carrying out of the measures that are considered necessary." The Keidanren has about thirty specialized committees to examine the various problems that concern it, ranging from international questions such as foreign trade and economic cooperation to those that have to do with finance, legislation, or indeed politics.

There are three other organizations that ought to be mentioned. The Nikkeiren (the Japan Federation of Employers' Associations) was founded in 1948 to withstand the growing power of the unions and has since somewhat modified its character; it now pays particular attention to the questions of productivity, modernization and rationalization in industry. The Nissho (the Japanese Chamber of Commerce and Industry) finds its members principally among the small and medium-sized firms. The Keizai Doyukai (Committee for Economic Development) was started as a kind of common center for modern-minded young employers; it is an association of manufacturers and businessmen, and they belong to it on a personal basis, as to a sort of club.

The influence of these great employers' organizations, above all of the Keidanren, becomes glaringly obvious when one observes the part they play in finding the money for political parties and elections. In Japan it is very expensive to be elected deputy or senator. It cannot be said that the votes are actually bought; it is rather a question of different practices and attitudes which arise from the fact that ancient semi-feudal customs survive beneath the surface of the modern democratic parliamentary system. Just as it was in the clans of former times, the loyalty of the rank and file creates an obligation in the chief—that is to say, the public figure who wants to be elected—to acknowledge his gratitude and to look after his followers. He is expected to shower the whole supporting clan with kindnesses. Feasts, presents and rewards of every kind, grants-in-aid to various middlemen who in their turn shower the followers at the lower levels—all these are usual, perfectly accepted practices. It is no less usual and accepted that the politician, who is rarely wealthy enough to cope with all these expenses himself, should have his election financed by openhanded benefactors, to whom he is then under an obligation.

Generally speaking the money comes from the political party to which the candidate belongs, but it can also come—at least some of it—in the form of direct contributions from the zaikai, from some employers' federation, or from some big private firm. The source of the funds of the party itself is also the business world. The Liberal-Democrats—that is to say, the conservative Right Wing—are the chief beneficiaries, and they receive very large sums indeed. The Liberal-Democratic leaders such as Sato or, before him, Kishi or Ikeda are, directly or indirectly, the party's main contribution seekers among the zaikai; and they are also the men who distribute the financial manna throughout the country. If the figures were known they would be found to be enormous, and everyone knows that this wealth is the prime reason for the long reign of the Right, which has been in power for twenty years and more. It is much less easy for the Socialist Party to acquire funds from sources of the same kind. The Socialists are largely dependent upon the contributions of the unions, and the unions are by no means wealthy. In the Diet there have been vain attempts—fairly hypocritical at times—to put an end to these practices by limiting the amount a candidate may spend and by supervising the parties' funds. In 1967 the Right put forward a bill that would have required publication of the parties' accounts—that is to say, if it had been passed—but in the end they took care not to bring it to a decision, and there is very little chance of its becoming law.

It should be added that the Liberal-Democratic Party, like most of the other Japanese political parties except for the Communists and the Komeito (a new party supported by a Buddhist sect), has no organized basis at the popular level and very few subscription-paying members. So, because of the way in which it is financed, its appearance is essentially that of a dependent upon the leaders of the economy. And these leaders must naturally look upon the government itself as a body of men who will as a whole always take care of the zaikai's interests and who will always be willing to agree to its wishes. Sato and his ministers are virtually the delegates of the managerial class, their representatives in power. To be sure, they were elected by the people's votes, but they were elected thanks to the contributions of this body that supports them, and while they were invested with authority by parliament, it was not without the obligatory consent of the economic leaders. From the time of Yoshida, who watched over the early days of the Japanese recovery, and on through Kishi, Ikeda and the others until we reach Sato, the leader of the government party or the premier (it has almost always been the same man filling both positions) has necessarily been a politician who was tacitly invested by the rulers of the economy and who enjoyed their confidence. During these last twenty years no one could have headed the government if the Keidanren had set its veto against his name.

The leaders' power in the state is rendered even greater by their very close relations with the civil service, or the bureaucracy—another highly important factor in the ruling complex. The strong links between the managerial and administrative classes arise partly from their common origins and recruitment. The graduates of the best Japanese universities go either into the civil service or into business and industry. Before the war there was a greater degree of separation, for the best private universities, such as the Keio, sent their graduates into private business, whereas the great state institution, the Imperial University, was chiefly concerned with supplying civil servants. The Imperial has been renamed Tokyo University (the Japanese call it the Todai), and it still provides the state with a great many officials (half the permanent undersecretaries in the ministries are old Todai men), but it also sends a good many into industry. In Japan that feeling of linking, of solidarity between men who have been educated in the same place, is of real importance, and it plays its part in this relationship.

The university graduates who make a career of the civil service reach high positions at a relatively early age, but in this overpopulated country retirement is early too (fifty-five), and many of them do not wait until they have reached that age but leave their ministries for the important posts that are offered them in big private firms; they are not allowed to do this, by the way, without official consent. So at the top level in these companies there are a good many directors who were formerly highly placed civil servants, men who are perfectly at home in the government offices they recently left and who remain in contact with the younger men who were once their colleagues. In 1967, for example, 121 higher civil servants moved over into private business. Among them there were four former vice-ministers and seven under-secretaries. Thirty-four of these migrants came from the treasury and most of them went into banking or finance; the others came mainly from the ministries of agriculture, public works and transport.

Finally, it should be mentioned that a certain number of civil servants, ending their official careers a little after the age of fifty, plunge into political life and get themselves elected to parliament. The civil service is a breeding ground for politicians, particularly those belonging to the Right; the Left finds its recruits more among teachers and trade unionists. But as we have seen, going into politics is just another way of coming under the influence of big business.

All in all, there is a complete alliance between the state and business and politics, and it is all the more solidly based and accepted since in fact it harks back to an ancient tradition, one that can be traced to the beginning of modern Japan and perhaps even to feudal days. For in the Tokugawa era the merchants managed to make their way into the courts of the daimyo, the chiefs of the clans. At the beginning of the Meiji epoch, the state itself built the first factories, got them on their feet, and then denationalized them, selling them to private firms usually run by government favorites who acquired them very cheaply. So the transition of modern times was carried out in an atmosphere of cooperation between government and business circles, both aiming for the same goal—industrialization. Today the primary aim of national policy is still industrial expansion, and therefore private firms can look upon themselves as being in many ways the instruments of this national policy. To some degree the distinction between what is public and what is private, between politics and economics, has disappeared. From the very beginning modern Japan was—and it still is—a country with none of the competition of hostility between state and business that is so familiar in the West. The relationship is like that between partners.

What kind of men are these managers of the new Japan, these men who brought about the country's extraordinary recovery and expansion? The first thing to emphasize is one of their most outstanding qualities, because it is a prime factor in the country's success—their daring. The soldiers of the former imperial army have vanished, and with their going people tend to forget the banzai charges and the lightning campaigns that aimed at "gathering the eight corners of the earth all under one roof," as a well-known slogan of the time put it— a Japanese roof, of course. Yet it would seem that their boldness of ambition, their dash and daring, survived them, that it migrated, still full of life, into these managing directors.

Certainly these captains of industry needed a most uncommon degree of courage to launch a general offensive on the economic front as early as 1951–1952, just after the defeat, and to suggest that their isolated, conquered country—a country poor in raw materials—should overtake the conquerors, wealthy nations that were so far ahead. They needed a surprising degree of ambition to aim at reaching the world's leading position, and most unusual skill to get there, having first accomplished feats that nobody would have believed possible.

A striking example of this is their extraordinary performance in steel production. In 1952 Japan set off with a modest production potentiality in this vital field—between 6 and 7 million tons, as it was before the war—and successively overtook France, England and Western Germany. The country aimed at producing 50 million tons in 1968; when that date came around, production soared higher still. This achievement was partly due to the fact that the Japanese managers are in the very forefront of modernization, continually on the watch for promising new techniques, and have managed to spot them as soon as they make their appearance, to acquire them, even at a very high price, and to apply them without losing a moment's time.

This applies to the whole range of their economy and production. The Japanese electronics industry was the first to see the immense possibilities of the American-invented transistors and to mass-produce them for the widest possible market. The shipbuilding industry discovered new techniques and organizational methods that allow it to outdo its European competitors; it was the first to plunge wholeheartedly into the building of gigantic yards for "superships," the vessels with six-figure tonnages. And although the automobile industry was somewhat behindhand, by 1967 it had managed to accumulate enough knowledge and equipment to launch the offensive that has now brought it into the international market. From their very first appearance, computers enchanted the Japanese, and the country's industry as a whole quickly grasped their revolutionary importance in the organization of companies and the coordination of production. Japanese dash and boldness are also apparent in the extraordinary new concepts and accomplishments mentioned earlier—the high-rise buildings, the superexpresses, the great newspapers whose circulation beats all records and so forth.

In more general terms, the leaders of the economy have managed to bring off rapid changes of direction and the most daring variations of emphasis. This was the case, for example, with the transition from light to heavy industries, which went so far as to give the last a truly prodigious weight—an importance that was of the greatest help in what has been called "the Japanese miracle." More recently, the Japanese manufacturers were able to foresee the coming of the twentieth century's "second industrial revolution" that is so much in the news today—the revolution of the highly scientific industries such as the petrochemical industry—and they quickly set about transferring the resources needed for this expansion.

In order to accomplish all this they have poured in money so lavishly that their country now leads the world as far as investment is concerned. In some of the most advanced industries, equipment is often renewed at a rhythm that leaves Western competitors breathless; it is renewed in spite of the risk of making nearly all machinery out of date before it has been written off. Japan is poor in capital, and the problem of investment—that is to say, the finding of money to finance the continued renewal of equipment and the race for new factories—might have been a great hindrance to development. But here the country managed to overcome the difficulty by the use of the most surprising financial methods, and it is here that the extreme boldness of the managerial class is most apparent. They never hesitated to run deeply into debt to set up their new installations, and they borrowed enormous sums of money from the banks. By agreeing to these loans, the banks in their turn displayed a most adventurous spirit, although it is true that it would all have come to nothing without the backing of the central bank, the Bank of Japan.

One of the most daring leaders of the *zaikai* is Soichiro Honda, the maker of the well-known Honda motor bicycles and cars. "A fertile mind and imagination, new ideas and well-based theories, and lastly the saving of time: those are the secrets of my success," he says. "The reason why the Honda company has grown to its present size is that Honda had no traditions. Since we had no past, all we possessed was a future. . . . It was as well for us that we lost the war. Otherwise we should never have had the freedom we enjoy today. We were able to start from scratch and to see big." *

It may be that not all the other big Japanese employers would agree with their colleague's total denial of tradition, but it is certain that a great many would also acknowledge that the country's defeat was for them a powerful stimulus to effort and to creative endeavor. Daring is one of the basic qualities of the Japanese character, and it has always managed to come into its own in times of adversity. But the defeat of 1945 and the American occupation, which lasted until 1952, did not merely stimulate energy; it also provided courageous and thrusting men with new opportunities for leadership.

When General Douglas MacArthur settled in Tokyo, his first care, once the remnants of the imperial army were dealt with, was to dismember and disperse the *zaibatsu*, the so-called money powers. The Mitsui, Mitsubishi, Sumitomo, Yasuda and other trusts had one remarkable feature in common: at the top they all had a holding company, a sovereign body that ruled over a pyramid of subordinate firms. The only shareholders in the holding company were the members of a single powerful family—the Mitsuis for the trust of that name, for example, or the Iwasakis in the case of the Mitsubishi trust. The occupying authorities' first measures against these trusts were very severe indeed. The trusts were purged—an operation that removed the members of the great families, confiscated their fortunes, and not only forbade them to carry on business but also did the same to their chief associates and their economic and financial advisers. At the same time the huge firms were split up, their component parts forming a great mass of small companies that competed with one another. MacArthur wanted to smash the trusts and to deconcentrate industry, because in his opinion the *zaibatsu* had been the militarists' accomplices; because at that time the American plan for Asia (ah, the irony of history) meant the restoration of great China, America's friend from earliest times, and the reduction of little Japan; and lastly because it was neces-

---

* From *The Japanese Miracle Men*, by Ralph Hewins. This book contains a series of remarkable and very well-informed profiles of some of the chief characters in present-day Japanese industry.

sary to strengthen the infant Japanese democracy by teaching it what the occupying forces called "the philosophy of free competition."

The American policy of deconcentration soon came to a sudden end, as it did in Germany. The cold war was beginning, and China was sliding toward communism. The Americans reversed their policy, began to help Japan build up its strength again, and allowed the scattered members of the great firms to come together in a long process of reassembly. The old groupings and the old names, such as Mitsui and Mitsubishi, began to reappear. Nevertheless, important alterations had been carried out, particularly in the composition of the economic staffs. New leaders were now in command of the *zaikai*. Often they were men who had formerly been in intermediate positions, under the orders of the family high command; now that their bosses were gone, these men stepped into their shoes. And often the leaders were new men altogether, whose emergence had been abetted by the upheaval of those days.

Naturally a good many of them either already had a business career behind them or found themselves at the head of a company that had a history of its own. But there were also many who had to start from scratch and build up completely new firms. A certain number of them were not only new to these commanding positions but were also self-made men; they had no links with the former *zaibatsu* but had been brought to the top by the current of history—though indeed they were also helped by their own ability, by their eagerness in grasping the opportunities that were offered, by their comparative youth, and by the wind of competition that was now blowing over the country's economy. More than twenty years have passed since then, and now the managerial generation is over seventy. (The usual retirement age of fifty-five does not apply to them.) But at the time when these men were reaching the top they still had all the energy of their fifties.

One of the latest examples of these new captains of industry in postwar democratic Japan is Masaru Ibuka, the founder of Sony, the great electronics firm. He started his company in 1958 in a little workshop with a capital of less than $500 and seven fellow workers, his "seven samurai," as he calls them. In under ten years the firm had a worldwide reputation. I have already mentioned Honda, the motor bicycle king and maybe one of the automobile kings of tomorrow. He is the typical self-made man of modern Japan. Until 1948 his life had been that of an ordinary mechanic, the son of a village smith, but that year, when he was thirty-eight, he chanced upon an idea that made his fortune. The country was still very poor, but it was intensely eager to work, full of vitality, keen to move about, and in a hurry; Honda's answer to these needs was to provide an inexpensive, modern and highly efficient working instrument—the motor bicycle. Some ten years later, Honda led the world in this field. But he had already turned his mind to the automobile. He plunged into this new venture in 1963 and in eighteen months produced his first model. As early as 1965 he brought off a daring stroke and a Honda racing car competed in England.

Soichiro Honda is not Ford's only rival in Japan. There is also Tsuneji Matsuda, the man behind the Mazda automobiles, an almost unknown little manufacturer in Hiroshima and Osaka who did notably well after the war, graduating in a little over twenty years from a three-wheeled van, perfectly calculated for a poor country that was just trying to get going, to the Cosmo, an exceedingly advanced pistonless car. Another instance is Taizo Ishida; he too is a self-made man with no more than a primary education, and now he is at the head of the great Toyota Company. He saw that the hour had come for the Japanese family car, and in 1955 he triumphantly launched the Crown, the first of a whole series of models.

Still another self-made man is Konosuke Matsushita, Sony's chief rival, a leader in the electronics industry and head of the company that is named after him. A former bicycle repairer and the son of a poverty-stricken peasant, he was put out as an apprentice when he was ten; he is older than the men I have just mentioned—born in 1891—and he was already making electrical machinery before the war. But he was one of those who brought new ideas, as Honda puts it, and who took off in a big way after the defeat, taking the lead and holding it. Rightly judging that his country was entering the consumer age, he provided Japan with its first cheap electrical gadgets, beginning with the famous electric rice saucepan that revolutionized the life of the archipelago; for the first time the Japanese housewife escaped from the bondage of the archaic pot that slowly cooked the rice over the embers of a wood fire and could stay in bed an hour longer every morning. A little later she was provided with a refrigerator and a washing machine, perhaps even an air conditioner; while her husband and her children had television, record players, tape recorders, electric pencil sharpeners, massage machines, heated trousers and so on. Matsushita produced all these goods under the brand name of National, offered them on deferred payment terms, and transformed the whole lives of the Japanese. He now employs forty thousand workers and office staff in something like fifty different factories. His firm ranks fourth in Japan and is included in the list of the hundred most important concerns outside the United States. And it is not yet over. Matsushita is now breaking into computers and color television.

Television—that is another industry which has sought out daring men and carried them to the top in the course of its fifteen years of astonishing expansion in Japan. The best known is Matsutaro Shoriki. A policeman who turned journalist, he was the first to launch commercial television in Japan, back in 1952, competing with the first state system, then just coming into existence. His particular stroke of genius was that he not only instantly grasped the fundamental importance of the medium but also stood out against the state's monopoly, setting up a rival private system. Even more important, he at once understood that the best way for the major newspapers to avoid what might be a losing battle with television was to found channels of their own or even perhaps many-channeled systems. Shoriki was the chief of the great popular daily *Yomiuri*, and so for him it was a matter of grafting a television system onto his own newspaper and doing so as quickly as possible, so as to withstand the semigovernmental chain, N.H.K. It was at this point that he began to display the agility and daring of a high-wire artist.

In order to launch his programs, for example, he had four hundred American television sets flown in and set up in the open air at the crossroads of Tokyo. Crowds gathered in the streets, gazing at the screen. In the evenings the cafés, bars and public baths were stripped of their customers; the campaign was shatteringly successful. But Shoriki still had to bring off the financial deals that were required for the setting up of his system. This was even more daring. I well remember the time when none of my journalist friends on the *Yomiuri* was paid at the end of the month; all they had was a note scribbled by the editor, promising that their salary would appear in time. "The paper hasn't a yen left," they said, horrified. "The Old Man has put it all into his TV." But in a few months' time the public was going all out for television; Shoriki, that old fighter, made a complete recovery, and the *Yomiuri* gathered even greater strength. Once his chain, the N.T.V. (Nippon Television), was going, the Old Man moved on to the next stage, that of color television; and here again he was the first in the field.

But not all these new business leaders are self-made men like those I have mentioned; still less are they tightrope walkers like the former editor of the *Yomiuri*. Many come from old upper-class families and started their careers with excellent degrees. Yoshihiro Inayama, for example, a graduate of the prestigious Tokyo University, became the president of Yawata, the best-known iron and steel company in Japan, at the age of fifty-three, in 1957. Or again, in steel there is Shigeo Nagano, who is famous for having the strongest personality in the industry and for having "raised the temperature of Japanese steel to fever point." He is the president of Fuji Steel, a firm he launched in 1945, which was Yawata's rival until the two merged recently. In shipbuilding there is Toshio Doko, the president of the gigantic I.H.I. (or Ishikawajima-Harima Industry); in heavy industry, Fumihiko Kono, the head of the firm Mitsubishi Heavy Industry; in engineering, Taizo Ishizaka, the former president of the Toshiba Company and, until 1967, for more than ten years the president of the Keidanren—that is to say, the leading figure among the Japanese employers; in banking, Wataru Tajima, the president of the Mitsubishi Bank, and Shozo Hotta, the president of the Sumitomo; in international trade, Chujiro Fujino, the president of the Mitsubishi Shoji; and Kogoro Uemura, the new president of the Keidanren. All these men are products of Tokyo University, the Todai.

The strong personalities of the magnates of the business world make a marked impression on all who come into contact with them, and many of them are well known even to the general public for their boldness, initiative and enterprise. This is the case with Takeshi Mitarai, for example, who is at the head of Canon, the pioneer company in Japan's great postwar success in cameras; and with Shinzo Oya, who was a minister in postwar years and who is now the best-known artificial-textile tycoon. Or Toshio Doko of I.H.I.: even before the Suez crisis of 1956, and therefore earlier than anyone else on earth, he led Japan into the adventure of building enormous ships. He was the first to launch one of more than a hundred thousand tons, and he followed that by another of over two hundred thousand.

The achievements of the Japanese builders of the supertankers (there are several of them now) are linked to those of the oil kings, which were striking enough in their time. Sazo Idemitsu made the first sensational entry into this field. He was a businessman who had the courage to stand up to Anglo-Iranian in 1953, taking advantage of the confiscation of the British oil interests to buy Persian oil cheap from Mossadegh. Since then his "independent oil" has been competing with the country's American and Japanese suppliers. But in 1957 Taro Yamashita, another oil king, brought off a still more striking feat: against the furious opposition of the Americans and of Shell he obtained a rich oil concession in Arabia and succeeded in bringing the Japanese into that part of the world; in doing so, he invested more capital there than Japan had ever placed abroad before.

Of course, by listing the names of these men, I do not in any way mean that it is they who form the "government of the managers." I repeat: that is a body which is by no means precisely defined, and although it would be possible to make a fairly exact list of the twenty or thirty most influential leaders in the country's economy, it is certain that several of the men I have mentioned would not be on it. But it is men of their cast and temper who do make up that "government." When we consider these men, together with their more important colleagues, we see that they constitute a positive class, a genus quite unlike those Japanese who ruled the nation for so long or who had a decisive influence upon it, such as the soldiers, the bureaucrats or the politicians. Even in their modified postwar versions, these two last categories often retain a certain number of the drearier features of Japanese behavior in human and social relationships—awkward self-expression, heavy-going conversation (particularly in a foreign language), unwillingness to answer questions or express ideas, and a liking for secrecy.

The foreign visitor who comes into contact with an important Japanese is often disappointed at finding him hard to talk to—"a man you can't reach." Indeed, it sometimes happens that the foreigner makes serious mistakes about the importance of the man he is meeting; this is because the foreigner does not know how to communicate with him and is unaware that even a highly placed Japanese does not care to shine in conversation or to reveal his inner being. Generally speaking, the representatives of the *zaikai* are not like this, and people from the West find relations with them far easier and more agreeable. The managers of the new Japan and their fellow workers of the new generation in postwar industry often stand out from their countrymen because they are what is called in English more articulate—that is to say, more open, more at ease with words, richer in ideas, more willing to talk, and capable of talking, too, even in a foreign language. In Japan's military days it was well known that the soldiers were closed in and dumb, whereas the sailors were far more open. Some of the qualities of the naval men of those days are now to be found among the representatives of the *zaikai*.

A Japanese businessman sometimes gives the impression of being Americanized, of resembling his colleagues on the other side of the Pacific. In my opinion this impression is largely or even wholly mistaken. One has but to remove a thin American veneer to discover a man who is profoundly unlike anyone produced by the United States. Certainly the influence of America upon the formation of the new top-level Japanese has been of the greatest importance, but there has been no imitation. Because of the defeat, Japanese businessmen were very much more exposed to the Americans than to their European equivalents, and no doubt this was very lucky for them. They have seen America much more clearly and closely than Europeans have; they are much more concerned with knowing the country, understanding it and learning from it. And generally they made this encounter of their own free will, unreluctant, meeting America with real pleasure.

It is not going far enough to say that the United States roused or rearoused Japan's drive and energy, assuming that the country was asleep. America gave Japan a revelation of the greatest importance—and gave it earlier and more fully than to Europe—the revelation of a new New World, an industrial and technological world racing along faster and faster toward the year 2000. America gave Japan an image of the world of tomorrow, at the same time preaching the vital importance of moving very fast, seeing very big, and thinking very new if the country wanted to take part in the race and share in the building of the world to come. In short, for the last two decades the "American challenge" has been an everyday reality for Japan and a potent stimulus to action. During the first years American aid played a part in Japan's postwar success, but what really counted after that was the American example and the urge, the drive, to come up to it and if possible to compete with and outdo it.

What the "Americanization" of Japanese businessmen actually consists of is an overdue modernization in their working methods and the adoption of more efficient programming and calculating systems, which were taken over not out of any love of America but rather love of progress. More pertinent than questions of Americanization or even Westernization is the point that Japan is modernizing itself. And in the end, after all, the most advanced countries necessarily come to look alike, since they are all shaped by the same adventure, all formed by the common goal they are hurrying so eagerly to reach.

The top men of the zaikai are, indeed, more unlike their American equivalents than are the Europeans. If capitalism is a system ruled by money and organized for profit, it may be said that the Japanese employer class is made up of a rather special kind of capitalist. A European industrialist in Tokyo said, while I was there, "Above all, their ideas of money and profit are different from ours. Basically they are not so interested in money as we are, and that is true for the Japanese as a whole. The almighty dollar and its way of ruling American life has no equivalent in the Japanese pattern."

It is a fact that money plays a far less important part in the private lives of Japanese executives than it does in Westerners'. They usually earn far less, and the setting of their lives is far more unassuming. Luxurious cars, high-powered social life, expensive vacations, millionaire's apartment—generally speaking they are quite untouched by all this. They receive a set salary, and in order to keep out of the top tax bracket it is usually not very high. Although it is true that they sometimes entertain lavishly on expense accounts—golf, presents, geisha dinners—their homes, personal expenditures and way of life remain unpretentious, and there is less of a gap between the big men and the ordinary people than there is in Europe or even in America.

And money is not all-powerful within the firm itself, either. One might even go so far as to say that money ceased to be the governing factor when the destruction of the zaibatsu after the war created a division between capital and management. In the prewar system the top power belonged to the ruling family at the head of the group, because it was the family that owned the capital. In spite of all their degrees and scientific ability, the technical and administrative directors were merely executives, supervised from above and given their orders by the family. At present, on the contrary, it is the managers who have the power, although they do not possess the money. They govern because of their degrees and their technical or administrative talents, and they do not need to dispose of large capital sums themselves. The executive class is mainly recruited from the university graduates, and a young man of poor and humble background who nevertheless has outstanding powers of work may reach a very high position with nothing but his own merit to help him.

In the same way the whole attitude of mind, the whole approach to the firm's work, is much less governed by questions of money and profit than it is in the West; the financial aspect is not the first consideration in any given problem, and the enrichment of the firm itself is not always the chief aim of those who run it. They often put progress before profit. They will distribute less money and they will appeal to their staff for a greater effort for the firm's expansion, for the modernization of its equipment, and for improving its competitiveness in home and international markets. With us, money is not at all inclined to move in the direction of activities that do not yield a profit, even if they are of great value for the community or the nation.

In Japan a firm will often manufacture some not particularly profitable line if that will improve the standing of the group the firm belongs to or even quite simply if it is for the good of the country as a whole. In comparison with the Western executive, the Japanese seems remarkably unaffected and unworried by the distribution of the firm's profits. What about his shareholders? He has relatively few of them, because his money comes from other sources, and unlike a Western director he is therefore free from concern for their demands for a dividend. His workers? Their relations with him are not primarily based upon wages and working agreements. Their age is the chief factor in their pay, so much so that from the very beginning they learn restraint, a kind of modesty about what they can claim. A young, very bright worker earns less and is given less responsibility than a senior man whose work is not so good; to get better pay the young man must grow older. This is not so unfair as it seems, for it is as the worker grows older that the expenses of his family increase, and it is then that he is well paid.

Broadly speaking, the attitude of a Japanese employer toward his workers is profoundly unlike the attitude of an employer in a liberal capitalist Western country, for the Japanese is far more influenced by human than by economic relations. Here we come into contact with the well-known Japanese employers' paternalism; we will speak of it in greater detail when we deal with the attitude of the workers themselves. The way this paternalism lasts is further proof that Japan is still very far from any advanced form of Americanization. A firm will often display a degree of harshness toward its office staff and workers with regard to discipline and working conditions—a kind of severity that does not exist with us—but often it will also behave with a generosity undreamed of in the West. When times are bad, for instance, it may keep on its redundant workers, paying them for doing nothing rather than dismissing them.

The old Japanese society which lasted more or less intact until 1945 was strongly stratified and pyramidal, with the authority coming down from a single ruler at the very top; in the same way the modern Japanese company is often run by a man who behaves like a minor emperor, insisting upon total loyalty from all his subjects. But he is an emperor who is as clearly aware of his duties as he is of his rights, above all the duty of acting as a father to those beneath him, one whose mission it is to protect them, look after them, and pay great attention to their needs. There are comparatively few employers who abuse their power.

Another field in which there is no Americanization among the Japanese employers, or even any plain Westernization, is that of decision-making. It would be a mistake to suppose that the "boss emperor" rules over his company with a wholly unshared monarchical power. The reality is more democratic, even though it does not correspond with the American or European practice. Paradoxically enough it is in the United States that the boss is absolute, for there decisions are usually taken at the top level, while orders for carrying them out are issued to the executives in descending order of rank; in Japan, on the other hand, a kind of collective decision rises up through the lower levels toward the man at the top.

To begin with, the suggestion that is likely to meet with most support is chosen, and then it is first circulated at the level of those who will eventually carry it into execution. This is the probing stage, and it is characterized by long, informal discussions and great numbers of meetings in which the plan may be taken to pieces and radically altered. It is only after this phase that it is put into writing and thus given the weight of an official proposal. The document is sent to the section heads for their approval; then it goes up to the heads of the divisions and departments concerned, reaching as high as the managing directors. At each stop in its rounds the paper is marked with the red seal of those who agree, the seal taking the place of a signature. In the end the plan, bearing fifteen, twenty or even twenty-five seals, reaches the topmost level of all, and here the final decision will be taken; in the majority of cases this merely amounts to approval, the head man and his immediate assistants not being required to make any choice but just to set the last seal on the paper. It should also be added (and this is most typically Japanese) that from the very beginning each man concerned has of course also wondered which plan was most likely to please the high command at the top of the pyramid.

All in all, the running of a business concern is easier in Japan than it is in the West. But this picture of the "government of the managers" would be incomplete without the additional observation that the running of the economy is also easier for the Japanese state. For the great Japanese employers agree that it is right that the state in its turn should treat them with a certain amount of paternalism. Even at this high level, there is still that thoroughly Japanese liking for direction from above; furthermore, there is the feeling that obedience to higher authority ensures a certain measure of protection by those higher authorities. We have also seen the interchange of personnel that exists between business managers and bureaucrats; it is clear that the same kind of men are going to have the same kind of outlook. Seeing that the government is to a certain extent a representative of the *zaikai*, and the bureaucrats to some degree the managers' cousins, the managers find it acceptable that the state should have the right to a certain amount of intervention in their concerns, and they are therefore comparatively submissive when they are given advice and guidance. The top men and the groups they direct are sensitive to the national interest and usually make no difficulty about agreeing with the government planners' directions. Taking it the other way around, the government is in very close contact with business circles, and its attitude and thinking are markedly "industrial." The officials in the most influential of the ministries, that of International Trade and Industry (well known to foreign businessmen by the initials MITI), are keenly aware of the problems of industrial development and have great experience with them. For all these reasons the relationship between government and industry is exceptionally easy and flexible.

Japanese planning is worked out by the Economic Planning Agency, a remarkable body that comes under the premier, and the plans it sets out are purely indicative. The plan tells private industry what production targets and what alterations in emphasis or structure the government would like, together with the information and forecasts that substantiate these wishes. The plan is in no way obligatory, but in fact it is very influential, partly because of the way the state can bring the Bank of Japan's credit policy and fiscal measures to bear to guide the economy in the desired direction and to make it move faster or slower.

The Japanese system is of interest to France, which has had indicative planning for years, but it is far more so to the United States and Great Britain, which have nothing of the kind. In the spring of 1967 the important English weekly *The Economist* published an inquiry called "The Risen Sun," enthusiastically describing the comparatively unknown system, in which it detected more penetration in forecast and analysis, newer thought, and greater efficiency in execution than anything that had ever been tried in London. According to the author of the inquiry, the main key to the Japanese success lies in "the world's most intelligent system of planned economy." In substance he says that one of its great virtues is that it is in a continual state of awareness as to which sector of the economy offers the highest yield and the greatest general utility, so that as soon as an industry shows signs of age, fresh resources are encouraged to move in the direction of newer and more profitable activities. At the same time a very close watch is kept upon foreign industries throughout the world, so that the country may be promptly guided in the direction it should take so as to stay in the race of international competition and keep well in front.

When we compare Japan's planned economy with that of the socialist countries, do we find the unpleasant consequences that are so often to be observed in them: uniformity and the death of the spirit of enterprise and of competition? Nothing of the sort. On the contrary, Japanese planning is successfully united with an unusually active competition, which is chiefly owing to the existence of the powerful industrial groups that have either reappeared or come into being since the war. In addition to the three main complexes already mentioned—Mitsubishi, Mitsui and Sumitomo—there are many others, such as the I.H.I. (the initials of Ishikawajima-Harima Industry) or Hitachi groups. Then again we have the Yawata and Fuji complex, whose firms gravitate around a powerful central company that specializes in one particular branch—in this case the working of iron and steel. And there are groups with no generic or family name that center around some great bank, such as those connected with the Dai-Ichi or the Fuji banks.

One striking feature of this competition is that instead of seeking the specialization and the division of labor that would allow them to carry on without coming into conflict, many of them do exactly the contrary. Each complex does its utmost to spread its activities over a very wide range of production, even if its competitor is doing the same; if one moves forward in some new sector, in a very short while he will usually see his rivals following his example. Mitsubishi's interests range from electric fans to atomic reactors, taking in such industries as mining, metallurgy, engineering, shipbuilding, cement manufacture, transport, trade and banking. But Mitsui competes with Mitsubishi in almost all these fields, and Sumitomo does much the same; the result is that in many sectors, where we would often have one important firm towering above the rest, the Japanese have three, four or even more.

This diversification—that is to say, the fact that the group includes companies with highly varied activities—brings with it a whole series of advantages. It allows certain sectors to be counterbalanced by others; one of them can run at a loss if there is another whose profits make up for it. When the goods circulate, being sold or exchanged, there is the advantage that the profits remain inside the group. As far as production is concerned, the subsidiary companies can make use of one another, grant one another favorable prices, and join together in combines or interlocking factory groups, going from the raw material right through to the finished article, for example, the whole train of production remaining within the same complex of companies. The system has another point in its favor: a Western manufacturer of ball bearings, for instance, is in direct competition with any rival ball-bearing firm, whereas in Japan a company that forms part of a group is neither alone nor in direct competition with the firm across the way; it is the groups that compete with one another, and the individual company, wrapped about as it were by the group, feels both protected and at the same time strong, since it has the support of all that power behind it. This is a still more important advantage in international competition with foreign companies.

The bonds within the complex network of companies that make up a group are highly varied: mutual holdings, main and subsidiary companies, affiliated companies depending on the same bank, joint companies that arise from the fusion of two parent bodies and so on. But over and above the financial or technical links, the personal relationships between the top managers of the various companies are of the first importance.

Much of the group's cohesion is derived from the bonds that exist between its top-level members, men who have passed their working careers together, who know one another well, who stand in for one another or take one another's places, whose directorships or plurality of directorships bring them to the same board meetings, and who are often together. A great deal of business, even very important decisions, is in fact decided upon at club meetings or at business luncheons. In the Mitsubishi group the top institution is quite simply the Friday lunch, a Western meal that every week brings together the twenty-five heads of the twenty-five most important companies that fly the house flag of the three red diamonds. And then again, talks between the representatives of rival groups, and contacts between business and administration—meetings that ensure close association between the great complexes, on the one hand, and between them and the government, on the other—often take place at informal encounters, on the golf links and during a geisha dinner.

When all these things are taken into consideration, it is not easy to class the managers of the new Japan according to the set categories of the political economy textbooks. Liberalism? Socialism? State management? Planned economy? Their system is no single one of these but includes something of all of them. Above all it contains a high proportion of nipponism—that is to say, patterns of thought and behavior that are unlike ours, patterns in which an often intense modernity is united with a deep attachment to certain traditions that are purely Japanese. The leaders of the zaikai quite happily combine attitudes that seem to us mutually exclusive.

A last feature, and one not without its importance: These leaders of the world's most dynamic country, these instigators of a permanent industrial revolution, are men who are not in a hurry. The chief executive is a man who has time to spare. He is much less harassed than his American or European equivalent; he is not the prisoner of a daily routine, and he keeps at a certain distance from his fellow workers. He delegates more responsibility for everyday decisions to them, so as to keep a better hold on the position and authority of the supreme arbiter, responsible for the firm's policy at the highest level. He sees to it that he has leisure. He plays golf. He reads, studies and thinks. He travels abroad. For all these reasons, his ventures are often conceived not merely in terms of Japan alone but in terms of the world market as well.

4.

A People at Work

Let us stop at a crossroads in Tokyo. The crowds are dense at all times of the day; the people are clean and well dressed in Western clothes. They are perfectly at home in this urban landscape amid the activity of a great modern city with its cars, its avenues lined with very tall buildings, its trains, its subways. And yet this setting contains one enormous paradox: There is not a single ounce of Japanese cotton on any of these people's backs, not a scrap of wool from a Japanese sheep. Every piece of metal in these automobiles, carriages, rails and bridges comes from distant countries in the shape of ore. Almost every drop of the gasoline in these cars has been imported in the form of crude oil, the rubber in their tires comes from abroad, and so on and so on. On the list of materials 100 percent of which are imported we see nickel, tin, bauxite, phosphates and many others; and, on the list of materials in short supply, coke, lead, wood, salt, potash and glass, to say nothing of food. Almost the only things that Japan has in satisfactory quantities are low-grade coal, building materials and electricity.

The paradox lies in the development and maintenance of a highly modern and industrial society under such conditions. It is an even greater paradox when one considers Japan's geographical position and its population statistics. If the world's large industrial concentrations were laid down according to reason, who would ever have installed one of the greatest of them all in this poor, remote country, cut off from the rest of the world by seas and oceans, less well endowed than England, yet so much more densely populated?

But one can understand this country only if one realizes that this paradox is in itself one of the strongest stimulants in Japan's economic life. I am tempted to say that every one of the people here, walking along the Tokyo avenues, is acutely aware of the problems raised by the cotton in his shirt or the metal of the subway car he is about to take. Everything in his daily life and of course in his papers and magazines tells him over and over again that, in order to live, the new Japan, which has turned in upon itself and whose swollen population means a kind of self-invasion, has but one course to take: that of becoming a many-sided, powerful processing factory and at the time an enormous import-export firm. The Japanese are obsessed with the idea of building up the Japanese factory and increasing the country's trade. But for this both drive and talents are required.

For years now the Western economists have been studying the reasons for the Japanese success, and they have put forward all kinds of often exceedingly interesting views on Japanese investment, industrial structure, population and labor, wages and so forth. I too will speak of these things later in this book, though with less knowledge of economics. But I was lucky enough to experience this Japanese success at first hand, to come to know it from the facts far more than through the specialists' surveys, and that is why it seems to me that in the accepted explanations one factor is either lacking or often overlooked, perhaps because it does not lend itself to statistical analysis. Yet it is the main factor and the chief explanation—it is the people themselves.

The people—that is to say, the Japanese, with their attitudes of mind, their behavior and their abilities. Why has Japan succeeded? Because of the Japanese. For the Japanese make up an intensely industrious nation, filled with a tenacious desire to get on, to progress, enthusiastically devoted to everything new, and capable of tireless exertion in order to succeed; they will work with a disciplined, obstinate steadiness and they will live with a frugality that is scarcely ever to be seen in the West today. A primary aspect of this all-important human factor in the venture of the new Japan, as we have seen, is the part played by the new heads of the economy, with their dashing spirit and their business philosophy, but those responsible for the Japanese success are not a mere handful of leaders; their name is legion. They are not only the top managers but also the great body of those who are managed, the countless workers at the lower levels. The Japanese success must be credited to the great mass of the Japanese workers, who, in addition to their other virtues and failings, are above all set apart by a wonderful driving zeal for work. This is probably instinctive. It is in the first place a characteristic of men of the yellow race in general, and in this particular case it is stimulated by Northeast Asia's cold but temperate climate and is therefore shared by Japan's nearest neighbors, the Chinese and Koreans. But more than anywhere else in Asia it is a conscious, self-imposed zeal, and this has been so for a long time. At present economic endeavor is of the very first importance for Japan, and the people understand this fact—not with a merely passive realization, as though it were some stroke of fate that just has to be put up with, but positively, as a stimulus to action and to the carrying out of great feats for the building up of the "Japan factory." It would be meaningless for the managers to put forward daring aims and plans if those aims did not in fact have their origin in the depths of the nation as a whole.

In the Japan of the military days, the country was extraordinarily united over nearly all the nation's problems, but this was an imposed unity, forced on the people from above by an oppressive political regime much given to the use of police. In our times the Japanese have lost their former unity of thought and action in many fields, and foreign observers may think them divided or sometimes even in a state of total confusion. But their disagreements are probably much less important than they seem. When it is a question of work they all fall into step again. Their natural cohesion returns in full force as soon as positive action is required, for every one of them has fully grasped the golden rule of the new Japan: all for the economy. In the last twenty years there are few countries that have shown so much steadiness and perseverance in the national effort—an effort whose great feature has been an unremitting drive in work and a continual upward progress in the level of education.

Are Americans a hard-working people? Unless one has lived among the Japanese one hardly knows the meaning these words can carry. If Americans work hard, the Japanese do so to a superlative degree. Yet here I must sound a warning note right away: it is not to be supposed that Japan is a country where the people are worked to death, dripping with sweat, engine oil and mud; or that they are so many robots. Rather, the opposite is true: one is surprised to see them smiling and relaxed as they work. But they work as automatically as they breathe, and when to this the often harsh requirements of the firm are added, then indeed there may be abuses. Work invades the daily life of the people to a degree that most of our workers would never tolerate, and this is the case in the offices, the shops, the factories and the fields. Quite recently the Japanese newspapers have launched a new word— or to be more precise, they noticed that their language lacked a word— the word for "vacation." So they borrowed it—from the French, just as they borrowed *chanson* (*shan-son*) and *après-guerre* (*a-pou-rei-gay-rou*); because of their way of writing they can bring the word *vacance* into their vocabulary almost without change: *va-kan-su*. Until recently they had never known what vacations were, and even now only a very small minority is beginning to discover their meaning.

Japanese workers and office staff have still almost no notion of such things as holidays with pay, a month at the shore, weekends or even half a day off on Saturday, to say nothing of our habit of taking the day between a public holiday and a Sunday. The almost total emptiness of Western cities during the months of July and August is unknown in Japan, and production does not drop in summer any more than the shops close their doors. At the most, economic activity may slacken a trifle at the New Year. There are about half a dozen public holidays in the year for the traditional feasts, but that is all. Sunday is usually a free day, but not in the big stores or in many of the small family shops, which know that Sunday is the best day for their customers. The law says that the working week is supposed to be forty-eight hours, but this limitation is ineffectual in the small and medium-sized firms, and there are a great many of them. Some top firms only require forty or forty-five hours of work from their staff, but many more call for overtime in addition to the eight-hour day, and the workers agree so as to make more money. Many of them work ten hours or more, and the peasants go on even longer.

The day starts very early in the morning. The Japanese are true children of the Rising Sun, for they and their symbol get up together. It has been estimated that by half past six in the morning 80 percent of the inhabitants of Tokyo are up. Most go to bed very early. Yet on the other hand there are countless bright-looking little shops that do not close their wooden shutters until between ten and eleven at night. And the world of the craftsmen's workshops and the family stalls is one of unremitting work; except for a funeral, the shutting of the shop is something that just never happens. At midnight, when the huge cities are all asleep, there are still great numbers of sites where the yellow-helmeted workers toil on beneath floodlights; these are the roadworks of a perpetually renewed communications system, with tunnels being driven, footbridges being hoisted over crossroads, huge metal scaffoldings where the electric welders spark and spit, new buildings where they pour concrete in the pitch-dark night.

For the Western visitor or resident, application and zeal seem to be the typically Japanese characteristics of all this multifarious labor. The old values of willingness, respect and conscientious work are all still very much alive and effective. Japan is a country where you stop at a filling station and in the twinkling of an eye four assistants clean your car without your having either to ask or to pay, where a nearby restaurant will send you in a meal as soon as you telephone for it, where the cab driver gets out of his seat to say good-bye at the end of the run, where hotel service goes on all night long, and where the papers are in your mailbox and the milk on your doorstep before six o'clock in the morning. It is a country where (apart from some exceptional cases that have to be sensed very exactly) tips are unknown —they would be politely refused. In this second half of the twentieth century, it is the country where, on the whole, labor troubles are least serious, where a firm's inner discipline is the most reliable, and where employees' loyalty toward their employers is the most widespread and usual.

Here we reach the heart of the matter—that is to say, the description of a Japan whose success is primarily due to its zeal for work. But this is also an area in which we see, behind the success, aspects of the social organization about which we have some reservations. I refer to the system of employment and to labor relations within the firm. The worker's position is still very much behind, very far from what would be generally accepted as normal in the West. The Japanese system has its bright side, such as the worker's loyalty and his devotion to the firm that employs him, but the shadows are sometimes very dark. These are the worker's strict subjugation to the company and, in the small firms (there are a great many of them) as distinct from the large, the extreme uncertainty of his position.

The subjugation of the worker to the firm is most apparent in the companies that employ a great many people, and it is the result of a particular state of affairs that became general only after the war and is little known today. It happens like this: once the worker is taken on, he does not leave the firm until he retires. If he wishes to succeed, he must make his whole career in that firm. Leaving one firm to join a rival, or simply changing jobs for some reason or other, just does not happen in Japan. The candidate for a job who tells the interviewer that he has left a firm after having worked there for some years is regarded with suspicion and given a black mark; he will not be employed except perhaps in some lower-grade firm that does not pay well. In short, there is only a very slight degree of mobility in employment, and there is virtually no labor market in the strict sense at all. The worker knows that if he loses his job he will be cast into outer darkness, so if he has been lucky enough to get into a big company, he has only one idea in his head: to stay there. And in order to stay there he will prove his loyalty by dint of hard work and patient submission to the company's requirements. What is more, the whole pay and promotion structure is calculated to imbue him with the necessary docility. As we have seen, the determining factor in raises and advancement is much less the worker's skill than his seniority in the firm, which implies loyalty and a right way of thinking.

Western standards should not be the basis for judging this system of lifelong employment and the consequent relationships between the company and its staff. It can be understood only in the context of a whole pattern of human relationships that is still very deeply influenced by the traditions of the Japan of former days. "It is an exceedingly complex matter: someone who does not know the country runs the risk of misunderstanding the nature of the problem and of forming mistaken or at least imperfect judgments," says Father Murgue, the author of an interesting monograph on the subject.

We often hear of the paternalism that is to be observed in Japanese companies, but in itself this notion is not enough. The family in Japan used to be very large, a "household," almost a clan, and it was arranged in a strict series of ranks under a single chief. Each individual's rights and duties varied according to his position, but all owed complete obedience to the head of the family. Everyone, even a stranger, who was allowed to share in the family life became an integral part of it. These family relationships were all vertical; there was very little in the way of horizontal relations—that is to say, with other families, neighbors and so on. This big family has vanished, being replaced by the smaller modern kind, but it has left deep marks upon the community. It is as though the Japanese find it very difficult to imagine any other kind of human relationship, even in this modern world where so many other kinds of societies exist, and as though relationships within the firm are in fact a transposition of those which used to exist within the family of former times.

The Japanese company does not look upon the employer-worker relationship in the light of a labor contract but rather as joint membership in the same family. The worker's main desire is to be an integral part of this second family, which is what the firm becomes for him. Without this membership, this belonging, he feels that he is a weak, orphaned, solitary creature in a world that is essentially based upon the group. With it, on the other hand—especially if it is one of the big firms—he knows that, like a family, the company will have the duty of looking after him for a considerable number of years, usually until he retires. He is not primarily concerned with the pay. It is by no means unusual for a new worker, on being asked what he is going to earn at his job, to reply, "I don't know; I'll find out when the first payday comes around." His chief preoccupation is to stay in the firm and, if he can, to move up through the grades. In order to be promoted and to be thought well of, he will display the utmost obedience, put up with great difficulties and constraints, work very hard, and pay court to those above him. What he asks of his superiors is above all to be good "elder brothers," and what he asks of the head of the firm is to be a good "father."

On his side, the chief also looks upon his functions as possessing this "family" character and considers that it requires him to be a just and watchful parent. Certainly he has all the rights, but he is also aware of a whole series of parental duties toward those under his orders. He feels that it is his duty not only to hand out wages and subsidiary benefits but also to endow the company with a canteen, for example, or a clinic or a playing field. He organizes trips and outings and arranges for courses in domestic economy, technical subjects and so on. His immediate subordinates share his outlook, and to be even surer of the staff's total loyalty they will often move right into the workers' private lives. Private life and working life tend to merge for some of the employees; many of the girls live in dormitories belonging to the works, sometimes the unmarried men are also housed by the company, and very often housing is provided for many of the staff's families, the accommodation improving with the rank.* Once a year the company has a great "family" gathering, at which everybody drinks and has fun.

Naturally the heads of the firm feel that in exchange for all they give their employees they have the right to expect the workers to share their views, and they bring very heavy pressure to bear on anyone who sees fit to stray from the company line. Usually the firm gets more than this: it wins the deep loyalty of all its employees, together with a strong "company spirit." The *Economist* survey that I quoted in the preceding chapter sees this as one of the incentives of Japanese zeal and drive in work. The worker feels that he is a part of the organization; it is a point of honor for him that the company should have satisfied customers or, better still, that it should, by a concerted effort of all of its members, beat its competitors, reach new records, and raise its standing higher still. The English magazine, referring to the wonders that the team spirit can accomplish in sport, says that in the West we no doubt underestimate the importance of this "group loyalty" as a stimulus to work.

It is in this "family" context, too, that we must consider relations between the company and the unions. For all the reasons that I have just mentioned, it is clear that the company will not look with a favorable eye upon the existence of any outside union, one that follows a line that is not the company's line and that claims to give it direction or advice. Like any other family, the company wants to integrate and take over everything in contact with it; it must therefore take over the union too. The union is welcome only as long as it forms part of the family—in other words, it must be a "house union," a company union very much under the control of the management. The Japanese trade union movement is in fact based upon a great number of single-company unions. In 1966 there were roughly ten million union members belonging to fifty thousand associations, 94 percent of which were house unions. It is these unions that have been promoting the system of lifelong jobs since 1945, in order to ensure steadiness

---

* Seventy percent of the big companies rent apartments to their workers; 80 percent, separate houses; and 90 percent, rooms for single people.

of employment for their members. So there is usually just one union in any given company, a vertical union that takes all comers: hands, office staff of various ranks, and even people belonging to quite different crafts. The firm's one union will group carpenters, metalworkers and clerks.

Membership in a horizontal union—that is to say, one based upon trade or calling—is most uncommon. Very rare, too, is the existence of two unions within the same concern. This scarcely ever happens except when the house union has come under strong Marxist or Communist influence, in which case the firm usually finds it easy enough to regroup the greater part of its people in another association, which then becomes the "right one" and does its best to drive out the first. The house union is usually supported by the firm, which provides accommodation for it, looks after its expenses and even withholds the members' dues from their wages. This means that most of the time the union leaders are men of whom the management approves.

All these employer-employee relationships and attitudes are summed up in a well-known Japanese formula, oyabun, kobun, which means the father-child relationship, or the relationship between patron and client, protector and protected. Lastly—and this is one of its most typical features—the class struggle is almost entirely absent from the Japanese workers' movement. There are strikes, but they are rarely motivated by a general movement of solidarity on the part of the working class or of a particular trade. Generally speaking, a strike is a movement within some given company, intended to remind it of its duty to give its family of workers an adequate wage or to persuade it to give them more. But it will not be found that two different house unions belonging to the same sector of industry and having the same problems ever combine to act in concert.

Father Murgue observes that in spite of all its drawbacks this system has real virtues, and it would be unjust to condemn it out of hand. But obviously, modernization is desirable. The great problem is the setting up of horizontal structures, above all at the union level, and the creation of conditions in which workers can move freely from one firm to another—or, in other words, the provision of a labor market like that in the West and a system of trade unions closer to ours.

We have not yet spoken of the intermediate employee grades, those that come between the management of the firm and the main body of the workers. The middle-grade executives in business and industry are taken on according to their school or university records and are promoted according to merit, amid strong and continual competition. Ferociously hard work, complete loyalty, and even toadying to their chiefs—those are the rungs of their ladder. They are the very model of efficiency, and they do a huge amount of work for the firm, usually for rather low pay. It would be too much to expect them to display much personality as well, and in any case the company's high command does not care for men with too many ideas of their own. What the management really wants is a competent and reliable carrier-out of orders, a trustworthy line of communication between the top and the bottom. These middle ranks are certainly capable and intelligent, but the company's discipline makes robots of them; the weight of the great family above them irons out their personalities, and they identify themselves wholly with their firm.

Their private family life is whittled away to such a degree that the real family, the one with a wife and children in it, comes far behind "the house," the employing company. All the social standing they may have, too, is derived from this company. If a man belongs to the Hitachi group, for example (the important concern with wide-ranging industrial and engineering interests that I have already mentioned), it means that he is of some consequence, no matter what position he holds in it. It can happen that the most important factor in a respectable family's decision about marrying a daughter is the firm for which the young man works. "He belongs to Hitachi!" the parents are told. This is a valid certificate of respectability and success, and once it has been produced the families will often carry on with the marriage, as soon as the traditional brief encounter for the engagement is over and done with.

While this system produces no strong personalities at the lower executive level, but rather a stereotyped and bureaucratic kind of official (Japan in fact brings forth few great thinkers and few philosophers), the country's strength lies in its middle-ranking executives, with their strong practical common sense, their experience, their discipline, their complete devotion, and the powerful solidarity that arises from their all having been educated in the same way—formed by the same molds. And while the big men at the top have a dash and spirit that makes one think of a more intelligent up-to-date version of the military leaders of former days, these middle-ranking executives remind one of the noncommissioned officers and subalterns who made up the strength of the old imperial army.

Comparison with the military era falls apart, however, when it comes to the question of education in Japan. The leaders of the Japan of yesterday exercised what amounted to Malthusianism applied to intelligence. They seemed to have worked out that it was necessary to give all the emperor's subjects enough schooling to produce a nation that could read, write and figure, but except for a chosen few it was scarcely desirable to go beyond a well-based elementary education. In this way critical attitudes of mind would not develop, nor would opposition, and the mass of the people would be easier both to govern and to indoctrinate. The new Japan has taken the very opposite course, and in a spirit of true democratization it has set about bringing the highest possible education to the greatest possible number of its citizens. As already indicated, present-day Japan is a country in which the citizen's sources of information are among the most highly developed in the world, and clearly, in our modern world, objective news and comment which keeps knowledge continually up to date and complete is a most valuable continuation of schooling.

Back in 1964 elementary education reached a level that can scarcely be surpassed, since it gave Japan the highest literacy rate in the world, with 99 percent of the children going to school for at least the obligatory minimum of nine years. This amounts to saying that there are no illiterates. As far as secondary education is concerned, the figure for that same year was rather more than 70 percent, which put Japan in second place, just behind the United States. The percentage has been rising since then, and in 1967 almost 75 percent of the pupils stayed at school until the end of their secondary education—that is to say, they had twelve years of schooling. The proportion of high school graduates is even higher in the great cities such as Tokyo (89.6 percent) and Osaka (82.3 percent). According to a Japanese Ministry of Education white paper, the proportion of young people throughout the country who will start earning their livings with at least a secondary education in 1973 will be 85 percent. The new Japan will therefore have succeeded in giving its citizens a secondary education as widely spread as the elementary was among the general mass of people for so long.

Then comes the university: 18 percent of Japanese students go on to this stage, entering the universities or other establishments for higher education which are so numerous in Japan. They leave when they are between twenty-two and twenty-five and have at least sixteen years of schooling behind them. The proportion of university graduates is growing fast, particularly as the number of young people has started to diminish, the bottom of the pyramid shrinking because of the strongly reduced birthrate. The Japanese Ministry of Education calculates that before 1973 between 25 and 30 percent of the young men appearing on the labor market will possess a university degree or its equivalent. As The Economist says, this is a genuine breakthrough on the mass education front. Norman Macrae, who wrote the survey for this important English review, does not hide his astonishment at discovering, there on the far side of Asia, a perfect example of what he terms "the educated society." Indeed, the comparison with his own country amazes him. "The British visitor always feels a shock," he writes, "when he realizes what the greatest advantage of the Japanese is: it is that the level of education in the Japanese community is now higher than it is in Great Britain." He says that, compared with the 70 percent of Japanese pupils going on to secondary schools, there are only 40 percent in Britain, and that as against the 18 percent of university students in Japan there are less than 10 percent in England. In 1968 the number of university students in Japan was approximately 800,000, and that of secondary school pupils 10 million.

There is still the question of determining the value of the teaching provided for this great mass of young people. The quality of the Japanese universities has often been challenged by the Japanese themselves, who state most emphatically that the degrees conferred by some of them are not as valuable as they should be and that they are worth less than the average Western degree.

And indeed the education reforms insisted upon by the Americans just after the defeat—reforms that aimed at extending the American system to Japan—did bring about an excessive increase in the numbers of universities throughout the country. The figures speak for themselves: there are 369 establishments having university status and giving a degree after two years' study, and there are 317 which give it after four years. This makes a total of 686 "universities"! There is obvious inflation here, and the title is being improperly used.

The Japanese reckon that in fact they have about ten "great" universities, whose degrees are highly valued, and a few dozen others that will pass muster; the rest are very uneven in quality, and many of them are at present substandard. The government is doing its best to reform the system and to improve it. But even with all its present faults, the Japanese feel that their system is not altogether without merit. The Japanese ambassador to France, Akira Matsui, in an address to the French National Defense Institute, quoted the opinion of the president of a great metallurgical company. "One of the reasons for the success of Japanese manufactures," said he, "arises from the fact that at every stage of production there are to be found university-trained technicians. Whenever there is a machine that cannot be put right by a workman you will always have the necessary university-trained technician right at hand. At a higher level you will always find other technicians working on ways of increasing production."

Currently, educational authorities are making great efforts to increase scientific and technical instruction in the secondary schools and universities (see Chapter 13). And there are a great many industrial firms that think the best diploma an engineer or a technician can have is the one they confer themselves. They have a whole system for teaching, improving and reorienting in the factory itself, and this school does its utmost to give its engineer students a very high degree of specialization, teaching them the particular skills that they will presently use. The big companies are always short of qualified staff, and this allows them to recruit students even before they have graduated, since the students can be sure of finishing their studies or of carrying them further when they are with the firm.

With the system of lifelong employment in which seniority is the chief factor in promotion, the most important thing for a young Japanese who is joining an industrial or commercial firm is to do so with the highest educational level that he can possibly attain. For it is this level that will decide what category he will be put in for good and all; the rate of his increases in salary will vary according to whether he was first classed as the product of an elementary school, a secondary school, or a university. In comparison with that, his social origins are of little importance, and a workingman's son has just as much chance of success as one from the middle class. It is understandable that parents should so passionately urge their children to study, for there is no country in which the children's career and even the social standing of the family's next generation depends upon it more. On top of this there are a very great many Japanese, and the last twenty years have seen the population figures reach their peak, so it is even more comprehensible that there should be savage competition at the school level. From their earliest days the young Japanese are plunged into an atmosphere of intense, even ferocious work at school, and this is still another reason why they are so industrious and persevering when they grow up. In Japan examination fever is a nationwide phenomenon. The whole of the country's youth suffers cruelly from it; it sows anguish in every family and poisons the life of the pupils from the first day they go to school. For just as there are good and bad universities, so there are good and not-so-good secondary and even elementary schools. There is competition for the places, and the classroom benches will not accommodate anywhere near the number of little candidates who appear. The result is that there are more and more examinations, even at the toddlers' level, and a rigorous selection eliminates a great many children, sending them off to schools with a lower standing. At the very top of the ladder, no more than twenty-five hundred to three thousand students, the cream of the whole country's youth, are admitted to Tokyo University, the most selective of them all.

The young people's long struggle also implies a long struggle on the part of their families. For university education is not free—this is one of the Japanese system's weakest points—it has to be paid for, and very heavily paid for at many of the private universities. Even at the secondary level parents prefer expensive private schools with high reputations to the free state establishments. This effort on the part of the families is still another example of the Japanese people's zeal for work. In their little straw-matted dwelling, a mother and father will sentence themselves to an even more frugal life so as to pay for their children's studies, but no doubt the continuous rise in the standard of living during the last twenty years has somewhat eased and softened this sacrifice. The opening of secondary and university education to continually increasing numbers of young people is therefore accompanied by a social rise on the part of their families. We have here a phenomenon of saving and of investment, an investment in education that is all the more striking in that it is carried out not by the state (since in this field the state does not do as much as could be wished) but by the people themselves, the ordinary people of Japan, who save part of their modest resources to finance it.

A desire to rise in the social scale is not in itself an adequate explanation. There is also a disinterested love for knowledge and progress among the Japanese. One of the greatest American authorities on Japanese questions, who was also the greatest American ambassador to Tokyo since MacArthur, Professor Edwin O. Reischauer, says:

It is probable that there is no country in which the people have a greater longing for education; and there are few that even come up to Japan in this respect. The importance given to education and the successes that have been gained in this field seem to be taken for granted in Japan, so much so that some Japanese do not realize what a great part they have played in the modernization of the country. The Japanese think it quite natural that when peasants are given the opportunity of doing so, they should want to learn new scientific agricultural techniques; but there are many countries where it is very hard to persuade the peasants to change their old ways. The Japanese think it quite natural that if young people are given the means they should be very eager to educate themselves; but in many societies the mass of the people are unenthusiastic about even primary schooling and downright opposed to all higher education.

Looking deeper, one sees that these Japanese attitudes toward knowledge and education are based upon the fact that culture is already widespread throughout the great body of the people. One has to have lived in Japan fully to appreciate the way culture "goes deep," penetrating all social levels right down to the humblest with a greater intensity than it does even in our most cultivated Western countries. Of course there are exceptions and gaps, and it would be possible to quote plenty of examples of Japanese coarseness or uncouth behavior. But when one lives side by side with the Japanese, one finds upon the whole that they possess not only a delicacy in feeling and action that is not often to be seen among our ordinary people, but also artistic, literary and intellectual taste and knowledge—in short, a cultivation, an openness of mind, and an interest in the outer world that is rarely to be found in the West among what are conventionally termed the common people.

Japan is a country where almost everybody can draw and even paint well; where there are great numbers of unbelievably well-attended art exhibitions; where open summer windows let out the sound of innumerable young musicians practicing scales upon the piano or violin; where a great many of the passengers on the trains and subways read not only papers or magazines but books; where a provincial high school boy can tell you at least something about Picasso, Dickens, Oppenheimer, Leonardo da Vinci, Bertrand Russell and Jean-Paul Sartre. An elevator operator reading Milton's *Paradise Lost*, a taxi driver interested in Matisse's painting, a secretary who reads Stendhal, the little daughter of a poor fisherman who has learned Japanese classical dancing, a mountain woodcutter who is interested in Swiss neutrality, the eleven-year-old son of a clerk playing the violin in a children's symphony orchestra, a factory mechanic listening to Beethoven on his record player—all these are cases that I myself have come across in Japan, and it is hard to believe that this would be possible in many other countries.

The omnipresent radio, television and newspapers and the generalized love of reading do a very great deal toward this democratization of culture. The press shows this very clearly. Which daily is looked upon as having the highest cultural level? Every Japanese will reply, "The *Asahi*." That is the paper that officials, important people, intellectuals and members of the learned professions read. And which daily has the biggest circulation? Again it is this same *Asahi*, which also has a huge following among the general public, since its 1968 figure, beating *all world records*, shows a daily printing of more than nine million copies. In other words, quality and mass production come together in the same newspaper. Mass production of high-quality objects is one of the new Japan's particularities, and this we see again in industry. But to confine ourselves for a moment to the press, the way television has seized a great share of the public's attention has not prevented the great papers from keeping their enormous circulations. In April, 1966, the average daily printing for all papers reached 43,988,412 copies, which gives an average for each family of 1.43. The circulation of the weekly illustrated magazines (there are about forty of them) amounts to an average of 6,622,000; that of the monthly reviews and periodicals (there are about thirteen hundred) to 58,405,-000. And all this for a population at that time of 98 million.

At the same time the Japanese are avid readers of books, in spite of their consumption of newspapers and magazines—and in spite of the difficulty of their system of writing. They are also among the greatest book producers in the world, coming third behind the United States and the Soviet Union. In 1962 it was calculated that each inhabitant of the country (counting even the babies in their cradles) read an average of 2.3 books and 13 periodicals a year. Twenty million families bought an average of 11 books in the year. In 1965 the number of titles published reached approximately 25,000, amounting to 280 million copies in all. In August, 1967, 3,036 books were brought out, a little more than half of them being reprints and the rest new works; and this gave a total of 19,070,000 copies printed during the month. A best seller often goes beyond the million mark. A historical novel about the first shogun, Iyeyasu, sold more than 6 million copies some years ago.

Japan has twenty-four hundred publishing houses, about twenty of them being very big, and sixteen thousand bookstores. At the moment there is a boom in encyclopedias; there are seventeen on the market. In spite of television—or rather, as some think, because of television—the number of books published has risen by 50 percent in fifteen years, and the number of books read by the Japanese has almost tripled. Paperbacks have increased and multiplied. This list of best-selling paperbacks, drawn up by the great Kunokuniya bookshop in Tokyo, will give some notion of the quality of what is read: (1) Plato's Apology, (2) and (3) two works by Engels, (4) Thomas More's Utopia, (5) another edition of the Apology, (6) Simone de Beauvoir's The Second Sex, (7) Kiyoshi Miki's Notes on Life, (8) Goethe's Werther, (9) Jean-Jacques Rousseau's Emile, (10) Kitaro Nishida's A Study of the Good.

The Japanese reader's insatiable curiosity naturally makes him a great consumer of translations, and this means that the Japanese publishers are the most "internationally minded" in the world. From the Greek Anthology to the French nouveau roman, by way of the Chinese classics and pieces by high-powered European and American journalists, every well-known work or widely circulated book ends up by being translated into Japanese (even though it is true that the translation is often rather poor). A well-known critic, Miss Michiko Inukai, states that Japan has translated more contemporary Russian literature, for example, than any other country. She insists that the reading public is in no way made up of snobs and intellectuals but, in the immense majority, is quite certainly composed of "average Japanese" men and women who save their by no means abundant pay to buy really good books. And she goes on to quote the example of a little town, most of whose inhabitants were miners, and whose bookshop had sold forty copies of the translation of André Maurois's and Louis Aragon's parallel history of the U.S.A. and the U.S.S.R. in a fortnight. A miner who reads books of this kind is no ordinary miner.

In short, the value of the Japanese workers lies not only in their zeal for work but also in their zeal for educating themselves and for the cultivation of their minds—still another proof that one of the keys to the success of Japan is the quality of its people. But although this is certainly true, their quantity, the great numbers of them, has also been a very important factor.

5.

Great Numbers
and Small Wages

In the shallow sea three hundred yards from the shore, there is a pretty little island covered with holm oaks and aborescent camellias that hide red-pillared temples; its name is Enoshima. There is a long footbridge between the mainland and the isle, the blue waves of the Pacific, and in the background the inevitable Mount Fuji. Enoshima has long been the favorite Sunday outing for the humbler people of Tokyo—who in the last fifty years have multiplied by ten thousand.

On a fine Sunday at the beginning of summer, between 150,000 and 200,000 Japanese will come here to take the air. The coast road is a total chaos of unmoving cars, the little station is embedded in a human jelly, and eighty enormous coaches make a line across the view of Mount Fuji.

For there is a danger threatening Japan; indeed, it already exists: the traffic jam. The superexpresses and superhighways are not growing fast enough, and presently they in their turn will be choked. Surely the time is at hand when Japan will be the first of the great modern countries to experience total congestion on a national scale. Will not trains, buses, homes, movie houses, theaters and public places all be completely full? Everything is full already, crammed, stuffed with three or four times the ordinary number of close-packed beings. Formerly, the overpopulated Japan invaded other countries. Now it invades itself.

Fifty million in 1912; 60 million in 1926; 70 million in 1937, the beginning of the war with China; 80 million in 1948; 90 million in

1957. . . . The inexorable progress goes on and on. For a long while people believed that the 100-million mark would not be reached without very serious upheavals.

The first effect of the 1945 defeat was to flood Japan with 7 million men that colonial conquest and war had scattered far over Asia. The second, with all these fathers coming home, was a sharp rise in the birthrate. From 1925 onward Japan had been producing a fairly regular 2 million babies a year. But the first period of postwar reconstruction opened with three even more fruitful years—three terrible years, say the Japanese. In 1947, 1948 and 1949 almost 2.7 million births were registered each year; in three years, that amounted to more than the overflow that the military epoch had exported as emigrants of all kinds!

After 1947 the Japanese began watching the curve of their population statistics with the concentrated attention of a patient who understands his illness and who sees the rise of his temperature chart. Month by month the papers and the radio told the country what degree the thermometer had reached, as it were. When it became apparent that Japan had never made so many babies at any time in its history, there was a general state of alarm. At the same time the country experienced its first slump, and the Korean War broke out. Was the fatal cycle of overpopulation, crisis and war going to begin all over again?

At this point observers were presented with an extraordinary phenomenon, one that still astonishes specialists in demographic questions: five years after the defeat there was the strongest and fastest drop in the birthrate that has ever been known in the history of the great nations. It had risen to 34.3 per thousand in 1947. In 1950 it dropped below 30. In 1954 it was at 20. In 1957 it was at 17.2; and, as we shall see later, the fall went on. In a few years the birthrate had dropped from an "Asian" one to the lowest European level, ranking with Denmark and Switzerland and only beaten by Sweden. It is obvious that an immensely powerfully restraining factor had begun to act in 1950, the middle of the century and the turning point in the nation's growth.

How did it come about? The explanation is very simple. Public information played a decisive part; it made the Japanese aware of the danger of this new inflationary rise in the population, and at the same time it told them that they had a legal weapon to fight it with—a war-time "eugenic protection law" that was broadened after the defeat to legalize abortion. In addition, the papers and other sources of information carried the birth-control campaign right into the remotest country districts.

At present abortion is allowed for "economic motives," such as the couple's poverty, but really the whole thing is so ill-defined that it amounts to unconditional permission. Under the influence of this law the midwives and gynecologists have in fact become birth-control agents and specialists in abortion, and in the same way there has been built up a body of specializing surgeons who are now the most skillful in the world—though this did not happen until after a period of readjustment that must have wreaked cruel havoc. In 1957, ten years after the alarm of 1947, there were 1.2 million officially registered abortions and probably half again this number that were not declared. It seems that this shocking rise in the number of abortions, which did in the end frighten both the government and a section of public opinion, is now receding because of the appearance of the pill and various other new contraceptives.

Another striking feature of the situation is that birth control has spread even faster in the countryside than it has in the towns, which is something that no other underdeveloped and overpopulated country, not even Mao Tse-tung's China, has ever managed to do. In Japan, the historic strongholds of rural society, although they were tradition-ally stubborn and conservative from the beginning of the Meiji era, have been shaken; they have not escaped the general movement. As for the cities, here is a fact that tells one a great deal about the spread of these practices: Many big organizations have themselves initiated a policy of birth control for their employees. This operates at the workshop or office level and is run by the company's social service. The organization provides contraceptives, education in eugenics, a nursing home and doctor for abortions, and even a financial grant.

The slowing down of the birthrate has now been going on for more than twenty years. So what is Japan's present position with regard to population? The capital fact, the great event that has not been suffi-ciently noted, perhaps because it is in a way a great "negative" event, is that in 1967 Japan did reach the dreaded 100-million mark without disaster. None of the catastrophes that had been feared took place—

no unemployment, no famine, no civil disturbances. Far from it; 1967 was a boom year. This untroubled passing of the 100-million mark merits an important place among Japan's current successes. It is very easily explained by the two factors that we have mentioned and that can be summed up thus: great increase in production, great restraint in reproduction. To be sure, not all these problems have been solved, but they are no longer alarming, and nowadays there is much less talk of the dangers of an abundant population than of the advantages the nation derives from it.

From the point of view of the man in the street, the new Japan must be given the credit for another advance that is indeed of vital concern to every Japanese. Just after the war life expectancy was still sadly inadequate; it was only in 1947 that the figure exceeded fifty years. Since then it has increased at an extraordinary pace: In 1960 it was sixty-five for men and seventy for women. Now it is even higher: A Japanese boy born in 1966 can normally expect to live until he is sixty-eight, and a girl until she is seventy-three. Japan has almost reached the level of Holland, Norway and Sweden, which are the countries with the longest average life.

The 1965 census (there is one every five years) was the final census to show an eight-figure population: It gave a total of 98,281,955 inhabitants. The birthrate had dropped to 16.6 per thousand. The annual increase had gone down to 10.4 per thousand, which is less than the world average of 19 but higher than the European figure of 9. The population was still increasing, of course, but only by about a million a year. It should be added that there has since been a tendency for the figures to rise a little faster; in 1967, the year of the 100-million mark, 1,974,500 babies were born and 670,300 deaths were recorded, which gives a natural increase of 1,304,200. (This was an exceptional rise. Because of an astrological superstition that would take too long to explain here, 1966 was an unlucky year for marriage. The number for that year therefore showed a marked drop, which was made up in 1967.) The birthrate was 19.7 per thousand, thus exceeding 19 for the first time since 1955, and the death rate was 6.7, the lowest since 1872.

What is the future outlook, and what heights will the Japanese population curve reach? The forecasts vary a good deal and must be regarded with caution; demography is a field full of surprises. The Japanese think that their country, like all great industrial countries that reach a certain level of success and material prosperity, will see its population stabilize or even diminish. They also believe that the top of the curve is near, both in time and in statistics. As to the question of when it will be reached and at what height, let me cite two 1966 opinions, the one "moderate" and the other "bold." Both place the peak at about 1985. But whereas the Institute of Population Studies, which comes under the Ministry of Public Health, calculated that the population of Japan would then reach 116 million, the experts of the Planning Agency foresaw 130 million—at first sight a somewhat alarming figure. Since that time the Agency has modified its forecast, and a long-term study put out in 1968 was based on the figure of 120 to 123 million for the year 1985.

Although these forecasts are by no means definite, it is clear from their attempts at looking into the future that the Japanese are finding that their demographic problem has limits and that it is possible to reduce it to an equation. In the long run, the terms of this equation are not as frightening as people had at one time thought. Even if the high point should be at a dangerous level, the country has a certain breathing space in which to get ready for it. It would seem that before the year 2000 Japan should have a stable population or even one that is beginning to diminish. The position is therefore quite different from that of China, where the rising curve forecasts a country with a billion inhabitants well before 2000, and there is nothing to show that the figure will stop there. No one, speaking with any certainty, can rule out the possibility of a human inflation going well beyond that enormous total.

In Japan there is no longer any talk of human inflation; the nightmare of the "population explosion" has vanished, and the people no longer fear that the country will be impoverished by too great a number of inhabitants. On the contrary, it is thought that the abundant population was a factor in Japan's success, a factor that favored the country's extraordinarily rapid expansion and carried it into one of the foremost places in worldwide competition. In round figures, out of the 100 million Japanese, 75.5 million are of working age—that is to say, they are over fifteen. Nearly 50 million do in fact work. These are the figures for 1967. They represent a high degree of economic activity and show the existence of a very hard-working nation. A clear proof of this is the unusually high proportion of female labor: in 1967 two fifths of all jobs were held by women, which is chiefly explained by the fact that in the country the work on the land is done principally by them, while the men go to the workshop or the factory. The distribution of the working population in 1967 was the following: primary sector (agriculture, forestry and fishing), 10.3 million persons; secondary (mining and industry), 16.9 million; and tertiary (retail trade, transport and services), 22.7 million.

From the point of view of population age levels, Japan is a remarkably young country. In relation to its total number, Japan has the advantage of possessing an exceptionally high proportion of young workers—that is to say, the men and women who are best at working hard and who also cost the least, since they are still only paid as beginners. Better still, the appearance on the labor market of ever-increasing numbers of young people—a consequence of the great post-war demographic rise—coincided exactly with the years of the Japanese economy's most rapid growth. Of these two concurrent increases, the first contributed to the second—that is to say, the demographic rise helped the economic growth—and the problems of the second were solved by the existence of the first—that is to say, the flood of newcomers was continually absorbed by the creation of factories and workshops.

As far as industry is concerned, for more than twenty years Japan has never ceased to be a country of full employment in spite of its numerous population. The abundance of labor has not depressed the economy to the point of causing serious unemployment or an under-employment that would have a bad effect upon the country's advance. Far from it; this state of affairs allowed Japan to escape the danger of a dwindling labor force—a danger that lies in wait for all rapidly developing countries—during the period of its greatest expansion. It has been an advantage that other great industrial countries might envy. West Germany, for example, has had its rate of growth slowed down these last ten years, partly because of its industry's lack of labor. In Japan, the emphasis has been on creating new jobs as new workers appear in very important numbers on the labor market.

The Japanese people's keen awareness of the problem has helped in its solution, particularly at the time when they saw the coming of the "new wave," the consequence of the high birthrate, the baby boom of the years just after the war. As was the case with birth control, this general comprehension was due to the effectiveness of very active and widely spread information media. The whole country knew that in order to cope with this demographic flood it was absolutely necessary to create at least a million new jobs a year, or even a million and a half at the highest point, and that this effort must not slacken for more than fifteen years.

Everyone knew that it was no longer possible to count upon any of the three safety valves for overpopulation that the Japan of military days had known—the army, colonization and emigration. A new safety valve had to be created, and this was expansion—speeded-up expansion. Or, better still, the mistaken idea of "overpopulation" had to be done away with by showing that the more people there were, the more work there would be. All the Japanese grasped this point, and they all consciously helped in making this solution possible. Statistics show that since 1960 the creation of new jobs has consistently gone well beyond the million mark annually, and this is between four and six times the corresponding figures for England, Germany or France.

Thanks to the drop in the birthrate that began in the 1950's, the population flood is going down, while at the same time the prodigious rise of production has continually increased the number of jobs. But everything changes very fast in Japan, and recently we have seen the rise of a new problem, the very opposite of what was expected for so long: Industry is now short of labor—that is, qualified labor. This, at least for foreign observers, is the great surprise—the unexpected price of the country's success—the other side of the coin. Whereas at the beginning of the sixties the working population was increasing by 1.5 million a year, in the seventies this growth will have dropped by half. And whereas at present the teen-agers number 45 million, it is reckoned that in 1971 there will be only 24 million of them. This inevitably means that the rate at which the country can produce an educated, trained labor force to meet the needs of its continuing industrial expansion is in for a progressive decline.

This change of tendency, which has exposed the great industrial organizations to a certain shortage of labor after their long period of abundance, started at the beginning of the sixties, the period at which both the great "speed-up" and the first near-inflation began, in the time of the conservative government under Ikeda, the author of the well-known plan for doubling the national income. In 1955 every industrial job offered attracted an average of 3.6 applicants, but in 1963 the shortage was making itself felt, and for every applicant there were three available places. And to an ever-increasing extent the jobs offered call for sound technical qualifications.

At the beginning of April, 1968 (April is the end of the Japanese school year and the most important time for taking on new employees), out of the 1,834,000 young people of about fifteen who had finished their elementary education, the 277,000 applicants for jobs had each an average of 4.9 available places. At the same time, the 847,000 (out of a total of 1,606,000) eighteen-year-olds who had finished their secondary education and who wanted to earn their living had an average of 2.8 jobs offered them. According to the Japanese Ministry of Labor the economy was short 1,800,000 hands and qualified workers in June, 1968. This shortage was 300,000 above the 1967 figure, and it was particularly evident in the medium-sized firms.

I hardly need say that this kind of situation in employment has necessarily given great strength to the movement for higher wages.

Japanese wages have been continuously rising for about fifteen years. Between 1952 and 1962, the rise in industrial wages was about 5 percent a year, twice the American rate and higher than that of all the other great industrial countries with the exception of West Germany, and since then they have risen faster still. From 1961 to 1969 it was above 10 percent each year in firms employing more than forty persons. In 1967 the rise was the highest ever recorded in Japan—a nominal 13.5 percent and (taking into account the cost of living) a real 9.1 percent over 1966.

In the ten years from 1957 to 1967, the starting pay of a graduate entering industry more than doubled. An even more astonishing advance affected the worker with no more than an elementary education —his pay almost tripled. So the advantages that large-scale Japanese industry may have had on the international markets because of rates of pay lower than those of its Western competitors have much diminished. The Europeans and Americans have a long-established belief that the expansion of Japan is due to low wages, but in the face of the far more complex reality this oversimplified explanation no longer holds water. Nevertheless, it would be an error to go too far in the other direction, unreservedly accepting another oversimplification— a semiofficial Japanese version, put forward by big business and government public relations in Tokyo—that, on the whole, Japanese workers' pay is now so close to the European standard that it is almost the same. This may be the case in certain sectors; it is very far from being so in all. The truth probably lies between the two. Or perhaps one should say that in the field of Japanese wages there are many possible truths; one has to be cautious, avoiding over-easy comparisons between East and West and distrusting the interpretation of statistics.

A great many years of familiarity with Japan and of interest in the complex subject of Japanese wages leads me to the conclusion that in this area everything is true and everything can be said, since every kind of structure, from the most "Western" to the most lamentably "Asian," is to be found, as well as every rate of payment, from the most rewarding down to the merest pittance. It is an area from which all logic has been long absent, one in which differences according to particular cases are unbelievably numerous. The pay for the same job will vary from one great organization to another. It may be higher in Tokyo than it is in a provincial town. It will vary a great deal according to the sex of the worker, the women being cruelly underpaid. The size of the firm will also make a very great difference. And within the same organization, it may vary widely according to whether the worker belongs to this or that category, whether he is classed as permanent or temporary, favored or unfavored. So averages and overall figures can be deceptive; objective returns are hard to come by. Disagreeable facts are easily covered up, and on the other hand it is not at all difficult to give a darker picture of the situation than is accurate.

The first thing to do to get a clearer view of the position is to draw the absolutely fundamental distinction between two very different economic worlds, that of the great organizations and that of the small and medium-sized firms. To be sure, this distinction is so well known that the Japanese themselves are the first to speak at length about what they call "the double structure" of their economy. But very often people will bring forward sanguine analyses of the workers' position or agreeable figures relating to their pay without making it evident that they refer to the workers or staff belonging to the higher range of the economy and that they give no information whatsoever about what is happening at the lower range.

When one is in Tokyo there is no need to go far to see a concrete example of the difference between the two classes, the two levels. All that is needed is to visit Kawasaki, right next to the capital, where only twenty years ago there were rice fields and where now the roar of the new expansion is to be heard; this former village has become the country's third most important industrial center. Kawasaki, bristling with high-tension towers and factory chimneys, has so thoroughly filled the ten or eleven miles between Tokyo and Yokohama that the three towns are now a single urban mass. Blast furnaces, steelworks, shipyards, factories that turn out chemicals, machines, electrical apparatus, food products and more are all to be found here, and most of them have very modern equipment. When the shifts change, hundreds of metalworkers may be seen coming out of the great Nippon Kokan steelworks. Apart from their Oriental eyes and a few Japanese touches to their clothes, they might perfectly well be the inhabitants of a European industrial town. There are twenty thousand of them working in this vast concern. Many of them belong to unions. The machines they handle, the safety and the healthiness of their workshops and the wages earned by some of them are scarcely inferior to their equivalent in a Western country. It is firms like this that make up the strength of the great "factory Japan" and allow the country to compete with the other industrial nations.

But a few hundred yards away from the great works, among the alleys between the wooden houses, is an immense labyrinth of factories, many of which do not employ as many as twenty hands and scarcely deserve the name, of little workshops, where the working conditions are indifferent or even primitive, and of little family enterprises which employ no outside labor. There are also a great many medium-sized firms here, and in their case too the technical level is pretty low and the financial position shaky; all this reflects upon the position of the employees. Yet the important firms, those having more than three hundred workers (which is not so very big), take up only a third of the labor force in manufacturing industry. Seventy percent of the force works in the smaller firms, at the lower level, and of these workers 33 percent are at the very bottom of it, in the little firms that employ less than thirty. The phenomenon is even more strongly marked in retail trade and services; one out of every two persons employed in this sector belongs to a firm that numbers less than five people. The statistics also show that the Japanese economy includes a great number of small concerns and very few big ones. In 1964 90.6 percent of firms fell into the class of those employing less than thirty workers and office staff. Those with between thirty and a hundred made up 6.4 percent of the total; between a hundred and a thousand, 2.9 percent; only 550 organizations, or 0.1 percent, employed more than a thousand.

It is easy to explain the coexistence of these two different worlds in the context of Japan's development. Economic expansion, carried out at great speed in a country that suffered from insufficient capital but was blessed with an abundant supply of labor, was possible only for the few big businesses which thrust far ahead while the mass of small businesses stayed behind, at a technical and social level that often corresponded to a time lag of more than half a century.

Looking at it from a sociological point of view, one might regard this double structure as a projection of the whole Japanese social system into the realm of the economy—a system that is not based upon the principle of equality but rather that of ordered ranks, of hierarchy. New Japan has learned to know freedom, but the same cannot be said of equality. Japanese society is made up of big people and little people, the protectors and the protected, and the client–patron relationship between them goes hand in hand with one of mutual assistance.

However that may be, working Japan is composed of two distinct worlds. In the first—such as the great Kawasaki steelworks—we are in a world that, in a great many of its aspects, is almost Western. In the second we are still in Asia, an Asia that has certainly been somewhat changed by technology but that has scarcely left the nineteenth century. So when we speak of wages, it is essential to state quite clearly that there can be no valid comparison between Japanese and Western —or at least European—pay except in the case of the "upper" Japan, the Japan of the great modern organization. There can be none with the "lower" Japan of the small and medium-sized firms.

Let us look first at the position in the higher sector. The Japanese rightly point out that the wage figures they publish are by no means blown up to bring them nearer to the Western level; on the contrary, they show an amount that is in fact less than the true total received. Far more than the law, it is tradition that causes the basic wage shown in the statistics to be no more than a part of the total real pay. For to the basic wage are added many special allowances in cash and kind that may increase it considerably; all these allowances, I should add, vary according to the firm's inclinations. Thus the salary may amount to no more than between 55 and 60 percent of the real total received, for the allowances will add an extra 15 to 20 percent and the grants in kind another 15 to 20 percent. The chief allowance is the semi-annual bonus, a traditional but not obligatory gift usually distributed in the summer and at the New Year; it may amount to several months' pay if the firm is doing well or be reduced to nothing in time of crisis.

Another addition to the basic pay is the productivity bonus, which the Japanese employer so oddly regards as of secondary importance; then there is overtime; then the various allowances for costs such as meals, transport and family lodging; and, finally, a modest capital sum for retirement, which happens usually—although it is not obligatory—at the early age of fifty-five. As well as all this, the executives have tax-free entertainment allowances, and for a man in the higher grades this may sometimes amount to a very considerable addition to his income. The allowances in kind may vary widely in nature—free or very cheap housing, free company transport, free working clothes, factory shops and canteens, playing fields and their equipment, company vacation camps and so on.

It is partly because of these untaxed allowances in kind that the workingman can lead a comparatively decent life, and it is they that attract the young beginner to the big organizations; generally speaking, it is the big organizations alone that grant them. Lastly we must add the social benefits: medical expenses are wholly covered for the worker, with 50 percent coverage for his family, and he is given 60 percent of his wages in case of a disabling accident. Apart from the few organizations in which generous employers have set up their own system of social insurance, the provision for such benefits is by no means common, and, at the workers' expense, its lack gives Japan a considerable advantage over the West in international competition.

Now, bearing in mind these various factors, let us take a look at some recent salary figures in the great Japanese organizations. The overall average monthly pay in these big firms as a whole for a thirty-year-old working man with eight years of seniority was 51,420 yen, the equivalent, in 1968, of $143. The highest-paid workers were those in the oil and oil-derivatives industry, with their $178; then came the iron and steel workers, with $166; transport, $161; gas and electricity, $160; paper, $155. The textile industry worker was among the lowest paid, with his $90 a month. The overall average for an industrial worker was $156.

What does a young man earn when he starts in industry? In 1968 a university graduate going into a big organization made $83 a month— more than twice what he would have been paid ten years earlier. A worker with a secondary education began at $66 in 1968, and one with an elementary education at just under $52. The 1968 summer bonus beat all records: the general average was nearly two and a half months' pay, and this came on top of almost the same amount at the end of 1967. (These figures come from an inquiry into wages conducted by the authoritative Japanese magazine *The Oriental Economist*. It has been publishing the same kind of survey every year since 1953.)

There is an appreciable increase in salary year by year, for, as we have seen, age is an essential factor in wage level.* Here, from the same source, are some figures on the average monthly earnings in July, 1967, of a male worker with a secondary education. If he was twenty he made $68 and if he was thirty, $122. The forty-year-old earned $177 and the fifty-year-old, $233. At fifty-five, on retirement, he made $257. For the same period a male university graduate of twenty-two earned nearly $80; if he was forty-five he earned nearly three times as much; and if he was fifty-five he finished with $387 a month. But the scale was considerably higher in the best-paying organizations; at the end of a man's career it would reach the level of $625.†

Is it really possible to compare the levels of pay in the upper section of the Japanese economy with those of the West? There have been attempts to do so, and here is the comparison put forward by the foreign ministry in Tokyo in 1963. Taking the figure of 100 for the hourly wage in United States industry in 1960, the other great countries would have the following indices: England, 32.7; West Germany,

---

* The system of wage rise by seniority, together with the low starting wage, means that Japanese factories employ a proportion of young workers that is almost twice as great as that in the Western countries.

† *The Oriental Economist*, February, 1968. In 1967 the graduate, on retiring from his firm at fifty-five, received a sum corresponding to forty months' pay; a man with a secondary education, forty-four months'; and an elementary education, forty-seven months'.

27.1; France, 18.5; Japan (for the firms employing more than five hundred), 17.4; and Italy, 16.2. An unpublished survey by French experts in 1965, on the other hand, made the following comparisons: The hourly wage in the Japanese manufacturing industry amounts on the average to 70 percent of the French figure, 50 percent of the German, 40 percent of that in Great Britain, and 15 percent of that in the United States. But taking into account the difference in purchasing power and in the pattern of living, these percentages could be raised to give 75 percent of the German figure, 70 percent of the British and 25 percent of the American.

But these comparisons of figures are dangerous, and their chief value is to show the general tendency. Here again we may grant that the Japanese statistics often lead to an underestimation of the true position. They should be corrected in terms of the many additional allowances in cash and kind that the foregoing figures do not take into account. It would then be seen that in the biggest organizations the real wages of the Japanese industrial workers are not very far from those that are usual in the industry of the Western countries.

The Japanese also have several other arguments when foreign competitors accuse them of exploiting a policy of low wages:

1. Japan has succeeded in joining the leaders among the great industrial countries primarily because of its big modern organizations. But these are the very firms that pay their employees well. There is therefore no "unfair competition" in this case.

2. The Japanese currency, the yen, has remained at the same rate of exchange for twenty years—that is to say, 360 yen to the dollar. But its real value is considerably higher. In just that proportion, therefore, the comparisons are weighted against Japan.

3. Even now the worker's productivity is lower, in general, than it is in the West. This justifies the lower wages. According to an American estimate, the Japanese worker's productivity is 40 or 50 percent of that of the American worker with the same qualifications.

There is a good deal of truth in these arguments, above all when they refer to the organizations big enough to stand up to the most important Western concerns. But they do not exhaust the subject or terminate all discussion, and even more eagerly than their foreign competitors the Japanese unions complain that in large-scale industry there are still many low-paid workers. Here are a few of the points the unions raise:

1. Female workers form an underprivileged class, paid far less than the men. And there are whole industries based primarily upon female labor and deriving their chief advantages from that fact. They employ only unmarried girls, taking them on at about seventeen and laying them off after five or six years without having to pay them a pension, the girls having received only the often trifling beginner's wage throughout. This is the case in part of the textile industry and in the manufacture of household equipment, toys and so forth.

2. Output is often low, yet in certain sectors it has risen fast because of the modernization of equipment. This advance was particularly rapid at the time of the boom between 1966 and 1968. In the one year of 1967–1968 it reached 18 percent in a whole series of important concerns and even 20 percent in iron and steel and in engineering. But the rise in wages has lagged behind the rise in productivity. For twenty years and more, the wage curve has been lower than that of output; for Japanese firms this is a great advantage over their competitors, to be sure, but it is an advantage that is gained at the expense of the workers. In most of the Western countries, on the contrary—in West Germany, for example—wages have risen faster than productivity.

3. The Japanese employment structure has one singular and rather shocking feature: the existence, within the great organizations themselves, of more or less seriously underprivileged inferior classes of workers. Membership in the firm, employment for life, the certainty of a regular basic wage and the allowances in cash and kind that come with it, membership in the union and so on—all these things are in fact reserved for a favored category of employees, the "permanents." Below them there are several classes of "temporaries" who are taken on for short periods, sometimes just for the day; they may be supplied and employed by people who rent out labor and who have nothing to do with the firm; and these workers are paid at a lower rate. They form a positive subproletariat, composed chiefly of laborers and unqualified workers, and one of the many

aspects of their inferior condition is that they are not allowed to join the firm's union.

4. The great organizations usually rest upon a whole pyramid of smaller firms, their subcontractors. The big houses pass down an order, say for spare parts, that can be executed in a small workshop and with inferior labor. By putting out work in this way to their vassal firms, the great organizations get a very considerable part of their production at cut rates; for these little firms pay their employees very low wages, since they belong to the lower level in the double structure of the economy—to the poor and somewhat underdeveloped "second Japan" of the small-scale companies where there are the "Asian" rates of pay—or even to an economy that has not yet reached the stage of salaries at all.

In 1967 17 million workers were employed in industry, mines and building—that is to say, the Japanese economy's secondary sector as opposed to the primary (agriculture) and to the tertiary (retail trade and services). It may be estimated that the middle level, that of the firms employing between thirty and three hundred hands, took rather more than 6 million of this labor force, and that the lowest level, that of the small and very small firms with less than thirty hands, took 5.5 million. This amounts to 11.5 million industrial workers who belonged to the lower levels of the economy and were paid less or, indeed, very much less than the 5.5 million who were lucky enough to be taken on by the great concerns belonging to the upper level.

Furthermore, this double structure is to be seen again in the tertiary sector—that is to say, retail trade and services, which employed slightly over 22.5 million Japanese in 1967. Here it is even more marked, for 70 percent of those employed work in companies with a staff of less than ten. One out of every two Japanese employees in this sector works in a firm or a shop in which there are five workers at the most.

All these workers on the lower level are "underpaid" in comparison with those belonging to the great organizations. And this state of affairs becomes more and more accentuated as one goes down the scale. If we take the figure of 100 for the wages paid by a big manufacturing company in 1964, the corresponding figure for a medium-sized firm was 75 and for a small one a mere 50. An average thirty-year-old worker, for example, earning $83 a month in a big firm, might find that another worker in a small factory nearby, doing the same job, was paid 50 percent of that sum. Fortunately these figures are better nowadays, because during these last years there has been a rise in the wages paid in the small firms—a rise that is in some cases proportionally even greater than that in the big firms, so that the 50 percent figure for the lower level has become 60 percent. It should also be pointed out that the difference between great and small concerns is much less marked when it comes to starting pay. In other words, at the beginning of his career a young worker earns much the same at either level. It is the progress by seniority that shows an ever-increasing divergence.

Finally, to present the problem in its entirety, there remains a factor that is not often appreciated in its full significance, a factor that does not exist in the same degree in any other great modern country. At the bottom of the scale of the very small concerns there is a mass of workers who quite simply receive no wages whatsoever. This mass is composed of all those who work with their families at home, in little booths and shops. The whole idea of wages is foreign to them. The household lives on its collective earnings; it spends almost all its income, and divides the rest when it can. But usually there is nothing left to distribute to its members once it has supplied them with food, shelter and work. This wageless group makes up one of the main bodies of Japanese workers, for, together with those in the lowest levels of trade and industry, it includes almost all those who work on the land and the fishermen who use traditional methods—that is to say, the primary sector of the economy. Their numbers may be reckoned at more than 20 million.

At the opposite extreme, the number of paid workers whose wages come close to Western standards, whether in industry, retail trade or agriculture, amounts to 10 million at the outside—a fifth of the labor force. Between the two comes the mass of workers and staff who more or less successfully make ends meet on typically Japanese pay and at a typically Japanese standard of living; there are 20 million of them, or rather more. This has one very important consequence. The wage-earning workers do not as a class occupy a dominant position in the social and economic life of Japan. They are greatly outnumbered by the huge, unorganized body of those who earn their livings on the family, or small workshop, scale and who still live in an almost unchanged atmosphere, in an almost wholly un-Westernized social tradition. The reason why the unions only reach about 10 million workers is therefore self-evident. Roughly speaking, these 10 million represent the upper level of the working class; below that level the unions come up against the difficulty of organizing and consolidating the great scattered mass of small concerns. And lastly, among those who do not receive wages, the unions have at present no possibility of success whatever.

Yet one of the particular features of the Japanese economy is that this lower level, in spite of its fragmentation into sometimes minute production units, nevertheless occupies a very important place in the gross national product. The output of each unit is small, but all of them together supply roughly half the nation's total production. In spite of the fact that this country is an impressive record-breaker in many fields and that it possesses industrial groups organized on ultra-modern lines that place it among the great economic world powers, it still calls on small-scale manufacturing units with an indifferent labor force, machines that are often out of date, and a low rate of investment for more than 50 percent of its production. This applies above all to every form of manufacture in which the finished article requires what may be called a high intensity of labor and in which manual work still plays the chief or at least an important part.

It would be possible to draw up a long list of articles that are almost entirely produced by small firms, such as gloves, hats, socks, shirts, toys, pencils, umbrellas, fishing rods, sporting goods, thermos flasks, costume jewelry, lighters, domestic hardware and so on. A high proportion of beads, spectacles, watches, fountain pens, electric fans and the like also comes from the small-scale sector; and even the output of important industries such as pottery, textiles, papermaking and cutlery is derived to a considerable extent from small and medium-sized firms. In the textile industry, although the spinning mills are usually important concerns, part of the weaving side belongs to a scattering of very small houses which often specialize in a single article.

This by no means is to imply that the lower sector of industry is almost wholly concerned with cheap manufactures or shoddy merchandise. For there is another particularly Japanese feature in the economy: It is not only the old, traditional, and what might be called folk-art fields of activity that are the realm of the small firms with their traditional craftsmanship and the little factories that manage without much in the way of plant; these small businesses also take part in modern activities such as metallurgy and the engineering industry. Highly advanced machine tools, for example, are made in small, backward workshops with a rudimentary organization at the cost of a great many hours of ill-paid labor. Also, as we have seen, large-scale industry itself entrusts part of its work to the great number of small craftsmen who toil in the shadow of the big factories. This happens to a surprising extent in the shipyards, for example, in the automobile industry, and in railroad supplies; up to 60 or 70 percent of the work is often carried out by subcontractors who make the parts that the big firms use or assemble.

Then again, we must emphasize the important part that the small and medium-sized firms play in the export of Japanese industrial products; their share is slightly under half the total. This is the case with the finished articles produced by light industry, such as sewing machines, china, canned goods and cheap cloth. There are some classes of export goods that belong almost entirely to this sector—for example, all those on the list mentioned that ranges from clothing to hardware. In the Japanese balance of trade, the export of the countless kinds of light goods is no less important than that of factory-produced plant and equipment or such products of heavy industry as steel and chemicals.

Finally, the lower sector of the economy is not only one of descending wages but also one in which the working conditions grow worse and worse the nearer one is to the bottom. This is the Japan of long working days, of weeks with no days off, of indifferent health conditions, of cut-rate labor—the hiring of temporary hands, day workers, women and old men. Official labor inspection, which is reasonably efficacious in the big factories, is almost nonexistent; if the legal rules were applied it would mean the ruin of the small workshops. Here lifelong employment is most unusual and the worker often changes jobs, looking for a stability that is hard to find. He has scarcely even heard of social security. This sector is a great impediment to progress in productivity and technology, and suffers economic crises more severely than the upper-level Japan.

All things considered, it is difficult to maintain that Japan is falling into step with the Western countries in the matter of wages. As far as the foremost ranks of its employees are concerned it is fairly close, but it is still a great way off for all the rest. Arguing the cause of Japanese wages by telling foreign countries that Japan is virtually Western is both clumsy and unconvincing. A better line of reasoning would no doubt lead one to admit frankly that in parts of the Japanese economy grossly inadequate wages do still exist, and to emphasize that, contrary to certain indictments whose anti-Japanese bias is equally clumsy, these low wages are seen not as an advantage to the country but rather a great hindrance to its development; that they are the result of a situation in which there is much more loss than profit; and that the Japanese themselves look upon them not as a source of strength but as a crippling blemish that they are doing all they can to cure.

No, Japan is not the West, because its abundant population is thoroughly Asian, and because this abundance itself does in a way maintain an Asian way of life embedded in a whole important sector of the Japanese economy. By making a powerful effort Japan has succeeded in prying the whole of another sector free from the Asian level at least and in raising it to the modern Western plane. The double structure that has thus come into existence is cruel, but for the time being it is inevitable, and it does have its positive aspects. It sets up sluices, as it were; locks that will gradually allow the lower and more backward parts of the economy to be raised to intermediate levels and then up to the top.

Another argument that the Japanese could bring forward is that in their country low wages are becoming rarer, whereas elsewhere other low-wage countries are beginning to make their appearance. The blame, if blame there has to be, has been sent to the wrong address and sent too late if it goes to Japan, for now it is Hong Kong, Taiwan and South Korea that are pouring out cheap goods based on very low wages, lower by far than those in Japan. And will not China soon produce an overwhelming flood? When the Chinese begin exporting in quantities and at prices that correspond to their huge numbers and their extreme frugality, will not Europe and the West abandon and regret their criticisms of Japan—and come even to hold it up as an example to developing countries?

It is of the very first importance to stress one seemingly paradoxical and even shocking fact, a fact that is nevertheless one of this nation's basic realities: The greater part of the poor and humble Japanese live comparatively happy lives and are contented with their lot. Because Americans and Europeans think in terms of their own way of life and know nothing about a very different Eastern pattern, they usually make the mistake of supposing that exceedingly large numbers of Japanese lead a wretched existence. There are poor and wretched people in Japan, but we must not draw too dark a picture of the Japanese working class. The drive and energy of the Japanese, closely packed in their little archipelago, overcome their difficulties, and the burden of the lower strata of the economy is not so great that it can hold back the impetus which is carrying the whole nation up toward a better life. Above all it is very important to realize that in this country misfortune and distress are diminished by the fact that social structures of great antiquity still survive, together with attitudes of mind that were formed, as one might say, before the days of capitalism. Many a Western country has its very poor people whose fate is worse than that of the most underprivileged workers in Japan. In Japan the family still acts as a unit of social solidarity and as a place of refuge—not only the family that has stayed in the village but also the family that has moved into the city. Village life does in fact carry on into the towns. Because of this, the notion of a proletariat as we conceive it just does not apply to a whole section of the poorest urban workers.

The Japanese is never a solitary, isolated individual. Several wage packets come into the family group. A part-time job or work at home or overtime helps out with slender means. The end-of-year bonus clears off debts, and children come to the help of their parents. Even in the small-scale firms the old paternalism eases personal relationships, for there the worker is often treated as a member of the family, and his trifling pay does not really reflect the nature of his life. As to the wageless men we referred to earlier, it is often they who come off best, working as they do in a compact, warm and united little family group.

Again, the Japanese lives in an economic, cultural and moral world that is quite unlike ours. His needs are modest and they correspond to his means. He is naturally Spartan, and he does not measure his happiness by the amount of money in his pocket. In Japan, right down to the bottom of the social scale, there is an art of living and of living happily that in spite of all the upheavals of modernization is quite without our Western material demands. An exceedingly austere life, without possessions or physical comfort, can still mean happiness.

Economists lay great stress upon the idea of the standard of living. But as far as Japan is concerned, I am tempted to put forward an additional idea that forms no part of statistics and that may nevertheless be essential—the idea of the "standard of contentedness." Japan is a country in which a high standard of contentment may be reached at a very low standard of living. A Japanese requires only a very slight improvement in his material well-being to derive great pleasure from it.

Now for the immense majority of Japanese there has been a continuous amelioration of this kind throughout the last twenty years or so; living conditions are far better than they were before the war— they are better than they have ever been, according to a white paper on the standard of living published yearly by the Planning Agency.

Until now the recessions have only been halts in a continual upward movement that has gone on from boom to boom, steadily raising the Japanese records for production, trade and standard of living. It is easy to give proof after proof of the prosperity that is staringly obvious to every visitor to the country—the abundance of food, the abundance of clothes, the enrichment of a great proportion of the country people and so forth. The best demonstration of the improvement of the working class's lot is the development of a powerful market for consumer goods. The Japanese worker is now no longer a mere producer; he is also a consumer.

Japan is the first Asian country to have had the privilege of developing a very large-scale consumer market at home, and here we find still another advantage that derives from its abundant population. This hundred-million-strong consumer market is a recent phenomenon. It provides industry and trade with ample reserves to fall back upon and is a factor in the country's vigorous expansion. It has also contributed to the stability of home politics, for the ruling Right Wing can boast of having raised the people's standard of living, which diminishes the charm of the opposition parties. And it has helped to guide the country's foreign policy in a moderate and peace-loving direction, since nowadays every Japanese knows that his own prosperity is directly linked to the peace that is essential for the smooth running of "factory Japan."

The expansion of this home market is shown by the figure for the outlay on consumer goods, which in real value—that is to say, with due correction for the rise in prices—rose by 70 percent between 1955 and 1965. Between 1960 and 1965 the total value of home sales doubled. In spite of his frugality, the average Japanese now eats more and better food. This advance provides the proteins and vitamins that were lacking in his diet for so long, and in a quarter of a century it has already obviously improved the nation's physique. Now that his family budget is less restricted, food does not take up so great a share of it, and other forms of spending increase in proportion. His spending on clothing is now higher, in relative value, than that of the average European in the Common Market countries. The cleanliness and neatness of the people's clothes is something that at once impresses all foreign visitors. Again, as we have seen, these last years have been remarkable for large-scale family investment in household equipment —modern devices of every kind, such as refrigerators, television, washing machines, which are bought out of the family savings. Lastly, the same Japanese whose pay seems so inadequate to us nevertheless manages to devote a comparatively important share of his budget to amusements and leisure: he often goes to the movies, he buys books and magazines, he stops off at the café for a daily drink of beer or sake, and from time to time he travels a little.

All this consumer expenditure is still sufficiently reasonable and carefully worked out to leave the family enough to put money aside. The savings rate in Japan is quite simply the highest in the world, both as regards the nation's total savings in the area of the overall economy and as regards private saving within the family. Private saving is almost twice what it is in the other advanced countries; it has reached over 17 percent of personal income, whereas the proportion for the Frenchman is 8.2 percent, for the American 5.7 percent, and for the Englishman no more than 5 percent. The share of private savings in the total of national savings is also remarkably high (30 percent) compared with other countries. One of the explanations of this high rate of saving is to be found in the wage system: a great deal of the money that families can put aside comes from the bonuses they receive twice a year, which amount to a kind of compulsory saving that the firm imposes upon its employees. But the way the great bulk of the Japanese economize their money is also explained by the universal need for making good the shortcomings of the state in such matters as education, for example, since it is not wholly free, and in social security, since social insurance is still in a rudimentary state.

This inclination to save is still another proof that the primary explanation of the Japanese advance lies in the human factor, the Japanese people themselves. The credit for Japan's achievements is due not only to the chosen few or to the middle classes, but to the whole body of the workers. In their struggle for existence, the small firms contribute to the mighty effort of the great organizations in building up a strong and modern Japan, and whether they belong to the upper level of the economy or to the lower, the workers are just as much the country's strength as the managers and executives. The nation owes a great part of its success to these millions of hard-working, low-paid toilers and their steady, unremitting effort.

When one has had the good fortune to live side by side with them and to know them well, one is obliged to come to this conclusion: Japan possesses nothing better than these ordinary common people, these polite, hard-working craftsmen, these loyal, disciplined, painstaking workers, these hospitable, tireless peasants, these good people, thrifty without meanness, stouthearted, civilized and kind.

6.

The Rush for Equipment

It was amazing. This was 1962, and I had gone to Yawata, which is in Kyushu, the southern part of the country, to see the famous steelworks there. "No doubt you mean you've come to see Tobata?" they said when I arrived. I did not understand, so I explained, "I've come to see the great Yawata iron and steel company, and at the same time to have a look at the town of Yawata from which it takes its name." "But Yawata is no longer at Yawata, you know," they said. "Or at least the greater part of the company's steelworks are not here. They are at Tobata, where the new installations are. What remains here is still in action, of course, but it is the old works." I asked for more information, and they told me that Tobata was a former fishing village which in six or seven years had become a town of a hundred thousand inhabitants, and that an ultramodern steelworks had been running there at full blast since 1960. It had all happened so quickly that in Tokyo one had hardly yet had time to notice it.

I could cite plenty of examples like this. At Hino, in the hills close to Tokyo, over toward Mount Fuji, I used to know a cluster of ramshackle workshops where trucks were made with equipment that was still quite rudimentary. Seven years later, instead of these workshops I found a huge concern with a production chain turning out private cars every bit as good as the best of the small European cars. (I may add that Hino learned the trade on the little three-horsepower Renault.) On the shores of Chiba Bay, north of the capital, I used to see picturesque family parties who had come out from Tokyo for the shellfish; a few years later, in the same place, I saw the Plutonian labors of the metalworkers in the midst of their great, newly risen steelworks.

Once again I must emphasize that the speed of Japanese industry's growth and modernization is explained by the prodigious amounts of capital that the country devotes to investment every year. During the ten years from 1954 to 1963 these sums amounted on the average to 34 percent of the gross national product, or a rate more than two thirds higher than the French (20 percent) and twice the British (17 percent; other comparisons: West Germany, 27 percent; Italy, 24 percent; United States, 18 percent). As housing occupies a much lower place in Japanese investment than it does in Europe, the *productive* investments are particularly high. In 1962 they amounted to 32 percent of the gross national product, or twice the average of the European member countries of the Organization for Economic Cooperation and Development (OECD). And it is significant that private investment represented more than twice the amount invested by the state, which was markedly inadequate in comparison with the private sector and distinctly lower than the usual rate in the great Western countries. This is still another demonstration of the degree to which the private economic world outweighs the state.

The spirited enterprise of the managers and the drive, quantity and quality of the workers—here again are two keys to the new Japan's breakneck expansion. But there is still a third: the extraordinarily rapid acquisition of very abundant and modern equipment. Ambitious leaders gave excellent workers the latest kind of industrial plant. In their calculations they must have determined to make the most of a particularly profitable situation that could not possibly last forever— that is, the simultaneous coexistence of advanced techniques and a comparatively low rate of pay.

But I believe that the determining factor in the investment boom was the intense attraction of the race to expand, a race in which Japan had to catch up with its foreign competitors or even outdo them, and in which each Japanese firm had to beat its Japanese rivals. The great employers laid a cumulative bet on the future and on success, for they could see big and see far, in time and in space. And it was a bet that must be won if it is true that all the years to come and the whole geographic extent of the world are to experience the adventure of an enormous industrial transformation until the end of this century—always providing, of course, that we have peace.

This has meant more and more great factories in Japan, built faster and faster; the feverish rhythm of the installation of ultramodern plant; the creation of new industrial centers. A striking feature of this has been that at all times the expansion has outrun requirements and the investment has come before the demand for it. Seeing that the world and the future belonged to the great powers, it was a question of going all out to acquire the means of producing a huge volume of high-quality industrial goods and therefore of providing the country with a range of great modern factories—a range as vast and as all-embracing as possible. If necessary (and indeed it was necessary), model installations and the latest technical patents would be bought from the United States and the West. Never mind if Japanese inventive capacities and research remained weak; ever since Meiji times Japan has economized on its own scientific research, having neither the resources nor the time to do otherwise.

Another feature of the investment boom has been that all this expansion was the result not of the natural efforts of an economy left to itself in a liberal climate but of a deliberate action on the part of a pilot sector of industry, that of the great organizations, within an economy that, in spite of its capitalistic nature, is to a considerable extent controlled and willing to be controlled. A flexible guideline planning played a most important part in all this, a program drawn up by both the men at the head of the state and those at the head of the zaikai (business circles), which are, as we have seen, part of the same whole. The government urges the manufacturers to expand, and at the same time the manufacturers urge the government to help them in their progress. Favorable tax rates encourage rapid growth and the very latest forms of investment. The government's fiscal and financial policies support the banks and make it possible for them to grant the most audacious loans. The setting up of the newest industries takes place under the government's immediate protection, and this protection goes on until they are fully grown, shielding them from foreign competitors, who are not allowed into Japan.

But although Japanese industry is perfectly capable of uniting when faced with world competition, in Japan itself it operates under conditions of strong and bitter rivalry, and this is still another factor that has played an essential part in the investment boom. The result of this furious competition is the proliferation of unnecessarily repeated investment, or even more often of a multiplication by three or four of equipment simply because each of three or four rival groups wants to avoid being behind the others. And we often find a company buying a new plant before its still recent installations have been written off; the company longs above all to remain among the leaders in national or international competition. Western observers are always struck by this overinvestment: one of them, for example, speaks of the *kamikaze* of the Japanese iron and steel industry,* and another, stressing the "investment fever," remarks, "The big organizations plan investment programs without taking the real possibilities of the market into account. There is no genuine economic calculation either of the investment cost or of prime cost or of absorption capacity." † The report of an inquiry speaks of the dangerous sequence of overequipment producing overindebtedness, which causes overproduction in order to pay the bills, which in its turn leads back to fresh overequipment.‡

So here we have industry launched upon a headlong race into the future. The Japanese themselves have an amusing expression for this state of affairs: the "bicycle economy." To stay upright the rider has to press onward, for if he slows down he topples over. The Japanese bicycle has never in fact slowed down to the point of falling. To change the image, there has certainly been overheating of the economic machine and the beginning of a certain amount of overproduction. But every time there has been a vigorous recovery, and the curve of growth has climbed even higher.

It is interesting to analyze the various phases of Japanese industrial progress through the long period of boom. During the first five years after the war, from 1946 to 1951, the country cleared away its ruins and got the remaining factories running. The Japanese did this very quickly, at the cost of a very great exertion, but even so they were still far from being in a strong position. Then, helped by the Korean War, there was another phase, extending from 1951 to 1955, in which

---

* Henri Rieben in the preface to Jean Bienfait's *La Sidérurgie japonaise.*
† Gérard Lauzun, *Le Japon nécessaire* (Paris: Office Franco-japonais, 1962).
‡ *Rapport d'information*, produced by the French Senate's financial committee after a senatorial mission to Japan (Paris: Senate documents, December 13, 1967).

the prime mover of the country's development was the massive introduction of new techniques.

Until that time Japan had not attempted to break new ground but only to make good the immense setback that was the consequence of its defeat. From 1955 onward, on the other hand, it wanted the increased size of its industry to be matched by a speeded-up modernization, and it took over great numbers of new foreign inventions. Electronics, oil derivatives, plastics, synthetic fibers and so on, which the West had taken years and years to develop, took only a very short time to come into full flower in Japan; it was a positive explosion. At the same time there was a great rise in productivity, amounting to 37 percent between 1955 and 1961. "Japanese industry has accomplished not one but two miracles since the war," says a 1967 OECD report. "The first, the rebuilding of the destroyed installations and plant, was easy to understand. . . . The second, the manufacture of wholly new products by means of the most recent industrial processes . . . is perhaps the more striking of these miracles."

From that time onward we were to see a continuous rehandling of the whole of the industrial structure designed to keep Japan at the spearhead of progress. And this reshaping was all the more remarkable in that the Japanese planners, both in the government and in business, were capable of foreseeing the new directions that were to prove valid in international competition, and to foresee them several years ahead. They therefore had plenty of time to carry out the changes that were required to channel the available resources toward those activities that had the most future and were the most profitable. Thus a whole series of transformations took place, either simultaneously or in succession:

1. Transition from light to heavy industry.
2. Transition from traditional to new industries.
3. Transition from industries requiring a great deal of manpower to those that are highly mechanized.
4. Transition from industries that export little to those that are likely to have the greatest number of outlets abroad at the most competitive prices.

It was a well-established policy in the military era to favor heavy industry. With the return of peace, Japan might have abandoned it and at least at the beginning have turned most of its attention to the development of light industry. But the country was still too ambitious to be satisfied with that, and just after the defeat, in spite of its entirely peaceful intentions, it put even more emphasis on the heavy and chemical industries. Whereas before the war these supplied 40 percent of industry's total production, this figure rose to 65 percent in 1967. Iron and steel, that pilot industry which governs the whole country's re-equipment, made a particularly powerful effort. During the first three plans for steel, investments in this industry rose from $356 million (1951 plan) to $1.9 billion (1956 plan), and thence to $3.2 billion (1961).

The transition from old industries to new started as early as 1950 with the development of synthetic resins, for example, and of man-made fibers, which began to compete seriously with the natural products from 1954 onward. The movement became stronger in the second half of the fifties, with the swift rise of the "super-boom industries," as *The Economist* of London calls them—household appliances, television and industrial equipment—and with the first "take-off" of petrochemicals (oil derivatives), electronics and "peaceful" atomic energy. The modernization of the shipyards won Japan the first place in this sector as early as 1956. There was a recession in 1961, caused by a swing in the trade balance—a swing in the wrong direction —and by an overheating of the economic machine. But 1962 saw a recovery, which in its turn was much helped by fresh prospects of freedom of exchange and therefore of stronger foreign competition, against which Japanese industry had to protect itself even more efficiently.

It was at this juncture that industry adopted more and more new methods and techniques: L-D (Linz-Donawitz) oxygen converters in iron and steel, huge ships, the first computers and so on. Petrochemicals "took off" on a very large scale in 1961, and the Japanese also made great efforts in the field of engineering and electronics. Investment was now directed less at increasing the total volume than at raising individual output, for it was plain that qualified labor was soon going to be in comparatively short supply. The general movement was in the direction of giving up activities that were based upon a very plentiful, relatively unsophisticated labor force and low wages, such as the production of low-grade textiles, for example, now valid only for Hong Kong or India. Re-equipment with new plant went on at an even greater pace.

In 1955 53 percent of Japanese plant was less than six years old. By 1964 this proportion had risen to 73 percent. Investment in current equipment and transports never slackened. And the result of this eager pouring in of capital was that Japan's industrial production doubled between 1960 and 1966. In a decade the output of machinery rose a thousand percent, whereas that of textiles only doubled. Iron and steel and the chemical industry produced five times more. Between 1955 and 1965 the average growth of investment was close to 20 percent each year. And in addition to all this, 1962 to 1964 witnessed the boom in public works that was brought about by the Tokyo Olympic Games.

Broadly speaking, Japan had finally caught up with the West by 1963, as far as its standard industries were concerned. To a great extent it had also begun its second industrial revolution with the setting up of its new highly technical industries such as petrochemicals, electronics, computers and atomic energy. But it had moved too fast; the country discovered that it was overequipped, that its industry was too heavily burdened with debt, and that a serious excess of imports had once more tipped the balance of trade in the wrong direction. A short recession had the effect of diminishing private investment in 1964 and 1965.

For a long time public investment had been inadequate, but now it took over, and public capital flowed into improving the country's neglected infrastructure—roads, water supply, housing and so on. This helped to bring the crisis to an end, and between 1966 and 1968 there was a fresh boom, a boom all the more vigorous in that the chief factor in the recovery was an increasing home demand. This was the moment for the triumphal entry of the "Made in Japan" private cars, whose production doubled between 1966 and 1967. In 1967 the Nissan Company increased its investments to a figure that was 70 percent above that of 1966 and Toyota to a rise of 40 percent. A new star appeared in the television sky—the very rapid spread of color television. Once again the oil refineries and the petrochemical works plunged into massive new investment. Even more powerful blast furnaces began to roar.

In 1968 the government grew alarmed at the prospect of still another crisis of overequipment and of imports and was obliged to apply its traditional financial brakes to avoid inflation. But no one has the least doubt that the race ahead is sure to begin again. The next phase will certainly be the development of the highly scientific industries, a field that Japan cannot possibly overlook. As I shall presently show, this phase will confront Japan with serious problems, the first of which will be that of at last making an effort of scientific and technical research worthy of its place in world industry.

The huge equipment that has arisen from this enormous amount of investment is, of course, equipment almost entirely manufactured by Japanese in Japanese factories. But this does not mean that it is the product of Japanese invention. A great deal of the plant in the factories of Japan is based upon Western inventions that the Japanese have acquired the right to use by buying the relevant patents or by coming to an agreement with foreign firms for technical assistance.

Even in this new industrial revolution of the second half of our twentieth century, Japan considers that it is cheaper and quicker to buy the most advanced technical processes from Europe and the United States. The country has never attempted to rival the giants of the West in the realm of discovery; for Japan's first task was to solve the preliminary problem of reaching at least the critical minimum capacity and the high technical ability that would allow its industry to stand a chance in international competition, and to solve this problem by every available means, including that of borrowing foreign technology. At times Japan imports foreign machinery as it stands, ready-made, but this has become unusual; nowadays it generally buys the patent rights and makes the machines at home.

As to the accusation that Japan has copied and plagiarized certain foreign inventions, before the war perhaps this was too often the case. But nowadays it is most unusual and indeed almost impossible; postwar legislation, the economic circles, and government supervision ensure the strict observance of the law in this field. But may not Japan at least be reproached with having followed the path of mere facility by turning so wholeheartedly to Western techniques? In my opinion the reproach would be unfair. As we have already seen, the borrowing, imitating and copying of foreign patterns are not only perfectly straightforward methods as long as the patents are bought, but they

are the inevitable procedure in the first phase of technical development. The West can expect to see a great many other countries turn
to the same practices in order to make their way out of their underdeveloped state—and here again China provides an example.

Moreover, having the ability and knowledge required to adapt a
foreign technique and bring it into one's own country is by no means
devoid of merit. It requires that a certain number of conditions should
be fulfilled and that certain qualities should be developed, qualities
and conditions that are not to be found in just any country but that
Japan possesses to the highest possible degree. For when Japan chooses
to do so, it can be the very epitome of the model pupil. Above all it
must be emphasized that Japan has long since gone beyond the stage
of imitation, pure and simple, and of the direct use of some technique
acquired abroad and applied without variation. It has become the rule
that before any manufacturing process is generally adopted in Japan
it must be the object of a great deal of study and research.

The aim is certainly to adapt new equipment to the local conditions
and to make it an integral part of the existing Japanese pattern. But
even more it is to extend the foreign technicians' invention, perfecting
it in various respects, modifying it, and generally broadening its field
of application. "Factories built according to foreign plans often end
up by achieving a far higher rate of production than that which was
foreseen by the supplier of the foreign process," says a Japanese author,
and he is right. He goes on to quote the example of blast furnaces that
were designed to produce fifteen hundred tons a day and that have
in fact raised their capacity to twenty-five hundred tons, and a certain
rubber factory that turns out seventy-five thousand tons a year instead
of the theoretical fifty thousand that were forecast.

Taken as a whole, the massive importation of foreign techniques has
been one of the essential bases of Japan's success. It has provided a
shortcut to an exceedingly rapid modernization; it has resulted in an
important saving of money and effort as well as a powerful incentive
to the setting up of new factories; it has made it possible for these
factories always to be equipped with the best plant in the shortest
possible time. And yet the Japanese do not often speak of the very
important part that this influx of Western—and especially American—
technology plays in their industry. Their official documentation upon
the subject is discreet, and perhaps this is also the reason why foreign-

ers' books on Japanese industry scarcely touch upon the question. But the fact is that the Japanese iron and steel industry, for instance, has built up its power largely upon patents bought from the Americans, together with a few processes acquired from the Germans, Swiss and even the Russians. The well-known Tobata rolling mills, for example, are the outcome of American techniques brought into action by Japanese engineers and American advisers. In the electronics industry, the great Japanese companies such as Hitachi, Matsushita, Sony and Toshiba make the widest use of patents bought in the United States. The manufacturers of artificial fibers—a field where Japan ranks second in the world—also make use of processes that they have acquired from the West: for example, nylon is produced under license from Du Pont de Nemours (U.S.A.), polyester from Imperial Chemical Industries (G.B.), and polypropylene from Montecatini (Italy). And the great complexes of petrochemical companies have been built upon a foundation of foreign techniques. The same may be said of the first reactors produced by the infant atomic industry, which looked to Calder Hall for the British processes or to General Electric and Westinghouse for the American.

To give some notion of the scope of the agreements between the Japanese and foreign companies concerned with heavy industry, here is the example of Mitsubishi Heavy Industries. M.H.I. is the biggest maker of iron- and steel-working plant and machinery; as far as these activities are concerned, this is only a partial list of its agreements with other countries:

High-pressure blast furnaces and sintering processes (preliminary treatment of ore)—agreements with McKee and Company, U.S.A.

Pure-oxygen-fed L.D. converters and Kaldo converters—agreements with Pintsch Bamag A.G., West Germany.

Continuous-casting plants—agreements with Loftus Engineering Corporation, U.S.A., and Erik Olsson, Sweden.

Rolling mills—agreements with Mesta Machine Company, U.S.A.; Schloemann A.G., West Germany; Loftus, U.S.A.; and Drever Company, U.S.A.

Machine tools—agreements with Innocenti-Berthiez, Italy; Oerlikon, Switzerland; Rockford, U.S.A.; Acme and Gridley, U.S.A.; Caterpillar, U.S.A.

The foreign techniques imported by Japan between 1950 and 1966 concern chiefly chemical products (801 agreements for patent rights or technical assistance), electrical machinery (805), and other forms of machinery (1,437). While giving these figures, the Keidanren (the Japanese employers' federation) emphasizes that the number of agreements for the exploitation of foreign patents or processes has increased year by year, following the curve of the nation's expansion, and that over the same period it reached a total of a little under four thousand contracts. As to the countries where these techniques originated, the United States easily comes first with 2,141 contracts, followed by West Germany with no more than 381, by Switzerland with 268, Great Britain with 194, and France with a mere 118—the French take little interest in selling the Japanese their know-how. These technical agreements mean that Japan has to send abroad dues and royalties that at present amount to something in the nature of $140 to $150 million a year.

A 1967 OECD report pays this handsome tribute to the new Japan's drive for technical modernization: "Twenty years ago Japanese technology could not be compared with that of the other OECD countries except in a restricted number of sectors of production; but now in most cases it has reached the same level or has even gone beyond it."

This means that Japan can now move on to a new stage in its development, in which it will provide an increasing share of inventions and discoveries worked out in Japan itself. There is already some progress in this direction. It may be said that even now the country has proved that its scientists and technicians are thoroughly capable of bringing their independent contribution to the progress of science and industry, in spite of easily adopted opinions to the contrary. Here are a few examples. Purely Japanese technology is highly advanced in many sectors of the electronics industry, such as transistors, color television, integrated circuits, telecommunications and computers. The firm of Sony alone, for instance, has three outstanding inventions to its credit: the Sony recording tape; the Esaki diode, which is a new semiconductor; and the Sony magneto-diode, which is the very latest semiconductor, between a hundred and a thousand times more sensitive than those made hitherto. Japanese techniques are also particularly well developed in electrical engineering, especially turbines, large-scale transformers, and heavy electrical machines. In the automobile industry, the Toyo Kogyo Company (the Mazda cars) has perfected a sensational rotary engine based on an improved version of the German Wankel patent. In chemicals and petrochemicals, particularly in the field of plastics, Japanese technicians are way ahead. One Japanese fertilizer firm has perfected a process for the manufacture of urea that is exciting a great deal of interest abroad. In shipbuilding, Europe is now buying certain Japanese techniques unequaled anywhere else in the world, especially as far as welding and painting are concerned.

Yet when all is said and done, the fact remains that Japan's contribution to the technical progress of our times has remained far below that of its Western rivals. This is evident from a comparison between the income the Japanese derive from their inventions which they have sold abroad and the cost of the techniques they have imported from foreign countries: the ratio is one to ten. This disproportion gives warning of a glaring inadequacy in research and of a degree of dependence on other countries, particularly on America, that is a danger for Japan's future and for the position it holds in the world. The Japanese are certainly beginning to realize this today, all the more so in that the liberalization of international economic relations is exposing them to the risk of no longer being in control of the foreign patents they use but of seeing them exploited in their own country by Western firms that will "invade" their market.

The Japanese foresaw the danger of an invasion of their economy by great foreign companies, and more specifically by great American companies, immediately after the defeat of 1945. It is scarcely known abroad, but one of the most remarkable achievements of their industry and their government has been to protect the country from this danger right up to the present. Japan managed to take up the "American challenge" in this field better than the European countries. On the whole it succeeded in keeping its doors shut to any large-scale influx of American capital. Its rule has been to devote a very great amount of Japanese resources to the purchase of American techniques and to Japanese-manufactured plant to operate them, but not to allow the Americans to invest massive capital sums in Japan and to bring in their own staff to operate these techniques to the advantage of the United States.

If government control, or rather the coordinated action of government officials and of private business, does exert itself anywhere—and it does—it is in this area of the importing of foreign technical processes. It has always been carefully limited by the MITI, the powerful Ministry of International Trade and Industry, and by the Ministry of Finance, in order to protect those sectors of Japanese industry that are not yet firm on their feet or sufficiently developed. Europe is totally mistaken in supposing that the almost entirely American military occupation of Japan (1945 to 1952) opened the doors to economic occupation by American businessmen. A fair share of the credit for this is due to General MacArthur; he saw that he had to allow the Land of the Rising Sun to protect itself against the designs of large-scale American capital if the nascent good relations between the two countries were not to be ruined by an angry reaction based on the still deeply rooted Japanese nationalism. The result has been that up to the present the American share in Japanese industrial capital, according to the specialists, represents no more than 2 percent.

To be sure, there have been exceptions to this closing of Japan, exceptions that mostly came about at the very beginning of the occupation and in those sectors where it was essential to get going without waiting for a then almost nonexistent Japanese industry. This was the case with oil, which is virtually under the control of the great worldwide companies; they have 70 percent of the Japanese market. Foreign interests also govern the aluminum industry. And the Americans have a dominating position in synthetic rubber and tires. The Japanese statistics for 1968 show that altogether there are 720 firms partially capitalized from abroad and that in 460 of these cases American capital is concerned. But there are only about 30 whose capital is 100 percent foreign, and 25 in which foreign capital amounts to more than 50 percent of the whole.

The MITI has generally refused, particularly since the great Japanese expansion began in 1955, to allow foreign shareholders to acquire more than 50 percent of the stock of any existing or newly founded Japanese company. Exceptions have been allowed only in the case of very powerful concerns such as Du Pont de Nemours, Dunlop, National Cash Register, I.B.M. Japan, Nescafé and Hillman. The next class, that of the "fifty-fifty" companies, numbers 71 individual firms. The next in descending order, the joint ventures in which foreign investment accounts for only 30 to 40 percent of the total capital, num-

bers 152. And lastly there are 452 companies in which foreign investment is under 30 percent. All in all, during the seventeen years from
1950 to 1966, the total direct American dollar investment in Japan
amounted to $207 million, whereas in the six years from 1961 to 1966
American investment was $735 million in France, $1.4 billion in Germany and $1.8 billion in Great Britain. Yet as far as Japan is con-
cerned we may add an extra $300 million of American capital that
comes into the class known as "yen-based investment," which may
be looked upon as a lower category, since it implies a "nipponification"
of the capital and therefore no guaranteed right to export its yield to
the country of origin. These American investments are comparatively
unimportant, but the contribution of the Western countries might
almost be called trifling. Between 1950 and 1966 Switzerland invested
$34 million in Japan; England, $22 million; West Germany, $4 million
and France, $1 million. (The French have not yet discovered Japan.)

Japanese industry has succeeded in keeping American capital at a
distance in spite of making continual use of American techniques,
and this success has been accompanied by another feat—that of finding the enormous capital sums needed for the "investment boom" in
Japan itself. What makes this all the more remarkable is that in the
general wretchedness and inflation of the period just after the defeat,
the country experienced extreme shortages of every kind, including
that of capital. The problem was solved in the simplest possible manner: the Japanese manufacturers ran into debt to an almost unbelievable degree, borrowing the greater part of the capital to build their
factories and make their plant from the banks, while in their turn the
banks ran into debt with the Bank of Japan.

It may be said that the financing of these investments was brought
about by an artificial creation of capital which took frightening liber-
ties with orthodox banking doctrines or which would at least seem
frightening in the Western capitalist countries. Methods that in any
other country would be regarded as disastrous—as leading to catastrophe—have been applied in Japan without the least mishap. In the
West, for example, it is a very important rule of caution for a company
to maintain a fairly equal balance between its borrowings and its capital
holdings and reserves. But in Japan the usual custom is for a company
to finance itself up to two thirds or more by borrowing.

In the West, companies usually provide 65 to 70 percent of their own financing, and the rest comes from the issue of shares and from loans, particularly debentures. In Japan the proportions are reversed. A big company will only call upon its own funds for 30 to 40 percent of its needs and will turn to loans for the remaining 70 or 60 percent; the money market will provide about 10 percent in exchange for transferable securities—a normal figure—but the 60 or 50 percent still to be found will be borrowed from the banks. I should add that more than half these funds take the form of short-term loans of less than a year at very high rates of interest.

The banks: they are the main source of the finance for Japan's enormous industrial equipment. For years now, industry as a whole has been heavily in debt to them, and the effect of this practice has been to create a very close liaison between the banks and industry. The banks primarily concerned are commercial banks; there are thirteen of them, and they, helped by some sixty provincial or local banks, funnel off the abundant savings of their private depositors. Immediately after the defeat the old family systems were broken up, as we know, and antitrust legislation shattered their companies. But since then the groups have come together again, and their chief connecting link is their common allegiance to the bank that finances them.

Now it so happens that the Japanese bankers' spirit of enterprise exactly matches that of the great industrial leaders. As soon as the possibility of modernizing the activities of some group or the need for outdoing a rival company by means of better plant has arisen, the bankers have shown no more hesitation than the managers but have instantly lent the necessary funds. It is because of this borrowing and overborrowing—a state of affairs agreed to by both borrowers and lenders—that the great Japanese companies have been able to grow and to renew both their plant and their factories at a speed hitherto quite unknown. Yet it is important to note that this very large-scale borrowing from the banks has not turned the bankers into the lords of the economy, nor has it given them sovereign power when it is a question of coming to decisions and of making overall plans.

Where the relationship between manufacturer and banker is concerned, in our Western countries there is a distinct separation of powers. The banker considers a proposition strictly on its financial merits; he comes to an independent decision, and in the end the manufacturer is obliged to accept it. In Japan almost the opposite is the case. The industrial leaders study the question and come to a decision at their level; then they turn to their bankers and say, "Find the money." The bankers find it, for the money they bring carries an annual interest rate as high as 9 or 10 percent or more, and the manufacturers accept this. That is the reason why in Japan a 5- or 6-percent rate of industrial expansion is not enough for the repayment of debts; the country requires an economy running at full blast. This gives what might be termed a funding rather than the balance-sheet economy of the kind that is usual with us. Then again we must take notice of the fact that the state does not tax this borrowed money, because that part of the company's profits used for paying interest on its debts is exempt. The true interest rate is therefore brought down to a more reasonable level. This strongly encourages investment.

These financial acrobatics, or what would look like financial acrobatics in the West, do not stop here. The commercial banks themselves indulge in practices that would be called extremely risky anywhere else, if indeed they could be imagined at all. To begin with, they "overlend" to an industry that is already overindebted, retaining only what other countries would consider a totally inadequate liquid position. It is perfectly usual for them to lend up to 95 percent of the deposits entrusted to them. Indeed, sometimes the amount of their loans actually exceeds the amount of their deposits. In the second place these banks run into debt in their turn, borrowing important sums from the Bank of Japan; the whole credit structure depends upon this institution.

Lastly, and this fact is not so well known, the Japanese commercial banks also turn to the American banks for loans; these loans are usually for very short periods and are very expensive, and their chief purpose is to cope with the difficult period at the end of the year when bills fall due. These operations provide the lenders with huge profits, not only because of the high interest rate but also because of the frequent practice of "offset." "You give me a loan of a billion dollars," says the Japanese borrower, "and I will leave half the amount in your hands." The U.S. banks are moving farther and farther into these profitable operations, so much so that in 1968 their experts were of the opinion that the total of very short-term American loans to Japan amounted to $3 billion. Of course the Americans could withdraw this money, but in fact that would certainly mean the collapse of Japan, which would be a disaster for the United States itself. One of the effects of these American loans to the Japanese banks—and this too is a phenomenon that is comparatively unknown in spite of its importance—is that although the American money certainly reaches the level of the banks it always stops there because of the splendid profit it earns, without going on to industry itself, a less simple and a less profitable form of investment. This system has proved one of Japan's most important shields against an eventual American invasion of its industry; it is one of the prime reasons why American capital has scarcely penetrated Japanese business. The European countries have had no parallel experience, and they have not been able to hold out so well.

A usual Japanese reply to people from the West who accuse their industry of having an unfair advantage because of low wages is that, even supposing this advantage to exist, it is in any case wiped out by the huge price Japanese industry has to pay for its financing, a price far higher than that paid in Europe or the United States. The argument is not without validity. The shortage of capital, the undeveloped state of the money market, and, it must be said, the eager greed of the banks, mean that Japanese borrowers are obliged to agree to rates of interest that seem usurious to us. Still, the usual rates of 8, 9 and 10 percent are nevertheless thought acceptable by the very important industrial groups. The smaller firms on the lower level have difficulty in finding lenders and they are even more harshly treated. Because of this same "offset rate" or "system of obligatory deposit," they leave part of the loan with the lender and therefore in fact pay a real rate that may be as high as 15 percent. If, as a last resort, they turn to the usurers, they pay as much as 20 or 30 percent a year; as far as they are concerned, bankruptcy is not very far away.

Many European observers utter frightened shrieks when they discover the apparent fragility of this whole financial underpinning, but events have not justified their pessimism; on the contrary, events tend to emphasize the system's advantages. It has been a prime factor in industry's extraordinarily rapid growth, for it has provided the remedy for the weakness of the money market. At the same time it has been a most important cog in the machinery of economic planning and financial guidance. While it gives the banks a very considerable share in the control of business and industry, at the same time it brings the banks themselves under the power of the central bank. For this reason the economy as a whole is unusually responsive to the directions of the state, which are exercised through the central bank by the raising or lowering of interest rates and by increasing or diminishing the advances made to the banks. These are the methods of holding back or of stimulating economic activity; they are brought into play according to favorable or unfavorable circumstances, and they work extremely well.

All things considered, what label might we apply to this system as a whole? Is Japanese capitalism really capitalism at all? The question may certainly be asked, for we see that it is at all events a very particular sort of capitalism, since according to circumstances it may be (as we showed when we were speaking of the managers) liberal, or devoted to planned economy, or somewhat given to socialism, or feudal. And in the last analysis, the sum of all this gives, as we said, not so much capitalism as "nipponism." When it was a question of an enormous acceleration in growth to overtake the other great capitalist powers, Japan, as far as investment was concerned, forgot all the rules of the capitalist game as played by its rivals, all their accounting maxims, all their calculations of profitability, and all their policy of liquidation.

The thing that really matters in Tokyo is the look in the borrower's eye, his personality and his connections. Do people agree that he is a leader? Is he a man of strong, firm character? Is he, as the Japanese put it, "sincere"? Is he an accepted member of the body of great managers? Above all, has he already plunged boldly into the adventure of industrialization and succeeded in it? If so, he may borrow freely. He is tacitly a member of a club in which credit has no limits and in which, apart from quite outstanding failures to observe the group's ethic, no member is ever allowed to fall by the wayside. And because he is one of those men who indirectly rule the country, in the last resort help will come to him from the state itself. He may be granted long-term advances amounting to millions, all on the security of his name and the look in his eye.

Thus when we consider investment, the third aspect of the Japanese success after the managers and the workers, we conclude that what counts more than anything else in Japan is once again the Japanese themselves.

7.

The Third Great Power
in the World's Economy

Japan is the third worldwide economic power. That is the discovery the world made in 1968, the hundredth year, the year in which the Land of the Rising Sun celebrated the centennial of its entry into the international community with the Meiji revolution of 1868. Once the country was wrenched out of its long isolation, it needed only a hundred years to raise itself to this position among the other nations. In 1968 its gross national product (GNP) brought it to the second place in the non-Communist world (it is the third after the U.S.S.R.), passing West Germany, which itself had outstripped Great Britain at the beginning of 1960. In 1968 the Japanese GNP reached $133 billion, as opposed to $132 billion for West Germany, $120 billion for Great Britain, $118 billion for France and $71.5 billion for Italy; these are figures published at the beginning of 1969, based on OECD statistics. Earlier estimates gave $130 billion for Japan and $125 billion for Germany. In any case, the only greater figures are those for the United States (an estimated $843 billion) and for the Soviet Union (1966 estimate, $350 billion). Japan was three years ahead of its planning forecast; the last Japanese five-year plan reckoned that the country would reach third place in 1971.

One has some idea of the distance covered, and the speed at which it has been covered, when one recalls that Japan started off with a GNP of $10 billion in 1950. This GNP increased tenfold in sixteen years, for it reached the level of $100 billion in 1966 and from that time onward Japan was in the ranks of the world's great powers. In 1964 it was still only sixth; to reach a position immediately behind the American and Russian giants it had to overtake France, England and Germany, and it did so between 1964 and 1968. The Japanese experts foresee that the country will reach the $200-billion mark—twice the 1966 figure—in 1975.

In speed of growth, as well as in magnitude of investments, Japan clearly outstrips the world, including the Communist countries, and this has been the case since it got under way in 1950. From 1950 to 1955 its growth rate was slightly above 12 percent, with Germany coming next (9.3 percent), followed by Italy (6 percent), and then France and the United States with 4.3 percent each. From 1955 to 1963 it was always above 10 percent, while the West had the following rates: Germany, 5.8 percent; France, 4.1 percent; the United States, 2.9 percent; England, 2.8 percent. The years 1963 through 1965 were difficult for Japan, but nevertheless the rate of growth stayed above 8 percent. From 1966 onward the earlier speed returned, in spite of the government's efforts at restraint, and in 1968 the increase in the GNP was 1 percent a month, or 12 percent for the whole year. The forecast for 1969 was a nominal 15 percent and (taking into account the rise in prices) a real 10.8 percent.

In addition to these international statistics, the Japanese themselves draw up purely national figures which show how present-day Japan has grown in comparison with what it was a few years ago. According to the Keidanren, Japanese industrial production as a whole increased almost four times between 1955 and 1965; metallurgy, engineering, chemicals and oil, five times; textiles and food, 2.4 times. It was this that induced *The Economist* to say in 1967 that Japan's growth represented "one of the most exciting and the most extraordinary forward leaps in the history of world economics." In 1963 the same English weekly had already observed that Japan was "the greatest laboratory for economic growth of our times."

If we compare Japan, industry by industry, with the other countries of the West, we find that the new "third great economic power" in fact holds the first place in many important fields of activity, and in the same way the sectors in which it holds second or third place are increasing rapidly. Its best-known record is the building of merchant ships, a record that it has held for some ten years now; year after year Japan stays out in front, having left former champions such as England and Sweden far behind. In 1967 Japan built 7,496,000 tons out of a world tonnage of 15,800,000, and these were record-breaking figures both for Japan and for all the other shipbuilding countries. Japan's share amounted to 47.5 percent of the world total, whereas Sweden, the runner-up, only built 8.3 percent of the world total, or 1,308,000 tons. Next came England (8.2 percent), West Germany (6.4 percent), and then France, Norway, Italy and Denmark, each with less than 4 percent of the world's total. In 1967 Japan was also the first in the production of fishing vessels, including the great modern factory ships. Still ahead in 1968, it launched 8,500,000 tons of shipping.

Japan is the world's top motor bicycle producer (2.4 million in 1966); the top sewing machine manufacturer (more than 4 million in 1966, which is 42 percent of the world production and six times that of Italy, which comes second); the top producer of cameras, a place that it wrested from Germany after the war (4 million Japanese cameras in 1966). Japan is now reaching the top place in piano manufacture; there are some Japanese factories that turn them out on a production line, like cars.

It holds first place in the manufacture of transistor radios and of electronic microscopes. It has many world records in the realm of iron and steel, for it has the finest steelworks for the production of ordinary steel (but not for the special steels). Thus the world's greatest blast furnaces are to be found in Japan, and in the same way Japan is the largest producer of steel by means of L-D oxygen converters.

Under this heading of "the world's greatest" there are any number of Japanese achievements, from the Honshu-Shikoku suspension bridge to a mammoth ship, a tanker of more than 300,000 tons, which was launched at Nagasaki in March, 1968. Another thoroughly Japanese record, one that shows this nation's extraordinary mobility, has been set in the transport of passengers by train. The figure is over 1.5 billion passenger miles a year, which is way ahead of the U.S.S.R., Germany, France, England, Italy and the United States. There are various other records concerning foreign trade: Japan is the world's top exporter of merchant ships, ceramics, sewing machines, toys, radios, plywood, cameras—and the list goes on.

In February, 1967, the MITI (Ministry of International Trade and Industry) put out a list of nineteen key products of which Japan was the second most important source, usually coming immediately after the United States. The list is mainly concerned with the products of the textile industry, particularly synthetics. Japan is second in both long- and short-fiber acetate rayon and long and short noncellulose fibers; in the field of natural textiles it is also second in wool and cotton yarns. It is second too in newsprint, in synthetic rubber (of which the country consumes almost as much as natural rubber), in sulfuric acid, the essential basic product of the chemical industry, in synthetic resins and plastics, and in cement.

In metallurgy, Japan is second in the production of ingot steel, cast iron, refined copper, aluminum and zinc. And finally, it is second in the automobile industry, if we take into account its heavy production of trucks and commercial vehicles, though it is less advanced in private cars.

In listing these records the MITI, to give the scale, adds the following comparisons: if 100 is taken to represent the sum of these Japanese products, the United States ranks 229; Germany, 67.7; France, 42. It will be noticed that there is no mention of the Soviet Union, and the MITI list should therefore be modified accordingly. For some of the products quoted Japan comes second in the non-Communist world but third for the world as a whole; this at least is the case for steel and cement.

On the other hand, the MITI list could be extended. Japan also takes second place in the world production of television sets (over 5.5 million in 1968) and of radios; it is second, too, for the number of telephones in service (13 million, as opposed to 93 million in the United States). Its electronics industry ranks immediately after the United States for the manufacture of semiconductors, including integrated circuits, and of electronic components. It is second again in the manufacture of bicycles (nearly 4 million in 1967), in ethylene, in toys, in wristwatches (coming just after Switzerland), and in beer.

I will not even attempt to draw up a list of the products and manufactures in which Japan is classed third or at any rate high enough to be among the leaders in international competition, because it would be far too long. Let me merely give the examples of electricity, oil refinery products, ordinary paper, copper wire and clocks, in all of which Japan is third. It is also third for the number of electronic computers in service.

But perhaps the most significant achievement—it is certainly one of the basic criteria for judging a nation's economic power and degree of modernization—has been the growth of the iron and steel industry, which has placed Japan in third place among the world's nations, immediately next to those two giants, the United States and the Soviet Union.

At the height of its power, military Japan never produced more than 8 million tons of steel in the archipelago itself. Who would ever have supposed that, immediately after the war, Japan—conquered, disarmed and stripped of colonies, poor in iron ore and possessing only low-grade coal—would dare to set about becoming one of the great steel powers and would succeed in doing so? When it reached its own prewar level, the general opinion was that in itself this was an honorable achievement; Japan had already made a very good showing. Those who said this did not know Japan. In fact the country was setting off on a metallurgical race of which this is the timetable: In 1956 Japan passed the 10-million-ton mark; in 1960, that of 20 million tons; in 1963, 30 million; in 1965 40 million. We see that the time needed to increase production by 10 million tons progressively drops from four years to three and then to two. But this was not the end. In the next two years, 1966 and 1967, it was not by 10 million tons that Japanese steel advanced but by 20. For in 1967 the 60-million mark was passed: The production of ingot steel in Japan reached the astonishing figure of 62,164,000 tons in 1967 and 66,890,000 tons in 1968.

With Japan moving at this breakneck pace, the European producers were left behind long ago: first France in 1959, then England in 1961, and finally West Germany in 1964. And Japan is not just a short way ahead, as these figures make clear: in 1967 Japan's 62 million tons of production exceeded that of West Germany and France together. As for the two giants at the top, the Soviet Union, coming second, turned out 101,900,000 tons, passing the 100-million mark for the first time, while the leader, the United States, gave the figure of 118,033,000 tons. In a decade, Japanese progress in steel production amounted to 300 percent while the rest of the world advanced by only a little more than 50 percent. The 1966–1967 Japanese leap forward amazed European and American competitors; in a single year the advance was close to 14.5 million tons, 30 percent higher than the 1966 figure.

Why climb so high and at such enormous speed? The Japanese reply that their very rapid expansion has also been healthy, for it has come about primarily in response to a continually increasing home demand. A few instances of the country's steadily growing steel needs are provided by the automobile boom, the record-breaking shipyards, the plant required by the manufacturers of electrical machinery, the requirements of the chemical industry and of building—for building, in a country that has many earthquakes, consumes more steel than it does in the West. And this is not the end; the curve will go on rising. "On the basis of our present information, it is reasonable to forecast that Japan will produce eighty million tons of crude steel in 1972." This statement was made by Yoshihiro Inayama, the president of Yawata, when he was addressing the International Iron and Steel Institute in Brussels. He added that some people were afraid of overproduction but that, in view of the growth of the underdeveloped countries, the expansion of heavy industry, and the increase in population, the Japanese were not. He might have gone on to say that in the opinion of the Japanese their own development was not yet over, since they certainly meant to raise themselves to the same general level as the great Western countries, a level that they had not yet reached, in spite of all their progress. And then again it is a fact that, taking into account the population figures, their present rate of steel production seems in no way excessive, since proportionately it is much the same as that of the West Germans.

Nevertheless, in the course of these last years Japan has been turning out steel in quantities too great for the home demand, and it has become an important export—so important, indeed, that it stands at the head of the list of sales abroad as a foreign currency earner. In 1966 Japan exported nearly 10 million tons of crude steel, which earned $1,377,000,000, or 14 percent of the total exports. In 1967 slightly over 9 million tons were exported. The chief buyers are the Asian countries, but the proportion of Asian sales is decreasing now that Japan has two new customers: Australia and the United States, which is an even more important purchaser still. American steel, with a demanding labor force and high prices, is growing less competitive than Japanese, and Japanese steel is getting a good foothold in the American market. It remains to be seen whether or not this outlet will remain stable.

The European producers are worried by the yearly Japanese surplus, and they are afraid that one day they will suffer from the dumping of Japanese steel on the European markets. What is more, they think that the Japanese surpluses are partially caused by the extreme competition among the great steel companies in Japan, which are constantly outbidding one another in modernization and in increasing size. Again they point out that the cars, the machinery, the ships and so forth, that Japan sells to the outside world are still steel—steel in another form and with a high degree of added value. And the ambitious plans of Japanese steel obviously foreshadow an increasing volume of these Japanese products on the foreign markets in the years to come.

However this may be, so vigorous an expansion could not have come about without a most uncommon degree of drive and skill on the part of both Japanese workers and management that deserves to be acknowledged and appreciated. "The Japanese ironmasters are not merely excellent metallurgists; they also prove formidable strategists in the organization and running of their business," says Henri Rieben in the preface to Jean Bienfait's book on Japanese iron and steel, *la Sidérurgie japonaise*. Two typical instances of this strategy are to be seen in the way the Japanese steel backed heavy industry and allied itself with the transforming industries such as shipbuilding and engineering. But above all, just as good generals know how to choose the right place for their battlefields, so the strategists of Japanese steel found one of the chief factors of their success in the siting of their works, in bringing off the "triumph of seaboard steel," in the words of Bienfait, who was the first to assess the growing importance of this aspect of the industry.

Apart from one exception just before the war, the Japan of the Meiji and the military eras were content with locating their steelworks close to local supplies of raw material, though they did their best not to be too far from a port. After the war it at once became evident that any revival of Japanese steel would have to be based upon massive importation of raw materials coming by sea from very distant foreign countries. The chief problem was therefore going to be that of transport. Logically, the ideal would be for the ore and the coal to be unloaded directly from the ship to the works, thus avoiding handling and movement by rail. From this point of view the fact that Japan is a collection of islands with a very long coastline was an outstanding advantage. So its steelworks began to move down to the sea and to stand "with their feet in the water," providing themselves to some degree with their own harbors, whose docks run right alongside the blast furnaces or workshops.

But there is still another factor that has drawn the steelworks down to the shore, and perhaps it has not been sufficiently emphasized; this is the fact that on the shore and only on the shore is there any possibility of finding abundant building sites for industrial complexes. True, it was not a question of the existing shore, which was already occupied and overcrowded, but of new shores artificially created, immense empty stretches of land rising from the sea, untouched and wonderfully flat, won from the deep by making polders, by damming and filling. Very often the steelworks have taken advantage of this to move nearer to other great concerns dealing with heavy industry, petrochemicals or shipbuilding, the steel either gravitating toward them or they coming toward the steel. In the end they all gather together on the seaboard in huge new complexes.

A third new aspect of steel's seaboard strategy is the development of a fleet of very large ships designed to supply the coastal factories. The consequent saving on freightage is more considerable and more profitable for Japan than for any other country. At the same time Japan is geographically better endowed than others for the use of these huge ships and for docking them along its coasts. Seaboard factories, polders and enormous ships—between them these three factors account more than anything else for the success of Japanese iron and steel.

Japan began the new coastal system as early as 1953 with the Chiba works, which made use of land won from the shallow Bay of Tokyo. Soon after this, seaboard installations began to multiply fast, growing larger and larger as they multiplied. In the southern island of Kyushu on the Shimonoseki Strait, there was Tobata, of which I have already spoken; in the Bay of Osaka, near Kobe, the Nadahama, Wakayama, and above all the Sakai complexes; in the new industrial zone of the Bay of Nagoya, the Chita works; in Tokyo Bay again, the Mizue works and the new huge Kimitsu complex now being built; and lastly, on the Inland Sea, which the industrial tide reached in 1968, the gigantic Mizushima and Fukuyama complexes, which are also new. The Inland Sea is becoming the fourth great iron and steel basin, coming after those of northern Kyushu, Osaka and Tokyo. The older Muroran steel-works in Hokkaido completes the list.

It may be said that at present all the great Japanese iron and steel complexes are on the coast and that they all date from the last fifteen years or so. Every great firm has set up one or in some cases several; for example, Yawata has three: Tobata, Sakai and Kimitsu. All these installations have quays with seven fathoms of water or more along-side, and depths of eight and nine fathoms are tending to become the rule. For indeed the great ore carriers already reach 78,000 tons and the coal carriers 59,000 tons; but several 90,000-tonners are being built, and ships of 125,000 tons are already planned. The docks are of a corresponding size, and the stocking areas are laid out according to the most carefully planned lines and dimensions. The great steel firms have been led to include shipping as an integral part of their own activities, and they have built their private fleets of ore and coal ships which they entrust to subsidiary companies. In March, 1967, the Japanese ore-carrying fleet amounted to seventy-nine vessels with a total of more than 3 million tons, and the coal-carrying fleet to twenty-four, totaling nearly 1 million tons.

At the same time as this labor of organization, the great Japanese steel producers also devoted a prodigious amount of effort to equip-ping their installations with ultramodern plant and to acquiring the world's most advanced technical processes. A first example of this is provided by the blast furnaces, which continually increase in size and efficiency. Not long ago it was considered that the best possible produc-tion was a thousand tons a day. At present they have reached thirty-five hundred tons, and since the summer of 1968 a new record has been reached by the huge new Fukuyama furnace, which turns out five thousand tons a day. There are others that will soon do as well; after the 1965 recession, a most striking feature of the year 1967 was the setting up of a whole series of new giant blast furnaces, all of a capacity of more than 2,000 cubic meters (2,600 cubic yards). At the beginning of 1969 the world's biggest blast furnace was that of Krivoy Rog in the U.S.S.R., whose volume capacity is 2,700 cubic meters (3,500 cubic yards). But it is going to be outstripped by the number-three furnace in the Kawasaki steelworks at Mizushima; its capacity of 3,300 cubic meters (4,250 cubic yards) is capable of producing seven thousand tons of ingot steel a day. Sumitomo has also decided to erect two 3,000-cubic-meter blast furnaces at Kajima.*

The Japanese have taken over and often improved the most recent processes such as oxygen blast, compressed air flow at the top, fuel injection, the sintering of the charge and so on; and these are among the causes for their success, since they provide an increasing economy of raw materials and therefore a drop in cost price. Their rate of coke consumption is the lowest in the world. If their production of cast iron by cubic meter of furnace capacity (1.71 tons in 1967) is surpassed at all, this is accomplished only by the Soviet Union. Since 1955, oxygen blast has been used in the furnaces and converters and has added greatly to their increased efficiency.

Another factor in their success is the fact that the Japanese lead the world in the production of steel by L-D oxygen converters. Japan was the first country to adopt them on a large scale, as soon as they came out in Austria in 1953, for they saw that the process would save them a considerable amount of scrap iron. In 1966 there were forty-eight of them (sixty at the end of 1967) and 42 million tons of Japanese steel, or more than 60 percent, was produced by L-D oxygen converters (United States 25 percent; West Germany 24 percent; France 14 percent). Electric steel, above all for the manufacture of special alloys, remained important (19 percent), but the production of Martin steel dropped heavily.

As far as the number of rolling mills is concerned, Japan ranks second in the world after the United States, and it has almost twice as many as West Germany. They have ultramodern plant, for a great deal of effort has been devoted to them, particularly to the development of continuous operation and to the checks that ensure a high degree of precision homogeneity. Automation is carried to a pitch that brings it to the level of the United States or even higher. Computers are freely used for the checking and the coordination of operations, particularly in the most recent installations such as the Fukuyama com-

* The world's biggest steelworks is that of Magnitogorsk in the U.S.S.R.: yearly production capacity, 10 million tons. The second, in the United States, is the Bethlehem Steel Corporation's installation at Sparrows Point, Maryland: 8.2 million tons. Out of the twenty-four biggest steelworks in the world, five Japanese and three non-Japanese have integrated production—that is, the full process from ore to semifinished product—and seven Japanese and one non-Japanese (Sparrows Point) are in coastal regions.

plex on the Inland Sea. The technique is to a great extent foreign, above all American; but Japan itself provides almost all its own plant, covering the whole range of equipment—blast furnaces, steel working machinery, rolling mills, subsidiary installations for sintering and the various processings, loading and handling machines and so forth.

This picture would not be complete if it did not emphasize the Japanese effort to reach the highest possible degree of integration in the various processes and of a logical organization of them. The ideal is to make a single entity on the same site, bringing together all the different concerns whose consecutive activities complete the cycle of processes, from the ore to the semifinished product. The ideal is also to minimize stocking and movement from one works to another and to ensure a perfect coordination between them, both in processing and in the flow of materials. The results the Japanese have obtained are in fact the admiration of foreign visitors, although it is true that there still exist a few out-of-date plants which have been handed down from the past and, of course, an assortment of small firms working at a low technical level.

At present it is reckoned that 75 percent of Japanese steel comes from integrated plants, each of which turns out 5 million tons a year; but each of these integrated complexes has a middle-term aim of a yearly production of between 7 and 8 million tons of crude steel, and this postulates a 19-to-22-million-ton consumption of raw materials, all of it, or almost all of it, being brought from overseas in huge ships. The iron and steel complex now installed at Fukuyama on the Inland Sea, in the Hiroshima prefecture, will turn out 10 million tons of ingot steel a year; apart from what may possibly exist in the U.S.S.R., this is a world record.

A typical example of these integrated works is given by the Tobata complex which I have already mentioned, the first of the "direct line" assemblies built end to end on the Bay of Dokai, now Asia's greatest artificial port, and feeding one another according to a perfectly logical program. Another model complex is that of Kimitsu, which is now being built at the far end of Tokyo Bay; here one of the blast furnaces is of a size that already constitutes a world record, beating that previously held by the great Sakai furnace near Osaka.

But I think the finest instance of integration is that which is to be seen in the Fukuyama complex. When the directors of the Nippon

Kokan group (or N.K.K.) first conceived the project, it is said that they called in the engineers whose job it was to draw up the plans and asked them to design the most logical and most efficient complex possible, to include all the various given processes, from the untreated ore to the finished product. "But where is this to be?" asked the engineers. "What site have you in mind? What is the nature of its surface? What is its shape and size?" The directors replied, "Don't you worry about that. In our view, none of these points has any importance, and you will see why. Design us the ideal works and we will find the site for you; for the moment we haven't got one at all." The engineers did what was asked of them and produced the plans for the most logical and best organized "dream complex" that could be imagined. And upon this the directors simply won the necessary site from the water, an area of 1,798 acres, trimmed to exactly the required shape and size as a tailor cuts his cloth according to his measurements, and that rose from the bottom of the Inland Sea. All the builders had to do was to erect the complex according to the ideal plan, with its excellently coordinated works running end to end in a straight line.

Here the essential problem of the rationalization of transport within the works is dealt with in the most economical way possible, with only about five and a half miles of track. Automation is carried very far, and the labor force required to produce 10 million tons of crude steel a year (a figure that I repeat deliberately) is among the smallest in the world, amounting at present to five thousand men, with an additional three thousand in the subsidiary services. Fukuyama is in a fair way to becoming the wholly rational complex: at the western end one can already see the huge ore ships discharging their cargo by means of ultramodern equipment (sixty-two thousand tons can be unloaded in twenty-four hours, which is twice the ordinary speed), while at the other end, a mile or so to the east, other ships sail off laden with the finished products.

Clearly only very powerful companies can launch undertakings of this kind; it is primarily a question that concerns the six Japanese leaders in steel. They are, together with their percentages of the total production in 1967, Yawata (18.5 percent) and Fuji (17 percent); then Nippon Kokan, Kawasaki, and Sumitomo, which are all on much the same footing with 11.5 percent each; and finally Kobe Steel with 5 percent. The first two hold an outstanding place in international competition; in 1967 Yawata came fourth, after two American giants and one huge English company, and Fuji fifth, ahead of Thyssen (Germany), sixth, and de Wendel (France), tenth.

And yet up until now the concentration of Japanese iron and steel has not been taken very far. The six great companies compete strongly among themselves for their share of the greater part of the market, and there are also the many medium-sized or small firms that provided about 25 percent of the total production in 1967. All in all there are about sixty companies that really count and are solidly established, either because of their massive production or because of their particular products. But a strong movement toward concentration for the years to come is now beginning, both on account of international rivalry and of Japanese ambition.

The supply of raw materials for Japanese iron and steel is likewise developing fast. Here again the great managers, backed up by their government and their country's foreign policy, have proved remarkable strategists, especially in their long-term views and the flexibility of their operations. It would be very interesting to run over the shifting history of Japanese iron ore imports in detail, for this would give a striking illustration of the country's problems of supply. As far as iron ore is concerned, as is the case with so many other raw materials, Japan is very heavily dependent upon imports; more than 85 percent of the ore comes from abroad. And Japan's vitally urgent needs are increasing year by year to a formidable extent. During the first half of this century Japan's consumption reached a level of 10 million tons. It reached this figure again after the war, in 1957. But as early as 1961 the figure had risen to 20 million; in 1964, to 30 million; in 1967, to more than 50 million; and it is calculated that the country will need 90 million tons of iron ore in 1971. As for coking coal, Japan consumed 32 million tons in 1967. By 1975 this will almost have doubled.

Before and during the war, the sources of iron ore were convenient and profitable, because they were close: China, Malaya and the Philippines. After the defeat Japan began to rely heavily upon its conqueror, the United States, and upon Canada; then it turned for large quantities to South America and India and again to Malaya. (In India the Japanese were chiefly interested in the former Portuguese colony of Goa; Japanese engineers undertook to prospect, equip and carry out the technical management, and they developed the port of Mormugaõ for their ore carriers.) In this present second phase the South American countries (Chile, Peru and Brazil) are the main suppliers (31 percent in 1966); then comes India (21 percent); and then the great newcomer, Australia (7 percent).

This last figure is small, but Australia's sales of ore are going to astonish the world; one of the most impressive deposits of high-grade ore on earth was discovered in Western Australia less than ten years ago, at Mount Newman, containing enough to supply not only Australia itself but also Japan for several centuries. From the Japanese point of view, the distance is comparatively short—less than twenty-five hundred miles—whereas on the average every ton of ore used in Japan travels nearly six thousand miles. The deposits are quite close to the sea, and Australia is politically stable—an important point. So the leading Japanese ironmasters combined, and in 1965 they signed an agreement with the Australian and American owners of the huge Mount Newman mine. This was the most important contract they had ever made, for according to the terms of the agreement, Japan will take more than 100 million tons of ore, spread over fifteen years starting in 1969, and the Japanese will play a considerable part in the equipment and working of the deposit, as well as in the setting up of its harbor, Port Hedland. Indeed, a second agreement, signed at the end of 1968, added another 37 million tons, this additional amount to be spread over ten years. The agreement stipulates that the Japanese engineers will so construct Port Hedland that it will be capable of receiving three 100,000-ton mineral carriers at one time.

This is not all. In 1966 the Japanese began to receive ore from the Hamersley mine, also in Western Australia; in this case too they are associated with an Australian-American group. In the course of eighteen years they will receive 65 million tons; they will load it at the port they are building at King's Bay, where they have already set up the biggest rotary ore crusher in the world. And lastly the Savage River mine in Tasmania will provide them with a total of 45 million tons of ready-crushed ore spread over twenty years; here again they are contributing a great deal toward the equipment of the mine and the development of the port. The third phase will see Brazil becoming a large-scale source of ore, together with various other South American countries, Australia and India. It was in order to carry the Brazilian ore from Tubarão that the Japanese built their first huge specialized ship in the 70,000-ton class.

The United States is still Japan's main source for scrap (between 4 and 8 million tons according to the year); but since the L-D converters have come into use and since the gigantic blast furnaces have become so usual, scrap has lost its importance in comparison with the other raw materials. Immediately after the war the United States was also Japan's chief supplier of coking coal—indeed, almost their only supplier. But here again Australia's appearance on the scene has made a great difference. The Japanese have gone into partnership with the Australians for the development of the Moura mine in Queensland; according to an agreement that came into force in 1965, in thirteen years they will receive a total of 30 million tons of coking coal. This was the biggest contract that Japan had ever signed as far as coal is concerned. There are agreements of great importance dealing with long-term supplies of coking coal, however. In 1968 Japan concluded one according to which the country will receive 45 million tons spread over fifteen years from Canada, starting in 1970; it will be supplied by the Kaiser Steel Corporation and it will come from the Balmer mines.

Wherever the Japanese customers appear, in Canada, South America or Australia, the ports for loading raw materials are enlarged (often, as we have seen, with the help of Japanese engineers) so as to admit the great new ships flying the flag of the Rising Sun.

The astonishing accomplishments of Japanese iron and steel are an essential factor in Japan's success in shipbuilding—a success that provides still another example of this country's drive, intelligence and capability in industrial undertakings. This is a somewhat less paradoxical success, since Japan's maritime character makes it natural for the Japanese to be shipbuilders, but it is a very striking success nevertheless, for this time the country stands first in the world. More than ten years have gone by since Japan reached this rank, and it is hard to see how it can lose it, since at present the Japanese are now building a yearly tonnage that is more than five times greater than either of its closest competitors, Sweden and Great Britain. Japan holds records of many different kinds: the country is the top builder of merchant ships and tankers, it is the top ship exporter, and its merchant fleet has grown faster than any other in the world. Its prices are the lowest, and although the quality of Japanese shipbuilding is very high the ships are still built faster than anywhere else. And once again we may add the record for rapid growth in this particular industry too, for it performed the extraordinary feat of doubling its output in the three years from 1964 to 1967.

At the end of 1967 the Japanese builders had two and a half years of work on their order books—17 million tons of shipping. In the *Glasgow Herald's* list of the world's biggest shipbuilding yards, six, including the four top ones (Mitsubishi at Nagasaki, I.H.I. at Aioi, Hitachi at Innoshima, and the other I.H.I. at Yokohama), are all Japanese.

What no doubt impressed world opinion most was the spectacle of the Japanese plunging wholeheartedly into the race for ships of enormous tonnage, in which they were the first to venture. At the end of 1967 there were 69 huge ships of more than 100,000 tons on the various oceans, and of these 51 had been built in Japan. At the same date 206 ships of more than 100,000 tons had been ordered, and of these, 103, exactly half, had been ordered from Japanese shipyards. Out of the 23 ships of more than 60,000 tons that were launched in 1967 (all but one were tankers), 16 were made in Japan. But this does not mean that the Japanese shipyards have given up the building of small or medium-sized vessels. Not at all: I.H.I. (Ishikawajima-Harima Industry) has begun what might almost be called the mass production of improved Liberty Ships, a Japanese version of 14,000 tons; they are built at a rhythm of eighteen a year. The aim is to replace the nine hundred aging Liberty Ships (they date from the war) that are still sailing the seas.

As far as the great European countries are concerned, the "over 100,000 tons" revolution—that is to say, the decision to set about building gigantic ships—dates from the closing of the Suez canal in November, 1956. For Europe had to offset the necessity of having to carry the crude oil from the Middle East around Africa by the saving on freight charges provided by these new monsters. But the Japanese had not waited for the Suez crisis to make this discovery, particularly since Japan's geographical position means that the greater part of its raw materials do not have to go through the canal at all. In fact they had conceived the plan of providing themselves with a whole fleet of huge ships as early as 1954 and 1955, the time at which the Greek shipowner Onassis astonished the world with a 50,000-tonner.

Ralph Hewins in *The Japanese Miracle Men* gives a very lively account of the way his first hero, the oil tycoon Sazo Idemitsu, set about it. He had brought off the feat of breaking the English and American monopoly of Persian Gulf oil and of securing a sound foothold there for Japan, and right away he wanted to be able to use giant ships to carry his oil; he wanted to have a fleet at his disposal. And indeed as early as 1957 the Idemitsu Kosan Company could boast the biggest ship in the world, an 85,000-tonner; the company held the record for eight years, not merely with one but with four great tankers—the first I have just mentioned, then two 75,000-tonners, and then the world's first ship of over 100,000 tons, the *Universe Apollo* of 115,000. They were all built at the Kure yards, near Hiroshima. In 1962 the glory of being the largest ship men had ever built passed to a "dinosaur," as the Japanese say, the 132,000-ton *Nissho Maru*, which was built for Idemitsu at Sasebo, in southern Japan, in the then incredibly short time of ten and a half months.

At this period the European yards were still far from being equipped for the age of gigantic ships; they could not even take them into serious consideration, so in 1964, when Royal Dutch Shell eventually made up its mind to order a fleet of these monsters, it had to turn to Japan for eleven 170,000-ton tankers! Japan drew even farther ahead of its competitors. This became strikingly obvious when at last the other countries "took off" with 100,000-tonners in 1965. In that year England laid the keels of five, Germany of four, France and Sweden of two each, and Holland and Italy one apiece; but Japan began twenty-six. That same year the world's record for tonnage passed to the *Tokyo Maru* of 150,000 tons, which was built by the I.H.I. yard in eight months! This time it was the oil firm of Caltex that could boast the world's biggest ship, but very soon Idemitsu took the lead again, having made the astonishing decision to go beyond the 200,000-ton mark. The result of this decision was the 209,000-ton *Idemitsu Maru*, which I.H.I. built in 1966, taking only ten months.

The *Idemitsu Maru* is 1,022 feet in length—only about two hundred feet less than the height of the Empire State Building in New York. In depth she measures just over 160 feet. Her hull is almost entirely made of a special high-resistance steel, and her enormous propeller is twenty-six feet across. Since automation aboard has been very carefully studied, her crew amounts to no more than thirty-two; and when she is sailing the high seas only two men are needed to steer the huge vessel. Both loading and unloading are automatic. In order to profit to the utmost from the heavy tonnage, these operations have to be carried out very quickly and the ship must move rapidly between the Persian Gulf and Japan. The *Idemitsu Maru* manages to make the double voyage nine times in one year, carrying a total of 2 million tons of crude oil.

Obviously one of the most daring strokes of the Japanese ship-builders was to put their money on the possibility of using these giant ships without accident or any very important difficulty, or rather to base their decision on the calculation that the problems of navigation and safety could be fairly easily solved. In practice the ships over 100,000 tons like the *Nissho Maru* have shown astonishing qualities, both as regards maneuverability and seaworthiness. Laymen might be afraid that these huge vessels would break in two in typhoon weather. Experience has shown that on the contrary they behave excellently; they withstand the stress particularly well because the very fact of their length means that they lie upon a whole series of waves at any given moment.

So as the experience of these last five years was decisive, as the 200,000-tonners were successful, the builders raised their sights to tankers of 300,000 tons. A range of six, varying between 276,000 and more than 300,000 tons, were laid down in the Mitsubishi and I.H.I. yards for American oil companies. Two were launched as early as the summer of 1968. The first, the *Universe Ireland*, is 312,000 tons and she is 1,135 feet long. When these ships are loaded they will be too big to go through the Strait of Malacca. They will have to go around by another route, through the Lombok Strait. The Japanese would like to deepen the Strait of Malacca, dynamiting various natural obstacles, setting up a system of sea marks and organizing the traffic through it with one-way passages; the plan would cost $275 million.

But the soaring rise of tonnage is not yet over. A 367,000-ton vessel has been ordered from I.H.I. by Tokyo Tanker, and the great Japanese yards are making plans for the building of the 500,000-tonners of the coming years. So the race for enormous ships goes hand in hand with a parallel race for enormous yards. In 1964 Japan possessed about three hundred shipbuilding yards, but out of these about thirty built more than 90 percent of the nation's total between them. It was in 1963 that the entirely new yards came into action, yards that were far better than old ones that had merely been enlarged and modernized. Like the steelworks, the shipbuilding yards have left their out-of-date clutter of equipment behind and have set themselves up on new land won from the sea; this makes sure of the necessary depth and space and an entirely rational layout. At the end of 1967 there were seven of these new Japanese yards designed to build ships of more than 200,000 tons. Three of the existing docks will be able to construct 500,000-tonners even before 1971. Many others of the same magnitude are planned, for each of the great names in shipbuilding, Mitsubishi, I.H.I., Mitsui and the others, wants to have its own.

The result of this Japanese experiment has finally convinced the European shipbuilders, and they have made up their minds to follow the same course. With some anxiety the Japanese see that at last the Western shipyards are launching a great counteroffensive to catch up with Japan. To be sure, each one of Japan's competitors is far behind, but their combined production might make life difficult for the Japanese in a few years' time. And then there is another danger looming ahead—that of overproduction. In mid-1968 Europe had four yards capable of turning out ships of more than 200,000 tons; a little later the number rose to seven or eight. It was foreseen that within two or three years there would be about fifteen such yards. Everybody has come to believe in these enormous vessels, and every shipbuilding country wants to provide itself with new yards of suitable size. There is talk of installations at Belfast and Rotterdam that will be able to turn out leviathans of a million tons! In Tokyo they say that there is a danger that by 1971 the world will have a total building capacity exceeding its requirements by 5 to 6 million tons.

Many European missions have gone to Japan to draw on its experience and to learn the lessons it has to teach, and to see whether its success may not have been brought about by an unfair exploitation of its abundant labor force. On coming home these visitors, who have included the ministers responsible for shipbuilding in France and England, have generally acknowledged that these suspicions were unfounded. Nevertheless they often stressed the fact that a lower standard of living and a lower level of wages than are found in Europe did amount to a subsidy for Japan. The Japanese, on the other hand, accounted for their record-breaking by their organization and their high degree of technical ability. No doubt there is truth in both arguments. The whole of the complex reality is made up of more factors than these.

It is unfair to attribute the "miracle" of Japanese shipbuilding to lower wages and to a system of sweated labor that victimizes the worker. On the other hand it does seem right to say that the outlay on wages and social security is less of a burden upon Japanese employers, although this does not make a great deal of difference to the position of the wage earners, living as they do in an atmosphere that is different from the West both in regard to work and to private life. Then again, the Japanese yards have found it very much to their advantage to adopt the system of nonstop work, with three shifts in the twenty-four hours and the machines turning without a pause. What is more, the "company union" system and the discipline of the workers mean that a Japanese firm has a more flexible and more diligent labor force than is usual in Europe, where the yards are often in difficulties because of the numbers of different unions and their delimitation claims as far as jobs are concerned. A Japanese welder, for example, can be turned over to the painters' shop for a while, and he will make no complaint. The average worker is younger than he is in the West, he has a high degree of training in his craft, and he is most conscientious. The middle-grade executives are employed in large numbers; they are very good workers, and they pay the closest attention to the highly detailed preparations and to the scrupulous checking of the execution of the work.

The success of the Japanese shipyards is generally to be explained by very highly developed organization and an excellent use of widely known processes, and not by the invention of revolutionary techniques that may well not exist. Indeed, it was by exploring every kind of imported technique to the utmost possible degree that Japan won its leading position. The shipyards offer a typical example of the Japanese skill in finding useful processes or patents anywhere in the world, in buying them, and in making free and intelligent use of them. In this field their policy with regard to patents has been singularly important and well managed. Japanese missions went shopping all over the globe, making positive collections of the most profitable or most advanced patents and paying the price that was asked.

Once they were equipped with the best possible plant, they developed and made a common practice of the block construction of ships—that is to say, the building of them piece by piece. The workshops set about what is almost a mass production of the prime elements of the vessel or they turn to such specialized parts as the engines. These parts are then assembled in the sheds, forming huge blocks of the future ship, though they are not yet in the dock. A very powerful system of transporter bridges and cranes that can lift six hundred tons (it is said that they will soon be able to manage blocks of eight hundred tons) moves them to the slip, where they are put together like the pieces of a jigsaw puzzle. Throughout the drawing up of the plans and all the various phases of the building there is constant use of computers and electronic checks. The planning is highly detailed and accurately followed; this applies not only to an individual ship but to a whole building program spreading over several years. This means that slack periods are avoided and oscillations in prices are minimized. Automation is very highly developed; this is particularly the case in welding, painting and the cutting of steel plate.

The Japanese, although basing themselves upon known techniques, have also made technical improvements and innovations. High-speed welding is a case in point. They were the first to use the method of welding on one side only, which means that the plates do not have to be turned over for the welding of the other surface. They have developed processes that unite photography, beams of light, and the use of magnetic powders to replace the painting of the shape to be cut out of the steel plate. And they have made many technical innovations of their own, including bulbous hulls, ship brakes, stabilizers and the welding together of the sections of a ship while it is actually in the water.

They have also devised the "lengthening" of ships. The vessel is cut in two from top to bottom, and then again horizontally on the plane of its decks, through the bows and the stern; when these pieces are put together again additional sections are inserted at the same time so that the result is a ship that may be twice the size of the original and, it seems, quite as strong. The latest revolution is that of the container carriers—that is, ships which carry only standardized containers.

The first thirty are to be built within five years. Improved processes and good organization result in a rapidity of production that has been an essential factor in the stream of orders to Japan, orders that come above all from Europe.

The well-regulated flow of operations means that not only is there no stoppage of work when one ship is left for another, but also that several ships can be built at the same time in the same slip. When one vessel is ready to be launched, the stern of another is already almost finished, just at hand, and as soon as the slipway is empty it moves into it, there to be given its bows. This method was first begun at Sakai, on the Bay of Osaka, in 1965, and it doubled the number of ships built there in a year. It was also in 1965 that the British minister responsible for shipbuilding came home from Tokyo and complained that the English took twelve to eighteen months to do what the Japanese could do in five. In 1966 I.H.I. launched 74,000-ton ships at the rhythm of six a year, building each in two months and finishing it off in two more. In 1967 the time needed for building a 100,000-tonner had been cut from seven months to four and a half.

The European missions who went to Japan to investigate this miracle of progress were determined to discover whether there was any truth in the accusation that Japan's advantage in shipbuilding was partly based on indirect help and concealed subsidies from the state. They concluded that this complaint, like the complaints about low wages, had no real substance. For one thing, it is public knowledge that the European shipyards, in counterattacking to catch up with the Japanese, rely heavily upon assistance from government funds. In a survey published in March, 1968, the London *Economist* acknowledged that there was virtually no shipbuilding country that did not grant its yards either tax relief or subsidies in one form or another. The survey ends by stating that in fact Japan's direct or indirect aid was considerably less than that given in England, for example, or France or Italy. The OECD made a thorough inquiry into this subject, and its conclusion was that the indirect subsidies granted to the Japanese shipbuilders did not exceed 10 percent. The Japanese dispute this figure, but even so it seems very moderate.

On the other hand, when European investigators are in Japan they usually discover a factor whose full significance they had not realized, a factor essential to the understanding of the Japanese shipyards' competitive strength: this is the country's industrial structure itself, and more specifically the fact that the shipbuilding companies form an integral part of far bigger combinations, powerful industrial groups that support them. The associated group, such as Mitsubishi, Hitachi, N.K.K. or Toshiba, is made up of parent companies that turn out an enormous variety of goods that may range from steel to pocket torches.

Generally speaking, a French or British shipyard is an orphan and has to make its living from the sale of its ships and nothing else. A Japanese shipyard is backed up by a huge family. The group can afford to make very little profit on the ships it sells as long as it compensates itself elsewhere. In this way profits arising from activities that have nothing to do with shipbuilding have done a great deal toward financing the equipment of the new ultramodern yards and increasing their size for the export trade.

Lastly, in their actual building the Japanese yards have an advantage over their European rivals that arises from their close links with all the other industries in their group—industries that provide them with services and supplies. In the new great coastal complexes the shipyards very often stand right next to the steelworks and rolling mills that provide them with the bulk of their materials, and to the engineering factories that are of such value to their block assembly works, and all these advantages have their effect upon the cost price of the ships.

8.

The New Industrial Revolution

Passing on from the shipyards, which show us that the Japanese are capable of extraordinary success in a traditional industry, let us look at electronics, one of the new industries of our time. Here too we find the Japanese equally skillful and equally ready to take the lead. Turning in this way from the one industry to the other also allows us to gauge the extent and the variety of their talents, since here we make a sudden transition from the enormous to the minute, from the building of the mammoths of the shipyards to the manufacture of integrated electronic minicircuits.

For a long time it has been said that the Japanese could see small and make small. The truth of the matter is that the Japanese can above all see big; this is a truth that has not yet been fully realized, and in our rapidly changing world it will certainly have many more opportunities for making itself clear. Nevertheless it is an undoubted fact that the Japanese do excel in scrupulous fine-scale work and that they have a particular taste for very small manufactured articles. Few of the world's artists and craftsmen have shown the Japanese genius for embodying their skill and their feeling for beauty in such a limited compass. The Japanese starts off, then, with a natural gift for succeeding in the manufacture of small-scale objects and for contributing a great deal to the miniaturization of techniques and the finished product.

Miniaturization is the new word, the new tendency, and one of the keys to the industry of the coming years. Now it so happens that the Japanese worker of today still possesses the skills, the aptitudes, of his ancestors in this respect; he still has the same meticulous care, the feeling for detail, and even that degree of shortsightedness that is valuable in these delicate manipulations. This applies especially to the Japanese working girl, with her skillful young fingers. The industries that are concerned with very small and delicate products are particularly suitable for the employment of women.

Electronics is but one of the many industrial sectors in which the Japanese ancestral talent for miniaturization has given the country still another advantage in international competition; it also comes into its own when the Japanese turn to watches and clocks, precision instruments, scientific apparatus, chemistry, engineering, photography and so on. At the same time it is above all these industries that in the last twenty years have reversed the notion, long held abroad, that most Japanese products were cheap goods of very low quality. On such products the label "Made in Japan" is now a guarantee—and this is particularly true in electronics.

Electronics, one of the trump cards in the new Japanese industrial revolution, provides a perfect example of explosive growth. To be sure, it did not start from scratch after the war. It had a past: starting in 1920, Japan was one of the first Asian countries to develop telegraphs, telephones and telecommunications. But just after the war there occurred what might be termed a graft of the most advanced Western techniques upon the well-prepared Japanese stock; this was the time of the modernization of the Japanese way of life, which was marked by the development of radio in the fifties and of television after 1953, and by a continually increasing demand for household and industrial apparatus. All this meant that the electronics industry got off to a flying start. Between 1956 and 1966 the value of its output increased by ten times. Its exports have brought it to third place in Japan's foreign trade, and although it is a consequence of the new Japan's economic revolution, at the same time it reacts upon it as a powerful stimulus.

The growth of electronics is closely linked to some of the phenomena that are the particular characteristics of this revolution—the galloping modernization of the whole industrial structure, the raising of the standard of living, the fundamental change in home life caused by household equipment, the creation of a powerful interior market for consumer goods. It is also associated with a shift in the economy's center of gravity, away from the traditional and toward the new, highly scientific industries, away from the village, and the oversupplied textile industry, into the factories. Electronics has been favored, too, by the fact that, in a country poor in raw materials, it calls for small amounts of these, drawing rather on the intellectual capabilities of an educated labor force—something that postwar Japan, thanks to its efforts in teaching and general culture, can supply in increasing quantities.

The first chapter in the development of Japanese electronics might be called the "transistor boom," or more precisely the boom of transistor radios. As is often the case, what we have here is a foreign invention, American in this instance, for which Japan bought the patent rights, saw its potentialities sooner than its originators themselves, discovered the right processes for mass production, and sold the product at a price well within the people's reach. Only a few months after the appearance of the transistor in the United States in 1955, the Japanese firm of Sony brought out a small-scale transistor radio in Tokyo. Soon they miniaturized it, and in 1957 they launched a pocket-sized set that was copied by many of their Japanese competitors; this has become a Japanese speciality, and it has turned the world radio market upside down.

From 1956 to 1959 the exports of transistor radios tripled every year and they broke into the American market itself. The second chapter of this story saw the "transistor boom" gradually give way to the "television boom," the transmission of television programs having begun in Tokyo in 1953. In 1957 the production of television sets rose to 600,000, two years later it reached almost 3 million, and two years later still, in 1961, it was 4.5 million. In 1964, at the time of the Olympic Games, it reached approximately 5 million sets, 4 million being for the home market and the rest for export.

The television boom was accompanied by very greatly increased sales of household equipment such as electric saucepans, fans, refrigerators, vacuum cleaners, record players and tape recorders—an increase that was particularly marked from 1955 onward. Because of mass production their prices are very moderate, and they often drop from one year to the next. It was at this time that Matsushita Electric made its fortune by equipping even the humblest Japanese homes with every kind of gadget, including television. Its president, Konosuke Matsushita, the former bicycle repairer, was to become the richest man in Japan, or at least the man who declared the highest income to the tax authorities, and his company was to rank among the hundred biggest concerns in the world outside the United States, a distinction it shares, by the way, with several of its competitors, such as Hitachi and Toshiba.

From about 1962 industrial orders for electronic devices and machines became more and more important; these were in addition to the private demand. The great works, particularly those concerned with heavy industry and chemicals, furnished themselves with electronic checking apparatus, computers and so on. The production of semiconductors, circuits, spare parts and accessories designed for industry increased, and by 1967 industrial demand as a whole accounted for 60 percent of the total electronic output.

But a third boom was already under way: this was the color television boom of 1966 and 1967. Just when the home market for black and white television was nearing saturation, color took over. The government encouraged this, for the good reason that the color sets also sold very well in the United States, which takes almost all that Japan exports. Color has reached such a stage that the first Tokyo channel (N.H.K.) sends it out half the time (ten hours a day), and several other channels do almost as much. As early as 1967 it had become quite usual to see modest working-class families gathered around the screen in the evening, watching color distinctly better than it is in America.

At this point I should strongly emphasize one outstanding feature of the industry: Unlike its Western competitors, Japanese electronics has never experienced the stimulus of military orders. In the United States these account for 60 percent of electronic manufactures, and the supply for civilian purposes takes second place. In Japan the industry has not been spurred on by the space race, either. Civilian manufactures alone have maintained it, manufactures that correspond to the popularization of electronic devices, to a peaceful industrial demand, and to a strong export drive. One consequence of all this is another remarkable feature of the industry, which is that the advanced techniques, instead of being directed toward the limited market of military users or of space research (which means that the productions are secret and highly specialized), have been turned toward the general public in the form of inexpensive mass-produced goods.

The most striking example of Japanese electronics' latest advance is the sudden wholehearted development of integrated circuits. These are made up of microscopic semiconductors that provide a circuit ten thousand times smaller than what is termed a conventional circuit; they make possible the application of microelectronics to the most complex techniques and the use of dimensions far more reduced than industry has ever known.

The transition from laboratory manufacture to mass production of these integrated circuits was an outstanding accomplishment. The Americans succeeded in doing it because of their huge efforts in atomic and space research and in armaments. The English could manage only with the help of a great deal of public money, and even so they are still quite a long way behind. The Japanese were bold enough to plunge straight into the undertaking with much less official help, meaning from the first to devote their integrated circuits not only to industrial equipment such as computers, electronic checking devices and telecommunications but also to gadgets designed for the general public, mass produced for the man in the street—things such as radios, color television, stereophonic apparatus, tape recorders and hearing aids. In Japan integrated circuits have a whole variety of civilian applications that just do not exist in other countries. A little while ago a typical success caused a sensation: this was the world's first mini radio with integrated circuits. It weighs 3.2 ounces and measures 1.2 inches by 3.5 inches; it is a high-quality radio no bigger than a matchbox, and Sony brought it out in 1967. It will not be long before Tokyo sees the first "wrist television"—a miniature screen to be worn like a wristwatch. Using integrated circuits, the same firm has already astonished the world with its little black and white sets, whose longest side measures no more than 8.2 inches, while Matsushita brought out a pocket-sized cassette tape recorder far ahead of anything else in the field.

The great Japanese electronics firms (and among these we should also mention others, such as Mitsubishi Electric and N.E.C.) have positively hurled themselves upon these integrated circuits and everything that has to do with them—so much so that Japan at once took second place in world production, coming after the United States (which nevertheless still has a great lead) and ahead of England; ahead of the Soviet Union, too, as far as we can tell. For the Japanese it was essentially a question of preventing the Americans from acquiring a virtual monopoly and of guarding themselves from an eventual invasion of their market by American integrated circuits when Japan, in accordance with international agreements, such as those which it signed in entering OECD or GATT, has to open its doors completely to American investment. This is why Japan held out so firmly against Texas Instruments, a great American company that was already trying to force its way in. Texas Instruments was admitted only in 1968, after a long wait, and then on conditions that limit the possible competition and turn it to the profit not only of Sony, with whom Texas is associated, but also the other Japanese firms, for the American technical processes that Sony makes use of are to be made public. What is more, Japanese apparatus embodying integrated circuits will also be able to be sold on the American market, which has been closed to them up until then.

So the Japanese can truthfully say that they have not been dozing behind the tariff barrier that they set up around their electronics industry until it should be strong enough to withstand competition—not dozing at all. Very far from it. Furthermore this is one of the fields in which they have proved not only their skill at adapting and improving the technical achievements of others, but also their inventive powers. In 1958 the diode (semiconductor) discovered by Dr. Leona Esaki completely changed all ideas upon the subject. In 1961 the Japanese were the first to put a transistorized device for recording photography on tape for use in television; this video magnetic tape recorder is a light, simple piece of apparatus, and it immediately made the heavy, expensive equipment that had been used up until then completely out of date. In 1968 they patented a new kind of diode a thousand times more sensitive to magnetism than any that existed, and this will be used in countless different ways. Then they invented another kind of diode which is sensitive to pressure; after that the "one gun" television tube for color television, the most important advance in this realm for the last twenty years and one that opens the way to cheap mass production. Yet another outstanding success is the Japanese electron microscope, an enormous, highly technical object that is capable of using a current as powerful as a million volts. Here Japan is very far ahead of the United States and on the same level as France, but the Japanese have an advantage over the French, since they have already begun turning out their electron microscopes in large numbers and putting them on the market—and what is even more striking, there are two models to choose from, made by two different firms.

Sheltered behind their high tariff walls and their protection against foreign investment, the Japanese also launched themselves with great speed into the manufacture of electronic computers, for they very soon grasped (far earlier than such European countries as France and England) that these machines would bring about a radical change in any great modern country's economic life and that it was of great importance not only to put them to use as soon as possible but also to make them in Japan itself. Six great companies devoted their energies to this task, the leaders being Fujitsu, N.E.C. and Hitachi. In March, 1966, there were 2,101 computers functioning in Japan, 1,204 of them being of Japanese manufacture. In September, 1967, there were 3,040, and of this number70 percent were Japanese. The Japanese survey that gave these figures reckoned that there were then 32,500 computers in the United States, 3,300 in Germany, 2,200 in England, 1,950 in France, and 1,400 in the U.S.S.R.; Japan thus took the third place after the United States and West Germany. Latest known figures for Japan, for September, 1968: 4,171 computers in operation, 2,990 of them being Japanese.

The manufacturers are helped by the state. As early as 1965 the number of large computers produced in Japan exceeded the number of those of the same size that were imported. It is foreseen that by 1972 Japan will have reached the highest international level for computers of all sizes. In September, 1967, there were 205 large computers in operation, of which 70 were Japanese, and 1,245 medium-sized machines, 544 being Japanese. Digital computers numbered roughly 2,000 and anologue computers over 300. The Japanese are making great efforts at developing desk computers for the home and export markets. Most of the important machines made in Japan are based on American patents or are manufactured jointly with American companies. Yet on the other hand Fujitsu does produce an entirely Japanese computer. All six big Japanese makers have an agreement with I.B.M., and there are other agreements linking some of them with various other important American firms in the same field—for example, those between N.E.C. and Rand, Hitachi and R.C.A., Toshiba and General Electric. With state help a company has been set up to manage the renting of computers, which does away with the financial difficulties that have been experienced in other countries; it is called the Japan Electric Computers Company, and in 1966 it looked after 650 machines. And let us add that informatics, or electronic data processing, that industrial and commercial activity which is concerned with organizing and making use of the memorizing powers of these new machines, is developing as fast as it can in Japan, urged on by the MITI and the important manufacturers concerned.

One last point should be emphasized: It is Japanese companies that have created and developed this powerful electronics industry in Japan. Of course, as we have seen, they turned to foreign and particularly to American technology. But they have successfully defended their independence; they have neither shared their capital with foreign companies nor allowed foreign companies to set up branches in Japan. The American penetration has been reduced to a minimum. However, the only important exception to the rule of Japanese independence is to be found in computers: this is the existence of I.B.M.–Japan, a subsidiary of the great American company, which put up 100 percent of its capital. This is explained by the fact that I.B.M. managed to get in at a time when Japan was still under American occupation and still totally unequipped; the country's urgent need for various products and forms of equipment was then even more important than the protection of its industry.

Although in the case of electronics foreign penetration is negligible, in oil and oil refinery—another new sector of Japanese industry—this is by no means so. Here is a field in which Japan has been compelled to share the market with stronger powers, partly because the country was faced with the virtual monopoly of the great Western oil companies and partly because these same companies were able to take up strong positions in a Japan conquered and defenseless after its defeat. The English and American companies supply the country with a high proportion of the crude oil it needs, and they have invested heavily in its refining industry, either by means of subsidiaries in which they provide up to 100 percent of the capital or by joint ventures in which they hold a very considerable part of the shares.

Oil has taken the place of coal as the new Japan's chief source of energy. In the process, petrochemicals—the industry based on oil derivatives—has become one of the country's foremost activities. Here, then, we have two aspects of the oil revolution that is being carried through at a great pace and is helping to bring about other "revolutions" such as that of the shipyards and the new seaboard combines. The fact of the development of oil has meant a great flood of orders for the engineering industry, which has been called upon to equip the new refineries and petrochemical works. Indeed, Japanese engineering has recently had such a superfluity of orders in this area that it has been obliged to turn some over to the shipyards, which now find themselves working for the petrochemical companies!

Once again we are faced with extraordinarily rapid development; the increase in Japan's oil requirements means that the Japanese market is growing at a greater speed than any other in the world and that therefore the international suppliers find it the most attractive of all. In 1955 the country looked to oil for no more than 15 percent of its energy. Ten years later the figure was over 50 percent, and it is still rising. In 1955 consumption was only a little over 10 million kiloliters (one kiloliter equals a thousand liters, which in its turn equals roughly a ton). In 1966 it passed the 100 million mark; in 1970, approximately 170 million; and it is still increasing very much faster than consumption in the Western countries. According to the forecasts, in less than twenty years it will go beyond 500 million.

But the amounts of oil that have been found in the archipelago until the present are so comparatively trifling that 98 percent of the country's requirements has to come from abroad. The greater part of what is imported is "Western" oil—that is to say, oil bought from the Americans and the English, who are the leading figures in the market. The Americans are way ahead; in 1966 they supplied 63 percent of Japan's imported crude oil, the three leading companies being Caltex (16 percent), Esso (13.7 percent), and Mobil Oil (8.7 percent). The English supplied roughly 15 percent.

Immediately after the war Japan was ruining itself by buying refined products from these companies. Very soon the country made an immense effort to provide itself with its own refineries, so that it need only import crude oil. As early as 1960 imports of refined products had dropped to 10 percent, and oil refinery had become a fundamental industry in the new Japanese economy. Today Japan stands second in the non-Communist world from the point of view of refinery capacity, coming after the United States. In 1967 Japan processed 2.2 million

barrels a day, which is slightly over a fifth of the American performance. But most of the country's present refineries are joint ventures,
partly Japanese and partly American or English. The big names in international oil, with Shell and Standard Oil (Esso) in the lead, settled
in Japan at the beginning of the American occupation and put up a
great deal of the necessary capital. For example, the two biggest Japanese oil companies, Nippon Oil and Toa Nenryo, are only 50 percent
Japanese, the rest of their capital having been put up by Caltex in the
first case and Esso and Mobil Oil in the second. The presidents of
these companies are always Japanese, but the vice-presidents and a
fair number of the chief directors are foreigners.

Other companies, some of them possessing refineries, sell the finished products through their own distribution networks, and in many
of these foreign capital also holds a commanding position. The country's most important refinery has a capacity of 180,000 barrels a day,
then come two with a capacity of 140,000, and after them four that
can deal with more than 100,000. But all the others are smaller; they
do not reach the average size of French or British refineries. For this
reason wide-reaching plans for extension are now being worked out.
It has been calculated that to meet the continually growing demand
there will have to be investment at the rate of a billion dollars a year,
six-tenths of it in Japan itself and the rest abroad, all devoted to
the discovery, exploitation and transport of the oil. It is scarcely
likely that Japan will have financial resources equal to an effort of such
magnitude.

Faced with these powerful foreign interests that control their supplies of oil, the Japanese have done their utmost to obtain at least a
certain minimum of independent provision. In 1957 a fearless businessman, Taro Yamashita (he has since become a Japanese oil tycoon),
caused a sensation in Tokyo by obtaining a concession in the neutral
zone of Kuwait on the Persian Gulf. In 1956 the Idemitsu Kosan Company had already won a footing in the Middle East by getting a long-
term contract for the supply of Kuwait oil: this was done in agreement
with an American company. Yamashita's new company, Arabian Oil,
settled in, despite the opposition of the English and American interests, and it dealt with the Arabs on the basis of a 55-to-45 division
of the profits instead of the traditional 50-50. Back in 1959 it found

oil at its first boring, and in 1965 it was providing the Japanese market with 13 percent of its needs.

But even so, this was not enough. In 1967 the government, together with private interests, set up the Japan Petroleum Development Corporation, whose essential purpose is to provide Japan with independent oil supplies amounting to 30 percent of the country's needs. A most important factor in this decision was the war between Israel and Egypt in the summer of 1967, which dramatically emphasized the vulnerability of Japanese oil supplies and caused a momentary panic in Tokyo. Not only does Japan depend too heavily upon the Anglo-Saxons, but the geographical distribution of its sources is very unfortunate; at least 85 percent of Japan's oil comes from the Middle East, and supplies are threatened whenever there is trouble in those unsettled regions.

The new corporation is therefore encouraging the prospecting for new sources of oil in other directions, particularly in Indonesia, Malaysia, Canada and Australia. The Japan Petroleum Exploitation Company (Japex) has undertaken this effort in Alberta, Canada; Queensland, Australia; and in Australian New Guinea. Another company is focusing on Alaska. But it is likely that Indonesia will be the most promising source. The Japanese are particularly interested in the oil fields of north Sumatra, where one of their companies already has a well, while others are still prospecting.

Finally there is one remaining possibility: the purchase of Russian oil. This could be supplied in great quantities, and it would deal with Tokyo's present disagreeable situation of having all its eggs in one basket. Until now, Russian oil has accounted for only 3 percent of Japan's requirements although Soviet offers have not been wanting. But acceptance of these proposals would put the Japanese in a very embarrassing position, for, as the Idemitsu Kosan Company found, any deal of this kind angers Washington for political reasons. Will a slackening of the tension between the Russian and American governments eventually change all this? The opposition of the American suppliers would still have to be done away with; as far as the Japanese market is concerned, they would have plenty of ways of hindering the intrusive flow of Russian oil, were it to come flooding in.

Meanwhile, for about fifteen years now the country has watched the impetuous development of the petrochemical industry, whose raw material is the naphtha from the refineries. As regards the chemical industry as a whole, after the war Japan had to rebuild the entire structure from top to bottom. The country made considerable use of foreign licenses, and the state helped in the process of modernization. The MITI has unfailingly encouraged rationalization and concentration by means of its very efficient methods of steering investment. Petrochemicals have advanced even faster than chemicals in general; indeed, this industry has moved more rapidly than any other in the Japanese economy. Petrochemicals began in 1955, and since 1960 the industry has increased its output tenfold. The other forms of chemical production have merely tripled, for fertilizers which kept up the progress of agriculture and were the main chemical activity for many years, no longer hold that position. Petrochemical products outstripped fertilizers in 1966, and this change caused a profound modification of the whole chemical industry. At the same time the Japanese moved over from acetylene chemistry, based on coal, to ethylene chemistry, which is based on oil.

The rise of Japanese petrochemicals was founded upon American technology, and its essential basis is the Stone and Weber process for naphtha cracking. At the very beginning four of the great companies launched themselves into petrochemicals: Mitsubishi, Mitsui, Sumitomo and Nippon Petroleum. Their new petrochemical companies made technical agreements with foreign firms, but the foreigners were not allowed to share in their capitalization—something quite unlike the earlier state of affairs in oil refinery. Japanese petrochemicals is an industry that has grown up behind the shelter of protection, and the Tokyo government has taken care to shield it from any new wave of investment.

As early as 1963 the first goal was reached—Japan was self-sufficient in a number of petrochemical products, including ethylene, which had been imported before that date. In that year five factories reached an annual capacity of eighty thousand tons, and in 1964 Japan rose to fourth place as a producer, coming after the United States, West Germany and Great Britain. The manufacture of polyethylene was increasing fast. In that same year the huge Japanese investments in petrochemicals reached $300 million, almost equaling the amount put into electricity, iron and steel, and the automobile industry collectively. There is no room for small concerns in this boom, only for the giants. Even so, the Japanese installations are not yet gigantic enough, for Europe is taking part in the same race and the Europeans are running very fast; Japan is still behind. As for a comparison with the United States, even the biggest Japanese petrochemical works are still far smaller than the American giants. The sales of Mitsubishi Chemical Industries, for example, scarcely reach a tenth of the volume of those of Du Pont de Nemours. So the country has to enlarge its factories, bring producers and consumers closer together, set up great combines that link the refineries, petrochemical works and the associated enterprises such as those that produce synthetic rubber, man-made fibers and plastics, and lastly diversify production so that it reaches out to other main branches—propylene, for example.

The year 1965 was one of recession, and production dropped, but the next year petrochemicals leaped forward, almost doubling output in twelve months. As far as ethylene was concerned, Japan's production capacity was second in the world. There are now eleven petrochemical installations, each one centering upon its own naphtha-cracking plant. A little while ago a hundred thousand tons a year was looked upon as the optimum capacity, but now most of them have doubled this figure.

But this is still not enough. In a few years' time Japanese industry will have to face the inevitable liberalization of foreign investment in the country. It has to prepare to stand up for itself without protection, and if, as it is very likely, Japanese industry is obliged to accept foreign participation, it must not do so upon a footing of inequality.

These are the reasons why the race for new plant and equipment was renewed with even greater vigor in 1967 and 1968. There are some very unusual features in this competition. In February, 1967, the MITI announced that Japan needed to increase its output of ethylene by almost a million tons a year. Immediately a dozen companies came forward, each producing schemes so ambitious that if all the planned production were put together it would amount not to the million tons required but to twice as much! In order to eliminate a certain number of candidates and retain only the most powerful, MITI then stated that the government would give its help and approval only to those new installations that had a capacity of three hundred thousand tons. But even so, the drive of the Japanese manager in the production race is such that no less than seven companies still maintained their candidacy.

In the end MITI had to eliminate three, and it was four huge centers of ethylene production that began building in 1968, three of them on Tokyo Bay, next to the great Chiba steelworks, and an even bigger one farther to the north, among the hitherto deserted sand dunes near the ancient temple of Kashima. They join the great petrochemical complexes that stud the Pacific coast, such as the Kawasaki works near Tokyo, Yokkaichi near Nagoya, and Tokuyama, in the neighborhood of Osaka. Their fantastically modern landscape of enormous towers and metal spheres, lit up all through the night, makes travelers stare from their trains as they journey toward the ancient temples of Kyoto and Ise, not far away. For these are the new shrines of the Japan of the year 2000, the prodigious temples of the god Industry.

This growth has been a powerful stimulant for the plastics industry. Here Japanese production regained its highest wartime level as early as 1950, between 1950 and 1955 it increased by more than 500 percent, and it did almost as well in the next five-year period. Its average annual growth has been greater than 30 percent during the last few years. This strikingly rapid progress, which has no equivalent among the other great plastics-producing countries, brought Japan into second place as of 1967; it comes after the United States, and West Germany has been pushed down to third. In 1967 Japanese production amounted to 2,675,000 tons, as compared with 6,000,000 tons for the United States and 880,000 for France. And lastly, as far as the processing of plastics is concerned, Japan is in many respects well ahead of the other industrial countries. To take only one example, its production of rigid vinyl-polychloride tubes in 1967 was in the nature of 150 tons, or twice that of Germany or the United States, and almost four times that of France.

While electronics and petrochemicals, those most advanced industries, were making their remarkable progress in Japan, still another boom was on the way. This was in the automobile industry, the most recent of the activities new to Japan, in which the industrialists have begun to move very fast indeed. An unusual feature of this fresh advance is that it has been taking place in an industry that belongs to the "first industrial revolution" and to the first half of the twentieth century. Here again Japan has scored a remarkable success; although it may be called "a success in catching up," it is none the less profitable and outstanding, for it has been achieved in a sector where all the places seemed to have been already taken. In spite of that, the Japanese are beginning to make their presence very strongly felt.

One of the paradoxes of Japan's expansion is that the country has often managed to turn its backwardness in comparison with the West to the advantage of its economic development and technical progress. Because Japan was last in the field or because it had to start from scratch (which was to some degree the case after its defeat in 1945), it was able to equip itself with the finest plant in existence and could choose the best sites, unhampered by earlier installations and out-of-date equipment.

The Japanese manufacturers not only had the valuable possibility of drawing freely upon foreign experience and the existing Western models but also found a wonderfully available, unencumbered home market—a remarkable stroke of good fortune. Japanese demand gives every promise of increasing steadily year by year, for it is spurred on by the impatience arising from this time lag and maintained by the increase in family incomes and the very rapid modernization of the Japanese way of life. What is more, Japanese cars can hope to win themselves a profitable place in the international market, especially in the developing countries. Now that Japan has made its way into the last of the "early stage" sectors where it had not yet carved out a place worthy of its new potentialities, it feels perfectly confident of success. As *The Economist* put it, for Japan the car is a new gold rush.

This getting under way, this new start, is quite recent, for it began only after the 1965 recession. When economic recovery came in 1966 it was the automobile industry that opened the most vigorous offensive. This offensive was stimulated not only by a most sanguine outlook but also by a sense of the danger that overhangs the future of the industry. This danger, which the Japanese wish to forestall, is that of the competition of foreign cars in Japan itself once liberalization has opened the market not only to the European and American sellers but also to the foreign manufacturers, who will then be allowed to place their investments in the country. Until that time (and this is a point that should be emphasized) the Japanese automobile industry will develop behind a rigid protective curtain; a limited quota for imported foreign cars; high customs duties of at least 35 percent; costly licenses; and prohibition of foreign manufactures, assembly factories, and direct investment by foreign companies.

Behind these walls, Japan has managed to take the preliminary steps of acquiring equipment, learning the trade, and expanding—to take such giant steps that in the early sixties the country joined the leading makers and exporters of commercial vehicles. It was by turning out trucks, buses and vans of every kind for the home market and for the underdeveloped countries that the industry prepared itself for the manufacture of private cars. After a long time of lagging far behind in this field, in recent years Japan has become the world's third producer of automobiles, counting its whole output of four-wheeled vehicles, including trucks. In 1967 it even outstripped West Germany and reached second place, but for private cars Japan only came sixth, coming after the United States, Germany, France, England and Italy.

Although there has been an extraordinary development in the use of automobiles of all kinds in the archipelago, this does not mean that there are very great numbers of private-car owners. In 1966 the average was one automobile of some kind for every twelve Japanese, but for private cars it was only one for every thirty-five. The explanation lay not only in the financial position of the average Japanese, who was not rich enough to indulge in more than a refrigerator and a television set, but also in the state of the roads, which were perfectly vile. Until 1962 or 1963 the Japanese highways were among the worst in the world. The Olympic Games of 1964 changed all that, for in order to welcome foreign visitors and to preserve their country's good name, the Japanese steadily improved their road system. The hour of the people's car was about to strike.

It was the Games that persuaded the leading manufacturers to set up very large-scale plant for the mass production of low-horsepower private cars and "family models," made available to the middle classes on the installment plan. In the spring of 1966 they launched a whole range of popular models—family cars of about 1,000 cc. selling at between 400,000 yen ($1,100) and 500,000 yen ($1,400) and light models of 360 cc. Mass production began in 1967, and in that year sales amounted to twice as much as in 1966. In 1967 the total output of private cars amounted to 1,131,000, and in 1968 to 2,050,400; by the end of 1967 the number of private automobiles on the road reached

3,840,000, out of a total of four-wheeled motor-driven vehicles that for the first time exceeded 10,000,000.

This was the beginning of a movement that is going to make a fundamental change in Japan, starting with the landscape and the tranquillity of the remoter countryside. Prophetic statistics—statistics that have no parallel in the world—prove the radical nature of the coming change: Japan has ten million drivers who possess no car! Ten million Japanese who have not yet been able to buy themselves an automobile have nevertheless passed their examination for a license in the driving schools, which have become a nationwide industry, and they drive now and then, either in a borrowed or a hired car, as the opportunity offers. Obviously they represent a huge market of buyers who are very eager to drive, sitting there behind the wheel of their own car. So according to the forecast, 1971, the last year of the current economic plan, will see 9.5 million private cars in the archipelago. One Japanese out of eleven will have his own (a figure that is still only half the 1966 statistics for France, Germany and England). The yearly output of private cars will reach 2.5 million, and the industry's total production 5 million. But the curve will go on rising, and by about 1986 or 1987 it will have reached or passed the 20-million mark for private cars.

Then again the Japanese driver has the quickest turnover rate in the world; it does not take him more than a year or eighteen months before he changes his car. Furthermore, he is a difficult, exacting customer, and he insists upon the latest improvements and the greatest possible number of gadgets for his money. Since there is the liveliest competition between the leading makers, they take very great care of their customers. The popular models have many recent advances and novelties that are just not to be found in their European equivalents.

When I arrived in Japan from France in 1967, I was surprised to see that several of the models on the ordinary market had an automatic gearshift. The salesman needed only a week at the outside to deliver whatever car the buyer wanted, in the color he asked for and with all the specified gadgets. To take a typical example, the Crown, which is one of the most popular makes of car, is to be had in a choice of a hundred and twenty different colors. The variety of models is very great, ranging all the way from 360 to 4,000 cc. The coachwork is elegantly designed, and the interior finish is excellent. For many years the prices were distinctly higher than those of equivalent European cars, but now, with the advance of mass production, they have come down. For example, Toyota's Publica (two cylinders, 800 cc., four seats) sells for a little over $1,000, and Toyota's Corolla (1,100 cc., four cylinders, five seats, eighty-seven miles per hour) costs $1,250.

The little 360-cc. cars have no equivalent in other countries. Their makers bet on a new potential market, the market composed of young people delighting in speed and starting with one of these little machines as their first car; then, after this initiation, they go on to more powerful models. The bet is paying off, and another reason for the success of the 360-cc. cars is that their owners are to some degree exempt from the troublesome regulations about parking and periodic inspection and do not pay so much tax.

It remains to be seen whether the quality of Japanese cars will allow them to withstand the competition of the great foreign makes and win a lasting place in the markets abroad. There is no shortage of ambition among the Japanese car makers. The motives behind their recent offensive were a drive for expansion and a desire to make a spectacular entry into the foreign markets. Even the outward appearance of their automobiles, their exact similarity to Western and particularly European models, and above all the names they have given them (Prince, Crown, Bluebird and so on) prove their intention of competing and of bringing all the well-known Japanese gifts of adaptation, imitation, infiltration and charm to bear. From the very beginning the leading Japanese exporters set about the business on a grand scale, equipping themselves with garage ships, especially built for carrying whole cargoes of automobiles across the ocean.

Opinions are still divided as to how they will be received in Europe and America. Sometimes one hears strong adverse criticism to the effect that Japanese engines are indifferent and soon show signs of wear, the suspension is too rigid, and the seats are not wide enough. The after-sales service is still rudimentary; spare parts do not reach the customer quickly enough. These critics say that the Japanese success is owing to curiosity and will not last. These are the same criticisms that were heard in Japan itself during the preliminary phases of the present expansion and that now are heard no more. The teething troubles that at one time made the Japanese buyer prefer a foreign car have mostly been dealt with, and there has been rapid and widespread improvement. It is reasonable to suppose that the Japanese makers will soon cope with the existing drawbacks and that they will prove formidable competitors for quality in the international market.

In the meantime they already have the right to feel pleased with their first results abroad. To begin with they made their way into the United States, Canada, Australia and the Southeast Asian countries (see Chapter 11). In the second phase they moved into Europe, starting with Scandinavia and going on to the Benelux countries and Germany. In 1966 the industry's total exports, including trucks, exceeded 250,000 vehicles, and in 1967 360,000, of which nearly 225,000 were private cars. The Americans have been Japan's best customers, taking 62,000 automobiles. Toyota has sold more cars in the United States than either Renault or Simca, thanks to the success of its Corona. In 1966 Australia bought 31,000 Japanese cars, South Africa 16,000 and Thailand 14,000. During the 1967 automobile shows in Paris and London the Honda sports car (N360 and N600) caused a sensation and at the same time provoked what an English magazine called "an anxious rage" in the bosoms of certain English manufacturers. Honda has set up a network of two hundred and fifty German agencies. The Japanese exported 406,250 private cars in 1968.

The same year saw the appearance of the Mazda sports car in Europe, and its rotary piston engine, an improvement on the German Wankel, caused a great deal of comment. In spite of quotas and customs duties, the Honda, as the Hong Kong *Far Eastern Economic Review* observed in the summer of 1968, is making its way into the Common Market countries. Honda competes with Fiat, and it is said that Fiat will no longer allow any Japanese to visit its factories. In Australia and South Africa it is the productions of B.M.C. and Volkswagen that suffer the most from Japanese competition. In 1968 the target for Japanese sales in the United States was already over a hundred thousand cars. In 1971, between 20 and 30 percent of the Japanese output will be exported. Great Britain foresees that, in 1972, fifty thousand "Made in Japan" cars will invade the country.

In this international competition the two major Japanese manufacturers—Toyota and Nissan—are at least capable of standing up to the great foreign companies as far as quantity is concerned. In 1965 Toyota held the twelfth rank among the world's automobile producers, in 1966 the ninth, and in 1967 sixth, coming after General Motors, Ford, Chrysler, Fiat and Volkswagen; Nissan, maker of the Datsun, came eighth. (These positions are based on total output, including trucks.) But the Japanese automobile industry is expanding a great deal faster than that of the European countries, because of its huge home market, which is still far from being saturated. It also has the quite outstanding feature of never having experienced a single strike for more than ten years! "We're too busy to find time for such things," observed a Nissan engineer. In this respect the European and American manufacturers are at a disadvantage, compared with their Japanese rivals.

The outlook is favorable. But it must be pointed out that the Japanese car industry has weaknesses and serious difficulties that make one wonder whether all will go as well as the Japanese makers suppose. The chief weakness is the almost ridiculously large number of manufacturers—there were twelve in 1965 and there were still ten in 1968—competing furiously among themselves. The result is an excessive number of various models turned out in far too small numbers and a superfluity of cars that are all very like one another, all competing in the same class, particularly that of the 1,000-cc. family models—no less than seven companies produce them. There are very few models that reach a production of twenty thousand a month. The two major firms completely dominate the market; in 1968 they left the others only one third of the home sales and 10 percent of the exports. It would be to the advantage of the medium-sized companies, such as Mazda, Mitsubishi Automobiles, Fuji Automobiles and Isuzu, to merge with the smaller firms, and the smaller firms would be well advised to disappear, since they are not strong enough to keep up in the competition.

A second problem, linked to the first, is the inevitable offensive of foreign automobiles in Japan as soon as the barriers against foreign capital and the importation of American and European cars are lifted. Concentration and liberalization: these, then, are the Japanese car industry's two great problems for the immediate future, and their solution will call for still further transformations and still greater efforts, which I shall refer to later on. In the coming years these problems will also apply to the last, the most recent of the "spearhead" industries.

This is an industry of whose birth and enormous future we have yet to speak—Japanese atomic energy.

In twenty years atom-bombed Japan has become atom-powered Japan—in other words, a country that can in its turn master the atom and make use of it, peaceful use. This is a striking symbol of the metamorphosis of a country that in less than a quarter of a century has passed from utter desolation to a position of overwhelming economic power.

But let there be no mistake about it. Here for once we find Japan quite far behind the other great powers, and here the "advantage of late starting" does not seem particularly obvious when it is compared with the difficulty of catching up with the huge advance of those who began first. Atom-bombed Japan was a heavy burden to atom-powered Japan, partly because years were required for the regaining of the industrial level that would allow the country to embark upon the use of atomic energy, and partly because both the traumatic experience of Hiroshima and the 1945 veto upon rearmament delayed Japan's start in the realm of even pacific atomic power.

This beginning dates only from 1957 and 1958, when several of the most powerful industrial groups began to take an interest in nuclear energy. Each working on its own, Mitsubishi, Hitachi, Sumitomo, Mitsui and Dai Ichi set many of their subsidiary companies to work on the study of nuclear problems—of atomic theory, Western achievements, plans for the development of the new industry in Japan and the manufacture of the necessary plant, the setting up of small experimental reactors and so forth. The Japanese had no illusions about their being able to produce any original work in atomic science for a long time. Before setting off on their nuclear career, each of the groups I have mentioned took care to come to an agreement with some foreign company that had been concerned with nuclear power for many years: General Electric in the case of Mitsui and Hitachi, Westinghouse for Mitsubishi, and British General Electric for Dai Ichi. Sumitomo did not manage to bring off a similar deal with any great American company, and in 1968 it provisionally retired from the race.

While these manufacturers of nuclear equipment were making their preparations, the consumers—that is to say, the nine great electric companies that divide Japan between them—were also making their plans and preparations for the nuclear generating stations of the future. To begin with they, together with certain manufacturers of electrical equipment, came to an agreement for the setting up of the Japan Atomic Power Company, whose function was to import the first reactors; these machines would provide the Japanese technicians with experience until the time when the country could produce its own atomic plant.

So it was this company that built the two first important nuclear reactors, both of them being based on equipment bought abroad. The first was built on the coast north of Tokyo, at Tokai Mura; the center houses a Calder Hall reactor bought from the English. I may add that the builders had a rough time of it, because there were all sorts of difficulties and unforeseen snags that delayed their work, and the station cost much more than the estimated price. It began to function in May, 1965, and on September 1, 1966, it produced the first commercial nuclear-energy electricity Japan had ever known. Since July, 1967, it has been producing at its full capacity of 166 megawatts. The Japan Atomic Power Company's second reactor was built in 1969 under license from General Electric on the Tsuruga Peninsula on the Sea of Japan; it is a "boiling water" type with an estimated output of 322 megawatts.

The end of 1970 saw the completion of two other reactors. One is being built by Mitsubishi at Fukushima, north of Tokyo, for the Tokyo Electric Power Company; this is also a boiling-water type manufactured under license from General Electric, and it will have a capacity of 340 megawatts. The other is for the Kansai Electric Power Company and is a pressurized-water reactor made under license from Westinghouse; its capacity is to be 340 megawatts, and it is being built at Mihama, near the Tsuruga atomic station. It is worth pointing out that these two electricity companies, which supply the Tokyo and Osaka regions, are the biggest private electric concerns in the world.

In 1971–1972 the construction of more and more new reactors will begin, and by 1976 there will be sixteen altogether. Japan will then rank among the leading atomic powers as far as commercial nuclear electricity is concerned, for in 1976 they will supply about 9,000 megawatts—some 11 percent of the country's consumption of current. According to the plan that the Japanese Atomic Energy Commission published in 1967, nuclear energy should produce a total of 30 to 40 million kilowatts in 1985; and this will provide 30 percent of the current required.

As we have seen, until now all the reactors that have been installed or that are being set up are based upon the use of American licenses— or of English, in the case of Tokai Mura. But for the years that follow this period of learning and experiment on foreign models, the Japanese industrial groups concerned are preparing for another phase in which there will be a steady development of purely Japanese atomic equipment. The country's principal aim is to provide itself with surgenerators (or surregenerators), because these will free Japan from its dependence upon the United States for its supplies of enriched uranium. The plans foresee an experimental reactor in 1973, and then in 1977 the first Japanese accelerated-neutron surgenerator, or fast breeder. To achieve this the industrial groups and the government set up the Atomic Reactor and Fuel Development Corporation in 1967.

In the atomic industry France and Japan have begun in a particularly interesting cooperation. Both countries will be in roughly the same situation as regards the experimental prototype planned for 1973, but France is somewhat ahead, having already learned from the French "Rapsodie" reactor that went into operation in 1967. Both countries are in a position to gain from the other's research. Japan has therefore signed an agreement with France according to which the French experts will report on the first Japanese experimental reactor. Furthermore, another agreement signed in December, 1968, states that French and Japanese atomic physicists are to exchange information and collaborate in general research, more specifically in fundamental research on sodium, equipment, and the precautions needed for this kind of reactor, which is cooled by liquid sodium—a difficult process. This collaboration goes hand in hand with the exchange of considerable numbers of experts; more than a hundred Japanese scientists had already studied in France before the end of 1968.

Japan is also making several other moves to prepare for the development of its peaceful atomic industry:

1. The construction of diffusion plant. In order to be less dependent upon America the Japanese technicians would like to develop their own process for the enrichment of uranium. They are

therefore planning the construction of a gaseous diffusion plant in Japan that will do just this.

2. The manufacture of uranium bars. Five great companies have set about this task, and in 1975 they will produce five hundred tons of bars. This figure will double by 1980, and in 1985 they will turn out two thousand tons; with the use of a fast breeder this will satisfy the whole of the Japanese demand.

3. The building of a cyclotron (atom smasher). This was decided in principle in February, 1967, but it has not yet started. It is said in Tokyo that the machine will be the biggest in the world, outclassing the cyclotron at Brookhaven in the United States.

4. The building of a ship propelled by atomic power. This was begun at the end of 1968, the vessel was launched in June, 1969, and it is to come into service at the beginning of 1972. It is based on Japanese technology and it will make Japan the fourth country to have a ship of this kind, coming after the United States, Soviet Russia and West Germany. This 8,300-ton ship is designed to carry uranium ore.

5. The use of nuclear energy in the steelworks. There is a danger that Japan will run short of coking coal when steel production reaches the level of 100 million tons a year; to deal with this situation the Japanese are conducting research into the possibility of using the direct blast of the high-temperature gases produced by nuclear combustion in certain furnaces. It may also be possible to replace ordinary electric current in the steelworks with that which reactors generate.

When Japan has a fast breeder, the potentialities of a given quantity of uranium will be increased by two or three hundred times, since equipment of this kind goes on running indefinitely on the same charge of fuel; it does not have to be renewed. When this happens the two or three thousand tons of uranium that Japan can find at home (these are the estimated figures for the meager quantities of pure metal that the country is likely to provide) will represent a very considerable wealth, perhaps sufficient for all needs. But until the epoch of the fast breeders comes around, Japan has to import and above all will go on having to import great amounts of uranium for use in its big reactors. The chief deposits of uranium in Japan itself lie in the Ningyo

Pass, between the Tottori and Okayama prefectures, and in the Gifu prefecture, where the metal was discovered in April, 1968. Canada is the main foreign country from which Japan buys uranium; a very important deal has recently been concluded, according to which $200 million worth of ore will be supplied over a period of ten years. Japan has also secured the right to prospect for uranium in the Lake Elliot region of Canada. And, finally, the country has come to a similar agreement with Australia.

The Japanese and Canadian uranium will be sent to the United States to be turned into enriched uranium in the American diffusion plants. An agreement that was valid until the end of 1968 laid down that to begin with the Americans would provide Japan with 2.7 tons of enriched uranium and 6 kilograms of plutonium; these were annual amounts and they were to be continued for ten years. A fresh agreement, signed in February, 1968, covered the thirty years up to 1997; according to this the Americans will sell the Japanese a total of 161 tons of enriched uranium. This is the largest amount of the metal that the United States has ever contracted to sell to a foreign country, and it means that Japanese reactors are certain of their fuel for the next thirty years. Part of this enriched uranium may come from metal that Japan will buy elsewhere and send to America to be processed. Furthermore, the agreement provides for the supply of 365 kilograms of plutonium over the same period, for research and for the development of peaceful nuclear energy. The International Atomic Energy Authority will continue to supervise the peaceful use of these supplies, as it does at present.

What part will nuclear electricity play in the solution of Japan's problems concerning sources of energy? The Japanese themselves estimate that in twenty years' time the country's total consumption of energy will increase fourfold. But the share of hydroelectric energy in this total will drop from 11.3 percent to just over 4 percent, and that from coal from 27 to 9 percent. Oil, on the other hand, will supply not 58 but 75 percent, and atomic energy will rise from 0 to 10 percent. In 1985 30 percent of Japanese electrical energy will be provided by nuclear generating stations. Taking everything into account it seems that unless there is some unlikely discovery of very important oil deposits in Japan itself, the country will be even more dependent upon imports for its energy than it is today. Atomic power will diminish this dependence to some extent (it would be far greater without nuclear energy) but will not do away with it altogether. This is only another way of saying that the smooth running of "factory Japan" will call even more imperatively for the preservation of peace and international trade.

To round off this description of Japan's setting out on its nuclear career, I should add an important achievement that dates from 1968. On May 17 the Japan Atomic Energy Research Institute (JAERI) announced that Japanese scientists had for the first time produced plutonium. The communiqué went on to say that they had produced eighteen grams of 95-percent-pure plutonium 239, using purely Japanese techniques, during the reprocessing of exhausted uranium from the Tokai Mura reactor. In giving this information the JAERI made use of an expression as concise as it is dramatic: "This means that it is now technically possible for Japan to make an atomic bomb with home-produced plutonium." They took care to add in equally laconic terms that the country had, however, no right to do so. The communiqué offered no further elaboration on these remarks.

In view of Japan's total commitment to a new industrial revolution and its determination to be one of the most advanced countries as far as the highly scientific industries of the second half of the twentieth century are concerned, it is perhaps surprising that Japan has kept out of the one activity that is after all the very spearhead of progress—the conquest of space.

Not that Japan, to be sure, has been wholly absent. Indeed, the country has even obtained some results that in some respects are looked upon as quite remarkable. For whereas the United States and the Soviet Union devote prodigious sums of money and the vast effort of great numbers of their scientists to space research, the Japanese have brought off the remarkable feat of making interesting discoveries over a wide range with a trifling budget and with very small teams who have had to work with almost no support from either the government or public opinion. But there is a striking contrast between Japan's effort in all other fields and its modest achievements in this. A meagerly equipped laboratory housing the obscure labors of a young Tokyo University professor, unfurnished with money or equipment; an almost ragged band of students or young research workers gathered around him, driving a beat-up old truck to the stretch of waste land that was their Cape Kennedy; rockets so light and thin that they were called "pencils"—this was what Japanese space research looked like when it first got under way in 1955.

Nevertheless, in the end the pencil-sized rockets excited widespread interest because of the fact that they represented by no means inconsiderable scientific experiments at a comparatively small cost. By 1958 the Japanese research workers and their rockets were already collaborating in the study of solar rays and spatial radiation. In 1961 a three-stage rocket of the Kappa type weighing a ton and a half and using solid fuel reached a height of 220 miles. In 1964 a Lambda rocket soared three times higher, and in 1966 it reached 1,125 miles. The pencil of the early days had become a kind of aerial torpedo, the forty-ton four-stage Mu rocket, well over sixty feet long; and since 1967 a whole new series of experiments have been made with its assistance.

With a shoestring budget, the independent research workers of Tokyo University obtained such striking results that finally the government authorities began to move. An already existing semiofficial body, the Agency for Science and Technology, turned over a number of scientists to research on the problems of space. A new commission for the development of space science was set up, with coordinating functions, and at the same time executive functions were entrusted to another new body, the Agency for Space Development. And then in the fiscal year 1968–1969 the first real budget for space research came into being, together with a program which is to be carried out by the research workers of both the university and the Agency.

For Japan it is now a question of embarking upon the adventure of sending satellites into orbit. According to the program, the Tokyo University specialists should send up twelve experimental satellites between 1971 and 1975, while between the present time and 1974 the Space Agency should launch thirteen for the purposes of scientific research. The successive stages are, first, putting into orbit a satellite at an altitude of about 250 to 300 miles in 1970; next, orbiting a really big satellite more than 6,000 miles up in 1971; and then a very high static satellite at over 22,000 miles in 1972. Several existing centers for the study of space are to be enlarged: there is one at Kagoshima (in Kyushu, the southern island), another at Tanegashima (an island still farther south), and others at Michikawa and Noshiro, in the northeast of the country on the Sea of Japan.

It is true that as far as space is concerned the Japanese would find it hard to feel the same pride that they legitimately display in other sectors. Their space research is still modest. The coordination is not yet well enough organized; research does not dispose of adequate funds and it is held back by the kind of rivalry that exists between Tokyo University and the Agency for Science and Technology. Above all, one vital element seems to be lacking—a straightforward decision, taken at the highest level, to make an all-out effort. Japan has not yet really joined the race; that is the heart of the matter. And the puzzled foreign observer wonders what can be behind this delay. Is the explanation to be found in some kind of carelessness, in an oversight or an error of judgment, or in technical incompetence? If so, this would quite certainly be the first time that we could accuse the Japanese of lack of ability in the realm of industrial techniques.

As I see it, the explanation lies elsewhere. It arises out of the very nature of the strategy for the development of the new Japan and involves a wider explanation that covers the whole of the present Japanese success. And this explanation can be summed up in a few words: Japan systematically refrains from any undertaking whose sole or chief aim is prestige. Progress in space will play a very important part in the future; for the moment it does not seem to have been given any urgent priority. Still less is it a matter for priority when it is a question of joining the race to the moon or of interplanetary exploration, for the Japanese look upon these as undertakings primarily concerned with prestige. The country distrusts ventures of this kind, even if they could be afforded. In the same way Japan will have nothing to do with greatness that is based upon armaments or the atomic bomb.

Finally, a postscript to this discussion. I have not attempted to draw a complete picture of Japanese industry but merely to describe the spearhead of enterprises. A complete picture would call for a detailed account of the rear guard, which is made up of the backward sector in the small and medium-sized industries which work on the craftsman scale rather than that of real industry. Between the two extremes I should also have to speak of the powerful array of the ordinary industries, those just behind the leaders. Here the gaps and the weaknesses are few: coal is losing ground as it is everywhere else; the film industry has been in a critical state for some years; airplane manufacture is still only at the budding stage (and this will no doubt be one of the successes arising from a late start that the Japanese have in store).

In other fields, on the contrary, there are a great many strong positions, and they cover the whole range of the industries of a great modern country in all its variety and complexity: railroad stock and equipment, telecommunications equipment, public works, agricultural machinery, pharmaceuticals, plastics, and synthetic resins. Industrial machinery is overwhelmed with orders coming from other sectors. The machine-tool industry has made a great leap forward, increasing its output by 63 percent in 1967. In heavy electrical equipment, Hitachi took the world's tenth place in 1966, while Matsushita stood fourteenth and Toshiba sixteenth. And lastly, there is the textile industry, which saw the coming of man-made fibers in good time and carried out a wholesale reconversion; Japan now holds second place in the world production of artificial textiles.

9.

Greatness Without the Bomb

The economy first: that is the law of present-day Japan; the economy first, and politics afterward. Indeed, one result of the economy's dominating position has been a kind of devaluation of politics, beginning with the politics concerned with home affairs. This is not treated at any length in these pages; it is comparatively uninteresting for the foreign observer, and even the Japanese themselves are not very deeply concerned, however much space it may take up in their newspapers. For the citizen of Tokyo or Osaka there is a profound difference between his interest in the country's economy, which for about twenty-five years has meant both a continual improvement in his daily life and a series of records and successes on a worldwide scale, and that which he may feel for politics, which has remained motionless for the same period—unmoving and difficult for nonprofessionals to understand, arousing no deep response among the working masses.

This is in no way to condemn Japanese democracy as a whole. Today the Japanese are profoundly attached to the democratic order of things. The oppression and abuses they suffered during the military period have left a lasting memory, and the people have recovered a deep and steady love of freedom. They carry out their electoral duties with the utmost conscientiousness, and during parliamentary elections the voting is usually remarkably heavy. It might also be suggested that the immobility of Japanese political life has its good side; it is just the result of a desirable state of affairs—that is to say, ministerial stability and continuity in the interaction of the political parties. For twenty years and more the electors have unfailingly maintained the Liberal-Democrats in power; this is a fairly moderate, conservative party, thoroughly attached to the democratic system. The political stability has been exceedingly favorable to the country's economic reconstruction, and this reconstruction has taken place under the aegis of the Liberal-Democratic Party.

Yet as already noted, the basic fact is that in reality it is not the politicians who steer the country but the business and industrial managers, together with their allies, the bureaucrats, whose minds are firmly turned toward the problems of economic development. Money governs elections, and often the politicians are no more than the mouthpieces, the front men, of the business world. Since the dominant position of the Right Wing has never been seriously threatened, its political activity amounts to no more than bickering between the many factions within the majority itself; its chief care is to make sure of a due succession of figures capable of assuming ministerial functions, so that each of the various smaller groups has its fair share of the sweets of office. The Left Wing, which has not the least chance of coming into power, is also torn by faction squabbles that turn about ideological points or personal rivalries.

The two-party system seems to exist, but the Right Wing remains perpetually in office, and the Left never gets there at all. Politics is a specialized calling, confined to a narrow circle that has little contact with the electors, and the political specialists have not much prestige in the eyes of those who voted them into place. Disagreeable incidents between the unconquerable Right and the powerless Left are frequent in the Diet; sometimes they are ludicrous and sometimes violent. Although there is no serious opposition to the parliamentary system, the public feels little respect for it. The political parties (the conservative Liberal-Democrats and the Socialists are the most important of them) are in fact leaders with no following, a high command that has no rank and file. Throughout the country their party machinery comes to life only during elections. Being a paid-up card-carrying member of a political party is something quite uncommon in Japan. The Socialist Party does not possess 100,000 members, and it is likely that the Liberal-Democrats hardly number more. For a long while the Communist Party was the only one to pay great attention to having genuine active members, and even so it has no more than 300,000 at the outside. Recently membership recruiting has also been undertaken by the Komeito, a new Buddhist political party.

Although they are in the majority and although they are in power, the Liberal-Democrats have little standing, even among those who vote for them, because the party is worn out by its twenty years in office and has often been shaken by thoroughly distasteful scandals involving the buying of votes and bribery. The paradox is that people go on voting for it. The chief explanation is that they do so from motives to do with the economy; the average voter is frightened of the dangerous economic adventure that a change to socialism would mean, and in fact he votes to perpetuate the advance that, in his eyes, is firmly linked to government by the managers. As to the Left, whether we consider the Socialist Party, the little Democratic Socialist Party (which really belongs to the center), or the Communists, its comparative lack of success is probably largely owing to the fact that it looks upon politics as more important than the economy, and ideology as more important than anything else at all, whereas ideology is of little interest to the voters, and in any case it is put to them in a very obscure and cloudy manner. In order to make headway, the Socialist Party would have had to possess imagination enough to conceive a new up-to-date socialism, adapted to an affluent society and working for the practical development of the community within the framework of collective existence. Instead of this, the Socialists have obstinately remained in the realm of ideology; furthermore, within this same realm their factions fight bitterly among themselves. This course of action means that they abandon to the Right Wing, all the electoral advantages of a solid policy of economic expansion directed at raising the standard of living.

During these last years the only opposition party that has brought something new to the political life of Japan, and has begun to look like a possible long-term threat to the Right's monopoly, is the Komeito; its name means "the party of clean government." It is the political expression of a recently formed Buddhist sect, the Soka Gakkai, which is carrying out a kind of revolution where religion is concerned. Its exceedingly violent proselytism and the way it conducts its popular propaganda (its opponents accuse it of using methods not unlike those of totalitarian regimes) have rendered it the most vigorous, the most prosperous, and the most debatable of all the sects.

Thanks to the support of the Soka Gakkai the Komeito has made steady progress in the elections, and it now ranks third in the Diet.

It is said to cherish the ambition of achieving a majority in the ten or fifteen years ahead.

A good deal of the Soka Gakkai's success arises from its active, efficient drive for the improvement of its members' economic and material position. It recruits its rank and file among the poorer classes of what is left of underdeveloped Japan—peasants and very small-scale craftsmen, day laborers, the members of the unprofitable miniature family businesses, and so forth. Until then none of these humble people had been of the least interest to any of the political parties, but the Soka Gakkai with its dynamic system of mutual assistance is bringing them a better life. The Komeito owes some of its rising popularity to its attempts at cleaning up the political and administrative world and to its struggle against financial corruption—all of which amounts to another way of giving the economy more importance than politics. This combination of a moral program with promises of material progress is well calculated to charm the many Japanese who are looking for guides in the hurry and turmoil of the present world.

There are violent struggles between these different parties and within each separate group, and this may give the impression that the country is deeply divided by political considerations. But as we have already emphasized, Japan is in fact more united than it seems, for as soon as the question at issue has to do with the economy rather than politics, a broad unanimity of opinion reappears. And this is also the case where foreign policy is concerned.

The overwhelming importance of the economy is no less apparent in Japan's foreign relations. In this area there is a striking contrast between the country's intense activity on the economic side and its holding back and even sometimes its sluggishness in diplomatic action. The practical part that Japan plays on the world's stage bears no relation to its industrial and commercial power, which every day grows more evident on the international markets. This is true to such an extent that it is possible to speak of a certain devaluation, in Japanese public opinion, of foreign policy—or at least the expression can be applied to foreign policy as it is understood by the other great world powers, which base their action upon ideological alliances and calculations of military strength.

At the very beginning of the postwar period, Japan's absence from the scene was easily explainable by its defeat. Until the San Francisco peace treaty, which was signed in 1951 and which came into force in 1952, Japan was a country subjected to the military occupation of its conquerors and almost entirely cut off from the outside world. Indeed, it seemed to be condemned to a lowered international standing forever. The 1947 constitution, most of which was dictated by General MacArthur, the all-powerful head of the army of occupation, forbade Japan ever to possess armed forces again or ever to have recourse to war. "Aspiring sincerely to an international peace based on justice and order, the Japanese people forever renounce war as a sovereign right of the nation, and the threat or the use of force as a means of settling international disputes." Such is the text of Article 9, the keystone of the constitution. A second paragraph adds, "In order to accomplish the aim of the preceding paragraph, land, sea, and air forces, as well as other war potential, will never be maintained. The right of belligerency of the state will not be recognized."

But five years after the defeat there was an astonishing reversal. It is almost unbelievable, but it was the Americans themselves who asked Japan to violate Article 9 or even to get rid of it altogether. Not only did the peace treaty put an end to the occupation, give Japan back its freedom, and provide the country with the United States as an ally, but the Americans proposed or rather begged that Japan should rearm. For indeed everything had changed: the cold war was now at its height, the revolution in China had triumphed, and the Communists had invaded South Korea. America released Japan from all its shackles and asked it to return to the Asian scene as quickly as possible, and even to return as an armed power.

The most paradoxical aspect of all this was that the Japanese refused. Tokyo has never forgotten the historic interview that took place in January, 1951, at the height of the Korean invasion—a meeting between John Foster Dulles, the American Secretary of State, and the old premier Yoshida, who is looked upon as the father of the democratic Japan. Dulles, who was very pessimistic about the outcome of the Korean fighting, thumped the table with his fist and repeated, "You must rearm!" With an ironic look from behind his spectacles, Yoshida mentioned the Japanese people's sincere attachment to Article 9 concerning perpetual disarmament and politely repeated his quiet refusal. His chief argument was that there was a total incompatibility between Japanese rearmament and the health of the Japanese economy, which was just beginning to get on its feet again. He granted *le Monde* an interview at this time, and in the course of it he humorously remarked, "One solitary Japanese torpedo boat, and there is our Japan torpedoed!"

Nevertheless, in the end the old statesman did make an important concession: acknowledging the state of urgency arising from the Korean War, he agreed to set up what he called a "reserve police force." But he did not wish it to have many members, and those few he wanted to be poorly equipped. At the same time he took care to announce that this was not an army but a police force and that, unless there were a nationally accepted constitutional reform, Article 9 would remain the guiding principle, the law, of Japanese policy. Was he sincere? Did he really want neither to cross nor to do away with this barrier that closed the road to rearmament? Or was the creation of this new force merely a hypocritical stratagem to disguise his determination to rearm? The last is what the Socialist and Communist Left maintains, and ever since then these parties have continually accused the conservatives of two crimes: (1) that under the Yoshida government they violated the constitution and (2) that under the subsequent governments they turned Japanese rearmament into a more and more hateful reality. For, says the Left, these governments have gradually strengthened the new armed forces and have reopened the door to the military clique.

On the first point, it is difficult not to feel that the accusation is well based. Article 9 is plain and categorical, just as the Allies' intentions were when they occupied the archipelago in 1945: they wanted to turn the Japanese into a nation that should forever be deprived of the use of arms. Unconvincing sophisms had to be used to circumvent Article 9, and the use of them was in itself a confession that the intention was to get around the prohibition. Much the same applies to the great argument that the conservatives have been producing ever since 1951, with the clumsy support of the Americans (who in any case seem to have invented it): that every nation has the natural right to legitimate self-defense, that therefore this right could not be done away with by Article 9, and that what this article meant to forbid was offensive—not defensive—forces. The value of this argument is self-evident. If a Western court had to take it into consideration it would probably not stand up for long, and old Yoshida's decision would be held unconstitutional.

As to the second point, it would appear that there is a good deal of exaggeration in the statement that rearmament is a fact and that it has gone so far as to put the military men "back into circulation." To be sure, it would be dangerous to deny the peril that does exist, once the first step has been taken in the forbidden direction and once the principle itself has been flouted. But let us also realize that in fact Japan has not moved far in that direction at all. Once Yoshida and his successors had violated the prohibition, they then displayed a most unexpected caution, as though they were frightened of treading farther onto forbidden ground and as though they were thoroughly aware of the strong disapproval aroused by their action. They had violated the constitution, but they hardly profited at all from their violation. Right away they sensed the nation's very strong and deeply felt resistance to rearmament, a resistance by no means confined to the narrow circle of the Socialists and Communists and their followers but far more widely spread and apparent even in the ranks of the Right Wing. They saw that unless a constitutional reform abolished Article 9, they possessed only a very narrow margin of action. They have been afraid of the Left Wing's unfailing watchfulness. As a result, the new Japan's "army," if it can be called an army, has been kept to very modest proportions, and the conservatives have never dared and (at least up until now) have probably never wished to make the clear-cut decision to move on to a genuine rearmament.

It is true that the reserve police force has shown that it is something more than a mere police organization, for it changed its name first to Security Force and then to the Self-Defense Force. It is also true that this body has been strengthened and has increased in size. But what do its numbers amount to in fact? For more than fifteen years they remained below the allotted ceiling, although that limit was not particularly elevated—180,000 men for the land forces. The ceiling was reached only quite recently. In round figures the force now amounts to 261,000, including 45,000 in its air force and 36,000 in its navy; and 261,000 is really a very low figure for a country of a hundred million inhabitants. Two thirds of the thousand-odd planes of its air force are out of date. The navy amounts to 144 tons of shipping, and the biggest vessels are no more than escort destroyers.

The men at the head of these armed forces are civilians. Tokyo has no War Ministry or Ministry of National Defense, but only a Defense Agency, under a civilian chief. His seven most important subordinates are also civilians. The Agency has a staff of three thousand civilians and only forty military men, and not one of these forty holds a key post. The chiefs of staff appear only at the third level of the hierarchy. The Military School and the Staff College are both headed by civilians. The last officers left over from the former wartime army are now retiring. The link that once existed between the army and the throne is now no more than a memory. The emperor has never once reviewed these new troops.

How long will this admirable caution last, and are there no Japanese who feel that it is out of date? These questions are discussed further on. But once again I must emphasize this basic fact: ever since 1945, the very great majority of Japanese have been deeply attached to disarmament, deeply opposed to any constitutional reform in the direction of rearmament, on guard against the least attempt at re-militarizing the country, and on the watch for any possible return of the soldiers to power. This state of mind, which has now lasted more than twenty years, is the outcome of sincerely held pacifist convictions, and its strength is in proportion to the event that brought it into being—the atomic bomb of Hiroshima.

Japan bears the atomic scar in its heart and in its soul. It is a wound that has never entirely healed. Even now it still hurts every day. It is not talked about, but it can never be forgotten. The Americans meant the bomb to be both a punishment for the past and a lesson for the future, a lesson upon the horror of war of every kind. The Japanese would not accept the idea of punishment, but the lesson went home. Its effect has been greater than anything that was ever expected. Perhaps it is easy for Americans to choose to forget; perhaps it is easy to tell the Japanese, brashly and unwisely, that "Everything is changed now, and we authorize you to rearm." The Japanese are the first to look upon this request as a piece of unblushing, shocking effrontery. It is not possible for them to have so short and so fickle a memory. Not a single prime minister for the last twenty years and more, including Yoshida, has dared to announce either rearmament or even the mere intention of rearming. Not a single one has stated or even vaguely hinted that Japan in its turn should possesss the atomic bomb. Any minister who had made such a statement would immediately have been swept away by the unanimous protests of the whole nation.

As they put it, the Japanese have an "atomic allergy," and this allergy has in fact an influence on the whole of their foreign policy. They are not only unwilling to have anything to do with atomic weapons but they are also opposed to conventional rearmament. Furthermore, if we look deeply into the question we shall see that until now they have been "allergic" to the carrying out of any foreign policy that is based upon the time-honored processes of international politics and diplomacy—ideological conflicts, political maneuvers, alliances and blocs, and the threat or use of force.

As soon as the country was free, Japan adopted as its foreign policy the having of no foreign policy, or at least the avoidance of all commitment and flight from all international responsibility. The country not only refused to go any distance along the road of genuine rearmament, in spite of American pressure and urging; but also escaped from any system of alliance, such as that with other Asian capitals, including Seoul and Taipei, which Washington had considered for some years. This would have meant an extension of the series of regional alliances with the United States that ring the Communist powers around: NATO, CENTO and SEATO exist, and they would have been completed by a pact covering eastern Asia; PATO, as some people already called it—the Pacific Alliance Treaty Organization—would have carried the ring right around the world. The Tokyo governments would never have any part of it. Their only membership in any system of collective security is in the United Nations, and they certainly show the greatest interest in this organization. But even in the UN their policy is remarkably effaced. They consistently refuse to join in any undertaking that implies military intervention, such as the peacekeeping corps in Israel or the sending of an international force to the Congo.

Japanese public opinion always reacts with the utmost hypersensitivity to the slightest suggestion that Japanese forces might one day be sent overseas, even if it were only on a pacific errand. It would no doubt rise up violently against any government that actively disregarded this feeling. All this means that Japan has remained at a great distance from the cold war, particularly the cold war in Asia. It has remained even more detached from the "hot" wars that have flared up in its neighborhood. When the Korean War was raging at the doors of Japan, the country made all it could out of it, from the economic point of view, but never stirred a finger to defend South Korea. The same applies to the war in Vietnam. A rumor in Tokyo that a few civilian sailors had unloaded goods in a Vietnamese port was enough to let loose a flood of angry journalism, denouncing an alleged Japanese participation in the conflict.

The one and only alliance Japan has signed is its treaty with the United States, which was concluded in 1951 and which is accompanied by a security pact, renewed in 1960 and extended in 1970. The American alliance, to be sure, is at the center of Japan's foreign relations, and it represents a most important exception to the rule of noncommitment and nonparticipation in the international politico-military game. But in fact Japan's part in the alliance on the political—and even more on the military—plane has throughout been entirely negative. The mutual assistance called for by the treaty has never come into effect; the only form of aid that has functioned at all is one-way assistance, from America to Japan. The argument that the United States itself was in danger in Korea or Vietnam and that their Japanese allies should have come to their help has never been accepted. Tokyo finds it absolutely unthinkable that Japanese should fly to the rescue of Americans in Seoul or go to fight side by side with them in the jungles of Indochina.

Of course, it would be unbecoming for the Americans to say that their Japanese alliance has been of no use to them in their Pacific and Asian policies during the last twenty years. The treaty gave them air, naval and military bases that have been of the greatest value in time of peace and even more in time of war. It would have been impossible to fight the Korean War without the rear base of the Japanese archipelago; and the war in Vietnam would have been even more arduous than it is. But the Japanese attitude has always been that these wars were none of Japan's business. The alliance obliged the country to put up with them, but it could not oblige it to do more. Many a time the Americans have more or less openly shown their irritation at this passive behavior. In the same way their patience has often been sorely tried when they have heard even government circles in Tokyo criticizing American policy in Asia and when they have seen the Japanese keeping markedly aloof from this policy—over the question of relations with North Vietnam, for example, or with North Korea, or even more with People's China.

The China of Mao Tse-tung has almost always been treated with great consideration by Japan. Japan has almost never spoken of it as an enemy; China is rarely criticized by officials, and indeed it is often held up for praise in the Japanese press. If to all this we add the Left Wing's hostility to the American alliance, the violent demonstrations against it in Tokyo in 1960, and the fresh outburst in 1969 against the 1970 renewal of the treaty, it becomes understandable that the Americans, behind their ostensible satisfaction with their relations with Japan, should often be filled with a gnawing doubt and uneasiness about their ally. Privately they wonder whether Japan may not be an associate whose trustworthiness is not to be relied upon: Will Japan just go on profiting from the security we provide without ever doing anything in return? Will Japan ever come to understand that, now it is economically strong enough, its duty is to support us more actively in international politics? Will Japan ever take its share in the tasks and the burdens assumed by the United States and the "free world," and raise its armed forces to an adequate level?

It seems to me that this way of stating the problem proves that the underlying motives that have until now actuated Japan are quite misunderstood. Once again, the country's experience with the atomic bomb is at the heart of its entire attitude. The bomb completely changed Japan's outlook; it is quite unlike ours. The country is already moving forward in a "postatomic" age, in a region "beyond the bomb" or, in other words, an age in which at all costs international relations must be built up again on new foundations and in which a new kind of understanding between the countries must be discovered unless we are all to perish in another Hiroshima.

Because it was Japan that had the bomb dropped on it, it knows some truths concerning this new age and this coming century that we, the Western countries, do not know with a full, total knowledge, for we do not know—we do not yet know—what it means to be atom-bombed. Japan knows far better than we do that from now on war is unthinkable and that unless we want civilization to vanish war must be wholly done away with, that the economic building up of the new world of the year 2000 and the development of trade to a hitherto unknown extent must be and shall be at the very heart of international life, and that in the future the only real power will be economic power. Some people believe that in this new age a country will be of importance only if it possesses atomic weapons, but this is not a really modern view, not a view that corresponds with the new realities of this present age of mankind. It is a view that still clings to out-of-date reasoning and calculation, and it is one that for the years to come quite certainly prepares the same disasters as we have known before, with the only difference that they will be even more savage. In the atomic age a country that wishes to be powerful must call upon the economy for its strength; it must no longer call upon armaments.

It may well be that the Japanese do not formulate these thoughts quite as clearly as this. As I have already observed, they rarely express general ideas in words, but these are the ideas they express in their lives and that they carry into practice, in spite of their clumsy violation of Article 9. That is why, when they are asked to go back to the old game of estimating relative strengths, their foreign outlook remains negative and tinged with a kind of noncompliance. But they do not leave it at that, they do not take refuge in static isolation; they turn toward a very different form of activity, one in which their approach is positive, wide open to the world and intensely dynamic. This activity consists of relying entirely—laying all their money—upon the economy, of launching themselves without the slightest reserve into international economic relations and foreign trade.

Once it is understood, Japan's attitude toward the rest of the world no longer seems to be deprived of all ambition. Immediately after its defeat, at a moment when it might have been thought utterly crushed by poverty and condemned to nothing but a humble rank forever after, Japan was already aiming at a fresh goal—that of making its economy catch up with the most advanced of the leading Western powers in the race of international competition. Once it had attained this goal, Japan raised its sights during the sixties and aimed at an even more lofty target; the country's ambition was now, by the strength of its economy, to reach the coveted third place among the world's great powers.

This is the true aim of the country as a whole. Here the rule of "all for the economy" unites the Japanese, just as it does where home politics are concerned. They all understand that their country's foreign policy and its relations with other countries must above all be an effort on the economic plane, an effort that is an extension of that which they exert at home. The task of building up a strong, prosperous, interior economy in a country with little in the way of natural resources, a country isolated in the Pacific, calls at the same time for an unremitting exterior effort in order to strengthen Japan's position still further in the matter of economic relations and international trade, to facilitate the country's access to raw materials, to expand its markets abroad, and to succeed in the peaceful battle of international competition.

How could Japan win this economic battle if it were to waste its strength as once it did in military battles or even in the mere preparation for them, in expeditions, or in projects solely designed to raise the country's standing? Here is a new key to the Japanese success, a key that must be added to those already discussed: part of the reason why Japan has made such astonishingly rapid progress is that it has escaped from the burden of continually increasing military budgets, from the arms race and, more widely, from the crushing expense of a policy of strength and prestige—from all of those burdens that weigh so heavily upon the other great powers.

One needs only compare the history of the other great powers since the war. The United States: an atomic arms race with intercontinental missiles and antimissile missiles, the cost of a powerful fleet and air force, the burden of a worldwide "policing" policy, cold war and military intervention, the war in Vietnam, and, if that were not enough, the cost of the race to the moon. . . . The Soviet Union: the same utterly disproportionate increase in nonproductive expenditure, armaments, atomic weapons, massive conventional armies, military support for the satellite states, and once again the race for the moon. . . . England: the labor of keeping up an imperial policy after the empire itself has been done away with, harassing "neocolonial" responsibilities, the cost of maintaining expensive bases east of Suez for years and years, the almost intolerable price of membership in the "atomic club." . . . France: the storms and the destruction of decolonization, war in Indochina, war in Algeria, and, when peace had come back, joining in the atomic and H-bomb race. . . . And then China: the economy of an overpopulated and still partly underdeveloped country crushed by expenditure on atomic weapons, the crippling economic effect of the strict rule of "policy first" both at home and abroad.

Compared with these countries how unburdened Japan appears, how free from these handicaps and how favorably placed for economic success! Japan runs in the race of international competition carrying as little weight as possible, while all its rivals are heavily loaded. In the first place, Japan no longer has any colonies; ever since 1945 the country has never had to worry about the least postcolonial responsibility. Very soon Japan realized that it should be grateful to its conquerors for their kindness in breaking up the empire; the country knows that every one of its former possessions would have become a hotbed of uprisings and war if it had remained under the Japanese flag. Japan would have had just as many "Algerian wars" on its hands as it had colonies, supposing it had been left any in Asia. But as things are, Japan has not conducted a single military expedition or fought a single war since 1945. Then again, it is the one great power that has not let itself be caught up in the more and more ruinous competition for atomic weapons. Finally, Japan has spent very little on its space program, consistent with its view of priorities. The country is realistic enough to feel no need whatsoever to go to the moon. When all its resources are put together, there is no surplus; everything is needed for the development of its own little territory.

However, there is the money that Japan does nevertheless devote to its "Self-Defense Force." Until the present these sums have been very moderate. A 1967 OECD report states that the percentage of Japanese military expenditure in relation to the state's total budget declined steadily from 1952 to 1962, dropping from 19.3 to 8.5 percent. In 1963–1964 the military budget represented 8.4 percent of the total budget, whereas in France it was 22, in Great Britain 26, in West Germany 34 and in the United States 53 percent. To complete this OECD report let us observe that the Japanese military budget for 1968–1969 was no more than 7.25 percent of the total.

The London Institute for Strategic Studies' report for the fiscal year 1966–1967 gave the following percentages for other countries' military expenditure as compared with gross national product: Japan, 0.9; West Germany, 3.6; France, 4.4; Great Britain, 6.4; the Soviet Union, 8.9; the United States, 9.2; China, 10. The per capita share of the same countries' annual military expenditure amounted to the following sums: $8 for each Chinese, $10 for the Japanese, $76 for the West German, $91 for the Frenchman, $120 for the Englishman, $129 for the Russian and $346 for each American. Lastly, military expenditure for the fiscal year 1966–1967 amounted to these figures: Japan, $0.963 billion; West Germany, $4.335 billion; France, $4.465 billion; Great Britain, $6.081 billion; China, $6.5 billion; U.S.S.R., $29.8 billion; and the United States, $67.95 billion. From these it appears that the top great power (the United States) and the second (the Soviet Union) spent respectively seventy and thirty times more on what they call their national defense budget than the third great power (Japan).

The saving achieved by Japan and the advantages the country derives from not imitating the other great powers in their traditional policy of strength are not to be measured merely by the budget figures for expenditure. There are a great many important advantages that cannot be put into figures: the fact that thousands of extra hands are available for positive, constructive work; that thousands of extra heads are devoted to progress by means of industry and trade; that industry, and particularly the heavy and engineering industries, instead of producing massive output for the stockpiling of war material, is working for the growth of production and of productive plant. A peace-loving policy produces what might be called more fallout than a policy of armament. What the economists term the cumulative effect of investment—the setting up of a new factory triggering off orders in all sorts of other branches of industry—operates to the full in Japan, with no loss in the direction of unproductive activity. Here we may really speak of what these same economists call a "virtuous circle" of investment—that is to say, a cumulative process of expansion the outcome of which, in the last analysis, is a rapid rise in the nation's standard of living.

And so much the better for Japan, after all, if the other great powers are so stupid or so enmeshed in out-of-date notions or in misadventures of their past history that they waste so many billions of dollars, so much work and energy, and so much intelligence and scientific ability in their search for a power based on physical strength. They leave Japan all the advantages of a unique monopoly—that of being the one power to follow a fresh policy that makes it the lightest, the most quickly moving and the most flexible of all the champions running in the race toward the year 2000. This is not the first time that Japan has gained from the mistakes, the muddles, or the violent conflicts of the

West. For the last hundred years, every time the West has squandered its strength in fighting, an Asian country on the other side of the world has at once profited from it, and this country has usually been Japan. The country's rise has come about partly because of the hostility between the members of the white man's world—World War I, for example, and then, between the two wars, the conflict between fascism and democracy in Europe. Every time the democracies retreated before Hitler, Japan instantly responded to the withdrawal by an advance in Asia.

Yet there was one occasion in the past when Japan was offered a completely different formula for success. Japan could have placed all its hopes on a policy of peace while the others placed theirs on war; it could have been the one country that grew rich by trade while all the rest were ruining themselves by violence. The nation's memory is filled with a bitter regret that it did not make that choice. The moment when it could have been taken was in 1941, and I was in Tokyo, following this little-known crisis of the days before Pearl Harbor. Half the world was already in a blaze. Japan was still undecided, but the alliance with Hitler was drawing it in the direction of war. And then suddenly, during the summer of 1941, when the country was yet at peace, it realized that it could still pursue a course that a wonderfully kind fate was offering: this was the adoption of a policy of shelving the alliance, coming to an understanding with Roosevelt, and, while the other powers were finally tearing one another to pieces, of becoming the one nation that carried on business and made money, the one peaceful trading nation in a world that had gone mad. A section of the zaibatsu, the trusts of those days, argued in favor of this policy. A handful of the remaining liberals led a campaign for it. Prince Konoe, the prime minister, was within a hair's breadth of putting this policy into operation. For a few weeks Japan could be felt to be hesitating, wavering between the two roads that destiny had opened before it, and then war carried the day.

"Oh, if only we had chosen peace!" say many Japanese, even now— Japanese who lived through those tragic times. "Today we might be the richest and the most powerful nation in the world!" Outside Japan few people know that, for a real understanding of the strength of the country's new economic and pacifist concepts of its foreign relations, we must add to the memory of the atomic bomb and the horrors of war the recollection of this magnificent opportunity that was lost.

We have yet to see whether these concepts can remain unaltered now that Japan is faced with a new development, one whose eventual consequences cannot easily be calculated. This is China's entry into the atomic club. There was however, one remarkable immediate consequence—or rather lack of it—when the Chinese exploded their first atomic bomb on October 16, 1964, in the central Asian remoteness of the Takla Makan Desert: Tokyo did not in any way react as though this were a disaster. The Japanese heard the news with extraordinary calmness. When Communist China first set off its still more terrible hydrogen bomb on June 17, 1967, I was in Tokyo. What was the reaction? Not the least sign of panic, or even of fear. A disconcerting calm. The huge neighbor over the way, Mao's China, now owned the terrifying weapon, but Japan, small and near at hand, refused to be frightened. Japan did not cry out, "Now I must have the bomb too!" Foreign observers had been of the opinion that the event would immediately bring about the appearance of a "pro-bomb" party, that this party would be discovered already in existence in the Japanese Right Wing, and that it would press very strongly for atomic weapons for Japan. Nothing of the kind happened.

Nevertheless, this does not mean that the event passed unnoticed. A certain change in the climate of opinion, a change that it would be unwise to disregard, has begun to show itself in different ways. In the first place it has meant the beginning of public discussion of the problem of Japanese security. For the first time the Japanese can be heard discussing among themselves both their own defense and the consequences of the Chinese bomb, two subjects that have up until now been almost taboo or looked upon as something above the reach of debate, just as everything to do with the emperor is left undiscussed. Then it became clear that the press was paying unwonted attention to a body that it had hitherto considered devoid of interest or even shameful—the Self-Defense Force. And finally certain important figures, both in the government and in the ruling party, for the first time showed a clearly expressed wish to increase this force and to give it better equipment. A new "five-year plan for defense" was drawn up, which is the third since Yoshida's time and which was adopted at the end of 1966. In July, 1967, the necessary sums for increasing the force by slightly over four thousand men and strengthening the defensive air force were voted, they having been held over for three years. This third plan has two central ideas: the replacement of the force's almost entirely obsolete equipment by modern weapons, and the manufacture, in Japan itself, of these weapons, almost all of which were supplied by America. Air defense is to be strengthened, and this will ensure the protection of the archipelago by short-range Hawk rockets (five battalions instead of three) and by the long-range Nike-Hercules and Nike-Ajax (two battalions of each). The main additions included in the plan are helicopters for the army, a few extra planes and submarines for the navy, and seventy-five F-104 fighters for the air force, until a new model is ready.

As for the manufacture of arms by Japan, the stepping up of the Vietnamese war since 1965 and 1966 gave certain Japanese firms the opportunity of trying their hands at this industry, working on orders for the Americans. It was only one step from that to the supplying of weapons for Japanese requirements, and this has now become the official policy, the ostensible reason being that it is necessary to save dollars by limiting imports of arms.

The Japanese make a light American rifle, machine guns, artillery, armored vehicles, medium tanks, rockets, and the Hawk and Nike-Hercules missiles that I have already mentioned. They make jet engines, assemble helicopters and F-104 planes for the Americans, and they are going to build jet fighters.

The coming of the Chinese bomb has also favored the development of an official campaign directed at public opinion, based upon the present inadequacy of Japanese defense.* One of the originators of this campaign was Premier Sato himself, and he has been criticized by a section of the conservatives both in the party and the government who are less to the right than he. In 1968 he made a great many declarations upon this theme, declarations that were often no doubt purposely obscure, muddled or contradictory. The primary intention is to persuade public opinion to reconsider its negative attitude toward rearmament. This campaign is also actively supported by Washington and the United States embassy in Tokyo, and the American press takes

---

* See articles on this subject in *The Far Eastern Economic Review,* June 20, 1968, and *The New York Times,* August, 24, 1968.

part in it, stressing the necessity for Japan to play a more important part in Asian politics. And, too, if we are to believe the Japanese Left, the campaign is secretly encouraged by the nascent armaments industry, which the Socialists and Communists accuse of already wielding a sinister influence.

Is it true to say that these new opinions, which are still only those of a minority, do in fact represent the first phase of a campaign whose ultimate aim, whose hitherto concealed aim, is to call for atomic weapons for Japan? The Left noisily asserts that this is so, and it particularly accuses Sato of secretly moving in this direction. We must not exclude the possibility that such may be his private intention, although those who are near him and know him well state that he is too shrewd a politician to compromise himself over a program that cannot after all be carried out until a time when he will certainly be out of office. At all events it is clear that he is taking pains to say nothing against atomic rearmament that may bind his successors; he is careful to leave them the possibility of coming out in favor of it.

In such a case Japan could make use of atomic bombs provided by the United States by abolishing the rigid prohibition that has hitherto forbidden the presence of all atomic bombs on Japanese soil, or it could make its own. It can scarcely be doubted that this would be a simple task for Japan, in view of the advanced state of its industrial technique; equally simple would be the manufacture of the carrying missiles. In 1968 General Yoshifusa Amano, the head of the Joint Defense Council, stated that if Japan chose to develop a system of nuclear weapons it would need between five and ten years to do so; the country would therefore possess them between 1973 and 1978. This estimate reckons that in such an eventuality the stockpile of atomic bombs might amount to five hundred by 1975. There has already been conclusive proof that this is possible. Since April, 1968, when Japan obtained plutonium by processing the exhausted uranium from one of its reactors, it has been perfectly clear that the country is capable of producing the bomb.

It is exceedingly probable that the debate on the nation's security that has been opened before the Japanese people will go on for a long time and that it will grow very heated. It might be less muddled if public opinion were to realize that at this present moment two wholly different paths are open. The first leads in the direction of giving

Japan what might be called a "muscular neutrality" similar to that of Switzerland and Sweden; this would be ensured by the increasing of the conventional nonatomic strength of the country's Self-Defense Force. The second is the path of nuclear weapons, and in fact it would lead Japan back to a policy of strength based on military power. Would the first eventually seem acceptable to the country, and workable, if there were really solid guarantees against any reappearance of the militarism of former times? This does not seem wholly impossible. But before the second—that is to say, Japan's entry into the atomic club—could become a reality, the country would quite inevitably be torn by a whole series of violent storms. It is likely that the Left and a large section of public opinion would put up a furious opposition to atomic rearmament.

The battle against the Japanese bomb might give the Left back the unity, the strength, and even the revolutionary force that have been so lacking for the past twenty years and more. It would also bring the support of wide sectors of moderate public opinion, great numbers of people quite outside the usual following of the Japanese Socialist and Communist parties. Millions of Japanese who went through the military epoch have bitter memories of the liberals' and the Socialists' weaknesses, renunciations, and defeats in the face of the increasing police oppression and the rise of military fascism during the thirties. For them the idea of beginning all over again would be a nightmare. It is reasonable to suppose that the experience of forty years ago would make popular resistance more general and more energetic this time. The Right could win no victory without savage domestic battles that, by once more making politics more important than the economy, would put an end to the admirable stability and general unanimity of opinion that have made the success of the economy possible.

Even among those of the Right Wing, there are great numbers of Japanese who are convinced that if they were now to join the atomic race it would bring the whole edifice to the ground and call the whole of the new Japan's success into question. Public opinion does not merely feel that an eventual atomic rearmament would have extremely dangerous political consequences, such as the dividing of the country into two hostile camps, the reappearance of arbitrary decrees—laws of exception—and of the military men, playing their former role in the state. It is also persuaded that this would mean abandoning the one valid formula for the success of the Japan of today and of the future, which requires absolute priority for the economy.

The managers, even those who from time to time make money out of the American wars, are the first to dread the spectacle of the military taking over the guidance of the country once more. Nations at peace, free navigation, a plentiful international trade—that is what the *zaikai* aim at. They know that peace always means better business than war. One of their leaders, the great industrialist Kogoro Uemura, with whom I had a conversation immediately after the setting off of the Chinese hydrogen bomb, said in substance, "We do not believe that China represents any menace to us as long as we ourselves are in no way threatening. China will be a powerful conpetitor, but the competition will be economic. Our two countries must both be able to work, to trade, for our mutual advantage. It is quite possible for small countries to live next to very big ones; and in any case we are *not* small. The real question is to find out what kind of a world it is that we want to create. Have we learned nothing from the past? Either Japan lays its hopes on the atom, in which case it helps to remake a madhouse like the world of yesterday and eventually perishes in an immeasurable atomic disaster; or it puts its trust in a world that has learned wisdom from past experience. In that case its strength will come from economic development in Japan itself and in the countries around it. Japan has chosen the second course. Japan trusts in peace." A little while later this same gentleman became the very active president of the Keidanren, the Japanese employers' federation, and he is therefore one of the foremost authorities in the country.

How would the Chinese react if Japan were to make an atomic bomb? The very great numbers of Japanese who believe in reconciliation between the two countries and in their future collaboration, and who work for this end, know that it would mean the immediate collapse of all their hopes and efforts. It was fine to see that up until the present the warlike Japan of yesterday had genuinely and sincerely disappeared, and that on the other side there were wonderful possibilities of forgetting the past and of renewed friendship. Is all this to be thrown away? A Japanese bomb would instantly change the whole climate of Asian opinion in a way the Chinese bomb has never done. The moment it came into existence China would blaze with anger, just as in Moscow a pitiless fury would arise if the Germans produced their own atomic bomb. A final uncrossable breach would open between China and Japan. The Chinese would feel that they were thirty or forty years back in time, faced with the warlike, aggressive "Greater Japan" of those earlier days. The breach would not only separate Japan from China; it would also cut the country off from the rest of Asia. From that moment on, China would see to it that Japan should be kept out of Asia, a continent that would become a private Chinese preserve. Having lost its vital markets upon that continent as well as all those Asian ties that might counterbalance its relations with the United States, Japan, reduced, dependent, and this time certain of being turned into a vassal state, would be thrown into the arms of the Americans.

From the military point of view Japan's position would not be improved; far from it. Instead of doing away with the Chinese threat, the Japanese bomb would accentuate it and make it more imminent. A Japanese bomb would also cause intense concern in the Soviet Union. Both Peking and Moscow know that a single atomic attack could wipe Japan out and that Japan would not have the same possibilities of retaliation. In fact, a Japanese bomb would only possess a very slight degree of dissuasiveness. Quite apart from its technical backwardness in nuclear weapons, a backwardness that would be difficult to remedy as far as the U.S.S.R. is concerned, Japan has overwhelming geographical disadvantages. An atomic attack launched from Japan would have to cover enormous areas, striking far behind the immense continental horizon. It would be exceedingly hard for such an attack to destroy the enemy's atomic bases, hidden in the desert solitudes of Central Asia or Siberia; and if on the other hand it were to be directed against the populated regions of China, that country is, as the world in general knows, the least vulnerable of all, for the very reason of its teeming masses. But Japan for its part would be shockingly open to atomic assault. The enemy, either Russian or Chinese, would have the advantage of a converging fire from many different bases, all aimed at an exact target. Indeed, the Japanese Megalopolis, with its extreme concentration of human and industrial resources, would be the perfect target for any attacker. A few bombs, and for all practical purposes Japan would cease to exist.

But happily—and this is a factor of the very first importance—there is a second solution, a completely different way of ensuring the country's security. The same geographical position that is disastrous for Japan in case of war is a protection and a safeguard if the country remains peaceful and neutral. It represents the strongest guarantee of safety, and it means that Japan can permanently remain a country that stays outside any kind of war. For indeed if there is one part of the world where, by means of an agreement between all the parties concerned, it is possible to ensure peace, it is certainly the region of Japan, the North Pacific; and peace can be ensured not by military pacts of the kind imagined by Foster Dulles but by a multilateral agreement designed to guarantee Japan's neutrality and its peaceful nature. The country is in a most extraordinary position, for it is surrounded by the three greatest atomic powers in the world. If there were a war it would be the most exposed region on earth. But then on the other hand it is entirely to the interest of Japan's three neighbors to maintain a peaceful balance in this area.

Theoretically each one of them could annihilate Japan, but each knows that it would instantly have the two others to reckon with. It is to the interest of each that Japan should remain at an equal distance from all three, that it should not join with any one against the other two, and that militarily it should be sufficiently weak to threaten none with attack. Japan's neighbors must know that it is impossible for them to combine either to bring the country into subjection or to destroy it, for both their rivalry and their common interests are opposed to any upsetting of the balance. If Japan were attacked by China, a sense of geographical reality would oblige the Soviet Union, although it is bound neither by treaty nor by alliance, to come to Japan's help, just as the United States is compelled to do by the present military pact. Even if there were no such pact, the United States has a vital interest in seeing that Japan should fall neither under Russian nor under Chinese domination, and that the country should be destroyed by neither of them. Lastly, it is exceedingly important to China that Japan should stay neutral, that it should not act as a military base for any power, and that in case of war the "factory Japan" should remain undamaged, with a view to the period after the conflict.

Japan's aim should therefore be the setting up of this balance—this equilibrium that is so necessary to everybody—by means of a treaty. Its aim should not be to equip itself with the atomic bomb but rather to negotiate a pact with its three awe-inspiring neighbors, the United

States, the Soviet Union and People's China, a pact guaranteeing its security. This Pacific pact would protect it against all forms of aggression by laying down that any attack by any one of its three neighbors would be followed by reprisals on the part of the other two. Japan itself would undertake to follow a neutral policy prohibiting any alliance, any share in a policy of military or ideological blocs, and any overseas expedition. Its neighbors might agree that this neutrality should be "muscular"—that is, that it should allow for the retention of small, purely defensive armed bodies of the same nature as Japan's present Self-Defense Force, and that they should be equipped with conventional weapons and placed under international control. It is worth recalling that, when the San Francisco peace treaty was being discussed in 1951, Stalin himself suggested that the Japanese should have the right to possess an army.

Although the conclusion of this Pacific pact between the four powers concerned may at present seem both difficult and doubtful in view of the uncompromising attitude of China—the China of the cultural revolution—it would nevertheless be possible to take steps in the desired direction, beginning with arrangements for a peaceful policy to be followed by the three powers, Japan, the United States and the Soviet Union. In 1964 one of America's most outstanding diplomats, George F. Kennan, made suggestions that caused a great sensation in Japan, and the moment for putting them into practice now seems to come nearer. Mr. Kennan, writing in *Foreign Affairs* for October, 1964, proposed that the United States should begin by helping toward the stabilization of Russo-Japanese relations by opening the way to a peace treaty between Tokyo and Moscow. He gave his readers to understand that the Americans could do this by handing Okinawa back to Japan, which has in fact since been arranged. The Russians, for their part, would then return part of the Kuriles, those northern islands whose restitution is, for Japan, an essential factor in any reconciliation. Once that was done there would be nothing to prevent the signature of the Russo-Japanese peace treaty, which has been awaited these twenty years and more. This would leave the road open—and here we come to Mr. Kennan's great idea—to an agreement by which the U.S.S.R. and the United States would, under the aegis of the United Nations, jointly guarantee Japan's security.

In order that Mr. Kennan's plan should have its full value, it would be essential to prevent this agreement from having the appearance of a two-power alliance against China; on the contrary, the arrangements should be so conducted that, even before China adheres to the pact, it should tacitly and indirectly form part of it. To this end, the pact should from the first be presented as a three-power treaty—or rather, since Japan is to be included, a four-power treaty, with an empty chair, waiting to be filled, for China. And above all, so as to ensure China's security in the new balance of power, the United States should carry out a military "de-escalation" in Japan, where it has hitherto retained a huge network of land, air and naval bases that constitute a permanent threat for China and that provoke anti-American feelings among the Japanese themselves. As we know, very strong opposition to the 1970 renewal of the security treaty with the United States was organized in Japan. This treaty is remarkably obsolete in its ideas, which date from immediately after the war, a time when the Americans still had the monopoly of the atomic bomb but when they possessed neither the Polaris submarines nor the intercontinental missiles that now allow them to dispense with bases.

The war in Vietnam is the last excuse for their retention, and once it is settled the Americans could begin retreating from Japan and closing their bases. The American alliance would be progressively replaced by the new, better balanced and essentially peaceful security system, and it is possible that China itself should eventually be included in it. Once China has emerged from the storms of its cultural revolution, it should be possible to open the way to a Sino-Japanese treaty and, at the same time, to settle the question of Taiwan on the base of the "one undivided China" thesis. Lastly, looking beyond the four-power Pacific pact, it would be possible to envisage an agreement still farther along the road to a lasting peace, an agreement that would make that particular area of the world a "nonatomic" zone. Surely this is not a dream too beautiful to be true.*

      ✿   ✿   ✿

* A statement made by Chou En-lai himself on October 1, 1960, shows that China may come around to ideas of this kind. In the course of one speech he made the unexpected suggestion that there should be a nonaggression pact between the Pacific powers, one that might be accompanied by the setting up of a "nonatomic" or "denuclearized" zone in that region. The suggestion was never subsequently elaborated.

Without waiting for all this, Japan, by means of the bold innovating experiment in peaceful expansion that it has been carrying out since 1945, has already given us an answer to the essential question, "What does a country without the bomb amount to?" Too often we have heard the categorical reply, "Nothing much; it is condemned to be no more than a second-rate power." Japan knows that it is a living contradiction of this theory. It proves by actual deeds that there are other roads that lead to the top—the peaceful roads of industry and international trade.

Greatness without the bomb: this phrase sums up everything in Japan's success that is peculiar to Japan and that is not to be seen in the advance of the other great powers of our time. Or if not greatness, then at least one of the highest positions in the world, for the word "greatness" has been banished from Tokyo ever since the total failure of "Greater Japan." The country is well aware that when it is referred to as the third great power this means the third great economic power. And it is perfectly happy that this should be so. In our days this is the only true greatness. Japan has hardly any interest in being the third great power in the sense that the first and second understand the words, and what is more, it knows that the facts forbid any such state of affairs. It has no claim to reaching such a degree of strength that its relations with the rest of the world, its international activity, could be entirely free and, as it were, 100 percent Japanese. For this to be so, Japan would have to get rid of its still very close ties with the United States. The chief of these links is commercial, for roughly 30 percent of Japanese trade is with the United States. Japan is also closely bound to the Americans in the matter of technical knowledge, since most of the patents Japanese industry makes use of are American. And a third bond arises from the exceedingly important fact that the United States provides powerful military protection in order to counterbalance Japan's own lack of strength. The country shelters under the American atomic umbrella.

To infer that these bonds negate greatness is, as far as the Japanese are concerned, an assumption based on an obsolete conception of what a great power can and should be in the worlds of today and tomorrow. Throughout the rest of this century and the century to come, we shall live to an ever-increasing extent in a world whose key word is interdependence—a world in which interdependence will become more and more widespread and essential, forcing us to reconsider and perhaps to discard the old notion of national independence. The Japanese would certainly say that it is desirable that the powers that achieve greatness by economic—not military—strength should increase in number and that Japan should no longer remain the unique specimen; the multiplication and tightening of bonds between the nations would then give peace a firmer, more certain basis.

More and more countries should understand that even if their territory is poor and remote, their labors can build up a strong and prosperous community, always provided that the world around them forms an interdependent society with trade weaving its peaceful bonds in every direction, rather than a world in which dependence brings the rival nations face to face in conflict. Indeed, how could Japan possibly claim to be "independent" when it has so great a need of abundant imports and exports, has so few resources at home, and runs the risk of choking to death if the surrounding oceans are not open to it? In one sense it is a perfect example of dependence. But that does not prevent Japan from being economically powerful. It could even be said that it obliges Japan so to be, for the country has to work hard to make its living, and a hundred million people who work hard necessarily occupy an important place in the world. At the same time Japan provides the perfect picture of interdependence; it demonstrates the necessity for it and proves the extraordinary advantages that it can give.

Japan's real problem is not to get rid of this many-sided dependence but to organize it as well as it can so as to ensure the best possible balance in the country's foreign relationships. The American atomic umbrella means an excessive and exclusive dependence upon the United States for military security, and Japan will be led to replace it by a system of collective security. No doubt American protection has been of the greatest assistance in helping Japan to reach the third economic place. But it is not an essential condition for holding on to that favored position. The American umbrella cannot be there forever, and we have seen that the substitution of a purely Japanese atomic system is also an impossibility. The solution of the collective guarantees, on the other hand, would allow the country to keep and to strengthen its place as the third great economic power.

In the area of its international economic relations, it is of primary importance that Japan should work for a better organization of its interdependence. In the first place this is a question of obtaining a greater freedom and equality within the framework of its alliance with the United States. But this is exactly what Japan is winning by growing stronger and by climbing into third place. At the beginning of its recovery the country was often an American satellite or vassal state; now it has become the partner who is treated with consideration and coaxed, whose advice is sought and who is even—we saw this at the time of the dollar crisis—appealed to for help. At the same time, Japan is now in a position to act with increasing independence of the United States with regard to the rest of the world. Here it is a question of balancing its exclusive and disproportionate American connection by the development of fresh links in other directions. The third great power can now venture to look for counterweights to the financial and economic might of the Americans, to seek fresh markets and new suppliers—in brief, to conquer a wide field of independent action apart from the United States.

10.

Diplomacy by Trade
and for Trade

The Japanese have been given such a thoroughgoing reputation as encroaching exporters that many Westerners are quite amazed when they learn that in this respect their own country is more of an encroacher than Japan. Yet in fact in 1967 Japan took only sixth place in international trade, exporting in round figures $10 billion worth of goods, and coming very far behind the United States ($32 billion) and Germany ($22 billion), quite far behind Great Britain ($14 billion) and somewhat after Canada and France, who were nearly equal with $11 billion each. It is true that in 1968 Japan outstripped France, but even so this third great economic power is not third from the point of view of trade; it is only fifth.

This fact is not sufficiently recognized. It is not foreign trade that means most to the Japanese producers today but the effort at home, the effort within this country that has to be made to thrive by means of industrialization and modernization. To be sure, import and export are the air Japan breathes, and without them it would stifle. But it is a mistake to suppose, as so many people do, that Japan derives its wealth and strength from foreign trade. In fact, Japanese manufacturers do not make their money abroad but on the home market. They do not try to make a profit out of their exports. What they look for in sending their goods abroad is primarily a source of foreign currency to pay for their imports.

All in all, we must reject the mistaken belief that foreign trade is the moving force behind Japan's industry and economic power. The driving force is within, and it could be said that foreign trade is a by-product of the growth of "factory Japan." The country's sales abroad amount to only 10 percent of its total production. We have a very different state of affairs in countries such as Holland, where the proportion is 32 percent, or England, with 15 percent.

It is worth noting too that the Japanese merchant navy ranks fifth in the world. At the end of 1967 it amounted to 12.5 million tons, coming after Liberia (22.6), Great Britain (21.7), the United States (21.3) and Norway (18). That year Japanese ships carried only 37 percent of Japanese exports and 46 percent of the country's imports.

But of course Japan's strikingly rapid economic growth has had its effects on the country's foreign trade. During the last ten years Japan has increased its exports fourfold while the rest of the world has only doubled them. In the three years from 1965 to 1967 inclusive, Japanese foreign trade increased by almost 80 percent, while that of Western Europe increased by 36 percent. During the same period Japanese sales to the United States mounted by 100 percent. And the rise will continue. Tokyo forecasts a 15-percent yearly increase in exports until the year 1973. Twelve years after that, in 1985, they will reach figures five times greater than today's. But world trade will also have increased enormously, and in this trade, considered as a whole, Japan's share will have grown to 8 percent instead of the present 6 percent. Will it then still be said that this figure expresses an encroaching attitude? The Japanese would reply that in a world which intends to build up a new age of peace this is a reasonable and healthy contribution from a country that means to place all its hopes on peaceful exchange between the nations.

However this may be, both Japanese buyers and sellers are wonderfully busy and diligent in international markets. This zeal is partly explained by the fact that they naturally behave abroad as they do at home. They are obliged to be very active in the home market, because competition in Japan is very keen indeed. The salesmen work furiously at home, and they carry this same state of mind with them abroad.

It is likely that the Japanese understand one basic truth better than anyone else in the world, and this is that mere production is not enough; the goods have to be sold. The Japanese manufacturers look upon the extension of their labors by the work of the salesmen as of the very greatest importance; what is more, on the foreign markets the salesmen act as the manufacturers' buyers, and they are also many other things—their ambassadors and observers, their scouts for information and for the latest manufacturing processes and the most interesting organizational methods. That is why so many Japanese missions travel all over the world, moving from Paris to London to New York and then on to the heart of Africa or the depths of Siberia, always going about in large groups composed of well-behaved businessmen, very free with their bows and civilities, incessant note takers, passionate photographers, untiring visitors of factories—people who have set out not to see one country but ten in immediate succession, and who are invariably to be seen in all the hotel lounges and on all the airlines.

But this merry-go-round of traveling salesmen, experts, buyers and engineers is only one aspect of a strongly organized and dynamic system of trade relations. Its great originality and its great strength arise from the fact that very large numbers of Japanese companies never concern themselves directly with their sales or their connections abroad, or even at home, but entrust them to other highly skilled and specialized bodies, the trading companies. This is so, for example, with many great industrial groups, which delegate the whole of their selling activity to a company that forms part of their own complex. It is also the case with the countless small and medium-sized undertakings that manufacture a large proportion of all the goods that Japan sends abroad. These firms, coming from the most disparate sectors of the economy and all converging upon the same trading company, can arrive at a collective solution of problems that they would be unable to deal with individually; they can discover outlets, organize overseas sales, approach the huge foreign companies for the purchase of technical processes or the importation of equipment, send out missions charged with buying or research and so forth. The trading companies do everything for everybody, undertaking the sale of gigantic merchant ships as cheerfully as that of ribs for umbrellas, negotiating the purchase of some very complex foreign process, and arranging the importation of vast quantities of any given raw material. The great Japanese firms themselves often turn to these companies rather than set up their own buying and selling organizations.

The trading companies are taking a more important place in the economy; they are no longer just middlemen, for now they are increasingly concerned with the problems of production, especially with expansion and the creation of new business. They are to be found, for example, taking a direct part in the development of such a spearhead industry as petrochemicals, occupying themselves with winning land from the sea, building great housing developments and so on. The very important groups such as Mitsui or Mitsubishi have their own trading companies (Mitsui Bussan, Mitsubishi Shoji), and these have become in fact the heart of the complex, the nucleus of the whole system. For example, Mitsubishi Shoji sees to the distribution and the prices of all Mitsubishi's products within the groups, in Japan itself and abroad; it coordinates the group's undertakings and does all it can to promote the setting up of industrial complexes within it; it collects and distributes information about the outside world; it directs the group's overseas enterprises; it imports foreign techniques and foreign capital. Between them these two companies have an annual turnover that amounts to four fifths of the national budget. Marubeni-Iida and C. Itoh are two other very important trading companies; after them come about forty more of very considerable size, and then ten times that number of small trading companies.

According to a Tokyo estimate, all these companies combined channel off about 65 percent of Japanese exports and over 50 percent of the imports. One of the results of this system is that every Japanese exporter can rely upon solid support. Every manufacturer can turn for advice to trading organizations that have exact up-to-the-minute information on the situation at home or abroad in all its aspects—the markets and their tone, techniques, finance and so forth. And every one of them has at his disposal a number of extraordinarily competent experts who specialize in the whole range of his interests on a world-wide scale. It often happens that foreign firms coming into the Japanese market also apply to the Japanese experts and deal with these trading companies. And the direction is also reversed; the Japanese trading companies are beginning to work abroad for foreign firms, not merely for those based in Japan. For instance, they might approach a Nantes or Düsseldorf manufacturer who turns out some attractive product and suggest that they should find him outlets in Africa or South America. They can sell no-matter-what to no-matter-whom.

But "no matter what" most certainly does not mean "no matter what quality." For foreigners, one of the postwar surprises has been to find that the Japanese pay the utmost attention—an almost fanatical attention—to quality. For many years their ambitions in this respect were brought to nothing by the military regime. The then rulers kept all the high-quality products for their own uses, leaving nothing but tenth-rate goods for the public and the foreign markets. Today high quality is available for all. I have touched on this point already; it cannot be overemphasized. Very great care is lavished on Japanese manufactures, particularly those for export, and the trading companies see to it that this is maintained. They have increased the number of checks not only at the selling level but also at that of manufacture, sending specialized teams into the factories. Apart from a few unfortunate, almost unavoidable exceptions that often come from small free-lance exporters, Japanese quality is now universally acknowledged, for example, in everything that has to do with photography, electronic apparatus, motor bicycles, steel, machinery, ships and watches. It is said that a watch manufacturer tested his wristwatches either by tying them to a hundred buoys and leaving them in the sea or by dropping them from a helicopter flying a hundred and fifty feet above a city square, and it is also said that they successfully survived these tests.

During these last twenty years, and in the context of this strenuous drive for success, a whole strategy of foreign exchanges has developed, a system that has been made possible by a wide measure of cooperation between the businessmen, the producers and the government agencies. A certain number of important objectives emerge from a study of this strategy:

1. The opening up of fresh markets, above all those that may counterbalance the excessive importance of the American market.

2. Economy in nonessential imports. In 1967 the London *Economist* observed that although Japan was in many ways comparable to England in its industrial structure, and had a greater GNP, it nevertheless succeeded in importing only a little over half the British amount. In particular, Japanese imports of food and manufactured products were very much less than those of Great Britain.

3. Export only after the raw materials have been given the highest possible "added value" or, in other words, when the transformation rate is at its maximum level. In 1966 Japanese iron and steel imported $1.3 billion worth of raw materials but exported $3.6 billion worth of its products, because a great deal of the industry's output

took the form of technically finished products such as ships, machinery and automobiles.

4. A progressive change in the structure of exports and, to bring this about, a certain degree of change in the structure of production within the country by means of selective guidance of resources, investment and labor. The goal is to encourage the technically highly advanced industries as opposed to those that call for a great deal of labor; to plan ahead for the withdrawal of those products that remain stationary and that are hard to sell—natural textiles, for example; and to concentrate effort upon new products such as electrical machinery and certain chemicals that can exert a strong and lasting competition.

5. The development of a long-term policy for raw materials, with the aim of improving Japan's dependent position as far as they are concerned, particularly by a geographical diversification of sources of supply and by Japanese participation in the exploitation of these materials in the countries where they are to be found.

At present Japan's ten main suppliers, in order, are: the United States, Austraila, Canada, Iran, the U.S.S.R., West Germany, the Philippines, Saudi Arabia, Kuwait and People's China. In 1967 Japanese imports were a little less than $12 billion. Food accounted for only 15.5 percent of this total; Japan is less dependent upon imported food than is generally supposed, producing 85 percent of its requirements at home. Manufactured products represented no more than 26.8 percent of imports; however, as Japan grows wealthier, this proportion has a tendency to increase. Raw materials amounted to 57.7 percent of all imports, and almost a third of this was crude oil. Wood took second position after oil, for Japan consumes a great deal and is particularly short of the hardwoods. The other chief raw materials imported are textile fibers, scrap for the blast furnaces, ores (above all iron ore), and coking coal.

As for exports, Japan's ten most important customers are: the United States, South Korea, Liberia (this surprising third position is due to the "flag of convenience" flown by many "Made in Japan" ships that are sold abroad), the Philippines, Australia, Hong Kong, Thailand, Taiwan, Great Britain and People's China. The composition of Japanese exports shows that the unremitting effort to make them more profitable and more "modern" has borne fruit to a remarkable extent. A great change has been brought about since the days before the war or even since those just after it, when textiles and the products of light industry took the lead. At present they amount to less than a third of the whole. Nowadays cotton goods are last on the list of the ten chief exports, artificial textiles come eighth, and ready-made clothes fifth. Conversely, heavy industrial products head the list, amounting to 66 percent in 1967, whereas in 1955 the figure was only 45 percent. These products include iron and steel, ships, automobiles and metal manufactures. In the sixth and seventh places we find radios and scientific and optical apparatus. The only product from the primary sector is fish, which ranks ninth and which is obtained by methods that may be called truly industrial. In 1967 the total value of Japanese exports passed the $10-billion mark for the first time.

The most important of all exports is machinery, taken in the widest sense of the word. This accounted for 40 percent of the 1968 exports, thus taking fourth place in the world, coming after the United States, West Germany and England. As well as machine tools and machines in the restricted sense, the list contains iron and steelworking equipment, chemical and other machinery and all kinds of products of high technical ability, ranging from oceangoing ships to wristwatches, and including such products as railroad equipment, automobiles, sewing machines, bicycles, binoculars and transistors.

When the Japanese premier Hayato Ikeda went to Paris some years ago, he was received by General de Gaulle. It may reasonably be supposed that he talked more about business than politics when he was with his illustrious host, for it is said that when Ikeda had gone the General observed, "A traveling salesman in transistors!" This crack (which may easily have been invented) was cabled to Tokyo by the Japanese journalists and caused a great outcry. Some looked upon it as an insult, others as a lesson that had been deserved but that was still extremely distasteful. As I see it, this was a great error, and they would have been better advised to think of it as a compliment, a tribute to the man who launched Japan into the international economic race. Would to God there were more traveling salesmen in transistors taking part, and that there were more prime ministers like

Ikeda who were deeply concerned with building peace upon balanced trade rather than upon the balance of terror!

For years the prime ministers of Japan have unfailingly assumed, as one of their major tasks, the encouragement of trade and its expansion, and all this time they have had the civil service behind them, as well as the ministers, including the foreign minister, who in his turn is seconded by the ambassadors of the Rising Sun throughout the world. To a very considerable degree, Japanese ambassadors are the ambassadors of their country's trade and industry. For Japan, the map of the world is primarily an economic map. No doubt they do see the political map showing through, though in many places it is rather vague. Often, on the political plane, Japan's activity seems obscure, ambiguous, and poorly connected with that of its allies and associates. But on the economic plane the country's activity is much easier to understand; it is exceedingly dynamic, and the whole is inspired by a logical singleness of purpose.

When Japanese foreign policy is given its economic explanation it no longer appears hesitant and paralyzed by what the Japanese call a "low posture." It goes hand in hand with the country's growth. It has evolved in three separate major phases. To be sure, it set off from scratch, from zero, and that is the reason why to begin with it was a policy that looked solely toward America. Until about 1960 and the advent of Ikeda, the world for Japan meant that of the United States, because the United States represented the country's one hope of salvation by means of the economy. The second phase in Japan's foreign policy consisted of getting itself recognized by the rest of the Western economic world—that is to say, primarily by Europe. But now we are beginning to see a third phase beginning, that is going to be central to the whole policy. It is the building up of a Pacific economic community, the great innovation of this latter part of our twentieth century.

One third of Japan's foreign trade is carried on with the United States: there, in round figures, is the great solid fact that we have to start with. This is by far the most important feature in Japan's foreign relations, and it gives full meaning to what is their essential basis—the American alliance. To move on to more exact statistics, in 1967 the United States took 28.9 percent of all Japanese exports ($3.108 billion worth) and provided 27.6 of all Japan's imports ($3.205 billion). The full importance of the trade with America becomes clear when we see that South Korea, the next on the list of Japan's customers, buys exports that amount to only a seventh part of those sent to the United States, and that Australia, Japan's second supplier, sells the country no more than a quarter of what America provides. In comparison with these two, England, Japan's main European customer, is one tenth as important, and France, with its trifling purchases from Japan, one fortieth.

So if there is any country that can complain of being "invaded" by Japanese goods it is the United States. The Americans' chief purchases are in the range of products that call for a great deal of manual labor. The importance of the American market for Japan can be gauged by the fact that it absorbs more than 70 percent of exported Japanese television sets, 65 percent of the Japanese production of skis, and 70 percent of the production of musical instruments; 30 percent of the knives, spoons and forks used in the United States are "Made in Japan," while 60 percent of foreign china and 40 percent of imported fishing rods are also Japanese. The Americans are Japan's best customers for canned tuna fish, sporting goods, cameras, secondary textiles, bicycles and electrical equipment. Japanese sewing machines, with their simple, ingenious "zigzag" models, have conquered 60 percent of the American market.

If the Americans were to stop buying Japanese cutlery or fishing rods or golf clubs, or if they were to buy less, it would mean ruin for thousands of small-scale family concerns in the Japanese countryside. There is for example a remote little town in northwestern Japan that sells three quarters of the cutlery it produces to the United States. And, too, American buying in the field of Japanese heavy industry is quite outstanding. The United States takes 45 percent of all the machine tools the country exports. Even better, Japanese steel has won itself an important place on the American market, for American steel is handicapped by high wages and strikes. Thus in 1967 nearly 10 percent of Japanese steel was sold to America, earning more than $500 million.

The United States is also by far Japan's most important supplier. Apart from Canada, Japan is the United States' best customer and without qualification the heaviest buyer of agricultural products. In 1967 82 percent of Japanese imported soya came from the United States, as well as 75 percent of the imported tobacco, 63 percent of the imported corn, and 54 percent of the imported wheat. Japanese industry bought 75 percent of its scrap from America, 51 percent of its wood pulp, and 43 percent of its coal. The chief heading in the list of American sales to Japan is machinery, in the wide sense of the term used earlier; Japan bought more than $400 million worth. In passing, it is worth pointing out that although one might suppose the contrary to be the case, Japan sold almost twice that amount to America.

Japan's is therefore by no means a one-way dependence. Japan has need of the United States, but the United States has need of Japan too, both as an important buyer and as an important supplier. For example, Japan sends America specially manufactured parts and elements such as "Made in Japan" transistors and electronic components, and American firms make great use of these products. At the same time Japan, because of its economic power, has become America's indispensable partner at the gates of Asia, a partner who fills many different functions—associate, agent, middleman, prospector, supplier of information and so on.

Strangely enough, for many years the United States was the only Western country that acknowledged the existence of Japan; the only one to try to discover the way of making use of it, as it were; the only one that grasped that the one way of doing so was first to be of use to Japan itself by helping it to rebuild its strength. At a time when the country was still crushed and feeble, America had the intelligence to see its potentialities—ten years before the rest of the world—and put its trust in Japan. After having compelled the country to be an American protectorate, the United States gave it back a wide freedom of action, at the same time keeping it almost entirely in the American orbit by means of aid. "Aid" and then "trade"—that is to say, first an injection of dollars and then a profitable commercial association. This liberal policy contained a paradoxical and very important element: in order to help Japan, the United States, a country that had attained the highest degree of development, consented to behave as though, in relation to Japan, it were an underdeveloped country. America opened its gates wide to the importation of Japanese industrial products competing with its own, and provided Japan with raw materials in great quantity instead of flooding the Japanese market with its own industrial manufactures. With Japan, America has carried out

the international division of labor, but it has done so to the advantage
of the protected nation and not to that of the protector, asking the
American manufacturers to make sacrifices and granting the Japanese
favorable terms. In a great many respects the United States has
handled the alliance intelligently and has done Japan much good.

Yet the United States, whose political analysts often lack subtlety
and insight into the psychology of other nations, has never fully understood that, as the Japanese see it, the American alliance has two
aspects, one of which is very strongly challenged and the other extremely popular. Insofar as it is, as Washington continually emphasizes, a politico-military alliance, many Japanese find it most distasteful; they look upon it as perilous, and it is the source of a great deal
of opposition. These Japanese think the treaty goes too far and does
much more than merely help and protect Japan. It makes use of the
country, turning the archipelago into the rear base for an undertaking
whose aim is the domination of the western Pacific by means of
planes and ships and the maintenance of a strong military foothold on
the Asian continent. There have been many points of friction—for
example, the air force bases, the mooring of American nuclear-powered
submarines, and the prolonged occupation of Okinawa. Many Japanese
feel that the alliance on this level involves a policy that can in no
way be called 100 percent Japanese but is rather 100 percent American,
and they think it puts their country, as America's ally, into danger.

On the other hand, from the economic point of view the American
alliance is accepted by most people and even welcomed heartily; they
admit that it is necessary and profitable. While there is no lack of
problems on the economic plane, these are almost always solved without conflict, all the more so since in this field Japan's position is no
longer subordinate but rather that of a partner. It has become strong
enough to speak more and more often to its former protector on a
footing of equality. Japan feels itself sufficiently necessary to the
United States to be able, if need be, to lay down certain uncrossable
boundaries to discussion, and even on occasion to stand up to America
with a friendly, unyielding steadiness.

Many examples of this could be quoted. Until the present Japan
has said no to the penetration of American capital. It has protected
itself from even very powerful American interests, such as the automobile industry. In spite of American displeasure it has increased its

exchanges with People's China. Only a little while ago when Sato visited the United States, he made overgenerous promises of Japanese help for the defense of the dollar and then, shortly after, was bold enough to withdraw them in part. Washington's need of Japan was too great for any protest, and nothing was said. Shall we soon see the partner turning into a competitor? And may not problems of a completely different nature arise from this change? It is not impossible, for after all there are latent tensions within the alliance, even on the economic plane. Tokyo is afraid that the presidency of Mr. Nixon may see the growth of a new American protectionism that may above all hit Japanese textiles, steel and transistors. American capital is also mounting a powerful new offensive aimed at opening the half-closed door of Japan at last.

But very few Japanese believe in the expediency and still less in the possibility of breaking the economic bonds that attach them to their partner on the other side of the Pacific. What is envisaged instead is a lasting continuation of the economic alliance as the politico-military aspect gradually fades away. And if the United States realizes that in any event Japan will remain an important, reliable partner on the economic plane, it would be far easier to make both a progressive reduction in the American air and naval bases in the archipelago and a loosening of the military ties to which Japan is still committed. The same realization should relieve the United States of worry when the Japanese, seeking to remedy the too great importance of the American alliance, try to counterbalance it by the active expansion of their economic relations with Western Europe.

The discovery of Europe, or rather the rediscovery of Europe—this was Japan's new plan at the beginning of the sixties. Feeling itself too much shut in by the American alliance, Japan turned toward Europe and found that it was an almost unknown continent. Still worse, the Europeans knew nothing whatsoever about Japan. Until the sixties Europe had conveniently left Japan out of its calculations. For them, the country had, as it were, been wiped off the map. It was Japan's task to induce them to discover or rather rediscover it all over again.

This was the period when the Common Market was beginning to take shape, and when the OECD was widening its field of action after the United States and Canada had become members. In a world in which these great entities were forming (and there was also the Communist bloc), Japan was seized with a sudden fear, the dread of being left "the orphan," as they put it, of the world's economy, alone and weak as soon as it started trying to find other partners outside the American orbit. For whereas the Americans had agreed to forget the past and to treat the Japanese magnanimously, the Europeans looked upon their reappearance with suspicion; discriminatory tariffs were still in force against Japan, clauses such as Article 35 of GATT (General Agreement on Tariffs and Trade) which allows the Europeans to refuse Japan the most-favored-nation status. With the birth of the Common Market, Tokyo was afraid that this exclusion would grow even more marked. Was not the Market going to turn itself into a private reserve surrounded with barriers? Would not the Western European Six become a new commercial giant on the foreign markets, its aggressive competition reaching out even as far as Asia?

Yet this initial pessimism gradually died away during the years 1961 to 1963, when there was a thaw in the relations between Japan and Europe. Japan began to make approaches to Europe, and it did so for several reasons. Besides seeing Europe as a counterweight to the American connection, it was finding that the American market would soon be saturated as far as Japanese foreign trade was concerned. At the same time Japan came to understand the growing importance of Europe, which, now that it had overcome its postwar difficulties, was in full, rapid development. And lastly, beyond all economic and political considerations, Japan felt that there was something else that counted—the powerful attraction that two ancient cultures exert upon one another. And in this realm too both Japan and Europe still had a great deal to gain.

And Europe came to meet Japan halfway. Even earlier than Tokyo had hoped, Europe proved that it looked upon Japan as the representative of the free world out there on the edge of Asia. It understood that Japan occupied an important and exposed strategic position and that it was an essential element in the Western world's system of exchange. It appeared to London, Paris and Bonn that it would be dangerous not to allow Japan to join the club of the leading economic powers of the non-Communist world, for if Japan did not succeed in achieving a place in this association matching its real importance, might it not be tempted to change direction and see whether it could do better on the Communist side? That would be a great pity, for by its extraordinary modernization it had joined the ranks of the most highly developed countries in the capitalist West. Japan was no longer the Far East, and indeed the shortening not only of geographical but also of political, cultural and economic distances had made the very notion of any Far East obsolete and ridiculous. Japan was no longer the Far East; it had become the farthest west of the Western powers.

That is why at the beginning of the sixties Europe showed by a whole series of international or bilateral agreements that it meant to neglect Japan no longer, that it meant to give Japan an increasing share in its trade, to plan with Japan in mind, and to give that country its place in the international economic organizations. The important Anglo-Japanese treaty of November 14, 1962, and six months later the Franco-Japanese trade agreement of May 14, 1963, marked the opening of a new era. From that time onward both Great Britain and France were to have a Japanese policy. Paris, London and Tokyo were to consult one another at regular intervals on the great international problems. Lord Hume and M. Couve de Murville went to Japan, thus inaugurating a subsequently uninterrupted series of two-way ministerial visits, among them M. Pompidou's, the first journey of a French prime minister to the Japanese capital.

Japan entered into relations with the countries of the Common Market. It joined the OECD, GATT and the International Monetary Fund. Experience has shown that protectionism, instead of gaining ground as Japan had feared, is on the ebb in Europe, and that there is now a distinct, progressive increase in exchanges with the European Economic Community. Both with the countries of the Common Market and with those that have remained outside it, Tokyo has negotiated the abolition of discriminatory clauses and the suppression of Article 35 of GATT. It has succeeded in persuading France, the Benelux countries, Great Britain and Italy to grant a steady relaxation of their former restrictive attitudes toward Japan. In the long run the exclusion of Great Britain from the Common Market was useful to Japan, because the British entry would have brought about a freeing of world trade so rapid that certain still-protected sectors of the Japanese economy such as the automobile industry would have been put into a most awkward position.

All things considered, Europe's share of Japanese exports, though it has not shown any spectacular increase, has nevertheless grown considerably. It amounted to only 10 percent before the war and even less in the early fifties; now it is nearly 15 percent, and in absolute value this represents a far higher figure, since Japanese exports have increased roughly fourfold in the last decade. The chief European buyer is England, which bought nearly $300 million worth of Japanese exports in 1967; then came Germany with over $200 million, and France far behind with less than $90 million. The new Japanese five-year plan for foreign trade predicts a fresh expansion of the European market; by this development, together with that of the Asian markets, the plan hopes to achieve a yearly increase of 15 percent in exports, thus helping to counterbalance Japan's trade with America.

Japanese foreign trade has also made great advances in "the other Europe"—that is to say, the Communist countries of the continent, a sector full of possibilities for the future. At the end of the fifties trade between Russia and Japan amounted to less than $100 million; by 1964 it had increased more than four times, exceeding $400 million; and by 1967 fresh progress brought the figure to $600 million. According to a survey in the *Far Eastern Economic Review* (November 14, 1968) many Japanese companies are installed in Moscow, at least fifty of them. In central Europe their offices are authorized in a semiofficial way, and they are to be found in rooms in the big hotels. Among them are to be seen the representative of Mitsubishi, Mitsui and C. Itoh. Japan's system of trading companies has proved very suitable for doing business with Communist countries, where deals are usually negotiated with the central government and take the form of barter. We hear of many recent sales of factories to Czechoslovakia and Romania: the supply of steel, technical agreements. And there have been very successful Japanese industrial exhibitions in Bucharest and Prague, the latter taking place in October, 1968, in spite of the political crisis.

There is one shadow, however: in their relations with Japan all these countries buy much less than they sell. Japan's exports to the Soviet Union have amounted to no more than $150 million, whereas imports from Russia have cost Japan $450 million. These have mostly been raw materials, for in fact Russia produces few manufactured goods that interest the Japanese, though they do buy great quantities of coal, oil and wood. In the same way Japanese trade with central Europe shows imports at twice the value of the exports. To correct this lack of balance, Moscow would have to make a very considerable increase in its purchases of Japanese manufactures, plant, and industrial equipment. Maybe this will happen, for the Soviet Union is much in need of such products, not for Europe but for Siberia. And this state of affairs is now making Japan realize how valuable it might be for the country to direct its efforts toward Asian Russia, its nearest neighbor on the Pacific.

However this may be, the progress that Japanese trade has made in capitalist Western Europe is by no means so great that it yet amounts to an adequate counterpoise to the trade with America. The exchanges with all the non-Communist European countries put together do not so far amount to half of those with the United States. There is one country in particular that has been a grave disappointment to the Japanese, and that is France, whose purchases of "Made in Japan" products have been strikingly meager; France takes only 0.75 percent of all Japanese exports. No doubt there has been a distinct improvement in the sale of these goods on the French market and in French sales to Japan, particularly since the fairly liberal trade agreement of April, 1968. But the figures are still absurdly small. England and Germany have a volume of trade with Japan three or four times greater than France's. Japan is a splendid market with 100 million potential customers, and yet France has managed to reach only the twenty-seventh place, coming after Holland and Switzerland, whereas in the export world at large France is Japan's rival for fifth place.

It is perfectly clear that the countries of Western Europe have no great inclination to imitate the United States' generosity as far as trade is concerned. Can they afford to do so? They have little in the way of raw materials to sell to Japan; on the other hand, they already manufacture a great many items that Japan produces. Above all they dread an invasion by Japanese goods. Their best line of approach would be to compete with the Americans as sellers of know-how to Japan—in other words, of advanced technical patents. None of them pays enough attention to this. There is little international division of labor between Europe and Japan, for to bring this about Europe would have to sacrifice a certain number of national manufactures. Each side looks upon the other not as its complement but more often as its competitor.

When all is said and done, Japan has certainly profited by drawing closer to Europe. But perhaps the most valuable gains in this respect are not those that can be shown in import and export statistics. What is of essential importance for Japan is the fact that it has been honorably received and has made a striking official entry into the international community. Today it has its place in the Western club. Now that it has become a member of OECD, the International Monetary Fund, GATT and so forth, it is an integral part of the great organizations that watch over and steer the economic and financial life of the Western world. There it has exceedingly valuable listening posts. Japan's voice is heard in the Atlantic world. Japan can see to it that its interests are protected there, and it is in the Atlantic world that it carries out part of its foreign policy, a foreign policy that is here again essentially economic.

Yet this policy is not centered upon Europe. The comparatively limited results achieved there cannot but encourage Japan to concentrate upon the third aspect of its foreign relations—its own hemisphere, the Pacific. After the period of tutelage in the shadow of the United States and then the interval in which it discovered Europe, Japan is now coming back to its own world, the world of Asia. It is finding that it no longer has any reason to feel small and isolated when faced with the blocs and the systems of the other powers; here, in Asia, there is the possibility of a splendid collective program of which Japan may be the heart, the prime mover.

11.

The Asia-Pacific Zone:
From Korea to Southeast Asia

It was Takeo Miki, a member of the Sato government until the end of 1968 and the most Westernized of Japanese foreign ministers, who made the "decision for Asia."

His plan, which he brought forward in December, 1966, was from the first summed up in a phrase that was to prove exceedingly popular: "the Asia-Pacific Zone." In effect the plan states that Japan must now create a privileged zone of economic and political activity for itself, and that naturally this zone is the region surrounding the country—nearby Asia and the Pacific. This is the ideal field for Japanese activity. But it must also be the scene of collective action, of international cooperative undertaking. Everything is propitious for such a course. It is a question of organizing and developing a whole region by means of an effort to which Japan is capable of making a very important contribution. Of course, Miki had not the slightest intention of saying that the whole of Japanese foreign policy must now be limited to the Miki plan. But for the first time foreign observers in Tokyo had the feeling that the nation was at last being offered a point of departure, a central position around which it could organize all the rest of its foreign policy and activity.

Actually, facts were a jump ahead of Miki; the Japanese businessmen had not waited for him. The representatives of the *zaikai* (economic and financial circles), who always move quicker than the representatives of the Gaimu-sho (the Foreign Ministry), had already thoroughly committed Japan to this new undertaking, and they had done so with the blessing of Sato's predecessors, Kishi and Ikeda. But

Miki first defined the great outlines of the pattern that was taking shape, suggested the general aims for concerted action, and gave this operation both a plan and a name.

It is tempting to say that the name alone has had more effect than the program. The formula "Asia-Pacific Zone" caused an instant sensation. The Japanese do not care for verbose plans, just as they do not care for verbose poems. In their opinion three lines can hold a masterpiece of poetry. Miki's plan was contained in three words, and these three words acted as a sudden catalyst for all the new Japan's still undefined hopes and aims. The sensation was quite as great outside Japan, though in some parts the reaction was anxious and disturbing rather than favorable. The slogan struck home in Asia, too, but it did so because it revived intensely bitter memories.

An important visitor who had an interview with Miki shortly after the announcement of the plan unwisely said to him, "But after all, isn't this just another version of your military leaders' Asian Co-Prosperity Sphere—the same thing in another shape?" The Japanese do not often lose their self-control, but this time Miki proved that there are exceptions to the rule. At once he flushed and burst out, "How can you speak like that! Let me tell you we shall never, never do any such thing again." We may certainly believe that his indignation was sincere. What is more, the foreigner's remark was unfair. The Asian Co-Prosperity Sphere of 1940–1945 was a ferocious campaign aimed at conquest and colonial exploitation; it was carried out by the army, and it was imposed by armed force upon the nations of Southeast Asia from the Philippines right down to Burma.

Between this venture and Miki's Asia-Pacific Zone there lies the whole of the distance that separates the Japan of the generals from the Japan of the managers. This is clear from Miki's explanations of his ideas; he has often spoken of them—he did so in Tokyo, for example, before the Keizai Doyukai, the Committee for Economic Development, on May 22, 1967. I may add that he always seems to take care never to put forward a "Miki plan" in any final, completed form, as though he would rather let the driving force of the slogan he has launched work by itself. In his various speeches he has merely sketched this aspect or that of his ideas, carefully leaving them somewhat vague—and this is very Japanese. It is in what Japanese policy actually does rather than in official declarations that the essential features of this new great plan are to be found—and this too is very Japanese.

Japan's first anxiety is to avoid isolation and at the same time to prevent itself from being drawn into ideological or politico-military alliances. Economic associations, on the other hand, do interest the country, because it is convinced that the coming years belong to very large-scale entities, and that the future therefore requires those countries that are not giants like the United States or the Soviet Union to unite their strength and to form great geographical unities for the sake of their common interests. If eastern Asia cannot build up a common market in the European manner, it can at least form itself into an economic association of a cooperative nature. With its hundred million inhabitants, Japan has no doubt grown beyond a certain minimum size, a certain critical level of population, that ensures strength in international competition. But it needs to belong to a far wider collective whole that will increase that strength. By entering into association with Asia it will create the desired counterpoise to the power of America. Furthermore, in Asia Japan will be at home, in a familiar world that it knows through and through.

But even within this Asian bloc there is a certain isolation to be feared. Will Japan not in fact be the only developed country, the only member that is rich, at least in comparison with the rest? Is there not the danger that it will therefore be continually harassed by the demands of all the poor and hungry countries in that part of the world, where most are both poor and hungry? During his 1967 tour of Southeast Asia, Sato, the Japanese premier, promised loans of $60 million to Thailand, $50 million to Malaysia, another $50 million to Singapore, and $100 million to the region's agricultural fund. Furthermore, Burma has asked Japan for $40 million, the Philippines for $30 million, and Indonesia for $100 million. Before this the country had already lent $150 million to Taiwan in 1965 and the same amount to Malaysia in 1966. All this is over and above reparations, which cost Japan more than $70 million a year. It also has promised to contribute a third of the cost of the $200-million program it proposed for the reconstruction of the two Vietnams after the war. From these figures it is easy to see that Japan has no wish to be the one and only Father Christmas of the Asian countries, but rather hopes for the support of other highly developed powers in this task.

This is the reason for Japan's appeal to the "rich" and "Westernized" countries—that is to say, primarily Australia, New Zealand and Canada. The result is that the composition of the Asia-Pacific association is entirely unlike that of Co-Prosperity Sphere of former times, which was directed solely at the Southeast Asian countries—the Philippines, Indochina, Indonesia (then called the Dutch East Indies), Thailand (otherwise known as Siam), British Malaya, and Burma—a list to which Japan very nearly added China. The new field of action will no longer include China, which has become a world apart, but it will not be confined merely to Southeast Asia. The idea is that of a bold extension, reaching out, as the plan's double-barreled name makes clear, to the three other countries I have mentioned—Australia, New Zealand, Canada—all of them, of course, giving onto the Pacific, but none of them Asian.

And then there is another aspect of the same question: Japan hopes that much of its activity in this region may be channeled through the international bodies of which the other great powers are also members, or that the country may make its entry on the scene as one of a team composed of Japan and some Western power—Anglo-Japanese or Franco-Japanese joint projects, for example—so that the flag of the Rising Sun will not always be too much in evidence.

In the same manner the racial character of the former organization has completely faded away. The Co-Prosperity Sphere was violently anti-white and anti-West. The Asia-Pacific Zone, on the contrary, is based upon collaboration between the races. Decolonization and the spirit of Bandung have not been in vain. For the men who sit around the conference tables where Asian economics are discussed today, the old distinctions of white and yellow no longer have any meaning. The cooperation between them is all the more striking since it could come about only after there had been a very far from easy reconciliation. A quarter of a century ago Australia and New Zealand were the appointed victims, the ultimate goal, of the conquering Japanese drive down through the South Seas. Today the position is reversed, and these countries are moving toward one another. The Australians, those "white men of Asia," now heartily welcome those same Japanese who, in Australian eyes, for so long stood for a feared and hated yellow Asia. This reconciliation is a heartening defeat for racism.

The Japanese leaders—and this is another point that needs emphasizing—have radically changed the nature of their relationships with the underdeveloped countries of the region. From now on there is to be no question of the "colonial pact" kind of connection, with its implications of a massive transfer of raw materials from the weak to the stronger country and the stronger country's refusal to allow the other to become industrialized. Tokyo is fully persuaded that the spirit of the present age as well as a proper understanding of Japan's own interests require that the countries with a Pacific seaboard should all enjoy a steady industrial development and that for this they should be given active assistance. This means that they will, to some degree, become competitors, and that Japan will gradually have to make over certain aspects of economic activity to them—light industries, for example, and a share in textiles. In a well-organized association the advantages of an evolution of this kind will very considerably outweigh the disadvantages, the most important of the gains being a rise in the standard of living and hence the expansion of an Asian market of enormous potentialities. Furthermore, Japanese industry is so far ahead of that of the south Pacific countries that it does not have to fear being overtaken for a long while.

The nature of the future relations between this Asia-Pacific association and the United States has yet to be determined. They will certainly not be without their contradictory aspects; the position may be summed up by saying that on the one hand there will be collaboration and on the other conflict. In the first place we should observe that the Americans have not been invited to become members of the body that is now coming into existence. Such an invitation would mean a distortion of the association's whole significance at the very outset, because the first thing that the Asia-Pacific countries are trying to do is to assert themselves, to show that they are tributaries to no other power whatsoever, and to counterbalance American power. Yet it is also clear that this new collective venture needs to remain on good terms with the United States and even indeed to make use of it and to have its support. Those who wish for the development of Southeast Asia, with Japan at the head, know that if they want to accomplish anything they cannot ignore America, in the first place because America is there on the spot in great force, both in Vietnam and all the neighboring countries, and secondly because the combined resources of the members of the association are insufficient for their needs. Their venture will still need a certain invigorating flow of dollars, at least to begin with. The United States will remain one of the chief lenders of money to Southeast Asia, and Southeast Asia will look to the other Pacific countries for manufactured goods and equipment. The outcome of these three-sided relationships is that Japan and its associates, benefiting indirectly from American aid to Southeast Asia, at the same time compete with the United States in that area. Since 1967 Japanese exports to Southeast Asia have exceeded those of the United States; this is a striking fact, but it is after all one that can easily be explained: the Japanese carry on business there, while the Americans carry on war.

We can therefore go farther and say that in fact Japanese policy runs counter to American policy. In the Asia-Pacific Zone Japan wants to pursue a businessman's and a manufacturer's policy, whereas that of the Americans is a soldier's. As the Japanese see it, the Americans have gone astray; thirty years ago the Japanese launched themselves on the same adventure and they know from their experience that it cannot succeed, because it means relying essentially upon arms to build the new Asia. The comparison must certainly not be carried too far, and the Japanese, apart from those of the extreme Left, would never presume wholly to equate the present-day American intervention with their own country's aggression of former times. Furthermore, Japan itself cannot boast entirely clean hands in the Vietnamese war, since the country makes a handsome profit out of the business the war brings to it. Nevertheless Tokyo's view is that war is an utterly mistaken way of trying to solve the problems arising from Vietnam and China.

What do the Americans want? They want to bring about the containment of China and the rollback of Asian communism. Very well, say the Japanese, there is only one effective way of ensuring the rollback of communism, and that is to set about the rollback of poverty. This is something that cannot be done by war, which merely increases poverty, but only by peace and trade, which cure it. There is only one containment that can succeed, and this consists in surrounding China not with a military dike but with a barrier of economic and technical development, high living standards and progress in education. Pouring billions of dollars into the war in Vietnam, as the Americans are doing, is a horrifying absurdity. A Japanese commentator, Professor Yoshizaka

Sakamoto, writes, "It needs an investment of three hundred thousand dollars to kill one Vietcong, and this in a country where the average per capita income is fifty dollars a year. . . . If America had put the daily sixty million dollars it spends on the war into the form of aid for the building up of the Vietnamese economy, then, even supposing that it were a Communist government that benefited from it, the United States would have won a decisive victory over communism."

One can, without falling into ludicrous anti-Americanism, say that since 1967 the situation in eastern Asia has been dominated by the American failure in Vietnam, and that the birth of the Asia-Pacific Zone represents the first attempt at profiting from the lessons of this failure. The Paris peace talks to put an end to the war in Vietnam are an acknowledgment of defeat. It is still not clear how far a compromise with Hanoi will succeed in lessening the effects of the failure; this must depend on the outcome of the negotiations. But one thing is certain, and that is that after twenty years of struggle the American military leaders have not succeeded in solving the two vital problems in this area—Vietnam and China. America's friends in the eastern Asian states understand these truths, and, stifling any possible lingering distrust of Japan, they welcome that country as the representative of a completely different policy.

Eisaku Sato's tour of the whole region in the summer of 1967 proved this. The head of the Tokyo government visited South Korea, to begin with, and this was the first time that Seoul had ever seen a Japanese prime minister; then he went on to Singapore and the capitals of Burma, Malaysia, Thailand and Laos, and so to Indonesia, Australia, New Zealand, the Philippines and South Vietnam. However tolerantly Sato may look upon the Americans' war in Vietnam (and his enemies call him their accomplice), this journey turned him into the traveling salesman for a policy wholly different from that of the United States, and it was this that earned him his success now that the methods of Washington had failed.

The new policy for the Asia-Pacific Zone is in the making, and as usual Tokyo advances by trial and error, feeling its way, rather than according to any clearly established program laid down in advance, even when it is a question of the Miki plan. Then again there is room for non-Japanese programs and suggestions coming from the other capitals in the region. This fortunate state of affairs is well worth emphasizing. As early as 1966 three events helped the scheme to "take off," as Miki himself put it:

1. In April, the first ministerial conference for the development of Southeast Asia.
2. In November, the setting up of the Asian Development Bank.
3. In December, the creation of a Fund for the Agricultural Development of Southeast Asia.

And 1967 witnessed an extraordinary amount of activity. The calendar of events for that year shows the economic diplomacy of the region in a state of effervescence, with a great number of different kinds of organizations coming into action. There was Sato's visit to Seoul and then his tour of the whole of the Far East; Miki's journey to Moscow, where the development of Siberia was discussed (of which, more later); the meetings of the Southeast Asia Development Conference at Manila, of the ASPAC (Asia and South Pacific Area Council) at Bangkok, and of the ASEAN (Association of Southeast Asia Nations), also at Bangkok.

The ASPAC is an association of ten countries, seven of which are more or less committed to the war in Vietnam while three are not. Here is the list: South Korea, the Philippines, South Vietnam, Thailand, Laos, Australia, New Zealand, Japan, Malaysia and Taiwan. The group came into existence at Seoul in 1966. South Korea, which took the initiative, is trying to endow it with a political character so as to make it into an anti-Communist league, with the ultimate intention, perhaps, of turning it into an alliance. It is typical that this move was blocked by the veto of Japan, applied as a consequence of Miki's views on the economic nature of the work to be done, the role of the region's developed nations in relation to the rest, and the links that have to be maintained with Canada and the United States.

The ASEAN, founded in 1967 at Bangkok, groups the foreign ministers of the following countries: Indonesia, Malaysia, the Philippines, Singapore and Thailand. It is a kind of union of the assisted countries of the region—those that are at the receiving end. It was Indonesia that took the initiative in this case: the atmosphere is rather anti-American, and it is also rendered uneasy by the quarrels between Djakarta and Manila. The Ministerial Conference for the Develop-

ment of Southeast Asia was founded at Tokyo in 1966, at the suggestion of Japan: it brings together nine countries—Indonesia, Malaysia,
Singapore, Thailand, Cambodia, Laos, South Vietnam, the Philippines
and Japan. It met again at Manila in 1967 and then again at Singapore
in 1968; in the opinion of the Japanese this conference may become
the most important body in the general scheme. During its sessions
all the great problems of the region, such as agriculture, industrialization, finance and technical aid, are discussed. Japan would like a
permanent committee to be set up, which would turn the conference
into the executive authority of the new regional organization, but this
suggestion still meets with resistance on the part of the other members,
who are afraid of seeing it assume an undue influence.

In addition to the three governmental bodies that I have mentioned,
there are private organizations composed of prominent figures in the
region's business world. One of these is the Pacific Economic Cooperation Committee, which was founded in April, 1967, by businessmen from Australia, New Zealand, Canada, Japan and the United
States; another is the Australia-Japan Business Cooperation Committee, which dates from 1963. Lastly, the Asian Development Bank
is designed, as its name implies, to be an important instrument in the
Asia-Pacific Zone's economic cooperation by financing its great national or international programs. It is particularly significant that
Takeshi Watanabe, the bank's president, is a Japanese, and that
Japan's contribution of $200 million equals that of the United States,
thus underlining the fact that Japan is the biggest Asian participant.

One of the most frequently discussed subjects in all these organizations is aid to the underdeveloped countries in the region. In the wider
meaning of the term, taken to include reparations, private investment
and technical assistance, Japanese aid is very considerable; it is also
increasing fast: Tokyo gave the figure of $583 million for 1967. But in
the restricted meaning, the Japanese government's aid to the underdeveloped countries amounts to no more than approximately 0.7 percent of the gross national product; in order to comply with OECD
requirements it should be raised to 1 percent. Japan is also blamed
both by the aid-receiving and by the other aid-giving countries for
insisting upon credit conditions that, by international standards, are
too harsh and ought to be made less rigorous. Like nearly all other
great powers, Japan uses its aid as a diplomatic instrument, of par-

ticular value in connection with its foreign trade. More than 60 percent of this assistance goes to Asian countries, and, together with the aid from America, it strongly encourages Japanese exports in that area.

When it is a question of showing the outstanding importance of the Asia-Pacific Zone to Japan, figures tell us more than all the plans put forward by Miki, Sato or other Japanese ministers.*

In 1967, 25 percent of Japan's exports went to its non-Communist Asian neighbors—that is to say, those in the Far East (Korea, Taiwan and Hong Kong), Southeast and Southern Asia, as far as Pakistan (Communist China and Siberia being excluded from this group). If we take the Asia-Pacific Zone, or the foregoing countries with Australia and New Zealand added, the proportion rises to 33 percent. It is interesting to note that this figure exactly balances that of exports shipped to the American markets (the United States, Canada, Mexico, Panama and El Salvador), which also took 33 percent of all Japanese exports in 1967.

If we consider the ring of countries that surround Japan on the shores of the North Pacific (still not counting China or Siberia and also leaving out India, Pakistan and Ceylon, which give on to another ocean), we shall see that altogether they account for roughly two thirds of all Japanese trade and that they buy 63 percent of its exports. The exceedingly important part played by the countries of the Asia-Pacific Zone becomes even clearer when we observe that the list of Japan's best customers includes six non-Communist countries in this region (South Korea, the Philippines, Australia, Hong Kong, Thailand and Taiwan), while the seventh is People's China. Five of these countries increase their buying from Japan by 20 percent a year.

So here we have thousands and thousands of Japanese setting off once more on the roads they know so well, roads that lead to Southeast Asia and the South Pacific, to Taiwan and Korea. But they are no longer the same Japanese. They are just a peaceful army of businessmen and engineers, followed by the diplomats whose duty it is to support them. Import-export, investment, trade agreements, arrangements for loans, technical aid—essentially that is what the work in the Japanese embassies in Southeast Asia consists of. From Hong Kong to

---

* See the excellent supplements in *The Far Eastern Economic Review* for October 31, 1963, February 23, 1967, March 21, 1968, and March 16, 1969, which include articles of Japanese and Southeast Asian trade.

Djakarta, from Borneo to Bangkok, in Manila, Taipei, or far to the north in Seoul, Japanese diplomacy is carried on as much by the businessmen as by the diplomats. Their activity, in conjunction with that of the local governments and business circles, has become one of the chief driving forces in the region's development.

The Japanese presence is everywhere apparent—not that of the Japanese themselves, who are lost in the teeming Asian crowds, but that of the country's industry and trade. It might almost be said that the words "Made in Japan" are to be seen on everything in the daily life of the region that means hope for a better material life and a raising of the standard of living: taxis like those one sees in Tokyo, buses, motor bicycles, movie cameras, watches, transistor radios, television, artificial pearls and so on. There are even big Japanese stores and Japanese restaurants. The tropical night of Bangkok and Singapore blazes with many-colored neon signs proclaiming the merits of Japanese brands of beer or fountain pens, or advertising Mitsubishi's heavy industrial equipment with its three red diamonds.

It is above all in the context of the export of merchandise that Japan asserts its importance throughout the whole of Southeast Asia. Japan is Thailand's chief supplier, Taiwan's chief supplier, and Singapore's chief supplier too. Although America is very strong in these various markets, Japan has now become the leader, particularly since the war in Vietnam. It is Burma's chief supplier, having outstripped England, the former champion. It is second to America in the Philippines, South Korea and South Vietnam; second to China in Hong Kong (although, as an indirect consequence of the cultural revolution, it outdid China in 1968) and to France in Cambodia. In Malaysia it comes third, preceded by the United States and England. In the other direction, that of imports purchased by Japan, it is the most important buyer in the Philippines, Taiwan, and Malaysia.

Let us examine the structure of Japan's trade with its Asian neighbors more closely. Do we find that it floods these underdeveloped countries with shoddy merchandise and consumer goods as it did in earlier days? No, there has been a great change. More and more Japan has become a provider of capital goods—of the industrial plant and equipment required by countries that are trying to get free from their underdeveloped state and speed up their modernization. Over these last years this class of goods has accounted for between 60 and 70 percent of Japan's sales.

Taiwan, for example, which is in a high state of boom and which, after Japan, has the second greatest rate of economic growth in the world, buys between 50 and 70 percent of its foreign industrial equipment from Japan: this includes machinery of every kind; electrical apparatus; the equipment necessary for the setting up of its chemical, iron and steel, and other factories; cars and trucks; building materials and the like. The Philippines looks to Japan for more than a quarter of its imports, particularly modern equipment for the archipelago's development, ranging from agricultural machinery to the plant for power stations, mines, textile mills, plastic factories and so on. Thailand buys iron, steel and cement for building and public works; engineering products and machinery of every kind; automobiles, trucks and buses; railroad cars and plant. Burma takes machinery for its oil fields, transport equipment, machinery and fertilizers. Singapore imports Japanese iron and steel, scientific instruments, telecommunications material and power stations.

South Korea, too, has become a splendid market for the Japanese, and in the single year of 1966 their exports doubled; this followed the signing of the December, 1965, treaty, an event of capital importance that restored normal diplomatic relations between Tokyo and Seoul. South Korea has become Japan's chief Asian customer. The Korean purchases—iron, steel, cement, machinery, motors and mechanical equipment, electrical apparatus, railroad plant, vehicles, chemical products, fertilizers—are typical of a country that is experiencing its primary development boom and that is making ready to "take off" economically and industrially.

From the other point of view, what does Japan import from the countries of the Far East and Southeast Asia? Has it returned to the wholesale extraction, the draining, of their raw materials? It is true that Japan does buy a certain quantity of their unmanufactured products, but in this field its chief suppliers are now rich white countries—Australia, Canada and above all the United States. For as we have seen, although these are all very highly developed countries, as far as Japan is concerned they are also great sources of raw materials. In comparison with them, Southeast Asia is not a provider of anything like the first importance. The Philippines can sell Japan rubber, corn, wood and copper ore, and Thailand has agricultural produce. Malaysia offers iron, rubber and tin and is the only country in the region that has a favorable balance of trade with Japan. Although Taiwan trades heavily with Japan, the balance is against it; Japan buys Taiwan wood, rice, sugar, half the exported fruit, almost all the country's bananas and its exported salt. South Korea sells Japan four times less than it buys (the Korean sales are chiefly agricultural produce and fish), and complains that the first products of its light industry are excluded from the Japanese market because they compete with the smaller Japanese firms.

Taken as a whole, Southeast Asia has therefore a markedly unfavorable balance of trade with Japan, and generally speaking it is foreign aid, chiefly American, that fills the gap. The war in Vietnam has strengthened the tendency, which provides the Japanese with still another reason for wishing this disastrous conflict to be brought to an end so that a new era can begin—one in which peace is restored and in which Southeast Asia, modeling itself upon Japan, will be able to work wholeheartedly for its reconstruction. It may be that the Japanese look upon the war as a paying proposition, since in 1967, for example, it meant deals and orders worth about $500 million to them. But, to repeat—they now know that peace is far better business than war.

Meanwhile, it is interesting to note that the war in Vietnam has never entirely interrupted the trade between Japan and North Vietnam. The American bombing of Haiphong slowed it down, but it did not stop at any time, and at the height of the war Japan still imports anthracite from Hon Gay and North Vietnamese cast iron, while it exports textiles, chemical and pharmaceutical products, fertilizers, steel and machinery. This provides a very good illustration of the Japanese view—a view not always appreciated by the Americans—that trade must always take precedence over politics. North Korea furnishes another example. In spite of protests from Seoul, these last years Japan has kept up a very small but steady flow of trade with the north, buying coal and cast iron and selling textiles, chemical and pharmaceutical products, steel and machinery.

In any case, Japan has a tolerably clear notion of the important part that it may play when the Vietnamese war is over, for it sees the ever-increasing number of factories its engineers have built in Southeast Asia in spite of the instability caused by the conflict, the great public works in which it takes a share, and the investments in which its capital forms a considerable part.

Let us try to draw up a list of these Japanese contributions to the development of Asia, although our list will probably be far from complete. At Prai, in Malaysia, we see the first integrated steelworks in Southeast Asia outside India; it was erected at a cost of $75 million by the Yawata group (hence its name of Malayawata), and a rolling mill, its first converter and first blast furnace are already installed. In Taiwan, another steelworks is under construction, with Japanese, Chinese and American capital. At Singapore, there is the biggest shipbuilding and repairing yard in Southeast Asia; and at Singapore again, the Matsushita factory (electrical apparatus, electronics, television). Again in Malaysia we find a steam power station and Japanese participation in the development of telecommunications, roads and harbor equipment. In Indonesia, an oil refinery at Sumatra will presently turn out a hundred thousand barrels a day. A petrochemical complex is under construction in East Pakistan. In Ceylon, the installation of the island's entire network of electric power is by the Sumitomo group. There are great dams and hydroelectric projects in Taiwan (Teng Wen), South Vietnam (near Dalat), Burma and Indonesia. In South Korea, Asia's biggest urea works with a capacity of three hundred thousand tons was built with the help of Mitsui; in East Pakistan another urea works is under construction; fertilizer factories are in Taiwan and India (one in Uttar Pradesh, two in Gujarat, and one planned for Rajasthan). The striking progress of Japanese cars throughout the whole of Southeast Asia becomes clear from the following list: assembly works in Singapore (Toyota), Thailand (Isuzu), West and East Pakistan, Ceylon, and another under construction in Burma; automobile factories in Malaysia (a joint venture by Mazda and Peugeot together with Malayan capital), in South Korea (Toyota), and in Taiwan. What is more, this advance goes well beyond Asia, reaching Australia (three assembly works) and Canada (one assembly works in operation and three more at the planning stage).

Throughout Southeast Asia Japanese capital is associated with local capital for the launching of joint ventures. Private Japanese investments in Thailand have been booming since 1966, amounting to four times the American equivalent. (Japanese investments in Thailand represent between 45 and 50 percent of that country's foreign capital.

America provides 10 percent; England and Germany together, 6 percent.)

In the Philippines there is still strong anti-Japanese feeling, and Japanese investment is not allowed there, but loans from Japanese banks and industry play an important part, and so does Japanese technical assistance directed at the industrialization of the country, particularly in textiles and the timber and mineral industries, including copper mining. In Singapore, Japanese capital is at work in many joint concerns, such as those in which Malaysians and Japanese collaborate in the manufacture of tires, for example, or cement, plywood, sugar, textiles, various metallurgical products and so on. In Taiwan, Japan has been in the lead ever since 1965, when the United States decided that the now-prosperous island could manage without American economic aid. Japanese technical assistance, credits and investment mean that Japan is the most important influence in Taiwan's rapid industrialization. The island has many joint Sino-Japanese firms, active in the chemical, engineering, textile and mining industries. There are numbers of them in Hong Kong, too, and they are to be found in textiles, import-export, and business. Then again, the big Japanese groups are taking an important share in the plans for the industrial development of Cam Ranh Bay in South Vietnam, the huge new port which is the future rival of Singapore.

South Korea deserves a long discussion to itself. After twenty years of intense hatred and enmity nourished by memories of the past, the 1965 treaty marked the beginning of a reconciliation beyond all Japan's hopes; it also meant the return of Japanese businessmen to Seoul. Japanese capital has been flowing into South Korea since 1966. The treaty lays down that $800 million provided by Japan will be spent in South Korea over a period of ten years: $300 million is to be given by way of reparations, and this is to be used primarily for the country's infrastructure; $200 million in government loans will be chiefly used for the financing of imports; and $300 million in the form of private commercial credits (this total will probably be exceeded) is to be directed mainly at the expansion of private industry, such as fertilizers, fishing, cement, engineering and so forth.

There is one Southeast Asian country that should be mentioned separately, and that is Indonesia. The reason why I have scarcely spoken of it is the abnormal conditions under which Java, Sumatra and the rest of the great tropical archipelago have been struggling since the collapse of the Sukarno regime. It was only in 1968 that General Suharto's new government began to restore a little order in the country's economy; its foreign trade is still partly crippled, and the foreign aid that the conference of Indonesia's creditors organized at Amsterdam in 1967 has hardly yet begun to function. Until it sees surer proofs of political stability, Japan remains very cautious, and the rather low figure of its aid so far—less than $100 million—has been a great disappointment to Djakarta. But in Tokyo everyone knows that in fact the Japanese are eagerly looking forward to the moment when it will no longer be too dangerous for them to devote very considerable resources and efforts to helping Indonesia to recover. Since they once exploited it by force, they know the extraordinary potential wealth of this collection of treasure islands better than anyone else in the world.

In an interview that was published in Tokyo, General Suharto himself told them that his country could provide the international market with a third of the world's rubber, sixth of its tin, great quantities of oil, bauxite, nickel and manganese, all its quinine (Indonesia has a virtual monopoly), vegetable oils, spices and tea. The Indonesian leader stressed the complementary, not competitive, nature of the economies of his country and Japan. He ended by stating that the two countries had "a common geopolitical destiny": if communism, already present on the Asian continent, were also to spread to the surrounding ocean by seizing Indonesia, the other archipelagos would follow, and this, he said, would sooner or later be the fate of Japan.

The Japanese, whatever reservations they may have about General Suharto's political opinions, share his hope that Indonesia will never turn Communist, and they are wholly in agreement with his economic views as to the complementary nature of the two countries. They believe that it is entirely to Japan's interest to help Indonesia to emerge from its underdeveloped state, and that they can do so without any fear of raising up a competitor in anything like the near future. Japan can give Indonesia a great deal of help by providing manufactured products, equipment for the modernization of the country, credits and investment. In the other direction, Japan is very well placed for furnishing itself with Indonesian raw materials and even for taking part in the exploitation of the country's resources in Indonesia itself. Tokyo business circles ask nothing better than to be able to invest in

Indonesian oil, bauxite, tin, nickel and timber, if only the risk is not too great. And in agriculture, too, Japan has made offers of technical aid, supplies of seeds and equipment and so forth. They have done the same where the hotel industry is concerned, proposing the building of hotels and the promotion of tourism. Trade and exchange between the two countries may show a very great increase. Even in circumstances as abnormal as the present, Japan bought more from Indonesia in 1967 than it did from either Taiwan or Thailand, and its sales were greater than those to India.

Japanese missions in Djakarta are increasing in number, and the first agreements have already been signed, such as that according to which I.H.I., the heavy industry company, will presently build an oil refinery in Sumatra. Recently the president of the Keidanren said, "Indonesia is important to Japan. It has great unexploited and even hitherto unprospected resources. We can provide considerable help for the country's development. Once Indonesia's political problems are solved, there is a brilliant future for our relationship." Talking to me, another Japanese, a well-known journalist whose name I will not mention, put it in a more striking manner. "Indonesia? Why, for us it could be another Manchuria!" He added that of course this would be on an entirely different footing and in a spirit wholly unlike that of Japan's former military aggression on the continent of Asia, which began by the conquest of Manchuria in the early thirties.

This echo of the past comes at the right moment, for I do not want to leave Southeast Asia without mentioning the grave problem of the persistent anti-Japanese feeling in this region and of the attitude of the Japanese themselves toward the natives of the countries to which they are now returning. Asians certainly do possess a remarkable and in many ways admirable power of forgiving and forgetting. Without this there would have been no possibility of the present reconciliation that we see in Seoul, Singapore, Djakarta, and Taiwan—a reconciliation between the people of those nations, who not so very long ago were harshly oppressed and often subjected to atrocities, and the "new Japanese" of the postwar generation. But this must not make us close our eyes to the persistence of anti-Japanese sentiments in some of these countries, particularly the Philippines. And let us also take care not to overlook the possibility of a sudden rise in this feeling, a deterioration for which perhaps the Japanese themselves would be to blame.

There could be two main reasons for this, the first being the very success of the Japanese "new wave," the flood of businessmen throughout the region. Their new importance, their over-easy superiority and their too-obvious presence may combine to revive enmity and jealousy. But the second reason is (and Japan should quite frankly be told about it) that there are some Japanese whose attitude is far too often both clumsy and disagreeable; far too often we see them shoving the non-Japanese around and behaving arrogantly.

Earlier I spoke optimistically of what I believe to be the sincere and radical changes that have come about in the outlook of the leaders of Japan and of the Japanese government; in their opinion Japan's expansion can no longer and must no longer be a one-way street. It is possible only if in return it promotes the development and prosperity of Japan's partners by means of a great collective program of cooperation. Unfortunately, the "new Japanese army," as we have called it, the army of newcomers from Tokyo, the businessmen and the engineers who are spreading through the zone, does not always possess such enlightened views. One thing that may hinder the success of Japan's new great scheme is the psychological makeup and behavior of the ordinary executive. Too often he has a totally inadequate experience of contact with foreigners, and he does not know how to behave outside his own country. He does not communicate well, he is wanting in perception and tact, he entirely forgets the scrupulous politeness of Japan, and in other countries he behaves like a boor. Only too frequently the people of these other nations blame the Japanese for not really having changed after all and for behaving in spite of their neat civilian suits as though they were in a conquered country once more; they say that the Japanese are harsh and exacting in their business negotiations, and that they are far too aware of their overwhelming superiority.

Now that this has been clearly stated, it is nevertheless interesting to observe that one of those countries where military Japan was most hated is now the very one that has forgotten the past most thoroughly and decided that the new Japan is a nation with which it is happy to have good relations. The country in question is of course Australia. And much the same may be said of its neighbor, New Zealand.

12.

The Asia-Pacific Zone: From Australia to China via Siberia

In October, 1967, for the first time in its history, Canberra, the Australian capital, received the visit of a Japanese premier; this was Sato, and like Seoul a little while earlier Canberra gave him a welcome that could almost be described as warm. This illustrated a twofold change: first, the new and exciting collaboration between Australia and Japan; second, Australia's new orientation toward Asia instead of Europe. Here we are in an area where the changes are very striking indeed, but they are still so recent that the outside world has hardly even heard of them and has not yet gauged their full importance. In 1965 Japan's sales to Australia amounted to $30 million; in 1967 they had multiplied by ten—$300 million. In 1965 Australia's sales to Japan amounted to $250 million; in 1967 they had almost tripled—$700 million.

It is also between these two dates that there occurred a very important event, one that might be described as Australia's disengagement from England. In 1965 England was Australia's main economic partner, just as it had always been from the point of view of import and of export. By 1967 everything was over; England had been outstripped both in the one and in the other. The United States had become Australia's chief supplier and Japan its chief customer. It is true that England is still Australia's second source of imports, far ahead of Japan, which comes third, for England still benefits from the old imperial preference tariff, and indeed the United States has only moved into the lead because of the sales of American arms to Canberra. But it is very curious to see England, for so long Australia's mother country, withdrawing from the Asian and southern hemisphere and knocking on the door of Europe, while at the same moment new links are being forged between Canberra and Tokyo—links that make Japan England's successor, at least on the commercial plane.

The trade between Australia and Japan shows one of the most rapid increases in the world. It is booming to such an extent that we may echo the words of the London *Financial Times'* foreign editor when he says, "Australia has chosen the Pacific." From now onward, he observed, after his return from a visit to the Antipodes, this is "the historic tendency." In 1960, 25 percent of Australian exports went to Asia. In 1967 it was 40 percent, and nearly half of them went to Japan. There is not only a change of direction, away from England, but also a change in the structure of these exports. The sales of the Australia of "the good old days," which was entirely pastoral and agricultural, consisted mainly of wool and wheat; the Australia of today, which is discovering the fabulous wealth lying beneath the surface of the country, sells industrial raw materials, iron and coking coal, and also a few manufactured products. There is a gradual turning from trade of the colonial type to the kind of exchange that takes place between developed or developing countries.

So here we have Japan as Australia's most important customer; or, returning to the even more interesting viewpoint of Tokyo, here we have Japan, that voracious consumer of raw materials, looking upon Australia as its newly discovered second most considerable source of supply, coming after the United States. In particular, Japan is now sure that Australia will provide at least a quarter of the iron ore that is needed for its top-ranking industry, the enormous iron and steel complexes.

I have already spoken of the very important agreements that have been signed since 1965 and that cover the joint development, equipment and exploitation of the great Australian iron mines recently opened up at Mount Newman, Hamersley and Savage River by Australo-American combines. Whereas in 1965 Japan was still importing no more than 300,000 tons of Australian iron ore, five years later, that is to say in 1970, the figure jumped to 15 million tons a year, and according to the forecasts the total will soon reach 25 million.

Australo-Japanese agreements for the supply of bauxite are also very probable. The huge Japanese aluminum industry is strongly attracted by the huge deposits that have been discovered at Weipa (Queensland) and on the Gove Peninsula (Northern Territory); it is said that they contain a third of the bauxite outside the Communist world. Among Australia's nonferrous metals, both manganese and zinc are of particular interest to the Japanese, who are also to take part in the search for uranium. As for copper, over a period of fifteen years, starting in 1972, the seven biggest Japanese firms concerned are to take almost a million tons of concentrates, according to the terms of a contract signed at the beginning of 1969 and providing for a payment of over a billion dollars; this is the biggest deal they have ever concluded.

In the last few years Australia has also become Japan's main source of coking coal, and Japan in its turn has taken America's place as Australia's chief customer for coal. Here again there has been a sudden rise in the import figures. In 1962 Australian coal satisfied a quarter of Japan's needs; by 1970 the proportion had risen to no less than 60 percent.* Australia's political stability is one of the great advantages of this new economic relationship; Tokyo compares it with the frightening unsteadiness of the Middle East, which provides such a very great deal of Japan's oil. Another advantage is the enormous scale of the mineral resources that have been discovered in Australia. Japan is going to take virtually the whole of the iron ore Australia produces in the coming years, but even if it were to take an annual 50 million tons the deliveries could still go on for three centuries, so it would be quite possible for the Australians to set up their own iron and steel industry without having to cut their supplies to Japan. The cost of sea transport between Australia and Japan is comparatively low, too, since the distance is only half that which is traveled by the average cargo of ore or coking coal for the Japanese steelworks.

As for agricultural raw materials, their increased sales to Japan are partly connected with the changes in the Japanese way of life. All the men now wear suits in the Western style, and this has greatly increased the demand for wool. What is more, the Japanese have in-

* An agreement for the delivery of 85 million tons of Queensland coal over a period of thirteen years was signed at the beginning of 1969. The Japanese will take part in the mining through a joint Australo-Japanese company that is to function for forty-two years.

vented a new kind of kimono, made of wool instead of silk and worn in the winter. Japan has therefore taken Great Britain's place as the heaviest buyer of Australian wool; it absorbs a third of the whole clip. In the same way the Westernizing of the bill of fare means that the Japanese buy very much greater amounts of Australian butter and other dairy products, sugar, meat (particularly frozen lamb and mutton), leather and hides. Because of all this trade, the Japanese buyers have become thoroughly popular in Australia, particularly as they buy more than twice as much as the Australians buy from them; yet this gives rise to a certain difficulty, for since the balance of trade is against them, the Japanese are beginning to ask the Australians to buy more. At present their imports from Japan amount to only 10 percent of their total purchases abroad; it is obvious that they could do better. But fortunately for Tokyo these imports are rising even faster than Australian sales to Japan.

Australia is now Japan's fifth most important customer. What are its main purchases? Australian iron, transformed, makes up a considerable part of them. The Japanese buy it in the shape of ore and send it back as heavy industrial products. Australia is the greatest buyer of exported Japanese steel. It also looks to Japan for great quantities of machinery and various kinds of mechanical equipment, automobiles and spare parts, agricultural machinery, synthetic and chemical products and scientific apparatus; it buys light articles and consumer goods such as cotton and other cloth, radios, cameras, china and ceramics. For the greater part of its imported cotton goods Australia now does its shopping in Tokyo and Osaka rather than in London and Manchester.

The spread of Japanese automobiles in Australia has raised some particularly significant questions. In May, 1967, Japan sold Australia nearly fifty thousand cars, most of them of low horsepower; this means that in spite of the rise in customs duties in 1966 they have a third of the market. The chief Japanese makers have opened three assembly works in Australia, and these have put together fifteen thousand automobiles shipped in separate parts. This success raises a grave problem: Are the Australians going to prevent themselves from ever having their own automobile industry? Then the far wider question arises: Will it not soon be time for them to make an attempt at industrializing their own country instead of being satisfied merely with trade and the sale of raw materials? A decision of this kind would not frighten Tokyo, for the Japanese feel that no Australian industry could be any menace to them for a great while and that Japan would be wise to help in its creation. Indeed, this help has already begun, since Japan not only invests in Australian factories but also takes part in joint ventures with Australia in various other sectors of industry such as electrical and electronic apparatus, textiles, chemicals, printing and public works.

Yet Tokyo still has to reckon with resistance on the part of Canberra. The Japanese are distinctly less popular as sellers than they are as buyers. This was made perfectly clear in the spring of 1968, when the progress of Japanese cars provoked a vehement attack on the part of Mr. Ewen, the vice-premier, who reproached Tokyo with closing its home market to foreign cars while so many Japanese cars were being sold to Australia, and with being downright mean in its purchases of Australian foodstuffs—of not buying nearly enough in Australia, in comparison with what it spent elsewhere. It is reasonable to suppose that this outburst was not unconnected with the anxiety of the five great foreign automobile makers (three American companies, one English and one German) who are all alarmed at the appearance of this Asian newcomer in Australia's present market of a hundred thousand cars.

As far as New Zealand is concerned, these difficulties hardly arise, and the relationship is untroubled. Here too since 1966 there has been an impressive Japanese boom, and in the course of it New Zealand's purchases from Japan leaped by 80 percent. New Zealand's imports from Japan, unlike Australia's, are twice as important as its exports, for this is a new country, and it has a voracious appetite for modern equipment—iron and steel in the form of bars, rails, sheets and other articles, machinery, electrical apparatus, telecommunications equipment, optical goods, automobiles, engines and railroad materials, plastics, man-made fibers, cloth and so forth. In the other direction, agricultural and pastoral New Zealand sends Japan much the same exports as Australia as far as raw materials and foodstuffs are concerned: in the first place wool, then butter and dairy products, meat, wood and wood pulp. Japan is now New Zealand's third customer, after England and the United States, and the country's fourth supplier, after the two I have just mentioned and Australia. New Zealand has made great use of the services of Japanese technicians, for the expansion of the radio and television system, for example, for the development of the aluminum industry, and for the widening of the Aukland bridge.

The two Pacific countries, Australia and New Zealand, are discovering Japan, and at the same time they are discovering, and being discovered by, Asia. It is particularly clear to Australia, just as it is to Japan, that there is everything to be said for expanding its Asian markets, especially as it has to find fresh outlets to offset its declining sales to England. In the fifteen years 1954 through 1968, Australian exports to Asia rose from 19 to 41 percent of its sales abroad, and its imports from Asia from 18 to 22 percent. Furthermore, its aid for the development of Southeast Asia has steadily increased over these last years; this aid is given mainly through the Colombo Plan, an association of members or former members of the Commonwealth, and by 1967 the total amount of this aid must have exceeded 500 million pounds sterling. India has begun buying Australian wool, and in this area Australian products have a huge potential market. India is also beginning to take Australian wheat; and Malaysia, Australian meat.

The Far East and Southeast Asia are outlets of very great potential capacity, not only for foodstuffs such as dairy produce and fruit and for nitrogen fertilizers and other products intended for agriculture, but also for the manufactures of the infant Australian industries, such as lathes and presses, metalworking plant and equipment, machinery for the food industry, and plastics. In the other direction, Southeast Asia is begining to sell its wares on the Australian and New Zealand markets, for it finds that there are great numbers of customers in those countries and that they are willing to import heavily. Australia and New Zealand buy oil from Indonesia and Borneo, tea from Ceylon, jute from India and Pakistan, cotton goods from Hong Kong and Taiwan, rubber from Malaysia and Singapore and so on.

Australia, New Zealand, Southeast Asia: in the last analysis all the countries in this area have one thing in common—their whole future depends upon their economy, and their economy can provide the solution for many a political problem. For Japan and Australia especially, economic development is the great answer to the pressures and the dangers that they both feel threatening them from either side of the Pacific and that are causing them to come together. In the first place, the pressure of America: like Japan, Australia has to resist the gravitational pull of the United States, avoid the peril of being drawn wholly into the American orbit. Is it not true that the understanding with Japan, Japan's collaboration in Australian development, and the raising of the Southeast Asian standard of living are a means of doing away with the danger of an American protectorate? And there is danger and pressure from the Asian side as well: the English are leaving their bases east of Suez, and when they have gone will not Australia also see the departure of the Americans, when they have reached some compromise in Vietnam?

There is the likelihood of a vacation of power in Southeast Asia, perhaps even of a vacuum. And the Australians do not want to move in entirely by themselves to take the place of those who leave. They would like the Japanese to share in this taking-over from the former powers. They know that the Japanese too are intensely concerned with Indonesia's recovery, since for them it is their first line of defense on the Asian side. And then, more than any other country, Australia is aware of the huge shadow that China casts over this whole part of the world. The Australians, like the Japanese, think that the best antidote to communism, the best answer to the "domino theory," is peace and economic revival and modernization by means of economic and financial cooperation between all the countries in the area.

The Australian papers and advertisements were recently filled with an eye-catching symbol: it is the badge, or perhaps one might say the arms, of the Australian pavilion at Expo '70 at Osaka. It is simple and conveys its meaning at once. A globe—the Pacific Ocean. A vertical line down the middle—the 135th degree of longitude. At the top of this line a dot which is Osaka, with Japan all around it. At the bottom Australia, with the 135th meridian running right through it. In other words these two great countries, Australia and Japan, have discovered that there is an axis that unites them. Their clocks tell the same time, literally and figuratively. They are on the same meridian.

Naturally enough, another country with a Pacific coastline also feels the gravitational pull of the Asia-Pacific Zone: this is Canada. It does not yet belong to the region's intergovernmental organizations, but its representatives are already to be seen in the businessmen's permanent committees and conferences; and, turning more and more toward the Pacific, Canada has arranged for regular economic consultations with

Japan. In many ways the increasingly close relations between Canada and Japan resemble those between Australia and Japan. Australia may have risen to the place of the Japanese economy's second most important supplier, but Canada, in third place, comes very close behind. The whole of the trade between the two countries, counting both imports and exports, has reached the billion-dollar level.

Japan buys very great quantities of agricultural products from Canada—wheat and meat, wood and wood pulp—and even more in the way of industrial raw materials such as iron ore, scrap, copper ore and concentrates, nickel and other nonferrous metals, and oil. The latest news is that Japan has begun buying coal and uranium from Canada.*

As we have seen elsewhere in the Asia-Pacific Zone, Japan's need to ensure abundant, steady supplies induces it to invest increasingly in the producing countries. Japanese capital is welcome in the insufficiently developed western provinces of Canada, which only ask that some of the raw materials bought by Japan should be worked up on the spot. In British Columbia the Japanese take an important share in prospecting for copper ore and the mining of the deposits; it does the same in the exploitation of timber. The Japanese are to be found in Manitoba, where they are interested in the copper and zinc. Japex engineers, collaborating with Canadians and Americans, are prospecting for oil in Alberta in the west of Canada (Zama Lake, Rainbow Lake and the huge areas of oil-bearing sand in Lake Athabaska). The Japanese are also investing in the fisheries and even more so in the automobile industry; Isuzu already has an assembly works, and in another Canadian works Toyota promises to put together a thousand cars a month. It is estimated that between 1972 and 1974 Japanese investments in Canada will have reached $200 million.

Japan sells Canada iron and steel, textiles, machinery and industrial plant, particularly heavy equipment for the British Columbian hydro-electric stations, automobiles, motor bicycles and cameras. But the volume is not enough to satisfy the Japanese. "Buy more from us," they say. "We have everything you want; all you have to do is to buy less from Europe." They are in hopes that their purchases, which are on a very large scale and which are exceedingly valuable to Canada, will

* On the subject of uranium, see Chapter 8. As for coal, a contract for the delivery of 30 million tons spread over fifteen years has recently been signed; it is to come from the Smoky River mines in Alberta.

eventually give them a wider outlet for their exports on the Canadian market.

Meanwhile Canada also buys from the Asian countries. They in their turn are discovering that Canada is a profitable market, one that is in full expansion. Canada is Hong Kong's fourth most important customer, coming before Japan and Australia. Canada buys tin and rubber from Malaysia and Singapore, cloth and ready-made clothing from Taiwan, the same, plus fish, from South Korea, tea and vegetable oils from Ceylon. It sells Southeast Asia wheat and other foodstuffs, wood and wood pulp, industrial equipment, airplanes and more. Canada, like Japan and at the same time as Japan, is becoming aware of the need for taking part in an international effort designed to make Southeast Asia prosperous, and in this respect it is fully conscious of the role it has to play as a wealthy country. Canada has increased its economic and technical aid to the region, particularly within the framework of the Colombo Plan. Instances of this are the supplies of food and raw materials to India and Pakistan, Canada's help in the agricultural development of Malaysia, its contribution to the expansion of power stations in India, Pakistan and Ceylon, the building of the Ceylon airport, or a great highway in Thailand.

Canadian loans and investments in Southeast Asia are considerable. They do a great deal toward the development of the region's mineral resources—copper and nickel in the Philippines, bauxite in India and Malaysia, nickel in Indonesia, zinc in India, and oil in north Sumatra. Canadian technicians and financiers are particularly interested in Malaysia. Another example of the way economic bonds are crisscrossing in every direction throughout this zone is that Canadian capital, in association with Japanese capital, has also invested in the Japanese aluminum, zinc and nickel industries.

It is quite fascinating to see how Japan's interest in Canada carries on to Canada's neighbor still farther to the north—Alaska. Here of course we are in American territory. But the Japanese seem to look upon it as a country apart and to offer it a kind of autonomous position in the Asia-Pacific Zone, where it can cooperate with them—a position which, as they see it, Alaska has already accepted. The chief wealth of this northern land is timber, fish and oil. Does it all go to the United States? Not in the least; at present almost 100 percent of Alaskan exports go to Japan. Japan buys everything, although there is very little it can sell in return. In 1966 Japan sold Alaska $2 million worth of goods, as against its purchases of $40 million.

The Japanese are also bringing capital into Alaska, just as though they had made up their minds to stimulate local production. A few years ago they started in the timber and pulpwood industry, sending all their produce back to Japan; then they moved into the fisheries, and Japanese fishing companies have bases at Anchorage and Cordova. A joint Japanese-American fertilizer works is in operation at Port Nikiski, using natural gas. The Japanese have been buying more and more natural gas from Alaska since 1967, and they use special ships to carry it in liquid form.* Since 1967, too, they have also been prospecting for oil, joint Japanese and American capital having set up the Alaska Petroleum Development Company. Has Alaska the impression of being invaded? American timber interests have complained that the Japanese push up the price of wood, and that by channeling Alaskan resources to Japan they have created a local shortage. But if we are to believe *Fortune Magazine* (September 1, 1967) the Alaskans themselves are quite satisfied with the situation. The Japanese have already invested several hundred million dollars in their state, and it is sure to go on.

Finally let us turn to the most striking, the newest and the most exciting aspect of the Asia-Pacific Zone: recently Japan has begun to widen its field of action in northern Asia by clearing the way for cooperation with the youngest of all these countries, Siberia. Even more remarkable is the fact that it was Moscow that made the first advances to Tokyo; Moscow took the initiative and asked the Japanese to share in the development of Siberia.

Relations between Japan and Russia were bad for many years after 1945. It is worth recalling that there never has been any peace treaty between Moscow and Tokyo, for the Soviet Union refused to sign the treaty of San Francisco in 1952. Diplomatic relations were indeed reestablished, but only on the footing of a plain "declaration ending the state of war" in 1956. No progress toward the conclusion of a treaty has

---

* As of 1969 two methane carriers, each gauging 85,000 tons, carry natural gas from Alaska to Japan. Two gigantic methane carriers are being planned. These 130,000-ton ships will be as big as the huge oil tankers, and they will be used for supplying Tokyo with gas from Brunei, in North Borneo.

been possible, for the Japanese insist upon the restoration of the Kuriles, or at least of the southern part of the chain, whereas the Russians, who have been occupying all the islands since 1945, refuse to give them up.

But since 1960 the conflict between China and Russia has had a profound effect upon the Soviet Union's position in the Far East. The visit of Mikoyan, Khrushchev's right-hand man, to Tokyo in 1961 and even more his return in May, 1964, marked the beginning of better relations. The Soviet minister described the wealth of Siberia in glowing terms; he told the Japanese, in substance, that the region was about to enter a period of remarkable prosperity, for the Russians had made up their minds to undertake the immense task of developing it with all their available resources. Since you are so near and since you are so efficient and well qualified, he said, we should heartily welcome your collaboration. This offer keenly interested Tokyo. The Keidanren itself, under the leadership of Shigeo Nagano, the president of Fuji Steel, set about studying the whole matter. Meetings between the two sides became more frequent: the Keidanren sent a mission to Moscow; Miki went to see Kosygin, the Soviet premier; Gromyko, the Russian foreign minister, came to Tokyo; so did Patolichev, the minister for foreign trade, and some others; and then there were the sessions of the Russo-Japanese Economic Committee, which was set up in 1966.

It soon became clear to the Japanese that the undertaking called for huge capital investment and long-term credit, that it would affect the whole of Japan's economic planning, and that it would have an influence upon policy. In short, it was so vast that it was a matter for the state, one that had to be dealt with at governmental level and that would need a great deal of time. The Japanese government also seized upon this opportunity to reopen the question of the relations between the two countries, maintaining that the affair as a whole could not be separated from the problem of the peace treaty. Nevertheless two questions have been set aside for independent consideration: one is the exploitation of the Siberian forests and the other that of the Sakhalin deposits of natural gas. Both sides reached agreement on the first as early as July, 1968. The Japanese saw this as the beginning of a satisfactory settlement.

In Tokyo it is said that the Russian offers are on a prodigious scale, one that matches the wealth of Siberia, which the eighteen million inhabitants of the enormous region have hitherto scarcely exploited at all. It appears that huge oil fields have been discovered in western Siberia, as well as enormous and easily mined deposits of coal, iron ore and natural gas (which is also to be found in very great quantities in Sakhalin); they also speak of copper, lead, tin, cobalt, tungsten, molybdenum, diamonds, bauxite, salt and the huge expanses of forest. Moscow and European Russia are a great way off, at the far end of the Trans-Siberian Railway. Japan is much closer, and the Japanese could be both the consumers of part of these resources and at the same time the engineers who would actively help in their exploitation by means of equipment and supplies of every kind. In Tokyo the main outlines of the Russo-Japanese negotiations are beginning to emerge clearly: if we include Sakhalin, we see that the matter can be resumed under six chief headings:

1. Oil. What the Russians want the Japanese to do in this case is to build them an enormous pipeline, together with the necessary pumping stations, which would link western Siberia (where an estimated 40 billion tons has been discovered) with eastern Siberia, which is short of fuel. This pipeline, of the remarkable diameter of nearly four feet and running some forty-three hundred miles, would go from Tyumen in western Siberia to Nakhodka, the eastern Siberian port near Vladivostok. Another, a little over twenty-eight inches in diameter, would run from Megion to Aleksandrovsk, a distance of about five hundred miles. All this amounts to an undertaking that might take twenty years or so, and the financing of it would be a heavy burden for the Japanese, particularly as the Russians ask for very long-term credit. Japan would be paid in crude oil and iron ore. To begin with, between 10 and 12 million tons of crude oil might be delivered to Japan every year—that is to say, twice as much as it receives from the U.S.S.R. at present.

2. Gas. The main reserves lie in north Sakhalin, in the region of Okha. They have been estimated at 875 billion cubic meters. According to the plan Japan would provide the liquefaction plant and a gas pipeline over six hundred miles long, reaching south Sakhalin; here special isothermic ships would carry it to Japan. The Russians have proposed that Japan import 2 billion cubic meters of gas over a period of fifteen or twenty years, thus doubling their resources in

this field. Less important reserves of natural gas, estimated at 60 billion cubic meters, have also been discovered in the Yakutsk region of Siberia, and the suggestion is that Japan should build a pipeline to Nakhodka. Russia could absorb $400 million worth of Japanese equipment, up to 10 billion cubic meters of gas in exchange.

3. The port of Nakhodka. The Japanese would undertake the development and the modernization of this port on the Pacific, as well as the improvement of the harbor facilities at Vladivostok, Vanino and Mago. Ever since it was founded in 1859, Nakhodka—the name means Discovery—has been a mercantile port on the splendid Bay of Vladivostok, somewhat to the east of that town. Stalin decided to make it the great trading port of the Soviet Far East, Vladivostok remaining the naval base. In 1967 Nakhodka had a population of a hundred thousand, and the amount of shipping it handles is making it the rival of Leningrad and Odessa. Japan lies opposite to it, and the merchant ships go either to Niigata, on the Sea of Japan, or to Yokohama, on the Pacific. In summer, a Nakhodka-Yokohama line carries Japanese passengers who then take the Trans-Siberian Railway. It is a sign of the times that the harbor is not only thoroughly equipped with "Made in Japan" material, but in the streets and hotels of Nakhodka one also sees many Japanese tourists who stop off to look at the town on their way to Europe.

4. The forests. The exploitation of the Siberian forests calls for a great deal of equipment for the sawmills and the wood-converting factories that the Russians want to build, particularly in the regions of Bratsk and Komsomolsk, on the Amur and in Sakhalin. The timber agreement signed in July, 1968, was the first tangible outcome of the Siberian negotiations. It stipulates that Japan will send a total of $133 million worth of equipment for the timber industry; Russia will pay 20 percent in cash and the rest in kind, delivering 8.8 million tons of wood over five years.

5. Copper. Japanese participation is needed for the equipment and the working of the huge Udokan deposits, near Irkutsk in central Siberia. The Russians have already made tentative approaches to the Mitsui group; they also hope that Japan will cooperate with them in the development and exploitation of the Norilsk mine, also in central Siberia.

6. Coal. The southern Siberian coal mines, particularly those of Chulman, are of special interest to the Japanese because they produce coking coal. The reserves in the neighborhood of Chulman are thought to amount to 3.5 billion tons. The four leading Japanese trading companies are concerned in this project. There is a scheme according to which the Japanese would provide up to $400 million and receive 5 million tons of Siberian coal a year. But the Russians seem rather lukewarm over this matter, and it is all still at the planning stage.

Perhaps the most attractive of these schemes is, after all, the one that deals with natural gas. It may be that the Sakhalin gas, added to the Alaskan and that which Japan might also get from Brunei, will provide a partial solution for one of the country's greatest problems—the diversification of its supplies of energy.

In addition to the offers of cooperation in the areas I have just mentioned, there is talk of various subsidiary deals. These include the building of railroads and the sale of various kinds of plant—for example, the equipment needed for the great Siberian hydroelectric programs, such as the huge Bratsk dam and another even larger dam on the Yenisey.

Finally, there is the very important new Russo-Japanese air agreement of February 13, 1969, which has granted the Japan Air Line the right to use the Tokyo-Moscow route. The Japanese have been allowed to fly over Siberia, using their own pilots and their own planes. Recently, the Japan Air Line and Air France received permission to carry their flights as far as Paris. Other foreign airlines will follow suit. This will outdo the polar routes and offer the shortest air link between Europe and Japan.

Under the guidance of the Soviet Union, Siberia, with its tremendous landscapes, its fabulously wealthy mineral deposits, and a climate that is in some parts not as bad as it is said to be, is going to become one of the giants of tomorrow. Foreigners who have recently traveled through the country speak of the magnitude of the Russian effort in this vast north-Asian area. It is clear that both this enormous undertaking and Russia's call to Japan for cooperation result from the Soviet Union's desire to hasten the development of Siberia in order to be able to withstand the growing might of China. The Russians feel that China, overpopulated and inimical, is a real threat to Siberia, which is almost empty and mainly inhabited by whites. Moreover, it is common knowledge that among the territorial disagreements that oppose the U.S.S.R. and China all along the endless frontier that they share, the Chinese have claims on the Soviet Far East, Asian Russia's opening on the Pacific.

In March, 1963, the Peking *People's Daily* stated that Mao's China did not recognize the unequal treaties concluded in former times with the Czars, and that it reserved the right to lay claim, at a date of its own choosing, to a great stretch of Siberia beyond the Amur and the Ussuri which constitutes the Soviet empire's façade upon the Pacific and which includes the industrial regions of Khabarovsk and Komsomolsk. The Russians, backing Japan in order to counterbalance China, choose to forget their old and lasting distrust of these Asiatics who beat them at the beginning of the century, and to overlook the fact that the Japanese too once cast longing eyes upon Siberia. Indeed, just after the 1917 revolution the Japanese military leaders, with the connivance of the great Western powers, tried to carve themselves out a kingdom in those parts. But all that is past history. The powerful, heavily armed Soviet Union of today no longer feels any particular apprehension when it looks in the direction of Japan, nor does it suffer from any uneasiness when it suggests profitable business deals to the Tokyo capitalists.

As between Russia and Japan, it is the first that is more eager to see the Japanese in Siberia, and the second that is in less of a hurry. The reason for this is not only that a venture of such magnitude needs time for discussion and the taking of decisions; it is also that the Japanese too look in the direction of China and wish to take account of the Chinese presence, but they mean to do so in a spirit quite unlike that of the Russians. They ask nothing better than to turn the Siberian project into a legitimate and profitable economic operation. But they do not want to have anything whatsoever to do with turning it into a mainly or partially political maneuver in which Siberia would become, as it were, the focal point of a Russo-Japanese alliance or understanding of an anti-Chinese nature. Tokyo thinks it right to say yes in economic and no in political matters that might involve Japan in its partners' quarrels, and this applies not only to Washington but also to Moscow.

*   *   *

China! The reason why I have not yet spoken of it, and the reason why it is now the moment to do so, is that at present the whole of the Asia-Pacific Zone is being built up without China and yet at the same time with China strongly in mind. There is no room for China at its present stage in the scheme of Miki and his successors, or at least there is no mention of Chinese membership; but the great plan which is being worked out all around China's coasts and land frontiers, and which has caused the earlier pages of this book to revolve as it were about that country, merely emphasizes the implicit fact that China occupies the central position, and that in this vast structure the Middle Kingdom cannot be indefinitely left out of account.

One of the unspoken laws that govern Japanese activities in the new Asia may be summed up in these words: Work with reference to China, but not in any way against China. Relationships with Peking— here again we have a major problem in which Japan stands aloof from the American policy of containment, and most particularly from the policy of surrounding Mao's China with a ring of military power. On the contrary, Tokyo's rule is to handle China very gently. This too is the deeply felt wish of most of the Japanese, even—and indeed particularly—when their premier is too pro-American for their liking, as in the case of Sato. Deal tactfully with China; this implies disassociation from Washington's policy of opposition by all possible methods. It also means refraining from criticizing the policy of Peking and the Chinese Communist leaders, in spite of all conflicts of opinion, it means accepting their abuse patiently and never replying, and it means keeping open the channels of communication through trade and of broadening them whenever it is possible through private contacts when relations between the two governments are ruled out.

Yet there are many things that could cause conflict and disagreement. At least in theory, Japan and China are still at war; after 1945 there was neither an armistice nor a peace treaty between the two countries. Tokyo has not recognized the Communist regime set up in Peking at the end of 1949, and the two capitals have never exchanged ambassadors. On the other hand, Japan, being America's ally, does recognize Marshal Chiang Kai-shek's government in Taiwan. For more than twenty years the Tokyo governments have invariably been conservative and capitalist, and Peking has never ceased to denounce the Japanese political leaders as the accomplices of American imperialism and as imperialists themselves. Although the great treaty of alliance and friendship that Mao Tse-tung and Stalin signed at Moscow in 1950 has been shelved, it has never been denounced, and this treaty is directed as much against Japan as it is against the United States.

And yet there we are: in spite of all these reasons for hostility, it is fair to say that of all the countries in the non-Communist world Japan is the one that ever since 1949 has spoken most understandingly of China in its press, rarely criticizing its policy and almost always treating its leaders with respect. Japan's effort to learn about People's China and to inform Japanese public opinion has been no less persevering than America's; it has been conducted far more objectively and often with sympathy. There have been countless Japanese commercial, cultural, parliamentary and other missions to China; considerable numbers of Japanese businessmen live permanently in Peking, and correspondents of the great Tokyo papers have been the most important body of journalists in the Chinese capital. Hundreds of travelers coming from Tokyo by way of Hong Kong have made the classic tour of China in officially guided bands. In the other direction, a certain number of Chinese visitors are allowed into Japan, and a semiofficial trade mission with a large staff occupies a whole building in Tokyo.

How is this tactful treatment of China to be explained? The first answer probably lies in the Japanese people's guilt complex. Even though they may not mention it, they know how revoltingly the Japanese soldiers behaved to the Chinese not so very long ago. One way of expressing their regret, of making an *amende honorable*, is to have a kindly and understanding attitude towards their neighbors today. What makes their shame over the cruelties and the vandalism of the Sino-Japanese War all the greater is that the attack on China was an attack by a pupil upon his aged master, to whom he owed the utmost respect. Great China was from time immemorial the mother of Asian culture, and Japan knows better than any other country how much it has owed to China ever since the beginning of its history. In addition to the cultural likeness between the two countries, which shows in countless ways ranging from the use of the same written characters to the same habits of life and thought, there is the fact of the likeness of race—a fact that makes the Chinese close kin to the Japanese, giving them a feeling of nearness that they can never experience to the same degree with other Asians, still less with men of another color.

There was a time between the two wars when it would have been possible to build up a lasting economic collaboration with China, that gigantic neighbor and cousin, a cooperative association that might have been immensely valuable to both sides. Even more important, a Sino-Japanese economic understanding might have changed the face of the whole world. Japan is bitterly aware of having missed that splendid opportunity in 1930 when the brutal methods of its military leaders overcame the patient approach of its businessmen. War and its train of wretchedness and hatred shattered the possibilities of the very close relationship that was, and still is, implicit in the very geography of the Far East itself—utterly dispelled them for a quarter of a century and maybe for longer. The Japanese long to bring these possibilities back to life, and their longing is all the stronger now that China has risen from the abyss of ruin and despair into which Japanese aggression had plunged it for so many years.

Mao Tse-tung and his companions have fought a battle far harder than the Japanese war of former days, a battle against poverty, hunger and ignorance; and, broadly speaking, they have won. No one on earth can appreciate better than the Japanese the unbelievable advances that the Chinese have made: the unity of the nation restored, the growing might of a great industry, military strength and, above and beyond all this, the atomic bomb. Faced with this enormous transformation, how could Japan conceivably fail to be struck with a prudent, cautious respect, to say the very least? It is a respect made all the deeper when they realize that soon there will be a billion human beings living and working in that vast expanse of China just at hand, a country twenty-six times the size of their own.

If other nations had to live in the shadow of China they would no doubt live in dread. Not the Japanese, however. We have seen, for example, how calmly they received the news of their neighbor's atomic experiments. This calmness, too, calls for an explanation, and here again part of the answer is to be found in history. Over the centuries China and Japan have never been hostile neighbors, as France and England were, or France and Germany. There never had been a war between them until the one that Japan started in 1895 and the other, also started by Japan, that lasted from 1931 to 1945. The only attack directed at the archipelago from the mainland was that of the Mongols in the thirteenth century, and that came to nothing. Since its beginnings in 1949 Communist China has never threatened Japan, and even though China now possesses the bomb Japan does not look upon it as a present menace. "It will never be China," they think, "that will commit the error or the crime of dropping the bomb on us, thus blackening its history and its good face."

Exporting communism by armed force is no part of China's system; for this it uses the strength of its example and its ideas. Although for a while the Japanese were deeply impressed, and some thoroughly convinced, by Mao's experiment and by its underlying ideology, they now, after their own success and the difficulties of the cultural revolution on the continent, feel that they are in little danger from the Chinese infection. They feel sure, too, that Peking is too much taken up with its own internal problems to launch any adventure abroad. Tokyo feels that China too has plenty of reasons for treating its Japanese neighbors with consideration. It has need of them; since the break between China and Russia and the departure of the Soviet experts, Japan is in the best position to supply China with equipment, to provide some degree of technical assistance, and to buy Chinese goods. It is entirely to Peking's interest to refrain from throwing Japan into the arms of the Americans and from turning that country into an enemy rendered dangerous by American support; on the contrary, Peking knows that it would be well advised to draw Japan into a middle or even into a frankly pro-Chinese position.

All this explains the apparently paradoxical persistence of the trade between China and Japan. No diplomatic relations; alliances with opposing sides in the cold war; radical disagreement between Peking's "politics first" and Tokyo's "the economy before everything"; the many incidents and conflicts, such as Peking's boycotting of the Kishi government in 1958, Chinese encouragement in the anti-American riots of 1960, the 1960–1963 Chinese crisis, the crisis that began with the cultural revolution in 1966, and Taiwan's repeated protests, threatening in its turn to boycott Tokyo as a punishment for trading with Peking and so on. In spite of all these storms the exchanges between Japan and Communist China have gone on and have even increased.

Much more interesting than the statistics and the mechanism of this trade is the fact of its steadiness and its continuation. Is it not extremely unusual, or even unique, to see two great countries whose relationships are deliberately thought out and pertinaciously developed by means of business, in direct opposition to the obstinate official hostility that exists between the two governments concerned? And is it not a striking illustration of what Japan has been able to accomplish by giving the economy such an important place in its foreign policy? In comparison, the mechanics of the trade seem of minor importance; in my opinion it is pointless for the specialists to pour out floods of words describing wonderfully strange Oriental complexity. In their jargon, two sorts of Sino-Japanese commerce exist—the L.T. trade and the F.F. trade. The first consists of those exchanges which fall within the scope of a private agreement first negotiated by Liao and Takasaki (hence the initials), an agreement to which the two governments had to give their tacit blessing, whether they liked it or not. The second covers the rest of the trade, the greater part, which the Chinese reserve for what they term the "friendly firms"—that is to say, those Japanese companies that they look upon as politically pro-Chinese and that are therefore the only ones that are allowed to engage in this trade.

As for the figures of Sino-Japanese trade, although they multiplied by seven in ten years, they still amount to only a moderate sum. The total (imports together with exports) exceeded $600 million in 1966 but fell below this level in 1967, when the curve dropped because of the cultural revolution. In 1967 Communist China ranked only tenth on both the list of Japan's suppliers and that of its customers. The goods Japan sent to China were slightly less than its imports from China. It is true that for Peking these proportions are quite different. Since the break with the Soviet Union, Japan has taken Russia's place as Communist China's main trading partner; this, incidentally, fully explains China's interest in the continuation of the relationship.

Then again, the Chinese market for certain Japanese products is by no means to be despised. This applies particularly to fertilizers, for half of those produced in Japan are sold to the Chinese; to special steels, which the Chinese buy in very considerable quantities; to insecticides, cotton yarn, rayon, man-made fibers and so forth. Eighty percent of Japanese sales to China are composed of heavy industrial products such as mechanical equipment and metallurgical and chemical products. These sales would show a considerable increase if the suppliers would grant long-term credit, but the Tokyo government forbids them to do so, being afraid of reprisals on the part of Taiwan, for in 1966 trade with that island amounted to a total of no less than $473 million. As for Japanese imports from China, 90 percent of them are concerned with raw materials, 50 percent being for use in industry and 40 percent for foodstuffs.

Japan pays the closest possible attention to the doings of its European competitors on the Chinese market, and recently they have been making progress. The chief of these is West Germany, which assumed second place in 1967, its chief sales being steel, machine tools and chemicals. Here again the figures are of no great significance; what really matters for Japan is that it should not be outdone by any European country. And lastly Japan looks upon Communist China's achievements in exporting to the world markets as a matter of great importance. China is becoming a serious competitor in Southeast Asia as far as certain products of light industry are concerned. In 1966 the country exported 960 million yards of "Made in China" cotton goods, a record figure that is slightly higher than the comparable Japanese exports, which are dropping.

The whole of the Japanese strategy with regard to the conduct of its relations with China is dictated not by the present situation, which Japan looks upon as provisional and for the moment disappointing, but by the prospects of the future, which give it hopes for a great increase in its trade with China, an expansion matching the tremendous size of that country. Japan never forgets the importance and the value of its exchanges with the China of the time between the wars. In the period 1930 to 1937, China took almost 20 percent of Japan's exports and supplied 15 percent of its imports. In the future, the Japanese think that they may get back to these figures and perhaps go beyond them, even taking into account the fact that the new China, which is turning itself into an industrial country, will retain a greater proportion of its raw materials for its own use and will manufacture its ordinary consumer goods at home. If there were good relations between the two countries, Japan could also strengthen its position as the chief supplier to the Chinese market, and it could do so far better than it ever did by means of the threat or the exercise of force.

The Chinese market! That is where the future lies. Seven hundred million potential consumers today; tomorrow, 700 million and more actually buying, or in other words making the transition from the deepest poverty to the beginnings of personal comfort and domestic plenty. What an enormous market this will mean, a market at the very doors of a Japan that is fully equipped to supply it! A pipe dream? Mere speculation? The Europeans, having waited so long, are beginning to wonder whether this may not be the case; they are beginning to lose faith. But the Japanese feel, or rather they know, that it is not an illusion; they know it from their own experience. The Chinese mass, even though it may be Communist, is going to represent a most prodigious consumer market, and even though much of the task of supplying it may be reserved for Chinese industry, that industry is far behind Japan's; its development will take a great many years, and in itself Chinese industry will be an insatiable customer for the Japanese manufacturers. And Chinese agriculture, too, will have to import huge quantities of fertilizers, quantities that will match its enormous future needs.

But the Chinese of tomorrow will be a rival as well as a customer, because the Chinese factories, following the example of the Japanese, will devote part of their production to the export market. So the Japanese traders must expect the competition of Chinese exporters on the Asian and possibly the worldwide markets, and it may be that they will come up against this competition quite soon. This is another factor that Japan takes into account when it looks into the future. The possibility of a break with such an important customer, with such a gigantic neighbor, must be ruled out; it is essential for Japan to treat China tactfully and do everything to remain on good terms with that country. Even more, Japan must certainly help its neighbor. Japan's first aim must be the rollback of poverty in China too. A prosperous China will be a less dangerous neighbor for Japan than a China falling back into difficulties or bogged down in underdevelopment. In short, China's weakness and its absence from the Asia-Pacific Zone can only be temporary. A China sound and well based once more, set free from its inner turmoil, modernized and at last making its entrance upon the stage of international economy, is an essential factor in the very concept of the region itself.

If the appearance of this new giant should make the Japanese tremble, there is no evidence that it does. And in any case it is not going to happen overnight; they have some time to make ready. The industrialization of China is not advancing as rapidly as some people thought ten years ago, and the cultural revolution has given it another check. It may be, too, that the Chinese are not going to carry it as far as they were expected to do. Once more agriculture is of the very first importance in their planning. They seem less ambitious in the sphere of industry than they were in the days when Russia was helping them; perhaps they have understood that it will take a long while before their industry is capable of doing everything for itself. The Japanese are of the opinion that it will probably take a whole generation before the full weight of the new China as a great industrial power is felt throughout the world.

And in addition to this, may we not hope that the passing of the years and the coming of the post-Mao period will to some degree sober the Chinese and calm their zeal? Without supposing that they may fall into the revisionism that they so detest and still less that they may come to doubt communism itself, is it not reasonable to hope that they will by then have done with the permanent revolution, that their inner dissensions will have died down, and that in business Mao's heirs will be more flexible and more realistic partners than the leaders of the China of the Red Guards? Again, will not the future leaders also be dealing with what they look upon as a more "acceptable" Japan, one that will have withdrawn a certain distance from the United States—a Japan unencumbered by American bases and therefore a Japan that, in its own interest, China will not threaten, since a frightened Japan would once more feel the temptation to rearm?

A really intelligent policy for Japan, one that deserves to be carried out with patient steadiness, would be to make an appointment with China for the end of the century, an appointment for coexistence and cooperation. This policy would mean leaving the road open for closer relations, advancing gradually toward reconciliation, and closing the paths that would lead back toward hatred. Such an objective would not in the meantime prevent Japan from profiting from its advance or from holding on to its lead as long as it possibly can. Not at all, for that is what the policy requires. At home, Japan would push on its industrial development to the highest attainable degree, and it would do so peacefully, without threatening its neighbors in any way. Abroad, it would come to an understanding with its neighbors to occupy the best possible positions in the economic, political and social life of Asia, China always being an essential factor in their planning.

But here we must take great care. This has nothing whatsoever to do with turning the Asia-Pacific Zone into a system of encirclement. On the contrary, it is a system of inclusion, of welcome, that is to be organized. The positions that are to be occupied or created are to be economic and not in any sense military; they are to be positions in which Japan will cooperate with the other countries, since it knows that they are just as anxious as Japan itself for the maintenance of peaceful relations with China. These are to be positions that have nothing to do with armed threat or with the military strategy for some eventual conflict; on the contrary, they are to be negotiating positions held with a view to coming to an understanding, and to China's peaceful attainment of membership in the Pacific system—to China's joining it, perhaps as the leading partner.

When that time comes it will be necessary to give China its due share and to work out a lasting system of coexistence or even of co-operation with China, an economic alliance, using the advantages gained in the meantime during these negotiations. Japan will quite certainly have to come to an agreement with the China of a billion men, but it must do so by yielding or sharing only on the best possible terms and with guarantees; it must not lower itself, must not dwindle to the status of a satellite that could be drawn into the Chinese orbit.

China will have to be given its rightful place. But when at last this great country wins through, what in fact will this place be? Most probably it will be the third, no less! The third place—that is to say, that same position which will by then have been Japan's for quite a while: the third place in the economy of the Asian and Pacific region, perhaps even in that of the whole world. It will no longer be Japan that comes third after the United States and the Soviet Union, but China. Japan's present place will have been only a temporary rank. Even now the Japanese are aware of this; already they accept this future state of affairs. We must not forget that they are an extraordinarily flexible nation. Success can certainly go to their heads, but probably not to such a point that they abandon their fundamental realism.

This is a fluctuating, changing world. The Japanese have learned this reality or this truth from all sorts of teachers: from nature, from the surrounding landscape, from the Buddhism that has formed them, from the history of former times or of our own. Who indeed can tell what alterations and surprises there will be in the relative importance of the nations in the headlong race toward the end of our century? For example, might not the relations of the great powers be wholly changed by a reunification of the two Germanies? It seems to me that there is more real caution in the Japanese rise than appears on the surface. It is pleasant to occupy the third place when that place is free, but it is not necessarily worth clinging to it indefinitely. Would not a well-assured fourth or fifth place be better than a tottering, threatened third?

As it is inevitably the case, we do not find these ideas in Tokyo's official plans and documents, but I believe that they underlie the whole of the Japanese approach to the Asia-Pacific Zone. They also coincide with the suggestions that I have put forward about an "after the American alliance" period. Somewhere in the future, in the years that lie ahead of us, this region's hour must come; and that will be the time of "the great negotiation," the conference that, having brought about some degree of "de-escalation" of American military power in the zone, will at last turn the vast area that surrounds Japan into a network of forces in peaceful equilibrium, all counterbalancing and respecting one another and oriented mainly toward economic exchange.

A lightly armed Japan, guaranteed by the United States, Russia and China, could still base its prosperity and strength upon the co-operative development of the whole geographic area that lies about it, collaborating with its immediate neighbors and with the particular countries concerned.

At present we in the West have lost much of the faith we once had in the rise of the underdeveloped countries and in their power of achieving development and modernization. When one looks at these things from Tokyo, however, it seems that perhaps we may be wrong. If ever there was a part of the world where economic development should soon begin to shine like a great spreading patch of sun, that part is Southeast Asia and the whole of the Asia-Pacific Zone. There are huge reserves of industriousness, zeal and intelligence, only waiting for peace to accomplish miracles throughout the whole region, from Thailand and Vietnam right up to Korea. The Japanese adventure, with the country rising from utter prostration to the pinnacle of success in twenty years, could be reproduced many times over. And when we reflect that, of the world's great powers, whatever may be their present rank, four are countries in this zone, we may reasonably conclude that whatever may happen, the coming century will be that of the Pacific—which means that Japan is extraordinarily well placed for the world of tomorrow.

13.

The Weight of the Past, the Dangers to Come

Japan has a good start, Japan is right up with the leaders, wholly committed to this race toward the year 2000 and already in third place; yes, all this is perfectly true. But still there is no lack of doubt, of uncertainty, about the distance still to be run. As we have just seen, many factors bearing on the country are changing fast. The issues are not all cut and dried. The greater mass of the Japanese are so thoroughly immersed in action and so filled with optimism that they hardly ever wonder about how their present adventure will end. Nevertheless there are pessimists and worried men among them, willing to admit that they have doubts and to ask questions.

Does not the burden of the past still weigh heavily upon this old country? Is it not going to check its run, chill its enthusiasm? We have described a Japan of the atomic era, and there it is indeed before our eyes. But we must acknowledge that there is also a whole section of Japan that does not come into this category at all. There are disturbing gaps between the spearheads of the Japanese economy and the backward sectors that do not by any means follow the great advance.

The future of the country does not seem to be without its dangers. May not the economy be endangered in those sectors where it is so obviously vulnerable? Are not the managers once again pushing the country on at too great a pace? Does not the future of the country seem to be threatened? Are they not overestimating its possibilities, just as the generals did in former times, and will they not run it onto the rocks? Already the current problems of today are piling up, growing more serious. Even if the economic machine does stand firm, will not the Japanese community, shaken and partly demolished by the shattering effects of the industrial revolution, suffer crises that will put the whole economic success in doubt?

The burden of the past does weigh heavily on the Japanese economy, and for this reason its advances are both incomplete and unfairly shared; here the most striking illustration is agriculture, that overlooked, forgotten industry. This certainly does not mean that the new Japan renounces its agriculture or looks upon it as an out-of-date pursuit. The Japanese will take great care not to copy the English example of turning it into industry's poor and unsuccessful relation. They value their agriculture very highly, and it is thoroughly alive. One simple figure shows this: Japan produces 80 percent of its food by its own efforts and at home. The country thus proves that its massive industrial expansion is not incompatible with the preservation of a high degree of independence in the matter of foodstuffs, an independence that is due to high productivity in the countryside. But nevertheless in agriculture we do see the burden of the past, since rural Japan is a world that is not altogether willing to accept the economic revolution. The reason for reluctance to change is connected with an age that has passed away. Those who work on the land take too small a part in the general advance in productivity. A great part of the agricultural revolution, unlike the industrial, has still to be accomplished, and this gives rise to problems that have no easy solution—a state of affairs reminiscent of more than one Western country, as far as agriculture is concerned.

I do not mean that the peasants have not accomplished extraordinary feats since the advent of the new postwar Japan. In former days they were tenants, farming the land under onerous conditions, but the agrarian reform that the Americans insisted upon and successfully carried through changed all that, and now 90 percent of them own their holdings. For more than ten years now they, as proprietors, have achieved a long series of records in agricultural productivity, particularly in rice. A most recent one is that for the rice harvest of 1967, the heaviest in the country's history: 14.5 million tons. The former record was the 1962 harvest of 13 million tons. These results have been obtained from a surface of about 13.5 million acres, a cultivated area that has scarcely changed for the last fifty years. The harvests from the same acreage are two or three times as good as they were at the beginning of the century.

What is the explanation of this advance? In the first place it is the intensive use of the most modern synthetic chemical fertilizers; the Japanese peasant is the heaviest user in the world, and the most experienced. He uses five times as much fertilizer for a given area as a French peasant and sixteen times as much as an American farmer. And then the general employment of insecticides and fungicides and, during the last ten years or so, of the new weed killers (which also save labor), has helped to improve yields. Every single Japanese grower makes use of transparent plastic sheets, and this has led to an enormous increase in crops grown in frames or under light covering.

All this amounts to a positive revolution in the two-thousand-year-old farming calendar; the growing time is considerably shortened, and the crops can be gathered before the typhoon season (September and October), which was once the time of harvest. The widespread use of little motor-powered plows now gives the lie to the former view that rice growing could make little use of mechanization because of the smallness of the plots and the flooding of the crop. These plows, together with a very great many motorized farming implements, mean that 90 percent of 7.5 million acres of rice fields are worked at least in part by mechanized labor. And it should be added that the state has put a great deal of money into irrigation and the improvement of the soil.

On the whole, Japan can boast of having given its peasants a better life than they have ever known. The rise in their living standard is marked, particularly where their land is fertile; a striking proof of this is to be seen in the extraordinarily general use of home appliances in the countryside. The government subsidizes rice heavily, thus making it an unusually high-paying crop for many peasants; the state takes their rice at a price far above that paid by the consumer, and the treasury makes up the difference. For reasons that are primarily political, this price has been steadily raised during the last few years. Families living in the country also improve their position by means of nonagricultural sources of additional income, and because of the boom in building sites near the rapidly spreading towns, some have carried out very profitable deals in land.

Finally, there has been a continually rising demand for agricultural

produce; the average Japanese now eats more and better food. A revolution—still another to add to the list—has taken place in his eating
habits. His diet is gradually growing more like that of the West, with
an increasing consumption of meat, eggs, poultry, bread, green vege-
tables, dairy produce, sugar and so forth. This explains why total consumption is outrunning production and why more food has to be
imported. Although, as we have seen, Japan's dependence upon foreign countries is moderate, the fact remains that this dependence has
increased over the last years. In 1960 food imports represented 13
percent of the total; by 1967 the figure had risen to 20 percent. It will
probably show a considerable further increase in the coming years if
the government makes up its mind, as it can scarcely avoid doing, to
speed up the sweeping structural reforms that are essential to Japanese agriculture. For the time has come to realize that the euphoria
caused by the record harvests of recent years and by the new prosperity in part of the farming world has disguised the approach of a grave
crisis brought about by agriculture's slow and difficult adaptation to
the new economy of an age of gigantic industry and urban civilization.

When we compare the situation of agriculture with that of the
Japanese economy as a whole, we note its relative decline and its
diminishing share both in the general advance and in the benefits
that arise from that advance. Work on the land is increasingly abandoned for work in industry and trade; nevertheless this does not solve
the problems of an overpopulated countryside and of the reorganization of the holdings so that they can be modernized and made more
productive. Then again there is the widening of the gap, particularly
the cultural gap, between the country and the town, between the underdeveloped rural background and the ultramodern, overdeveloped
façade of the Japan of the Pacific coast.

Some time ago it was estimated that the contribution of what are
termed the primary occupations (agriculture, forestry and fishing) to
the Japanese gross national product amounted to no more than 14
percent, whereas that of the secondary occupations (industry) was
39 percent, and that of the tertiary (retail trade and services) was 47
percent. But these figures refer to 1964, and since that time the situation has grown worse. Between 1955 and 1965 industry's contribution
to the national income was multiplied by 4.5, trade's by 3.6, and agriculture's by only 1.8. This is reflected in the income of the peasant

family, and although it is true that part of rural Japan is doing well, there is also a great deal of poverty in the least developed farming provinces. The purchasing power of those who live off the land in southern Kyushu, for example, does not amount to a quarter of that of the average inhabitant of Tokyo or half the Japanese overall average. The agricultural north and northwest are poor too. The yearly income of an inhabitant of Niigata is scarcely half that of a citizen in the capital.

Agriculture's relative setback is also clearly to be seen in the evolution of employment. The statistics show a striking diminution in the number of active workers in the agricultural sector, which lost 33 percent of its numbers between 1955 and 1965, whereas the industrial sector grew by 45 percent and the commercial by 40 percent. The Japanese countryside undoubtedly had far too many people in it. The cultivable area, even taking into account the recent advances, amounts at the most to only 18 percent of the country's surface. This gives a density of over five hundred people to the square mile of arable land. But even this is only an average, and in the fertile regions the density often reaches eleven hundred.

The decrease in the overabundant agricultural labor force should therefore be a subject of satisfaction, and here Japan is going the way of all great industrial countries. Before the war the workers in the agricultural sector amounted to between 50 and 60 percent of the whole labor force. The proportion was still nearly 50 percent immediately after World War II. But by 1954 it had fallen to below 40 percent; seven years later, in 1961, to below 30 percent, and then in 1967 it fell for the first time to less than 20 percent. Japan is therefore rapidly nearing the most advanced Western countries; it is about as much of an "agricultural country" as France.

But a closer look at the way in which this evolution has come about shows that it has created more problems than it has solved. During the first half of the twentieth century Japanese farming provided work for an almost unvarying number of peasants—14 million. (This is the total number of workers; the total number of country dwellers was far higher.) From 1952 onward a serious movement toward the towns began, a movement that no longer merely drained off the surplus from a countryside that remained at saturation point but for the first time caused a lowering in the figure of the total peasant population.

The drift grew faster in 1955 and became really important from 1960 onward. Two million workers left the land between 1955 and 1960; then almost 4.5 million did the same in the following five years— between 800,000 and 900,000 each year, drawn by the factories, industrial wages, and the pull of the towns. In 1967 the agricultural workers numbered no more than 9,660,000. To begin with it was the young who left the rice fields, but since 1960 it has been middle-aged peasants too, and sometimes even the eldest sons of peasant families, a thing that would have been quite unthinkable in former days.

Insofar as this movement is counterbalanced by modernization in farming methods, the family holding should not suffer. And indeed the increasing use of machinery and fertilizers has meant a rise in the farm worker's productivity that reached 60 percent for the country as a whole from 1957 to 1964. But mechanization is far from being either general or adequate, and there has occurred what amounts to a positive revolution, one that marks a turning point in Japanese history—Japanese agriculture is short of labor and particularly of young labor. Nowadays only women and old men are to be seen in the rice fields. In 1967, 78 percent of the workers on family holdings were women. In the course of a few years there has been a change from the everlasting tradition of a superfluity of hands to a genuine scarcity. The authorities could have and should have avoided, or at least palliated, the harmful effects of this unburdening, this decongestion, of the countryside, a phenomenon that was in itself to be hoped for. There was one essential condition for this: the number of holdings would have had to be cut. In other words, the size of the individual holdings would have had to be increased, at the same time encouraging the modernization and the mechanization of farming. Prime Minister Ikeda made this an important point in his plan for doubling the national income in ten years, when in 1960 he published his unduly optimistic forecasts of movement of population from the countryside to the cities. Unfortunately the attempt at increasing the size of the holdings was a failure, and the modernization of production methods has made little progress in those hundreds of thousands of holdings that have remained extremely small.

After the agrarian reform of the years 1945 to 1952, the Japanese countryside emerged as a minutely subdivided collection of innumerable small properties, whose owners were now the men who worked them. But 70 percent of these were smaller than 2.47 acres, and on each 2.47 acres there dwelt an average of 5.7 persons (1960 figure). That is why a law of 1962 allowed and encouraged the formation of holdings larger than 7.4 acres, as well as the regroupment of holdings to be sold to form "agricultural corporations" run on modern lines. In 1968 there was another law to the same effect. But until now all these schemes have come to nothing because of one solid fact: the Japanese peasant does not want to sell his land. It is a good investment, particularly since the price of real estate rises all the time, it is an insurance for the children who have gone off to the city, it is dear to the whole family, and lastly the peasants can always somehow manage to make both ends meet.

For the peasant family has a way of coping with its difficulties, and here is a most important factor in the present situation, one I have already mentioned: in order to bring in extra money for the family purse, its members devote part of their time to a secondary, nonagricultural job. They will work for a craftsman or in some workshop in the village or the nearest small town; or, since the cities are never very far away, they will find temporary work in a factory or in trade, building, transport and so on. In 1965, this was the only way 70 percent of peasant families could get along, and as a matter of fact their extra income exceeded their income from the land.

The result of this pattern is that although the total number of people earning their living from the land—the total number of agricultural jobs—has fallen sharply, the number of peasant families working the land has not shown the decrease that was hoped for: it decreased by only 400,000 families between 1955 and 1965, and in 1967 there were still 5.5 million, a figure that is even higher than the prewar total. Japan, therefore, is still a country in which the agricultural holdings are far too small, in which there is an important wastage of farming capital and labor, and in which the agricultural workers' productivity is too low.

The government planners, faced with a situation that threatens to grow worse and to widen the gap between the Japan of the fields and the Japan of the factories, have seen the right answer: a gradual transition to an agriculture based on bigger, modernized holdings and also the state-aided reconversion of a considerable percentage of the rural population. What is needed is a far-reaching subsidized reform of the whole agricultural structure. Unfortunately the conservative governments have been following a completely different policy for years now—a shortsighted policy. In every budget they provide great sums of money that have in fact no other aim than the maintenance of the present state of affairs, for the Liberal-Democrats—that is to say, the conservatives—dread a lessening in the numbers of their peasant following, of the voters who are of great importance to the party in the elections and in political life. In fact this money is used for the policy of artificially keeping up the prices of agricultural produce by means of subsidies paid to the rice growers.

The real effect of this is to keep the peasants on the land instead of helping them to change to another pattern of life. It means that by paying a very high price it is possible to postpone the basic solutions; it also means that the sums that ought to be spent on structural reform are used for palliative measures, costly though they may be. The consumer and the taxpayer foot the bill. The continual rise in the official rate for rice is one of the causes for the present rise in retail prices, and the cost of this subsidized Japanese rice is twice that paid in the international market. As a consequence the country is obliged to put heavy customs duties on agricultural foodstuffs as a whole, so as to protect the home market from the cheaper goods that might otherwise come in from abroad—from Australia, for example.

Absurdly enough, Japan has ended up with a surplus of rice. At present the acreage under rice is greater than the country needs. The result of the official maintenance of prices has been the gradual accumulation of important stocks in the government stores. In 1968 the government had 2.5 million tons on its hands. A policy directed at putting things back on a sound basis would have the following aims:

1. Bringing rice down to its normal price by putting an end to the present subsidies.

2. Trying to lower the price of food, to the great advantage of the consumers, by lowering the tariff walls that keep out foreign produce.

3. Putting the money now used for keeping prices high toward basic reform.

A policy of this kind would undoubtedly give rise to new and difficult social and political problems, and it would distinctly increase

Japan's dependence on other countries for its food, but at least it would allow Japanese agriculture to share in the country's general advance toward modernization.

The burden of the past, backwardness, and uneven development—these same difficulties are to be seen in another sector of the economy, one that also finds it very hard to stand the pace. This is the sector of the small or medium-sized firms and the craftsmen's or family workshops. It will be remembered that this category still plays an important part in national production (see Chapter 5). Yet here again we must first acknowledge that the situation has its good aspects.

Some of the firms belonging to this class have succeeded in raising their efficiency and productivity faster than the huge companies. They have improved the quality and the educational level of their managers and top executives. They have found better markets for their goods. Their labor is better paid and more highly skilled, and the state has helped them in their financial problems. Those that are well managed and that turn out good work can do well either as subcontractors to the great firms who have chosen them because they are the best, or as members of cooperative associations of enterprises all in the same business. But there remains the great mass of small or weak or badly organized firms—factories that scarcely deserve the name or little workshops, many of which employ fewer than ten hands. These fight a continual battle to survive with inadequate and out-of-date equipment, with poorly paid labor that is neither particularly efficient nor productive, and with a heavy burden of debts that have to be repaid; it is a battle that never ceases, and every day it claims its victims—an ever-present threat of bankruptcy hangs over this whole sector.

There are great numbers of firms and of small family undertakings that cannot manage to bring themselves up to date, to adapt themselves to the mass production methods that make their appearance in the companies they supply, for example, or to follow the successive changes of structure in their own line, such as the current revolution in synthetic textiles or the sudden triumphant advent of plastic in household goods. In addition to their technical problems, these firms also have to deal with serious difficulties caused by the labor shortage and rising wages. And lastly they are faced with the question of finding an alternative market for their products, since many of them are at the mercy of the company they supply. Often enough this company is their only customer, and if it chooses it can cut off the orders the firm lives on with scarcely a word of warning; indeed, this is quite a usual practice among the biggest concerns in bad times.

When the leaders of the economy denounce the "double structure" as one of the curses of Japan, their words are not always wholly sincere. In fact the double structure is very useful to large-scale industry. When times are good, the small men can provide the great companies with a source of fresh supplies at very profitable rates. In times of slump, they soften the blow for the big companies, who can pass on the effects of the depression to the small men, stopping their orders and letting the subcontractors weather it out as best they can. Many great firms scarcely make the least effort to do away with this lower level; their inclination is rather to profit by the facilities the lower level provides, and to profit quite unfairly. For the economy as a whole the vassal or inferior companies form a cushion that helps it to absorb the shock of recession.

Since the crises that Japan has gone through up until now have only been dents in the continually rising curve and have never been very alarming, the dubious benefits of the double structure have outweighed its disadvantages. But if there were a really serious depression, and above all if the upper level itself were badly shaken or if the slump went on too long, the fact that part of the economy is built up on a great complex of far too many fragile units, all of them too small, might show that the whole Japanese structure has one shockingly vulnerable side.

There is also the vulnerability that arises from the extreme density of the population. Although it is true, in this economy full of contradictions, that there can be a labor shortage during a time of expansion, nevertheless the pressure of the massive and still growing population makes itself felt all the time, and in the event of a bad slump this too could be a source of grave danger. One way in which this pressure is evident is in the excessive size of the tertiary sector— retail trade and services—in comparision with the primary and secondary sectors (see the employment statistics in Chapter 5). It is to be seen, for example, in the extraordinary proliferation of stores and boutiques, in their astonishingly numerous staff, in the wonderful numbers of food shops, the quantities of serving girls, delivery boys, hostesses and so on. This is a particular characteristic of the Japanese economy, and it is another of its weaknesses.

A general slump would hit this sector very hard indeed by bringing about large-scale unemployment; it would affect the great commercial and insurance firms, with their countless employees, and at a lower level it would ruin great numbers of little shopkeepers who only just make a living even in normal times. Perhaps the people to feel it worst would be those engaged in an immense range of completely artificial activities that can function only in prosperous days and that include, for example, the vast "amusements industry" that is so typical of the new Japan. The reason why the towns of Japan have whole districts given over to amusements and night life, the reason why there are hundreds of thousands of little cafés and bars, tiny night clubs, tea shops, restaurants and so on, the reason why so many Japanese go on tourist trips, exchange so many millions of little presents during the year and buy so many minute objects that serve no purpose whatsoever—the reason for all this is that millions of Japanese have to take in one another's washing; they have to help one another to live without producing anything at all. The most striking example of this kind of quite pointless activity is also a proof of the existence of an immense army of workers who may so easily lose their jobs: it is pachinko, a kind of pinball, a national institution that astonishes foreigners. Pachinko is the billiards of modern Japan, and it fills the idle hours of millions of Japanese every day. In hard times, clearly nothing could be so vulnerable as this huge world of the wholly useless.

It would be unwise to overlook still another vulnerable aspect of the Japanese economy, one that is to be found at the topmost level of the whole system: that of the very important companies. The vulnerability lies in the weakness of the financial underpinning of investment and production. The equipment and the expansion of large-scale Japanese industry are based, as they were in the past, upon massive borrowing by the companies from the banks, a running into debt that would be looked upon as extremely rash in other countries. As we have seen, the system is extended by borrowings between companies of the same group and by the banks themselves borrowing heavily from the Bank of Japan. All these practices give the foreign observer the impression of a card house that would collapse in the event of a serious crisis.

Although, because of the very special nature of the Japanese business world, the country has successfully resisted this weakness and has emerged from the various recessions without suffering too much, this does not mean that a worse slump, particularly one arising from an international crisis, might not bring this fragile, credit-based structure to the ground. Might there not be a financial crisis with potentially disastrous consequences? Might not the failure of an important banking or industrial group start off a chain reaction that would lead to the collapse of whole sectors of the economy? In normal times one of the reasons for industry's continual efforts to increase production is the fact that it is obliged to reckon with its many heavy debts, and this is a factor in the speed of Japanese industrial growth. But if production were to stop or to slow down badly, the "bicycle economy" would become impossible; the bicycle, coming to a halt, would fall, and the situation might become disastrous.

It is from a foreign crisis above all that the shock might come, for although the Japanese economy is vulnerable to attacks from within, it is even more so to those that come from without, and it is unusually sensitive to the difficulties that arise from its balance of payments. Although for the last twenty years or so it has expanded continually, we cannot forget that one of its particular characteristics is that it shows very important periodical fluctuations. Every boom begets a slump, and the cycle is always the same—a boom throughout the whole economy, an upward leap in home consumption, excess in imports and deficit in balance of payments, strong official countermeasures by means of the restriction of credit, hard times and stagnation. Until the present the country has successfully emerged from these crises, and usually it has done so fairly quickly, but there have been many of them—1954, 1961, 1965, 1967.

Every time there has been a sudden outburst of constructive activity, it has endangered the balance of payments with the outside world. This is a balance made all the more delicate by the basically adverse balance of invisible trade and capital, which necessarily requires a correspondingly favorable balance of visible trade. Furthermore, the exchange reserves have long been inadequate, and this has been a permanent source of anxiety. For a long while they stood at the level of $2 billion, and it has not been easy to raise them to that of $3 billion, as the Tokyo government wished. And these reserves contain only a very low proportion of gold; it did not amount to $350 million in the spring of 1968.

Japan's dependence on the outside world makes it very sensitive to crises in other countries—that is to say, to the infectious consequences of any depression in the international situation. If there is a recession in the United States, if sterling finds itself in serious difficulties, or if some international conflict such as the Suez crisis of 1956 or the troubles in the Middle East in 1967 disturbs the circuit of world trade, Tokyo is filled with anxiety. There is even greater anxiety about any crisis that might arise in the United States, and this is natural when we consider the very great importance of America to Japanese foreign trade. Tokyo is perpetually on the watch for signs of weakness in the dollar and for any appearance of an international financial crisis. Nervously the Japanese wonder just how solid the whole American structure really is, for perhaps there too the building was run up too fast.

Since the war in Vietnam and the simultaneous worsening of race relations, it is not merely an economic crisis in America that the Japanese dread; they also wonder whether a more general, farther-reaching crisis, both social and political, may not be on the way, a crisis that would disrupt or at least disturb the whole fabric of America. Some of them, remembering how tragically the Japan of yesterday underestimated the United States, feel that perhaps the Japan of today errs in the other direction, relying too much on American strength and overvaluing its soundness. If the United States were really to experience a depression like that of 1929, Japan itself might be very seriously shaken, at least for a time. But even without making such dismal prophecies, we may say that shocks of a far less violent nature in America would create an extremely unpleasant situation for Japan.

The Japanese wonder, for example, if the Nixon administration will cause a wave of protectionism that will strike Japanese exports of steel, textiles and electronic apparatus. In this respect Japan's position is particularly awkward, since, as we shall see, the country is most unwilling to do away with the tariff barriers that still shield some of its new industries. Japan is also uneasy about Europe; it fears the strengthening of the protectionist policy and is alarmed at the least sign of distrust or hostile feeling with regard to its trade. To begin with, the formation of the Common Market terrified Japan, and even now that it has found that its fears were ill-founded, since the Six buy more and not less from Japan, it is afraid that its products may be subject to discrimination or restriction and that the "miserly" attitude of which it accuses France may spread to all the other members.

Even if there is no crisis, the Japanese foresee the coming of a stage in international competition when, as they put it, "Things will no longer be so easy." They are discovering one of those thoroughly Japanese paradoxes that have been the partial cause of their success: many earlier and almost feudal characteristics of their social and economic system are still present in the new Japan, vigorously alive in the most modern sector of production, and they have given the country many advantages over its rivals. I have already spoken of the low wages and the peculiarly Japanese tradition of employment, the overflowing abundance of labor, though much of it unskilled, the weakness of union organization. But it seems that these advantages are destined to vanish. Technical modernization is bringing with it a social and economic modernization that tends to replace this outworn pattern by that which is common to most of the developed economies of the Western capitalist type.

In the first place the huge demand for skilled labor, together with the steady shrinkage of the younger age groups and the aging of the population, is beginning to change the atmosphere in the industrial firms, and this is true even of the sector of small companies. Unless the serious crisis that we have just mentioned actually occurs, a period of labor shortage has succeeded the traditional abundance. Japan, unlike the European and American countries, cannot turn to foreign reserves of labor as it did in former times, when it imported Chinese and Koreans at exceptionally low rates of pay.

The continuing tendency toward higher wages is not very far from completely wiping out, in the upper level of the economy, the advantages that Japanese industry may have derived from paying "Asian" wages, which were lower than those in the West. One of the effects of this evolution is the undermining of the old system of employment and of the structure within the firms—promotion by seniority, "lifelong" employment, and the hiring of temporary workers of lower status. Some degree of mobility of labor is making its appearance and with it, therefore, the beginnings of a labor market. Some firms have brought in a modern system of promotion according to merit and of pay according to skill. Japan does not yet possess a full operative scheme of national insurance, but the social service charges are going up. Will not the unions change both their organization and their ideas of something nearer the Western model and restate the claims of the working class in terms of the international and Marxist formula? This is one of the things the Japanese employers are most afraid of for the coming years.

Finally, is not the notorious double structure destined to vanish, swept away by the modernization of the whole setup? From the long-term point of view, does not the twofold process of the bankruptcy on the part of the weakest small firms and the take-over of the soundest by their all-powerful associates mean the eventual disappearance of the lower level? And will not this at the same time deprive the economy of its chief "shock absorbers" in the event of a depression? "The success of Japanese capitalism is partly based upon the utilization of the archaic aspects of Japanese society," writes Hubert Brochier, the best analyst of the "Japanese miracle." It will take some ten or twenty years, or even the span of a generation, for these aspects to vanish, and the managers of the economy are doing their utmost to check and slow down the process, but sooner or later it seems that it must inevitably run its course.

Another fresh problem has arisen, a new danger on the plain of international competition, and this time it is a matter for urgent consideration; by no means will it wait for the passing of a generation. Hitherto Japan has successfully reduced the penetration of Western and particularly of American firms, but the country is now faced with an almost immediate threat of an "invasion"—a twofold invasion by foreign capital and technical processes, which will compete fiercely in Japan itself. Ever since Japan joined the great international organizations and above all since it was admitted to the OECD in 1964, it has been subjected to strong pressure from its fellow members, who insist that it should implement the engagements to which it provisionally committed itself, engagements that require the "liberalization" of its economy, especially in the free admission of foreign investments. The arguments that are brought forward have the full force of logic. There is a striking contradiction in the attitude of Japan, which on the one hand states that it has an imperative need for unhindered navigation and open frontiers, while on the other retains wide areas of protection in its own country. There is contradiction again when Japan asserts that its economy is still too weak to stand up to the full blast of international competition, when at the same time the country's economic strength has raised it to the world's third place.

The OECD is therefore perfectly within its rights when it urges Japan to adapt itself to an international economy that gives free passage everywhere else to capital and technique. As it happens, a good many of the countries that belong to the OECD have little more than a theoretical interest in the argument, and they are probably quite willing to give Japan time. But for practical purposes the leading spirit in the OECD is the United States, and the Americans are not pulling their punches. For some years now they have been making a powerful drive in the direction of the Japanese market, and the obvious purpose of the operation is the successful installation of American big business. This is also the reason for the prolonged resistance of the Japanese; ever since 1964 they have been fighting a rearguard action to limit American penetration and to delay it at least until they have organized their defenses against this future competition in the archipelago itself.

Since the Americans cannot in decency bring pressure to bear solely for their own interests, they do so within the international framework; they call upon GATT, the International Monetary Fund and the OECD, and, in Japan itself, the Western businessmen whom they have tried to form into an international chamber of commerce. Their own business community in Tokyo, which was already very active, has been mobilized for this present offensive. For in American eyes Japan is now "the last Garden of Eden for investment," as one of their own journalists put it. The American companies dream of getting into Japan and there finding comparatively cheap, skillful, industrious, undemanding and docile labor, a fiscal paradise, a consumer market a hundred million strong, and lastly—a most significant factor—a jumping-off point for the penetration of the Asian markets.

The Washington government supports its businessmen in their drive. Every one of the periodical meetings of the Japanese-American Economic Committee hears the impatient arguments of the American delegates, who refer bitterly and at length to what they call their opponents' ill will or obstructionism. At the same time they call for an establishment agreement, and this Tokyo will not grant. In short, they cannot break through the tenacious defenses of the embarrassed Japanese—embarrassed, and therefore all the more polite.

One of the battles fought by American business was that waged by the Texas Instruments Company, which hoped that it would take up a dominating position in the Japanese electronics industry if only it could get into the country. The Americans did not win the battle, and it ended in a compromise favorable to the Japanese.

Another was that of the automobile industry, undertaken to open what still another American journalist called "this tantalizing market of four million cars" to General Motors and a few others. Not unreasonably, the American makers complain of the excessive charges (17.5 percent duty, 35 percent tax) that an American car has to pay in Japan, of the quota restrictions on the importation of engines, and above all of the closed door shutting out American capital that would like to invest in the industry. The Americans have not won this battle either; after some acrimonious meetings in August, 1968, the Japanese succeeded in obtaining another three or four years' respite. Liberalization was in fact postponed until 1972. Although they agreed to a progressive lifting of restrictions on the importation of engine parts so that by 1972 seventy thousand engines could be imported,* they still examine each separate demand for permission to invest "on its own merits," which means that they either block or delay it. What is more, they have clearly stated that American capital will never be allowed to control a mixed American-Japanese automobile company in Japan itself.

"We have seen how Ford dug himself in in Germany in 1958," they say in Tokyo, "and in England in 1960; and we saw the way Chrysler bought its way into Simca in France and Rootes in England." They feel that in addition to automobiles there are some other industries and manufactures (computers, for example) that are still too young to be able to manage without protection, and that still others need time to strengthen and organize themselves for the coming of liberalization. They are also afraid that the powerful American companies—

---

* This has been interpreted as meaning that the MITI may be willing to yield a tenth of the Japanese private car market to the Americans, but not more.

and this applies not only to the automobile industry—may get into "joint ventures," owning less than 50 percent of the capital, and then increase their holdings so as to transform the firm into a mere American subsidiary; another fear is that joint ventures may stray from the field of distribution and encroach upon that of production, or the other way around. And lastly they are afraid that these companies may use Japan as an advanced base for making their way into Southeast Asia.

A menacing reply has come from Detroit, and in December, 1968, Henry Ford himself rebuked his Japanese colleagues in the industry. He accused them of being unreasonable and warned them that they would find themselves in trouble because of the reactions they would provoke in the United States. It is a fact that Tokyo's attitude did supply fuel for a flare-up of American protectionist feeling as well as arguments for the lobbies that are busily at work in Washington, bringing pressure to bear for reprisals against Japan. There is a real danger that the Japanese will have to learn a thoroughly disagreeable lesson. "Since you will not come to an understanding with us," their American allies may say, "we are going to raise our duties on the steel, textiles and various other goods you sell us."

In the end Tokyo yielded somewhat to pressure and, in July, 1967, announced a preliminary slice of liberalization intended to set the door ajar to foreign investment. As far as some seventeen named industries are concerned, American or other businessmen will only have to make a demand and it will be automatically approved. Unfortunately this list includes nothing but industries that have not the slightest chance of attracting foreign capitalists, either because Japan is already there on the spot as an overwhelmingly powerful competitor (steel and shipbuilding, for example) or because they have nothing but a purely local interest—the manufacture of some peculiarly Japanese foodstuff, for instance. There are also two other categories of industry, and as far as these are concerned it is fair to say that the Foreign Investments Council in Tokyo carries on with its sifting and delaying tactics; in any case foreigners are only allowed under 50 percent of the shares in the joint ventures that are provided for, and foreigners cannot be directors.

Generally speaking, the firms that want to set up factories in Japan wish to bring in their own patents and technical processes at the same time as their capital; these are of great importance in their plans. But although, as we know, Japan is very fond of foreign techniques when it buys the patents and exploits them itself, it is not nearly so pleased when it sees foreigners exploiting them in Japan for their own profit. Here again the Americans and others never cease complaining that the Japanese are obstructive. When the door was opened a little way in the summer of 1967, therefore, some technical processes were also admitted. It was stated that there would be automatic approval where only small sums (those of less than $50,000) were concerned. As for the other cases, there is in the first place a "negative list" in which the importation of foreign processes is strictly forbidden: aviation, munitions, explosives, the atomic industry, the space industry, computers and petrochemicals. In these areas permits are allowed only in the most exceptional cases, each of which is considered on its merits. In other fields, the permits are supposed to be granted automatically, but the minister concerned can always oppose them or lay down conditions, so long as he intervenes within a month.

Clearly, the 1967 liberalization was merely relative, and once again the Americans and the OECD complained of the restrictive nature of Tokyo's provisions. An OECD inquiry on the subject gave rise to a report which came out, I should add, a little earlier than the July, 1967, decisions; in civil terms, it was very severe upon the Japanese manufacturers and government. It singled out for blame the delays and the discreditable shifts employed by the Tokyo ministries to discourage foreign requests and to shelve great numbers of them for good.

One essential point that is almost never clearly expressed is that the Japanese manufacturers and government are afraid not only of American competition but also of another danger—the social consequences of the entry of American businessmen into the national economy. They fear that American directors or co-directors will refuse to play the game as it is understood in the Japanese business world; that in particular they will not adapt themselves at all well to the flexible planning system that is so widely respected in Japan, that the delicate cooperation between administration and business will not work with them, and that they may not be amenable enough voluntarily to follow the guidance of the government planners. They also dread the American companies' bad influence on the labor market. They feel that there will be ill-timed increases in wages, completely new kinds of conflict within the firms, in which the whole traditional structure—methods of hiring, promotion, wages—will be turned upside down in an overly hasty revolution carried out by American capitalists who know nothing whatsoever about Japanese psychology.

However this may be, early attempts at liberalization have given the Japanese business world a considerable psychological shock. The businessmen now have the feeling that a new era has come. Some degree of liberalization is inevitable, even though it may come slowly; it will go hand in hand with the greater competitiveness in the West caused by the effects of the Kennedy Round and its lowered customs duties, with the greater strength of Japan's European rivals—a strength that has grown since the inception of the Common Market—and with the ever-increasing concentration of American industry. All this calls for a fresh effort on the part of Japanese industry; it is essential that it too should grow stronger, and in order to do so it must also set about further concentration.

To succeed in international competition today, a country must have larger production units, larger companies, larger groups of companies than any that exist in Japan at present. The great problem of the immediate future is the lowering of manufacturing costs by means of huge units; it is no longer rapidity of growth, as it used to be. But only a third of the Japanese factories are the size of their American rivals. Petrochemicals, steel, fertilizers and so forth, all need tighter concentration. The widely scattered machine-tool industry needs rebuilding. In some sectors there are too many firms producing too many different objects. And, too, the great industrial and trading groups are not very firmly structured; the constellation of subsidiaries that revolve about the nucleus of a bank or trading company is often both somewhat amorphous and possessed of centrifugal tendencies.

So the time is ripe for mergers, closer relations, consolidation and reorganization. The ministries are deeply concerned with the question; they do their utmost to help, and the MITI encourages the tendency. The commercial banks support it, since they lend more money more willingly to big firms than to small. The important industrial groups such as Mitsubishi lead the movement. During the fifties the great trading company Mitsubishi Shoji recovered its power by means of an operation that regrouped twelve companies into four and then turned these into a single entity. The tendency is continuing: Mitsubishi Heavy Industries has come into existence (or rather has come back into being, since it was there before the war), as the result of the fusion of three separate sections of the former company; there is also the formation of Mitsubishi Electric by means of mergers between separate firms, and of Mitsubishi Chemical Industries. The same tendency is to be seen in the new postwar industrial groups: Toshiba is vigorously setting about the concentration of its subsidiaries and strengthening its connection with I.H.I., Hitachi is tightening the coordination between its many affiliates, Yawata is increasingly centralizing the direction of its associated companies, and Fuji is busy with a series of reorganizations, mergers and unifications.

The movement toward concentration has been ever faster since 1967. In petrochemicals, as we know, the present tendency is to build enormous works, but it is something new to see the increasing number of agreements for cooperation between the groups. Mitsubishi and Sumitomo, for example, have been making a joint effort to set up a very big installation. And then there have been several mergers in the shipbuilding industry. The medium-sized yards have grouped themselves around the six companies of international dimensions, and the fusion of two smaller firms has brought a seventh of these great companies into being.

In the heavy engineering industry, the fusion of three companies belonging to the Kawasaki group, one making ships, another airplanes, and another rolling stock, has provided the gigantic I.H.I. with a companion of a size comparable to its own. The formation of unified or cooperative groups is giving the machine-tool industry a new structure; in 1968 ten of these groups embraced some fifty companies. In textiles a far-reaching movement toward concentration is taking place; first it affected some ten big cotton goods manufacturers, which formed nine and then eight groups, and now it is reaching the medium-sized firms. The spinning mills, too, are combining in cooperative associations so as to modernize and rationalize their sector. And many other instances could be mentioned.

Of them all the automobile industry calls most for mergers and consolidation, both because it is one of those that run the greatest danger of American competition (and even "invasion," after liberalization) and because, as we have seen, it is one of those that have remained too scattered and ill-organized. There are still far too many makers, and most of them are too small. In 1967 there were ten automobile manufacturing companies; but only the two big firms, Toyota and Nissan, exceeded what is said to be the minimum profitable production of two thousand cars a week. The concentration began in 1965, but it has not gone far enough. Nissan absorbed the car firm of Prince and has recently signed a business tie-up with Isuzu. Toyota took over Hino, Renault's former partner in Japan. It is probable that the companies at the bottom of the list are destined to vanish or to be taken over in their turn.

Since 1967, one of the characteristics of the tendency to concentrate has been greater size in the companies that result from these fusions and therefore the appearance of new industrial giants. Indeed, this is one of the very reasons that has caused the failure of some of the mergers that were planned. One of the biggest paper manufacturing firms on earth was about to be formed as a consequence of the regroupment of the Oji complex, which fell apart in 1949. The operation was not carried out, for it seems that the Japanese Fair Trade Commission was against it, but it is likely that we shall hear more of it. Then again, the Mitsubishi and the Dai Ichi banks were just about to join forces during 1969, but resistance within the Dai Ichi, the older and more conservative of the two, caused the failure of the deal, which was favorable to Mitsubishi. Success might have had international repercussions, because the combined deposits of the two would have made the resulting body one of the largest banks in the world.

Another merger of worldwide importance caused a sensation in Japan when plans for it were first announced; this was the fusion of the two steel giants, Yawata and Fuji Steel, both of them already among the five biggest iron and steelworking companies in existence. Their union created the second largest in the world, coming after Bethlehem Steel in the United States. Between them they had been producing as much steel as the whole nationalized British industry, and 35 percent of the Japanese production. Professors and economists were particularly opposed to the merger, saying that it was a betrayal of the sound policy of deconcentration that the Americans had imposed upon the country after the war, would strike a dangerous blow at the freedom of competition, and would encourage the tendency toward monopoly. Banking and financial circles, on the other hand, welcomed it, the MITI was in favor of it, and the unions (Yawata had forty-six thousand workers; Fuji, thirty thousand) raised no objections.

Those who favored the merger, including the president of Yawata, Yoshihiro Inayama, asserted that its purpose was not so much to strengthen Japan in international competition as to stabilize prices within the market; it would do away with duplication, such as of blast furnaces, and would encourage technical development and a lowering of costs. The Fair Trade Commission weighed arguments for and against the plan for a long time and finally granted authorization for the huge company in 1969, on condition that certain guarantees and alterations were made. Apart from the Left Wing antigovernment circles, there were few protests in the end.

In the presence of an unmoved public opinion, the difference between the power of the few great companies and the weakness of the countless little ones is growing even more marked in Japan. The interests of the consumer are certainly protected in some degree by the fact that these great companies generally compete very strongly between themselves. But this is not always the case, and cartels are often formed. And above all, the smaller firms living in the shadow of the great companies are subject to an overwhelming domination.

An inquiry into the present state of concentration published at the beginning of 1968 made a distinction between the "very highly concentrated" sectors of industry and those in which there was "powerful concentration." The output of the three largest companies in the first category amounted to 90 percent of the national production. This was so in part of the metallurgical, chemical and petrochemical industries, in engineering, and in foodstuffs. The second category contains, among other manufactures, that of films, watches and pianos. Three film manufacturers share the whole market between them, and four in the watchmaking industry do the same. Four companies provide the entire output of aluminum, and so on. In this state of affairs, still further concentration must necessarily be dangerous. Yet it must be acknowledged that it would be useful in such sectors as that of textiles, where the output of the ten biggest firms does not amount to even half the total production.

Although concentration provides an answer to the liberalization and the increasing competition that the Japanese economy foresees in the coming years, there remains another difficulty to be dealt with, another area in which "things will no longer be so easy." This is the obtaining of the latest foreign technical processes. The Japanese are finding that the Western world is now less inclined to let them make use of Western scientific discoveries and technology in return for buying the patents.

For it is no longer to the Western countries' interest to strengthen Japan by selling it their most recent techniques. They prefer to let Japan wait; they prefer to sell only those processes that are not the very latest. Or again, as another way of bringing pressure to bear so that Japan will let them in, the owners of these ultramodern processes say, "We are quite willing to sell you this process or that, but only on condition that in return you will sell us your Japanese techniques; or, even better, that you open the door to us and accept us as partners in your firm or in a new joint venture that we will set up together, with our money forming part of the capital."

May this go so far that one day Japan will be faced with a kind of embargo on the part of the foreign and particularly the American firms, all combining to deny the country access to their new techniques, in order to keep Japan behind the times or even to bring it to a standstill? The Japanese do not really think so. They believe they will always find Americans or Europeans who are ready to sell a process, as long as they make a profit out of it. Besides, the Japanese are very skillful at making the most of the competition and the conflicts between their European and American rivals. However, if Japan wants to maintain a competitive position in the international market, if it wants to avoid falling farther behind, and if, to put it at the lowest, it would like to have its own valuable patents as a bargaining point in negotiation, it is clear that in its turn Japan must engage in discovery and research. And now that the country has become thoroughly aware of this, it is going to plunge into both wholeheartedly.

Japan is to commit itself to invention; Japan is to produce great numbers of inventors and research workers. Here we have still another revolution beginning, and perhaps it will prove to be one of the most important of them all. It must be admitted that hitherto Japan has been far behind, with the governmental contribution to research being far too small in comparison to the help provided by private sources (30 as opposed to 70 percent, whereas in the great Western countries it is approximately 60 and 40 percent). Again, too small a share of the gross national product has been devoted to this kind of expenditure (1.7 percent in 1966 as against the United States' 4.3 percent), and the total budget has been inadequate—in 1965 it was only a little over $1 billion.

But the new course has already been set, and in this respect everything is going to change very rapidly. Although the real value of the total Japanese budget for research is still scarcely more than half the French or the German, its rate of growth has become the highest in the world, and the state's share is increasing very fast. In 1968 the Japanese spent $1.7 billion; from 1971 onward, according to the new plans, they will spend more than twice as much. The aim is to devote 2.5 percent of the gross national product to research.

Japan already in fact has a sound basis for its "revolution of scientific discovery." The country's great strength will lie in its wealth of young men who have a technological and scientific education, many of them possessing university degrees. The universities prepare a high proportion of their students for an industrial career; their connection with industry is far closer and their courses have a far more practical bearing on the student's future work than can be said of most universities elsewhere. Generally speaking, the universities have a technological faculty in addition to their faculty of science. The Tokyo faculty of technology, which has been compared to the Massachusetts Institute of Technology in the United States, trains nine hundred students a year in special technical fields such as naval engineering, atomic sciences, metallurgical engineering, and aviation construction. In 1961 the new technical high schools—or rather, schools of higher technical education—were founded, taking their students from the age of about fourteen and educating them to the level of a university degree. These schools train great numbers of engineers of the lower category—assistant engineers—and, since these young men start work at a very low salary, industry will absorb them all the more easily.

A recent French mission of inquiry into Japan observed that the average intellectual level of the technical staff in the factories was distinctly higher than a French equivalent; in France the Japanese foreman would be an assistant engineer, and the Japanese assistant engineer would be a full engineer. One French visitor had the impression that 65 percent of the workers on the factory floor had been to an advanced technical school. There are some works, such as the Mazda factory at Hiroshima, that no longer take on any workers who have not reached the level of high school graduation.

There is another aspect of this "technological democratization" which is favorable to research: for a given budget, the number of research workers is distinctly higher than it is in most of the West, and there are three reasons for this—lower salaries, greater economy, which means that an equivalent amount of work is done for less money, and a natural gift for teamwork. Finally, it must be added that Japanese education is very democratic in its intake, and that any man can rise to the highest position without his social origins being taken into account.

In round figures, the number of students graduated from the Japanese universities in 1966 was 190,000: 42,000 had studied science (this includes a very great number of scientific disciplines, but it excludes medicine and scientific agriculture); 29,000, literary subjects; 57,000, political economy, commerce and law; 50,000 in diverse other disciplines; and 12,000 intended to go into teaching. (It should be observed that because of the great increase in the numbers of universities after the war, these graduates are admittedly of unequal value.) In 1966 there were also 75,000 students graduated from the "junior colleges," which give a shortened course of higher education and whose enrollment is chiefly girls.

According to the official Japanese figures given in a 1967 OECD report, the total number of persons connected with scientific and technological research in 1965 was about 289,000, of whom 43,000 were in research institutions, 67,000 in the universities and advanced schools, and nearly 179,000 in private concerns. Leaving out office workers and the like, the report states that the numbers were 18,000 in the state organizations, 36,000 in the universities, and 60,000 in the private firms: this gives a total of over 114,000. A report of the Japanese Agency for Science and Technology gives 139,000 as the figure of research workers in 1967.

Of the three categories—state, universitiy and private—at present there are at least a hundred institutions for scientific and industrial research that come under the state, or more exactly under either the MITI or the Agency for Science and Technology, which takes its orders from the premier. Among the most important are the Atomic

Industry Research Institute, the Institute for Metal Research, the Institute of Industrial Research, and the Electrochemical Laboratory. The universities, both state and private, have also set up several research organizations. These include Tokyo University's Institute of Nuclear Studies, Institute of Aeronautical and Spatial Sciences, and Institute of Industrial Sciences. Two winners of the Nobel prize for physics, Yukawa and Tomonaga, have worked at the first. The Institute of Industrial Sciences is devoted to the advanced study of space. Tokyo University also has its well-known Institute of Fundamental Physics, while Nagoya University has its Plasma Institute, for the study of the physics of gases.

The third category—institutes or laboratories belonging to private industry—began to be of real importance only some ten years ago, but now it is expanding fast. Some of the laboratories belonging to the great companies are outstanding and powerful organizations. This is particularly so in electronics. The Toshiba laboratory was founded in 1962, and it employs 1,200 research workers, a good third of whom are engineers; it has been compared to General Electric's laboratory in the United States. Both Sony and Hitachi have their own, Hitachi devoting 10 percent of its budget to research. In heavy industry we have the Yawata group, even before its merger with Fuji in 1969 the biggest producer of steel, and employing 700 scientists and engineers engaged in research. The Mitsubishi Heavy Industries had 3,000 research workers in 1968. This company has sold many technical patents to British and American firms.

One fault that has been observed in the Japanese research workers and their organizations is that hitherto they have shut themselves off from others, sometimes surrounding themselves with an atmosphere of secrecy. There is not enough communication between state, university, and industrial laboratories; each works on its own and there has often been duplication. Or sometimes, again because of lack of communication, research has not been carried out in a particular branch that called for it. But since 1966 and 1967 the government has at last waked up to its responsibilities in this area, and it has taken the lead in a general drive directed at bringing new order and fresh energy into research. This drive has two principal aims, the first being to coordinate the work of the separate laboratories and the second to increase the effort in certain sectors that should have priority.

Four very important plans have been decided upon: the first centers about giant computers, the second is a nuclear program based upon the fast breeders that are soon to be built, the third is concerned with the desulfurization of oil to decontaminate the atmosphere, and the fourth is a plan for oceanographic research. The grants for the leading programs are quadrupled as early as 1968. State financing of research is increasing fast and will reach 50 percent of the country's total budget in this field. Research workers' pay is to be raised, and expenditure on research is to be relieved from tax. Working through the relevant ministries, the authorities are also steering private research toward the areas of high priority, especially those concerned with semiconductors, nuclear energy, synthetic fibers, metallurgy, chemistry, the automobile industry, the study of very high frequency waves and so on. A five-year plan for science published in 1966 lays stress on a dozen disciplines in which research workers are particularly needed. A "City of Science" is rising on a ten-thousand-acre site at the foot of Mount Tsukuba, near Tokyo, and it will house two universities and some thirty science institutes. A $140-million fund for industrial research has been set up, the money coming from private capital and a government grant. A technological information center has come into operation.

The Japanese have many qualities of great value in research, such as steadiness, tenacity, the power of concentration and scrupulous attention to detail; they are perfectly willing to set twenty men to work on a problem where we would set two—twenty men who will form a team intensely eager to succeed; they are passionately interested in everything that is new, and science draws them like a powerful magnet. When we take all this into account, it is clear that we may expect them to make a spectacular "take-off" in this whole realm of activity. Those Westerners who still cling to the longstanding fallacy that the Japanese are a race of imitators have surprises in store for them.

Freedom of economic exchange, the growing concentration of industry into huge units, the rise of a scientifically and technically educated younger generation, the great drive for research and invention—here we have some of the factors that are speeding Japan along the road to the year 2000. At the same time these are the reasons why the country is more than ever obliged to spur on its spearhead industries, together with all its other most advanced, forward-looking activities, and the result of this is to emphasize the backwardness of the entire rear guard that we spoke about at the beginning of this chapter: agriculture, the craftsmen's workshops, the small firms and so on.

Yet although dangers lie in wait for Japan, perhaps those which arise from its economic vulnerability are after all neither the most formidable nor the hardest to deal with. The most serious of all the problems that the country has to solve, the most dangerous of all the perils it must face and overcome, are those that are due to the tensions and conflicts from which it suffers in its social life, in its cultural life, indeed in its very soul, torn between the old Japan, the burden of whose traditions it can no longer bear, and the new Japan of the futuristic Megalopolis, a Japan for which the country has yet to make the most difficult of all its discoveries—the new man, the new Japanese of the years to come.

14.

Old Japan, New Japan

A quarter of a century with no serious disaster, no lasting political crisis, no grave social disturbance, no revolutions—surely this amounts to the most outstanding of all the feats accomplished by the Japan of postwar days. Apart from the sudden outbreak of riots against Kishi and the American treaty in 1960—a flare-up rather than a lasting blaze—the country has displayed an extraordinary stability in home affairs. The Japanese governments may congratulate themselves upon having the world's most easily governed nation, the kindliest nation to its rulers. And although the Japanese citizen may have had a very rough time of it in the years of extreme shortage immediately after the war, he too may congratulate himself upon never having had any deeply worrying, unstable periods to live through—no great strikes in transport or the public services, no general strike, no violent conflict between the parties, no political unheavals. This wisdom or this passive acquiescence on the part of the Japanese has of course been of the very greatest help to the country's economic expansion. And no doubt wisdom is the right word, for this same development of the economy has proved that there is no passiveness about them, but that on the contrary they are filled with quite extraordinary energy and drive.

Yet for some while now the Japanese have been wondering whether this peaceful time may not be drawing to its close. They remember that in spite of the tranquillity of the last twenty-five years, Japan did go through a period of violent turmoil in 1960, with the demonstrations in front of the Diet and the anti-American riots, and they feel that the seventies may yet bring disturbances of the same kind.

The extension of the security pact with the United States was accomplished with much less controversy than had been foreseen; the return of the American-occupied Okinawa group has been promised; yet there still remain strong feelings against the American alliance, opposition to Premier Sato, the campaign for closer relations with Communist China: all these suggest that a whole series of domestic and foreign problems may come to a head in the 1970's.

In the great adventure of the new Japan the economy may stand the strain without cracking, and most Japanese think it will, but even so this may not be enough to do away with the danger that this bold and dashing country may come to grief in its race into the future. Many Japanese are wondering whether after all it may not be that the country's most vulnerable side is to be found in its social and political life. Is not this the plane on which all these sudden radical changes may eventually cause disasters? Is it not reasonable to fear that the tensions arising from these changes may even reach breaking point, endangering the whole process and challenging its very aims? Politics has been left out of account these many years and seems, for that very reason, to be trying to struggle to the surface again; the emergence of politics may have a bad effect upon the continuity of the economic advance—it may even check it. The social problems have been looked upon for a great while as something that can wait, but now they too may become insistent; they too may make it clear that their solution is no longer to take second place because of the rule of "the economy first."

It is not mere chance that makes the seventies the decade in which a whole series of problems have reached the point at which they must be dealt with. There was without doubt a great deal of wisdom and intelligence in the rule of "the economy first," and it has had all manner of laudable consequences. But there is certainly harmful exaggeration in carrying it to such a pitch that politics bogs down altogether or degenerates into a mere devious, complicated game played by professionals. Today it is possible that the political life of Japan may not only come to life again but also take its revenge. Can a great country indulge itself in the indefinite postponement of the discussion and solution of a variety of problems in home and foreign policy? The country has acquiesced in a phony "multiparty" or bipartisan parliamentary system, one that has brought about not alternation of government, since it has left the Right Wing in power for more than twenty years; it has got around Article 9 of the constitution all this time, never attempting a revision that would bring facts and the law into harmony; for years on end it evaded the duty of frankly confronting public opinion with such challenging and difficult problems as the recognition of Communist China, the future security of the archipelago, and the Moscow treaty; and for years it believed (like the simpleminded or perhaps shortsighted Americans) that the Japanese would forever go on putting up with the out-of-date conditions that the 1952 security pact imposed upon a Japan scarcely free from the American occupation. Now surely all this amounts to a piling up of the problems to such a dangerous extent that there is a far greater risk of the whole mass coming down in a sudden avalanche of trouble.

The danger is all the more real because of the fact that during this period while politics has been kept on ice, many Japanese, whose educational level has risen with their standard of living, have become more aware of the inadequacy of their participation in the country's affairs. This participation is considerable where the economy is concerned, as I have said, but they feel that it is slight or almost nonexistent in politics. All of them are by no means resigned to having the second-rate puppets controlled by the managers as their politicians, or to seeing these politicians acting as though the party's till and their own purses were the same thing, or to watching them evading the questions they are asked in parliament.

As for the country's foreign relations, whether or not Japan follows the path traced out in these pages (politically, the gradual replacement of the American alliance by a system of peaceful collective security; economically, the setting up of the Asia-Pacific community), the vast scale of the undertakings calls for real statesmen and not mere politicians, even if these do have big business behind them. Yet it must be acknowledged that since 1945, with the possible exception of Yoshida, Japan has not produced a single man of worldwide caliber. Now it is not hard to see the dangers that lie in wait for Japan, particularly in international relations, if the country is badly steered; with Right Wing pilots, for example, it might take the easy way out and rearm with atomic weapons and follow a policy of military blocs; with Left Wing pilots it might make such strong attempts at escaping from American influence that it would fall into the Chinese orbit. Nor is it difficult to see the mistakes it might make in its economic activity abroad. It would be dangerous for Japan to have arrogant representatives and an overbearing attitude; this could mean the revival of active and really organized anti-Japanese feeling. In any case, this feeling might arise from nothing more than the jealousy and fear caused by Japan's strength and success, and from the hostility aroused by the conservative and rightist nature of its policy. It is only too easy for Chinese propaganda, and indeed the whole of the Marxist press throughout the world, to ignore the very different views of the Tokyo of today and to hold up Japan's fresh economic expansion in the Asia-Pacific Zone as a hateful reworked version of the Co-Prosperity Sphere of former times. Whether anti-Japanese feeling is justified or not, it can sometimes have very disagreeable consequences for that country, putting it into difficult situations that call for outstanding diplomatic qualities in its rulers and its representatives—for a much broader outlook than is needed in merely economic diplomacy.

At home the pressure of many problems is increased as a result of a new type of opposition: this opposition, which challenges the whole present conduct of the nation, has some strikingly new aspects, and although it represents no more than a minority it displays a most unusual degree of virulence. It arises not only from political disagreement but also from deep and long-standing social frustration. It no longer has any faith in the normal course of elections and parliament but falls back upon violence and rioting in the street. It has brought a new factor into play—the power of the students, or rather, the power of a certain section of the students. In all this we see the Japanese version of "contestation," of the student unrest, the rebellion of youth, that we now know so well—revolution's brand-new face.

The Japanese might almost boast of having discovered contestation, or at least of having been among the very earliest to invent its methods and to give the world the movement's image. In a great many ways the activity of the formidable Zengakuren (students' union), which came to the front during the anti-American and anti-Kishi demonstrations of 1960, gave a foretaste of the worldwide phenomenon, but in fact they were in action even earlier than that, in 1956 and 1957, ten years before the Red Guards in Peking and years before the recent student uprisings in the West. In Japan, as in other countries, the movement has one very important weakness: those who call the whole establishment into question, who contest the entire present order of things, want to destroy before they have found out what they want to construct. And here too it brings with it a serious danger, that of provoking the reaction of fascism and repression. But it may also have the great merit of opening the eyes of the Japanese to the seamy side of their success, of forcing them to think about the future and to ask themselves just what kind of world it is that they are hoping to build.

The truth is that contestation should find a wide field of action in Japan. Many of the country's present defects arise primarily from the manner in which its expansion has been carried out, making the vanguard thrust forward at full speed, while letting the rear guard follow behind as best it can. Many of the inadequacies and negative aspects of Japanese society also stem from a feature that is by no means new, since it is one of those that the country inherited from Meiji times and the military epoch. Just as Japan was once a strong state based upon the docile weakness of millions of obedient subjects, so now it is a rich or at least a prosperous state based upon the more or less resigned frugality of millions of those who earn very little. On this subject the statistics are eloquent, and the Japanese themselves often quote them. "As a country, we are the third great power," they say, "but when it comes to the private individual our poverty ranks us at about the same level as Venezuela—we do not even come twentieth!" An inspection of the per capita national income does indeed show that this is the order. In 1968 Japan's per capita GNP amounted to less than a third of the United States'. Even now, in this period of modernization that has so improved their lives, the Japanese know that for the sake of their country's progress they must lead a modest and often a difficult life; what is more, they may think that to some extent all their countless efforts and sacrifices are partly lost, since the average individual productivity is low, meaning for the nation a heavy waste of energy. A report of the Ministry of Health shows that in 1965 more than 20 percent of Japanese households lived at subsistence level—that is to say, at the extreme limit of poverty. At the same date the Public Assistance helped 640,000 families, and yet, as everyone knows in Tokyo, this assistance reaches only a fraction of the families in difficulties. And the number of families whose incomes could not even reach the category of "modest" was put at 1.5 million.

So successful Japan has its forgotten men, its underprivileged, unfortunate people. While most are to be found in the small and very small factories and craftsmen's workshops that I have referred to so often, others come from the ranks of the crippled, the sick, the retired workers, the widows and the aged, for whom, often enough, the only social assistance is their family's help, if indeed their families are capable of providing any. They are also to be found in one particular proletariat whose life is almost outside that of the community as a whole, a proletariat made up of street sweepers, etas, Koreans and so on. And lastly there are very great numbers of them in rural Japan, above all in the Japan that turns its back to the Pacific and faces either Siberia or the north, and in the underdeveloped Japan of the mountains and the barren lands.

Until now the Japanese community has done little enough for this bottom layer, which may not include a great many people but which is left very much to itself—which is abandoned. The Socialist opposition can fairly blame the conservative party, or what it calls the "big business" party, for its excessive neglect of these underprivileged people. But the Socialists and the other Left Wing parties are wide open, too, to criticism for having done little to help them. The Left looks for support primarily to the unions, which take care of their own people well enough—that is to say, of the ten million workers in the great firms—but which have scarcely attempted to organize and protect the mass of little men who belong to no unions at all. There is only the Socialist-Buddhist Komeito, "the party of clean government" and the political expression of the Soka Gakkai sect, that tries to protect their interests; that is where the Komeito's great merit lies. It is in fact a party of nonviolent "contestation," in the particular sense we have been using for the student movement—a nonviolent but very active contestation that embraces a great many other aspects of present-day Japanese social life.

For in addition to the more or less inevitable sufferings caused by a breakneck expansion there are also the tensions, the muddles, the inequalities and the illogicalities that arise from the same cause and that are felt not only by the underprivileged but also by the middle classes and indeed by the community as a whole. This is so much the case that in Tokyo one often hears people say that, while the great majority of the Japanese live better, every day sees the number of the discontented rise higher still. For many the housing problem is probably one of the most trying; the reason for this is not only the poky discomfort of a badly built and yet expensive dwelling but the inconvenience of its position in an overpopulated environment. An official 1963 report stated that 4.5 million Japanese families were badly housed. The average is five persons in each dwelling, and the reality is even worse, since many workers live in dormitories.

Another inquiry says that in Tokyo 630,000 families live in a four-and-a-half *tatami* home—that is to say, a place with an area of about a hundred square feet. The total number of badly housed people in the capital amounts to 757,000 families, or one person in every three. In order to be a little more comfortable and to pay less rent, a man working in Tokyo will sometimes move to one of the dormitory towns surrounding the capital, but this means that he has to undergo two, three, or even more hours of packed trains, buses or subways every day; the crowds are so great during the morning and evening rush hours that the stations have a special body of "shovers," men whose job consists of standing behind the travelers whose backs protrude from the overfilled carriages and pushing as hard as they can so that the doors can close and the train set off.

This rush hour can be taken as a valid symbol of all those aspects of Japanese life that are subjected to the intensely disagreeable consequences of the huge and extraordinarily active population: traffic jams, accidents, fierce competitiveness. The fact that younger people —particularly the students, although they live in a society that offers them greater possibilities of education and more jobs than many a Western country—feel that they are being frustrated and so join the ranks of the contesters, is partly explained by the extreme pressures of the surrounding community: pressure of population, pressure of the ferocious rivalry in examinations, physical pressure of overcrowded schools, intellectual pressure of overloaded programs, psychological pressure of the group—for the individual always lives within a group. Catching the train for a career and thrusting others aside to get into it—this is a problem loaded with intense anxiety and one that calls for feats of mental acrobatics. And in this particular train, as well as in the hurly-burly and the struggle to catch it, there is hardly any room left for the good manners of former days.

It was the insurgent young soldiers of 1936 who launched the first assault upon the smooth and even ways of the old Japan and upon its rules of exquisite, unhurried politeness, which no longer had any place in their age of destruction. Although they proclaim themselves pacifists and although they execrate the memory of the days of the generals, the insurgent students of today are once again creating a violence closely related to that of the soldiers, but they are doing so in a feverish age of construction. It would have been too perfect if the huge torrent of violence that flowed during the military era had suddenly plunged underground in 1945 with the defeat and the coming of peace, never to reappear at any time or place. In fact, violence is never far from the surface in Japan; it will spring up almost everywhere, and indeed there is a broad section of the public that likes to see it, though without necessarily recognizing it for what it is. The unbelievable frequency of scenes of violence on television, on the official almost as much as on the private channels, is a striking instance of this. Another is the shocking number of road accidents.

According to the newspaper *Asahi,* present-day Japan has an average of 3.3 people killed for every thousand cars on the road. This is a world record. The number of cars is not very high compared with the United States or Europe, yet the death toll in accidents was above 14,000 in 1968, and the total number of people hurt or killed was 827,000, a rise of 50,000 over 1967. More than a tenth of the victims were children—pedestrians. It is hard to imagine what the situation will be like when there are 10 million cars on the roads of the archipelago. The Western observer has little doubt that a great deal of this butchery is due to the psychological makeup of the Japanese drivers; they are wonderfully skillful when they have had a good deal of experience, but they are terribly rash and they deserve their nickname of "the *kamikaze* of the wheel"; when they are driving heavy trucks they are mercilessly violent, and when they are beginners they are filled with reckless dash. For most of them the highway code might just as well not exist. In addition to this, there are not enough traffic police in the cities, and on the great roads there are even fewer, while the punishments for traffic offenses are both lenient and seldom imposed. To Western eyes, a Japanese at the wheel looks as though he were obeying jungle law.

It is only fair to add that the authorities are responsible for a good deal of the slaughter; as I have said, the state has taken little care to modernize and develop the road network, which is far behind the expansion of the automobile industry. This is only one aspect of the disproportion and unevenness of Japanese development; the main features of this distortion are the inadequacy of the public as opposed to the private sector, the distance and the increasing lack of balance between the rural areas and the industrial Megalopolis, and the inadequate protection of the general interest against the selfishness of big private concerns.

One instance of this selfishness is the indifference or the scandalous negligence of great numbers of factories and works whose chimneys pollute the air and whose waste products pollute the water. A more general case is the way industry entirely disregards the hardships its installations inflict on the community as a whole. One could compile a very long list of examples in which these abuses go on and on in spite of the repeated complaints of those who suffer from them; whole towns have to breathe an air that is literally poisoned by the unbelievable quantities of smoke poured out by certain industrial processes. A petrochemical town in central Japan has had for years on end an unusually high death and sickness rate from lung infections. A country district has been fighting ever since 1945 against a great mining company that pollutes its river with dangerously poisonous cadmium by-products; there have already been nearly two hundred deaths and a great number of cases of a strange and very painful disease completely unknown elsewhere. One industrial town has stated that every day its great numbers of steelworks and factories pour out enough soot and other air-borne waste over the city to fill a hundred and forty of its garbage trucks. In the same way Tokyo has calculated that the Sumida River, which runs through the city, carries a daily load of 1.3 million tons of waste products and filth thrown in by the factories or by the city and its inhabitants, for throughout much of the huge capital the sewer network and the system of collecting and destroying urban rubbish is still totally inadequate.

Speaking to me, one of the chief members of the opposition, the Socialist leader Saburo Eda, said, "The main reason for all this damage and this exceptionally great power of industry—no other major country has anything like it—lies in the antisocial behavior of big capital. It has never paid its social debt, the quota that it ought to contribute to society; and it derives much of its profit from this nonpayment. Its tax contribution has been much less than it would have been in

Europe or the United States. During the time of our rapid expansion, since there was no Socialist Party capable of taking office, there was no organized force to work systematically for the protection of the community against the evils that arise from an all-out advance. What party and what men will be able to create a democratic movement that can defend the nation against the social evils and abuses created by the economically powerful interests? That is going to be the great question: and that is going to be the battlefield for the political struggles of the years to come."

Japan is a country full of surprises. It has often proved this in the course of its history, even its very recent history. Sometimes, having moved along for years and years in the same direction, it will abruptly change course . . . it is a country capable of sudden reversals. It is also capable of setting fire one day to what it worshipped the day before, or at least this is so when it is suffering from the effects of a serious shock. Japan is a country of unexpected explosions, usually of the same general nature; it is hard to tell whether we are to explain them by the natural surroundings in which the people live—earthquakes, volcanoes, typhoons—or by the philosophy that has formed them—Zen Buddhism, Shinto and so on. Silent, long-enduring patience will explode into sudden shattering action that changes the entire situation. And then we have a Port Arthur or a Pearl Harbor. Shall we one day see Japan exploding inward in the same way that it exploded outward on those two occasions so close to our time?

Once more I must emphasize that Japan is a land of contrasts. When one makes any particular assertion concerning Japanese affairs, the statement may be based upon undeniable facts and it may be correct; but up to a certain point one might just as well have asserted the contrary. For so great are the differences between opposing situations that may both be found in Japan that this contrary can certainly exist. And this again is what makes it so difficult to forecast Japan's behavior. The country takes far less care than the West to provide itself with reasonably coherent social and economic structures, in tune with one another from the point of view of logic and organization. Contradictions whose injustice would make us cry out with indignation and which would be really dangerous in our world are accepted as normal in Japan. But even so, is there not a grave risk in the accumulation of these anomalies?

When one knows how this patient nation will suddenly lose its patience, and when one also knows that at home the Japanese citizen is apt to be something of a weathercock, liable to sudden change with the changing situation, and that in the mass he is often sheeplike, surely it makes sense to fear that he may find himself in the midst of disaster. The real danger of a crisis arising from Japanese weaknesses on the economic plane would lie in its social repercussions. A crisis of this kind would act as a catalyst for discontent that is hardly at the conscious level and would set off a process which in its social aspect would have a deteriorating effect upon the economic aspect, and the economic upon the social—a hopeless vicious circle of hard times and social protest, and therefore still harder times followed by even more violent protest, and so on. This is obviously what some of the new "contesting" revolutionaries count upon, and if necessary they do not hesitate to make use of sabotage if it can trigger the process of upheaval and change of direction. We have a notion of what these changes of direction might be, and they would not necessarily lead toward the Left. If democracy were under a very serious stress in Japan, just how firm would it prove to be? Are the Japanese now entirely immunized to the temptation of totalitarian order and discipline? Will these bold, dashing people always be careful in their international relationships? These men are still filled with a warrior's karma; how long can they go on being the champions of pacifism and disarmament? Is it possible, either at home or abroad, that these lovers of violence can really be nonviolent?

Having said all this about the darker side of the picture—and what country is without its darker side?—and having gauged the theoretical chances of those who are in favor of a total change of direction in Japan, I am obliged to admit that in practice there is not a single movement of opposition, contestation or revolution that has hitherto succeeded in rousing the Japanese or in winning a majority of their votes.

The Japanese are more clearly aware of their country's faults than anyone else, but right or wrong the greater number of them are convinced that these faults do not justify the perilous adventure of a revolution. Although the new "contesting" movement takes up a great deal of space in the papers, it is still no more than the expression of a very small minority of young people and intellectuals, and it is itself "contested" and criticized by the great mass of public opinion. The traditional opposition, the Socialist opposition, seems to have less chance ever of settling firmly into office. For the present the new opposition of the Socialist-Buddhist Komeito does not have the look of a movement that means to overturn either the establishment or the capitalist system. The Japanese Communist Party is perhaps the strongest of the Left Wing parties, but a maximum of three hundred thousand members and three million votes after twenty-five years of effort in a country of heavy industry, massive capital, and a huge working class can scarcely be called much of a success.

So side by side with the reasons that might push the Japanese in the direction of total violent change, it is important to try to list and to explain those which have hitherto held them back from such a course. The first of these is probably fortitude, courage in the acceptance of a harsh and rigorous life. Let it be stated right away that in Japan this courage is by no means resignation, but on the contrary it is a determination to change that life. It arises from this industrious nation's deep, instinctive conviction that the real cure for very hard times is very hard work—the conviction that effort pays and that the last quarter of a century has proved it, whatever reasons for discontent may still remain. In this country discontent is not readily transmuted either into protest or rebellion. The system has glaringly obvious faults, but the majority of the Japanese feel that this is the price that has to be paid for the speed of the national success and that the faults can be corrected. The means for doing so may not yet be at hand, because Japan still has to live austerely, but they will come later. The real way of achieving this is not to sabotage the present advance but to persevere with it. Many Japanese think that the future will reward them for their patience, because it gives promise of wonderful new advances no great way off. What is more, their courage arises from the whole of their past history, and their endurance is bound up with their most ancient, deeply rooted social concepts.

For in fact the second explanation of the Japanese nation's long suffering is the tenacious survival of the Confucian ethic. The ancient Confucian culture that came from China long ago formed a world in which there **was no** place whatsoever for protest—one in which protest was, generally speaking, inconceivable. Its prime law was the harmony of outward social relationships. In Japan even more than in China, Confucianism was something greater than mere ethics; it amounted to an aesthetic system of human relations. Disharmony remained below the surface, unseen, because it would have been ugly to express it in words or deeds. Men accepted the rule of unfailing, invariable politeness and of respect for the formalities and rites corresponding to their rank. There was nothing offensive about the inequalities, since the harmonious balance of the consequent rights and duties compensated for them. Passion must never be allowed to disturb the even-tempered expression on the face of the man who felt it.

In this silky smoothness of social harmony the community saw the smallest possible amount of naked suffering or hatred. The rule demanded a smiling face, by no means a false or hypocritical smile but, I repeat, a smile of courage, the smile exchanged by men who are determined to bear with one another and to avoid inflicting the ugliness of their dissensions, their bitterness or their sadness upon the community. These were some of the attitudes of mind that the Japanese derived from Confucianism, and Buddhist fatalism has also made its contribution.

On the Asian mainland the new China of today abominates these habits of mind and of behavior, looking upon them as a factor in their long-drawn-out humiliation of former times. In Japan too they have no doubt been seriously shaken, and I shall return to this, but upon the whole the rule of harmony in human relations has remained wonderfully strong and vital among these people whose way of life finds one of its most important explanations in the aesthetic principle. Obedience to this law was unfortunately of great service to the dictatorship in prewar Japan, when it was exploited to ensure the lasting submission of the masses. For fifteen years, and right up to the days of the blazing cities and of Hiroshima, there was not a sign of revolt, even among those who knew that their chiefs had led them to destruction; the nation's harmony survived the universal catastrophe. It is striking to see that in the extraordinarily different world that has emerged since those days something of much the same nature has continued.

The new venture of the Japan of the managers certainly makes far fewer victims and causes less disaffection than that of the Japan of the generals, but sufferers still exist. Yet among them, those who protest are in the minority, and their influence is small; the great harmony goes on, and for more than twenty-five years the majority of the Japanese have said yes to the conservative governments; what is more, these governments have found a high proportion of their supporters among the most underprivileged classes. American sociologists, considering the Left Wing parties' lack of success, have seriously wondered whether Japan, in its high state of modernization, may not already have reached what they term a post-Marxist age; it rather seems to me that it is almost proof against the theory and the practice of class struggle because of all the factors that survive from the old Japan.

Over and above the persistence of these historic attitudes of mind, the country's stability is explained by the actual day-by-day functioning of the "Old Japan–New Japan" complex. This provides a third major reason why the Japanese have hitherto managed without revolutions. The notion of the "double structure" dear to the Japanese economists for describing their economic environment deserves to be broadened to take in the whole Japanese world, including its mental and cultural aspects. At the beginning of this book it was pointed out that since the Meiji period the Japanese citizen developed in two separate yet contiguous worlds, the old Asian Japan and the new "Western" Japan. Other countries carry out their revolutions by substitution, replacing the old system by a new one built where the other had stood. Japan does so by juxtaposition, setting up the new system that it adopts next to the old, which it preserves; and this it has done time out of mind, since well before the year 1000, for example, when the same thing happened in the field of religion. This has been Japan's form of resistance, its way of defending itself against the powerful impact of Western civilization.

The country has become a combination of two Japans which, far from banishing or excluding one another, coexist in the Japanese citizen's daily life and indeed in his innermost being. His astonishing double life has often been described, the classic example being the businessman who passes his day in Tokyo surrounded by all the ultramodern gadgets of his calling and who, in the evening, changes his Western suit for a kimono and reverts to the Japanese Japan of his traditional home. This division dominates the whole of the Japanese way of life. It is not a schizophrenic behavior but a duality, a sum, a multiplication by two. The old Japan provides static acquiescence, the Confucian acceptance that we referred to, the realm of tradition. The new Japan means change and mobility, and here everything that makes the Japanese so passionately eager for new things, for the ultramodern, can function without the least restraint.

Why revolution? After all, every single day *is* a revolution for the man of Japan. His life is more filled with revolution than that of any of our protesters and dissidents. A good half of the world in which he lives is one that might be said to specialize in change; it is a world of perpetual, tangible mutation that will soon run far beyond anything that we are acquainted with. Is it still possible for anyone to go on saying that the Japanese is not an inventor? He invents his life every day—that is to say, the changing world in which he lives obliges him to renew his life, to "revolutionize" it continuously. In the United States and Europe life does not change so fast or so completely. The new Japan is a discovery and a revolution carried out every single day by every single Japanese. And one of the reasons for the unenthusiastic response of the average Japanese to the systems of political or ideological revolution offered him is that he has already moved into action; he has in fact carried out so many immediate, concrete changes that he has little time or liking for mere ideology.

There is another aspect to this phenomenon: the sudden bursts, the daring advances of this country would never have been possible, especially during the first fifty years of its rise, if there had not been the old Japan always there as a starting point or as something to fall back on. The new Japan is an acrobat who has never performed without a safety net under him; he has always had the old Japan to protect him if he falls. It is easier for a Japanese to launch into the hazards and the upheavals of the new Japan when he knows, as he does know, that the old Japan is always there, a base and a refuge in which he will be safe, with his feet on firm ground. There he can seek shelter from the savagery and the cruelty of capitalist industrial society, a shelter that the Western man has all too often lost. Although the Japanese works in that grim society, every day he can go back to a world in which happiness is both easier and more available, and in which frugality does not exclude contentment. Every day the old Japan acts as a tranquilizer. It soothes the unhappiness of those who come back to it from the new Japan; it heals the wounds of the daily turmoil. It recivilizes the barbarian who emerges from the struggle in the crowded trains. On the other hand, if a Japanese feels that the old kind of life is narrow, out-of-date and poverty-stricken, he can move over to the new Japan and experience the delight of stepping into the rich, powerful, ever-moving, ever-new world of modern life. One can see every day the beaming satisfaction of the many Japanese of the poorest class, from the town or the countryside, when, having just left their humble house, they enter without much expense the rich concrete and steel world, filled with all the wonders that technology and science have provided for them as members of the community as a whole.

In order to display the works of this surprising "Old Japan–New Japan" machine I have somewhat oversimplified it by presenting the two elements as though they were in a state of balance and by speaking of a situation that is likely to change as though it were permanent. In fact the center of gravity has been steadily shifting from the old to the new Japan. To begin with, the rule was certainly to keep the traditional Japan quite away from the changing Japan, firmly protected by the shields of belief, custom, tradition, manner of speech and so on. And for a long time this separation held firm, because when it began in the Meiji era the old was very much stronger than the new; compared with traditional Japan, solidly established in the midst of its ancient structures, the modern Japan, or rather the Japan that was making its first hesitant steps toward modernization, was no more than a blundering, lean newcomer, an upstart that did not seem at all dangerous. By the time half a century had passed and the country had reached the years between the wars, the new Japan had already assumed great weight and size; the old and the new were in a state of equipoise. This continued. It even went on throughout the military period, which counterbalanced the increasing importance of the industrial economy by a systematic reaction in favor of tradition.

The partition between the two Japans was holding fast; indeed, it can be said to have held firm until roughly the time of the defeat in 1945. Now, a hundred years after the accession of Meiji, we must acknowledge that the country's radical changes are forcing the dividing wall to yield. The barriers are beginning to give way before the tremendous thrust of postwar industrialization and modernization. The old rule that forbade the mixing of the old and the new is increasingly ignored, and often the coexistence of the two cultures, the purely Japanese and the Western, is being replaced either by a mongrel or by a fully Western culture. The former realm of tradition is shrinking; the Japan of iron and stone is driving back the Japan of wood and lacquer. In short, the old Japan is retreating, and this is one of the most important facts in modern Japanese history.

How far will this retreat continue, and what will tomorrow's Japan be like? If it is no longer to be the richly endowed, enchanting country of two cultures that it has been for so long, will not this change, this upsetting of the balance, have deprived it of some of its finest qualities, those that made it unique among the countries of the world? Earlier, in considering Japan's economic, political, and social vulnerability and in trying to gauge how dangerous they might be for its success in the coming years, I expressed justified optimism. But if its material success is to be based upon a civilization that is still unsure of its aims, and if the Japanese carry on this headlong career without knowing what kind of society and culture it is going to lead them to, will not the country suffer from a new and very special weakness, one that might be termed cultural vulnerability?

What will be the value of this success if the Japanese citizen is to become a human robot in an overindustrialized society, itself made up of mechanical robots and gadgets? What is the worth of its economic victory if it is to be accompanied by a cultural defeat, and if a mechanized society devoted to production, consumption and material comfort is in the end to destroy the personality and the unique quality that the country defended for so long, preserving them until our present age? At present, whether they know it or not, many Japanese seem to be going in that direction without being fully aware of the danger. Almost unconsciously, many of them are fast losing some of their ancient ways and habits; they have abandoned their disregard for physical comfort, for example, yet they used not only to endure discomfort but to welcome it, because for them it was one of the frugal virtues. They now forget the peace of their traditional way of life and plunge with disconcerting ease into the din, the roar and crash of machinery, as though their former deeply rooted submission to the tyranny of fate and men had made them indifferent to the new tyranny of the mechanized world. Their old hankering after discipline and the way some of them love parade-ground regulations (the barrack image sometimes reappears; it does so, for example, in the lining up of the supporters in certain political rallies)—are not these still other traits that may help in their transformation into robots?

Yet after all, these disturbing questions can be met with the optimistic reply that the nation seems to possess a certain number of characteristics and qualities that protect it from the advent of the Japanese robot. There is no doubt that they are too artistic, too spontaneous, too much in love with pleasure and with freedom to undergo any such change. It is indeed the new Japan that has brought them this gift of freedom; in fact this is the most significant change that it has made in the lives of the majority. And their memory is not so short that they have forgotten the war and the military epoch, either; as I have said, they are still haunted by the recollection of those years, whose history was that of an attempt at "robotization" that ended in disaster and that gave them a deeply rooted love of liberty. The Japanese character is full of contrasts, and all these different beings—the aesthete, the poet, the intensely sensitive man, the one who is apt to make sudden changes of direction, and the new lover of freedom— who live together in the one same person, will not easily allow themselves to be turned into a mass-produced robot.

It would be another danger for the culture of the future if the possibly inevitable relinquishment of the old Japan were to take place without protecting the finest cultural and natural treasures that it bequeathed to the men of today, and without the recovery of a certain number of spiritual and aesthetic values that flourished then, and their grafting upon the spirit of the new era. As far as the first point is concerned—the protection of the natural and cultural inheritance —it is time to sound the alarm and to tell the Japanese that their best friends are horrified at the way this legacy is being frittered away. They are afraid that the unequaled beauty and the unique quality of these fortunate islands may suffer irreparable damage before the end of the century. An explosive expansion accompanied by a second explosion—that of the population—all happening within a very limited space: these are factors that in forty years, and particularly since the war, have jointly caused a very serious change for the worse in the Japanese scene, one of the happiest and most lovely in the world.

Many of the best-known beauty spots and some of the most famous ancient buildings have been gradually surrounded by modern ugliness, by the spread of houses and the swarming mass of humanity. Tokyo is engulfing everything that surrounds it. Industry and new buildings have spoiled almost all the countryside along the Pacific coast as far as Nagoya and beyond. Ancient towns such as Kyoto and Nara, cities of an incomparable beauty, the repositories, the thoroughly living monuments of the old Japan, are surrounded and spoiled by the pressure of the new cities built next to them—by the process of duplication. Industry is beginning to seize upon one of the finest landscapes on earth, the shores of the Inland Sea, that other Mediterranean at the far end of the eastern world. A dark ring of tall, smoking chimneys is already creeping toward the most famous site in Japan, Miyajima, the red temple near Hiroshima whose porch stands with its feet in the sea. In addition to all this the automobile boom will make things still worse, for hordes of tourists will invade the more unspoiled and distant countryside; the thought of what the "gas pump Japan" may be like makes one tremble.

Japanese tourism is exceedingly well organized and has been brought within everybody's reach, but for this very reason every well-known place is now crammed with jostling sightseers. The famous garden of meditation in the Ryoanji at Kyoto—a few ageless rocks on a spread of white sand—is no longer visible at any hour of the day unless one peers between the legs or over the black heads of two or three hundred school children or peasants on an outing. Another scourge is the Japanese tourists's habit of leaving picnic rubbish behind him. And then wherever crowds gather, merciless commercialism sets up its buildings and its advertisements without the slightest regard for the surroundings; an example of this is the notorious Disneyland which wrecks the ancient site of Nara.

Strange as it may seem, this most artistic of nations is little affected by these crimes. No one protests when a hideous tower rises against the Kyoto sky, when the splendid Buddha of Kamakura is surrounded by a revolting covered gallery of concrete, or when a wicked imitation Le Corbusier construction is built within the precincts of the very sacred temple of Izumo. Although Tokyo was destroyed twice in a quarter of a century, it still had some ancient buildings and gardens that might have been preserved; they have been allowed to vanish piecemeal, overwhelmed by the flood of gigantic offices and apartment buildings. There is no adequate battery of laws and regulations for the protection of ancient artistic monuments and the landscape.

This acquiescence in the wrecking of the landscape or damaging of cultural treasures cannot wholly be explained by the habit of bowing to the inevitable with a smile. I think that the explanation lies in the fact that a very great many Japanese, faced with the immensity of the explosive changes all around them, are in a state of total confusion, above all now that these changes are no longer confined to the modern aspect of their existence but reach the underlying bases of their way of life and their processes of thought. For in the end the thrust and drive of the modern world have broken through the defenses of the old Japan; that sanctuary, that stable refuge, has been shaken to its depths. Its unchanging quality is now itself a fatal disadvantage. More and more the social rules it provides, the philosophical ideas and the moral laws that it insists upon, are becoming out of date, outworn, irrelevant, meaningless to the completely different, perpetually changing modern world of today. It is the young who are most struck by these inadequacies, for they have not their elders' need for bridges linking the present with the past.

Nowhere is the gap between the generations so sharply defined as it is in Japan. For many of the younger generations there appears to be an irreconcilable conflict between staying Japanese and being a man of the modern world, at least if staying Japanese means remaining attached to the past. Japanese history, with its relics and its ancient monuments, seems to them without validity for the present age; they must therefore escape from it. The same applies to the whole structure of the formal moral and social obligations, such as those which were based upon the important notions of the *on* and the *giri*, more or less feudal concepts of the debt every Japanese owed to society, of his honor and his duty. Among some of the young people there is a dislike and even a hatred for tradition that surprises and often shocks the foreign visitor. It is easier to understand the strength of this feeling and perhaps to excuse it to a certain extent when one has known how crushing and even deadly the weight of tradition can be in this country and in other parts of Asia.

Shohei Imamura, the *enfant terrible* of Japanese films, is a representative of the new generation; a little while ago he observed, "The Japanese are in a state of conflict. The intellectual, moral and social values by which we live have nothing to do with the Japanese reality of today." And one of his colleagues, the "committed" producer Kei Kumai, added,"Intellectually, Japan is still an underdeveloped country. The industrial and political revolutions have been accomplished. We still have to attack the ethical, philosophical and cultural revolution, because up until now the ruling classes and the disasters of the war have prevented any progress."

Cultural revolution! The word has been uttered at last, and uttered by a Japanese. For it is indeed a Japanese cultural revolution that is in question. To be sure, the phrase was not invented in Japan, nor does it belong to that country, but the thing itself is well known there. In its particular way Japan too is deeply engaged in its own cultural revolution. However great the distance from the Land of the Rising Sun to the Middle Kingdom, there are certain striking parallels between them. In various ways both countries are the most advanced countries in Asia, and both have reached a point of historical maturity at which their problems are somewhat the same. As the year 2000, a new age for mankind, comes nearer, both are in a difficult phase of mutation or metamorphosis, one in which they must throw off the last remnants of the old Asian chrysalis, assume their new forms, and take to the air. The ideal of rejecting outworn notions, as the Peking Red Guards put it, of no longer clinging to a more and more outdated ethic of immobility, of preparing for the great take-over by the new world's vanguard (a take-over that is already foreseen for the end of the century) and of giving this new age a new culture—this ideal belongs not solely to the Chinese new wave but to the new wave in Japan as well. But I must add, and add most emphatically, that the Japanese cultural revolution was not set off by that of China and that it is in no way whatsoever under the remote control of Peking. It did not wait for the beginning of Mao's revolution to get under way, and it goes ahead under its own steam, having taken over none of the Chinese style or methods. Here there are most important and deeply interesting differences between China and Japan.

At the end of this century there is a finishing line, a tape waiting for the great powers who are running in the race of this epoch of ours; and on the other side of the line there is a remodeled world, the result of an industrial revolution that has been carried through to its end, an industrial revolution terminating in the postindustrial age of the economists. Mao's China set off in 1950 far behind the other competitors, but its first burst of speed was so great that the astonished world thought the country's zeal would allow it to catch up with the rest and even perhaps outstrip them, as the Chinese themselves boasted they would. And then suddenly, fifteen years later, Mao Tse-tung surprised all observers by saying to his people, in effect, "Stop running, or slow down. This is not the race we want to win. It is not this victory that matters, if this victory just means knowing how to make the fabulous machines of the coming millennium like everybody else. What is important, and what must matter to us, is the creation of the new man who will make use of these machines."

So the outside world was mistaken when it thought that China, having scorned the spirit of discovery and of industry for four thousand years, had at last determined to plunge wholeheartedly into the economic and industrial revolution of our day. China has only gone in halfway; it feels no great urgency. Mao—and in this he is profoundly Chinese—betrays something of the ancient Chinese distrust of merely technical progress. For him it is a matter of secondary importance that the cultural revolution slows down his country's industrial development, losing it years of the utmost value. The machine that he is primarily concerned with is the political machine for the mass production of men. This is the production that must have priority over the other; politics is to have precedence over the economy.

Quite unlike China, Japan has flung itself headlong into the economic revolution and gives it every sort of priority, and if the country does not know exactly what kind of Japan will finally emerge, that cannot be helped. Japan above all believes that it is forbidden to let up even for a moment. Japan feels that unless it carries out its task of modernization with a speed equal to its zeal, the country will never have the important position it longs for in the new age. To succeed in our day you have to run as hard as you can, and because of its re-restricted size and meager resources Japan has to run faster than anyone else. Slowing down would mean weakening, and weakening would very soon mean having to drop out of the race.

Does this amount to saying that Japan, unlike China, is not concerned with what the "new man" will be or should be? Not at all. Japan too is continuously and deeply committed to this same inquiry, but it carries out its research in the full heat of action, making use of perpetual trial and error, for millions of Japanese are engaged in the quest, and every single one follows his own line. Mao Tse-tung has a ready-made plan, a plan that covers his whole nation. He provides just one mold, based upon himself, and this mold is intended to produce seven hundred million replicas of the original. Japan is carrying out its own cultural revolution without any plan and without any model, and there is a good deal of confusion. But this revolution is an unceasing daily series of experiments and improvizations; the whole muddled process is spontaneous and free.

And so Japan, having discovered its new love for discovery, is also possessed by the ambition of inventing not only new machines but new men too. Some of the more forward-looking Japanese intellectuals have a half-conscious longing to create the new Japanese and to give him a new culture. Here their ambition closely resembles that of the Chinese leaders on the other side of the water. For the old Asia is being reborn; it feels that it has an important part to play in the discovery of this new man of the third millennium, and that the setting free of this man that Asia is forming will liberate more energy than anything that Europe could give the world—always supposing that Europe ever finds itself.

Yet can some ideas, some formulas, some techniques be saved from the old Japan? And how are they to be grafted on to the Japan of today and tomorrow? What intermingling of the old Japanese Japan and the new Westernized Japan is both possible and acceptable, and in what areas could this synthesis occur? What wholly new formula is the country capable of discovering; what can this country discover to make its contribution to tomorrow's culture? The innumerable questions all lead in these directions. But it is we outsiders who see the logical pattern. For their part the Japanese behave empirically; as I have often said, they usually think out what they have done only after they have done it, having acted in the first place under the impulse of feeling and intuition.

We surely look upon the confusion, anxiety and muddle that often result from this state of affairs with sympathetic understanding. It is a painful metamorphosis that the country and its people are going through, and there is a striking contrast between the material success of present-day Japan and the spiritual and intellectual disquiet and unhappiness of some of its best minds. Part of the reason why the

Japanese are so feverishly busy is that in this perpetual activity they escape from the difficulty of thinking out their world or of re-thinking it. And let us avoid having only blame and criticism for their desertion of the past; often enough we should do the reverse and congratulate them. Modernization is at last attacking their ancient social structures and changing their manner of thought, whereas for many years it had been concerned far more with machines and tools than with the men who operated them. Now that it is affecting the organization of labor, conditions of work, the legal status of women and so forth, it is freeing Japan from many a chain that has long been burdensome to it.

The new era is wonderfully encouraging for Japanese creative artists: architects, writers, painters, musicians and others are producing powerful work in which the nation's inborn delicacy and love of beauty appears in new and different forms. There is no doubt that it is the artists who, both by their eager, fruitful questioning and by the value of their answers, are contributing most to the shaping and the enrichment of the culture of the Japan of the engineers.

Yet still the old Japan strongly holds out against these invasions and this process of amputation, and one feels this very clearly among working people. Here again we have the separation and the contrast that is so typical of Japan, for if one watches and listens to the intelligentsia, the avant-garde whom the Japanese call the "intelli," one often has the feeling that the bulldozing of the ancient culture has already gone terribly far. But if one lives among the people for a while, one sees how very little they are affected by the intelligentsia and how strong a hold tradition has upon them still.

I should like to illustrate this contrast by a recent personal experience. There was a UNESCO conference at Kyoto on the subject of artistic and cultural interchange between Japan and the West. The greater part of the Japanese who attended—artists, professors, writers, architects—were suspicious of their old culture or even hostile to it. It was the Western members of the conference who defended the old Japan, or rather some of its permanent values, while many of the Japanese condemned it out of hand. In the heat of the debate one of them shouted, "Tradition must be destroyed!" There was another Japanese who also thought that the examples and lessons of Europe were utterly out of date; he went on to say, in effect, that the values of the new world were now being worked out in Japan and the United

States, and that old Europe was no longer in the running. If these ideas are realized, the Japan of the day after tomorrow will be neither a new growth springing from the old Japan nor an adaptation or copy of the modern West merely called the new Japan, but a "third Japan" far in advance of the other two—something entirely new that may perhaps already be trying to find itself and to take form in this flight of a whole nation toward the years to come.

My mind was busy with these reflections as I left the conference, and I was wandering through a working-class district in the old Japanese tradition when my eye was caught by a group of Japanese in morning coats; they were getting into their cars at the bottom of a great flight of stairs. At the top of the stairs some ceremony must just have come to an end, and in my curiosity to see what it was I walked up. On the upper terrace, in front of an ancient wooden shrine beneath the trees, there was an astonishing, motionless figure that seemed to fill the whole scene, like a character in a No play. It was a provincial bride in all the glory of her ceremonial kimono. Its train spread in a torrent of gold and crimson silk around her; her relatives and servants were bending to arrange the long folds; they were tying the immense brocade sash and giving the last touches to her hair, piled high in the traditional manner. She was posing for the photographer. The whole splendor of the old Japan flowed streaming from her shoulders and its whole burden weighed upon them, too; this astonishing apparition—astonishing for me but perfectly natural in those surroundings—was a total denial of all those speeches I had just heard about the imminent death of ancient tradition.

Amazing country! In every aspect of life and culture it can present us with answers completely unlike our own, as though to say, "Yours was not the only solution: here is another; it is wholly different. And it is more than a thousand years old." Japan has two forms of everything—two ways of life, two hotel systems, two different ways of cooking, two architectures, two ways of dressing, two styles of painting, two kinds of music, two theaters, two sorts of writing, two cinemas and so forth. And all this is not merely to please us Westerners; it is not just for visiting tourists but for Japan, for the Japanese themselves. The country is "bicivilized," as some are bilingual. Is it true that this is no more than a fleeting moment in Japan's history, that this system is becoming intolerable, and that the intelli are right when they say that this split personality, this double image, is a notion almost as out of date as the old Japan itself?

Whatever the answer may be, let us frankly admit that for foreign observers, transitory or not, it is a moment of quite extraordinary fascination, and that the twofold system is exceedingly interesting. It will no doubt last for a good many more years, thus giving us the chance of discovering a world so remote from our own, this other world of the traditional Japan, and of discovering it still very much alive. Simultaneously and in the same place as this exotic, legendary Orient, we also discover its twin, the Westernmost of all countries, one that in its turn astonishes us with its style and its accomplishments which already differ from ours and which are sometimes better. The twofold experience is so interesting and so rewarding that I am often astonished to find how, although it has been open to the world for a century, and although it makes such efforts to know us, Japan is still so very little known in the West.

Some travelers may suppose that the Japan of today is already no more than a kind of almond-eyed America, drowned in the victorious roar of machinery and deserted by beauty and poetry, and perhaps my book may have contributed to this false belief; but let them be comforted, for the old Japan, I say again, is strongly alive, and it still has an immense hold on the people's country and their hearts. Western visitors still have plenty of time to come and immerse themselves in the old Japan. The remoter parts of the country, a wonderful and little-known countryside, comparatively unspoiled and recently opened to traffic, is waiting there for the visitors who like to keep off the beaten track, carefully avoiding the agencies' ready-made tours. The whole country is scattered with artistic treasures. The most widely spread of all qualities in Japan are good taste and aesthetic sensibility, and every day there is a continuous creation of beautiful things. In the provinces, folklore and popular traditions are incredibly full of life. And no one would believe that such universal, delicate good manners and polite attentions were still to be found in this world of ours.

But the visitor to the Land of the Rising Sun should not go only to see that particular Japan, nor should he suppose that it alone deserves the name of Japan. The intention of this book has been to show that Japan is primarily modern Japan, the Japan of today. When all is said and done, in spite of all the faults one may find in it, it is one of the most outstanding successes of our age. We Western people can all draw solid lessons of optimism and splendid examples of daring from this ancient country that has managed to grow so young again, from this poor, overcrowded and until lately underdeveloped land that has become so prosperous in only one century, from this Asian nation that has proved itself so capable of doing everything that we can do, and lastly from this people that has so far had the wisdom to renounce armed force and to base its strength upon industry.

REFERENCES

Chapters 3 and 4: The Government of the Managers and A People at Work

Ballon, Robert J., "l'Effet dynamique du sentiment national et de l'action de l'Etat: la société japonaise," Sociologie du travail, April–June, 1966.
———, "In for Life," The Far Eastern Economic Review, June 1, 1967.
Brochier, Hubert, Le Miracle économique japonais. Paris: Calmann-Lévy, 1965.
Dore, Ronald P., "Education in Japan's Growth," Pacific Affairs, July, 1964.
Hakayama, Ichiro, "la Modernisation des relations professionnelles au Japon," Sociologie du travail, April–June, 1966.
Macrae, Norman, "The Risen Sun," The Economist, May 27 and June 3, 1967.
Murgue, R. P., Rapports humains dans l'entreprise au Japon. Tokyo: published by the author, 1957.
Reischauer, Edwin O., lecture given to the Educational Research Union in Tokyo, quoted in The Japan Times, November 7, 1964.
Tokuyama, Jiro, "Decision Making in Japanese Business," in The Japan Business Guide. Tokyo: Diamond Publishing Company, 1964.

Chapter 5: Great Numbers and Small Wages

Article on population in Japan Quarterly, No. 2, 1966.
Articles on salaries in The Oriental Economist, December, 1967, and December, 1968; in The Times of London, May 27 and June 17, 1963.
Economic Planning Agency, Economic Survey of Japan (1965–1966). Tokyo: The Japan Times, 1967.

Hetman, François, "l'Economie et la Société du Japon en l'an 2000," *Analyse et Prévision*, January, 1968.

"Le niveau de vie des Japonais," special number of *Nouvelles économiques du Japon*, March, 1964.

"Les petites et moyennes entreprises," *idem*, February 10, 1969.

Wage Problems in Japan. Tokyo: Ministry of Foreign Affairs, 1963.

Wilcox, Nestor, "Where Are the Japanese Wages?" *The Far Eastern Economic Review*, March 14, 1963.

Chapter 6: The Rush for Equipment

Akita, Saburo, "la Croissance rapide du Japon d'après-guerre," *Analyse et Prévision*, January, 1968.

Articles on foreign techniques in Japan in the *Bulletin de la Chambre de commerce française de Tokyo*, March, 1954, and October, 1956.

"Banking in Asia," supplement of *The Far Eastern Economic Review*, April 1, 1962.

Bienfait, Jean, *la Sidérurgie japonaise*. Lausanne: Centre de Recherches européennes, 1965.

"Equipment Investments by Key Industries," article in *The Oriental Economist*, September, 1967.

Politiques nationales de la Science: Japon. Paris: Organization for Economic Cooperation and Development, 1967.

Chapter 7: The Third Great Power in the World's Economy

Article on the iron and steel industry in *The Oriental Economist*, July, 1968.

Article on the iron and steel industry in *The Oriental Economist*, July, 1968.

Article on shipbuilding in *idem*, March 2, 1968.

Bienfait, Jean, *op. cit.*

Consider Japan, The Economist, 1963.

Japan Steel Notes, monthly bulletin of Nippon Kokan Company.

Lloyd's Register for 1967, April, 1968.

Mitsubishi Heavy Industry Review, bulletin of the Mitsubishi Heavy Industries Company.

"The Shipbuilders," in special number of *The Economist*, March 2, 1968.

Yawata News, monthly bulletin of the Yawata Steel Company.

Chapter 8: The New Industrial Revolution

Articles on space research in *Look Japan*, November 10, 1967, and *This Is Japan*, 1968.

"L'Automobile en Asie," supplement of *The Far Eastern Economic Review*, April 13, 1964.

"Changing Pattern of Petrochemical Industry," in *The Oriental Economist*, April, 1968.

"The Computer Revolution," in *Industrial Japan Quarterly*, July, 1968.

"Livre blanc sur les ordinateurs," summary in *Nouvelles du Japon*, August–September, 1968.

Special numbers of *Nouvelles scientifiques et techniques du Japon*, a publication of l'Office franco-japonais, principally on the Japanese automobile, 1965; the petrochemical industry, March 7, 1966; electronics, March 16, 1967; the technical and scientific development program, March 11, 1968.

Chapter 9: Greatness Without the Bomb

Brochier, Hubert, *op. cit.*, p. 185.

Buck, James H., "The Japanese Defense Forces," in *Asian Survey*, September, 1967.

Cary, James, *Japan Today: Reluctant Ally*. New York, Frederick A. Praeger, 1962.

Examens des politiques scientifiques nationales: Japon. Paris: Organization for Economic Cooperation and Development, 1967.

Kennan, George F., "Japanese Security and United States Policy," in *Foreign Affairs*, October, 1964.

Matsueda, T., and George Moore, "Japan's Shifting Attitude Toward the Military," in *Asian Survey*,

Melchior de Molènes, Ch., "Prolifération et non-prolifération nucléaire en Asie," in *Revue politique des idées et des institutions*, March, 1968.

Mendl, W. M. L., "Japan's Defense Problem," in The Yearbook of World Affairs, 1968.

Chapter 10: Diplomacy by Trade and for Trade

Allen, George C., Japan's Place in Trade Strategy. London: Atlantic Trade Study, 1968.
Article on U.S.-Japanese economic problems in The New York Times, October 8, 1968.
Articles in The Oriental Economist on trading companies, January, 1968, and on industrial exports, May, 1968.
"Le Japon et l'Europe," supplement to le Monde diplomatique, June, 1963.
"Le Japon, la France et la Communauté européenne," supplement to le Monde, June 4, 1963.
White paper on the commerce of Japan. Tokyo: Ministry of International Trade and Industry, June, 1968.
Wilson, Dick, "Second Wave Export Attack," in The Times of London, October 23, 1968.

Chapters 11 and 12: The Asia-Pacific Zone

Articles on Australia in The Far Eastern Economic Review: November 4, 1965; May 23, 1967; February 23, 1967; May 23, 1968.
Articles on Siberia in Articles et Documents, November 4, 1966, and in Nouvelles économiques du Japon, July 7, 1968.
"Asian Development after Vietnam," Proceedings of the Asian Development Symposium, Asahi Shimbun, 1968.
"Australia and Asia," supplement of The Far Eastern Economic Review, November 4, 1965.
"Canada and Asia," idem, December 5, 1968.
Giuglaris, Marcel, Visa pour la Sibérie. Paris: Gallimard, 1963.
"Japan into Affluence," supplement of The Far Eastern Economic Review, October 31, 1963.
"Japan 1967," idem, February 23, 1967.
"Japan 1868–1968," idem, March 21, 1968.
Japan's Future in East Asia. Kyoto: The Center for Southeast Asian Studies, 1966.

Jones, J. D. F., article in *The Financial Times*, June 25, 1968.

Sakamoto, Yoshizaka, "Peaceful Coexistence in Asia," reprinted in *Guerre et Paix*, the organ of the French Institute of Polemology, 1968, III.

Chapter 13: The Weight of the Past, the Dangers to Come

Allen, George C., "Japan's Economic Problems and Prospects," *The Three Banks Review*, December, 1967.

Articles on concentration in: *The Oriental Economist*, March and June, 1968; *The Far Eastern Economic Review*, May 30, 1968; *Nouvelles économiques du Japon*, September 5, 1968.

Articles on foreign investments in Japan in *Nouvelles économiques du Japon*, May 14, 1968, and *Bulletin de la Chambre de commerce française de Tokyo*, January and February, 1964.

Brochier, Hubert, op. cit., pp. 296ff.

"Les Engrais chimiques du Japon," special number of *Nouvelles économiques du Japon*, January 12, 1967.

Examen des politiques scientifiques nationales: Japon. Organization for Economic Cooperation and Development, 1967.

"Japan's High-priced Rice," *The Oriental Economist*, August, 1967.

Libération des mouvements internationaux de capital: Japon. Paris: Organization for Economic Cooperation and Development, 1968.

"Livre blanc agricole," article in *Nouvelles économiques du Japon*, March 21, 1968.

"Livre blanc sur la recherche scientifique," *Nouvelles économiques du Japon*, November 28, 1968.

Ripelle, Fabre de la, "la Recherche scientifique et industrielle au Japon," *Revue de la Défense nationale*, February, 1969.

"The Small Men's Revolution," *The Economist*, June 3, 1967.

Wilson, Dick, article on invention in Japan in *The Financial Times*, August 8, 1968.

Chapter 14: Old Japan, New Japan

Articles by Jean de Baroncelli on the Japanese cinema in *le Monde*, August 16 and 20, 1967.

Benedict, Ruth, *The Chrysanthemum and the Sword*. Cleveland, Ohio: World Publishing Company, 1967.

BIBLIOGRAPHY

Introductory Works

Allen, George C., A Short Economic History of Modern Japan. New York: Frederick A. Praeger, rev. ed., 1963.

Borton, Hugh, Japan's Modern Century: From Perry to 1970. New York: Ronald Press Company, rev. ed., 1970.

Fairbank, John K., Edwin O. Reischauer, and Albert M. Craig, East Asia: The Modern Transformation. Boston: Houghton Mifflin Co., 1965.

Ike, Nobutaka, Japanese Politics: An Introductory Survey. New York: Alfred A. Knopf, 1957.

Reischauer, Edwin O., Japan: Past and Present. New York: Alfred A. Knopf, 1964.

——, The United States and Japan. Cambridge, Mass.: Harvard University Press, 1965.

Sansom, George B., A History of Japan. 3 vols. Stanford, Calif.: Stanford University Press, 1958–1963.

——, Japan: A Short Cultural History. New York: Appleton-Century-Crofts, rev. ed., 1962.

——, The Western World and Japan: A Study in the Interaction of European and Asiatic Cultures. New York: Alfred A. Knopf, 1950.

Storry, Richard, A History of Modern Japan. London: Penguin Books, 1960.

——, Japan. New York: Oxford University Press, 1965.

Yoshida, Shigeru, Japan's Decisive Century 1867–1967. New York: Frederick A. Praeger, 1967.

General Works

Abegglen, James C., The Japanese Factory: Aspects of Its Social Organization. Glencoe, Ill.: Free Press, 1960.

Allen, George C., *Japan's Economic Recovery*. New York: Oxford University Press, 1958.

Benedict, Ruth, *The Chrysanthemum and the Sword: Patterns of Japanese Culture*. Cleveland, Ohio: World Publishing Company, 1967.

Bennett, John W., and Iwao Ishino, *Paternalism in the Japanese Economy: Anthropological Studies of Oyabun-Kobun Patterns*. Minneapolis, Minn.: University of Minnesota Press, 1963.

De Vos, George, and Hiroshi Wagatsuma, *Japan's Invisible Race: Caste in Culture and Personality*. Berkeley, Calif.: University of California Press, 1967.

Dore, Ronald P., ed., *Aspects of Social Change in Modern Japan*. Princeton, N.J.: Princeton University Press, 1967.

Hewins, Ralph, *The Japanese Miracle Men*. London: Secker and Warburg, 1967.

Hirschmeier, Johannes, *The Origins of Enterpreneurship in Meiji Japan*. Cambridge, Mass.: Harvard University Press, 1964.

Jansen, Marius B., ed., *Changing Japanese Attitudes Toward Modernization*. Princeton, N.J.: Princeton University Press, 1965.

Kawai, Kazuo, *Japan's American Interlude*. Chicago: University of Chicago Press, 1960.

Lockwood, William W., *The Economic Development of Japan: Growth and Structural Change*. Princeton, N.J.: Princeton University Press, expanded ed., 1968.

——, ed, *The State and Economic Enterprise in Japan: Essays in the Political Economy of Growth*. Princeton, N.J.: Princeton University Press, 1965.

Marshall, Byron K., *Capitalism and Nationalism in Prewar Japan: The Ideology of the Business Elite, 1868–1941*. Stanford, Calif.: Stanford University Press, 1967.

Passin, Herbert, *Society and Education in Japan*. New York: Teachers College Press, Columbia University, 1965.

Stoetzel, Jean, *Without the Chrysanthemum and the Sword: A Study of the Attitudes of Youth in Postwar Japan*. New York: Columbia University Press, 1955.

Ward, Robert E., ed., *Political Development in Modern Japan*. Princeton, N.J.: Princeton University Press, 1968.

—— and Dankwart A. Rustow, eds., *Political Modernization in Japan and Turkey*. Princeton, N.J.: Princeton University Press, 1964.

Studies on Contemporary Japan

Beardsley, Richard K., John W. Hall, and Robert E. Ward, *Village Japan*. Chicago: University of Chicago Press, 1959.

Curtis, Gerald L., ed., *Japanese-American Relations in the 1970's*. Washington, D.C.: Columbia Books, 1970.

Dator, James Allen, *Soka Gakkai, Builders of the Third Civilization: American and Japanese Members*. Seattle: University of Washington Press, 1969.

Dore, Ronald P., *City Life in Japan: A Study of a Tokyo Ward*. Berkeley, Calif.: University of California Press, 1965.

——, *Land Reform in Japan*. New York: Oxford University Press, 1959.

Fukutake, Tadashi, *Man and Society in Japan*. Tokyo: Tokyo University Press, 1962.

Glazer, Herbert, *The International Businessman in Japan: The Japanese Image*. Rutland, Vt.: Charles E. Tuttle Co., 1968.

Henderson, Dan F., ed., *The Constitution of Japan: Its First Twenty Years, 1947–1967*. Seattle, Wash.: University of Washington Press, 1969.

Levine, Solomon B., *Industrial Relations in Postwar Japan*. Urbana, Ill.: University of Illinois Press, 1958.

Morley, James W., *Japan and Korea: America's Allies in the Pacific*. New York: Walker Co., 1965.

Morris, Ivan I., *Nationalism and the Right Wing in Japan: A Study of Postwar Trends*. New York: Oxford University Press, 1960.

Olson, Lawrence, *Dimensions of Japan*. New York: American Universities Field Staff, 1963.

Osgood, Robert E., George R. Packard III, and J. H. Badgley, *Japan and the United States in Asia*. Baltimore: Johns Hopkins Press, 1968.

Packard, George R. III, *Protest in Tokyo: The Security Treaty Crisis of 1960*. Princeton, N.J.: Princeton University Press, 1966.

Passin, Herbert, ed., *The United States and Japan*. Englewood Cliffs, N.J.: Prentice-Hall, 1966.

Riesman, David, and Evelyn T. Riesman, *Conversations in Japan, Modernization, Politics, and Culture.* New York: Basic Books, 1967.

Scalapino, Robert A., and Junnosuke Masumi, *Parties and Politics in Contemporary Japan.* Berkeley, Calif.: University of California Press, 1962.

Taeuber, Irene B., *The Population of Japan.* Princeton, N.J.: Princeton University Press, 1958.

Thayer, Nathaniel B., *How the Conservatives Rule Japan.* Princeton, N.J.: Princeton University Press, 1969.

Vogel, Ezra F., *Japan's New Middle Class: The Salary Man and His Family in a Tokyo Suburb.* Berkeley, Calif.: University of California Press, 1963.

Yanaga, Chitoshi, *Big Business in Japanese Politics.* New Haven, Conn.: Yale University Press, 1968.

Yoshida, Shigeru, *The Yoshida Memoirs: The Story of Japan in Crisis.* Boston: Houghton Mifflin Co., 1962.

Periodicals

Asahi Evening News (daily).

Asian Survey, University of California, Berkeley, Calif. (monthly).

Contemporary Japan, Tokyo (quarterly).

Daily Summary of the Japanese Press, Translation Services Branch, Political Section, American Embassy, Tokyo.

Economic Survey of Asia and the Far East, E.C.A.F.E., Bangkok (annual).

Economic Survey of Japan, Economic Planning Agency, Tokyo (annual).

The Economist, London (weekly).

The Far Eastern Economic Review, Hong Kong (weekly).

The Far Eastern Economic Yearbook, Far Eastern Economic Review, Hong Kong (annual).

The Financial Times, London (daily).

Industrial Japan, Dentsu Advertising, Ltd., Tokyo (annual).

Japan Economic Yearbook, The Oriental Economist, Tokyo (annual).

The Japan Quarterly.

Japan Report, The Japan Information Service, Consulate General of Japan, New York (fortnightly).

Japan Socialist Review (fortnightly).
The Japan Times, Tokyo (daily and weekly international edition).
Japanese Economic Statistics, Economic Planning Agency, Tokyo (monthly).
Mainichi Daily News.
The Mitsubishi Research Institute Monthly Circular: Survey of Economic Conditions in Japan, Tokyo.
Monthly Bulletin of Statistics, Bureau of Statistics, Office of the Prime Minister, Tokyo.
Nippon, A Chartered Survey of Japan, Kokusei-sha, Tokyo (annual).
Orient/West, Tokyo (monthly).
The Oriental Economist, Tokyo (monthly).
Summary of Selected Japanese Magazines, Translation Services Branch, Political Section, American Embassy, Tokyo.
This is Japan, Asahi Shimbun, Tokyo (annual).

INDEX

ROBERT GUILLAIN, permanent correspondent for *Le Monde* in Tokyo, is a Doctor in Law of the Sorbonne University and a graduate of the Institute of Political Science in Paris. He covered the Sino-Japanese war in 1937 and 1938, served as information officer at the French Embassy in Tokyo and, when Pearl Harbor came, was trapped in Japan for the duration of the war. During the years since the end of the war he has been present at all the major events of the multifaceted Asian drama. Mr. Guillain has been decorated by the Japanese government for his contribution to Franco-Japanese relations. He is the author of several major books on the Far East.

DATE DUE

JUL 14 '72		
FEB 28 '73		
E H		
not to leave lib.		
JUN 2 '74		
E H		
FEB 2 2 1983		
FEB 1 4 1983		
NOV 17 '87		
NOV 12 '87		
NOV 3 0		
BY 27 '90		
DEC 1 8 '91		
		PRINTED IN U.S.A.
GAYLORD		